WOMEN OF TROPICAL AFRICA

CONTRIBUTORS

Ethel M. Albert
Marguerite Dupire
Solange Faladé
Monique Gessain
Anne Laurentin
Annie M. D. Lebeuf
Denise Paulme
M. Perlman and M. P. Moal

WOMEN OF TROPICAL AFRICA

Edited by
Denise Paulme

Translated by
H. M. Wright

UNIVERSITY OF CALIFORNIA PRESS

Berkeley and Los Angeles

Translated from the French
FEMMES D'AFRIQUE NOIR
© *1960 Mouton & Co.*
First published in the U.S.A. in 1963
by the University of California Press of
Berkeley and Los Angeles, California
First Paperback Printing, 1971
Second Printing, 1974
ISBN: 0-520-02052-9 (paper-bound)
0-520-00989-4 (cloth-bound)
© *1963 Routledge & Kegan Paul Ltd*

CONTENTS

PLATES

(Between pages 230 and 231)

TRANSLATOR'S PREFACE

I SHOULD LIKE to thank all those who have helped me on various technical points.

Dr D. W. Arnott very kindly gave me advice on English transliteration problems in general, and on transliteration of Fula words in particular; M. de Dampierre and Professor A. N. Tucker did the same for Nzakara terms. If their recommendations have not always been followed to the letter, this is because in order to simplify matters for printers and readers, some diacritical marks have been omitted, and the French system of using capitals instead of special letters in words such as WoDaaBe has been retained. I have sought to give the English form for tribal and geographical names where this differs from the French, but, at the request of the editor, Mme Denise Paulme, an exception has been made for the Coniagui (the English form for which would be Konyagi), on the plea that this is the spelling accepted by the Coniagui themselves. Further exceptions have been made for Sultan Bangassou and his wife Natélégé, on the grounds that they are historical figures known under these names.

Dr K. P. Wachsmann was most helpful in supplying information about the *usir*, the bar zither used by the Coniagui. I am greatly indebted to him, as without this information I should have been lost to know how to translate the description of the instrument.

I have been fortunate in being able to consult Dr Judith Djamour and Dr Maurice Freedman on problems of anthropological terminology as they arose, and am grateful to both for giving so generously of their time and expert knowledge. If I have not always found the correct English equivalent for French terms, this is my fault, not theirs.

I am also grateful to the International African Institute for allowing me to consult their catalogues and use their library, and to the staff for their unfailing helpfulness in answering my queries. This greatly facilitated work on the Annotated Bibliography, which I have occasionally supplemented by giving reference to English editions of works cited.

The essay "Women of Burundi: A Study of Social Values" was translated by its author, Ethel M. Albert.

H.M.W.

ix

INTRODUCTION

Denise Paulme

THE SIX ESSAYS collected here are all by women who are professional anthropologists (two of them being physicians in addition), and are based on fieldwork carried out in Africa by the authors within the last ten years. Avoiding the usual preconceptions about the inferior position of women in a traditional African setting, each essay deals with woman in her everyday life and with the problems that particularly concern her. This is a new approach, for, since ethnographic research has almost always been exclusively carried out with the help of, and among, the male part of the population, the picture that has emerged has to a large extent been the image which the men, and the men alone, have of their society. It is well known that travellers in a foreign land, whether men or women, find difficulty in making contact with the womenfolk and in getting into conversation with them; and when, to the barriers of language and custom, are added those arising in a colonial situation between rulers and subjects, the difficulty becomes almost insuperable. When African women see a female foreigner making a direct approach for information to the men of the village, starting discussions with them, and entering places and sometimes even attending ceremonies to which they, as women, are not admitted, they show no interest in her at all at first. But, once their curiosity is aroused, they tend to be ironical and severely critical: how can a woman, whose proper tasks are looking after the home and the children, behave in a way that seems to deny her very nature? Besides, why should any attention be paid to the opinions of this foreigner who, from the very moment of her arrival, has taken the men's side in the eternal battle which is every day liable to flare up through some incident, either trifling or serious? And there can be no doubt as to which side she is on: has she not lent a sympathetic ear to the men's complaints—shame on her, shame on them!—and already written down on paper the reproaches that husbands and fiancés are forever casting at their womenfolk as if they expected the women to allow themselves to

1

be treated like servants? And when the foreigner finally comes to visit the women, she will be met with reserve or even open hostility, and as often as not will find her efforts rewarded by a refusal to admit her.

The relationship is vitiated on both sides by deep-seated prejudices. During my first period of fieldwork in Africa, after nine months spent in an area of the French Sudan I was able to follow the general trend of a conversation without understanding every word or venturing to speak very much. One day, crouched in the shade of a wall in the courtyard of a house, I whiled away the hot hours half asleep, while near me two young women were delivering vigorous blows with a pestle, pounding millet for the evening meal. Comparing their lives with mine, I was vaguely congratulating myself on not having to do a chore like theirs, day in and day out, when I overheard one of the women say something like this to the other: "That girl makes me tired with her everlasting paper and pencil: what sort of a life is that?" The lesson was a salutary one, and I have never forgotten it.

This difficulty in making contact with the womenfolk may explain the paucity of material concerning African women. It was only as a result of her unusual qualifications and of the exceptional circumstances of the serious riots in Aba in 1929-30 that Mrs. Leith-Ross was entrusted with the task of conducting an enquiry among Ibo women, the results of which appeared in her book *African Women*.[1] Its interest and charm are as fresh as ever, but at what cost! We only know something about the Pondo women of the Cape because Monica Hunter happened to have learnt their language in her childhood.[2] These are isolated examples, and we have to admit that nothing exists in French to compare, for instance, with the astonishing biography of *Baba of Karo*, whose story, although she actually lived in Nigeria during the first half of the twentieth century, might have come straight out of the Arabian Nights.[3] The essays which follow are a first attempt to fill a serious gap. We hope that they will be succeeded by others.

The first thing that strikes one on reading these contributions is how widely varied the modes of life are which they describe. There are agriculturalists of more or less permanent settlement, pastoralists living in straw huts and following their herds from one grazing land to another, or again a complex stratified society with masters, servants and slaves and a strict system of clientage where subordinates provide subsistence products for a patron who is bound to protect them from the exactions of others, this being the mode from the bottom of the pyramid to the solitary sovereign at its

Introduction

apex. No society is the same as another. Each one regards itself as, and is and remains unique. What is there in common between a Coniagui peasant and a Fulani herdsman, a Nzakara princess and a Twa slave?

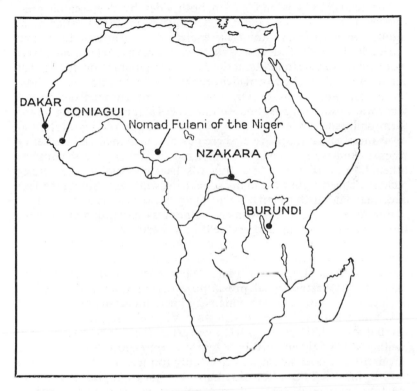

All the more remarkable, then, is the persistence of certain common features in the life of women. Almost everywhere a large measure of pre-marital sexual freedom is permitted to girls—provided they use it with discretion. Almost everywhere, too, a married woman shows an enduring attachment to her natal family, while the members of her husband's family, among whom she lives, continue to be strangers to her, and often hostile strangers. Marriage is regarded as a lesser evil, the necessary but imperfect means of concluding alliances and of ensuring the survival of the group by providing it with legitimate offspring. Finally, everywhere we see the primary importance of the mother, the very core of the African family, even for her adult and married sons, even in

Denise Paulme

Muslim societies. It was to her mother that Camara Laye dedicated the account, barely disguised as fiction, of her childhood: "Woman of the fields, woman of the rivers, woman of the great riverbanks, O you, my mother, I am thinking of you . . ."[4]

*   *   *

African marriage customs have often been condemned on the grounds that they debase women: polygyny, child-betrothal, widow inheritance, and all methods of transferring women without their consent are cited as evidence. Further on in this book will be found the comments of Dr. S. Faladé, a psycho-analyst, herself an African, on polygyny and on marriages arranged by parents for their children.[5]

Writers who disapprove of these customs also mention the heavy burden laid on women by the division of labour; the submissive attitude a wife must adopt towards her husband; the generally acknowledged right of a man to beat his wife; and finally the fact that marriage gives rise to little intimacy between spouses. The usual conclusion drawn is that women are oppressed and exploited, have no freedom of action, and are held in low esteem.

In this judgment by the outside observer there lurks a hidden assumption: that any divergence from the Western ideal necessarily implies a lower status for women. What is left out of account here is that the Western ideal presupposes a fairly high standard of living, with a household in which the husband is sole provider and the wife is supplied by him with domestic help or with appliances for coping with the rough work; and further, that in actual fact such a standard is only enjoyed by a minority. Far more common is the type of household which we know only too well in our part of the world, in which the wife contributes her earnings and in addition performs, without help, all the domestic tasks; and this type of household is never found in Africa. There, a wife's contribution to the needs of the household is direct and indispensable, and her husband is just as much in need of her as she is of him. Thus in some respects her status is higher than that of a wife who is entirely dependent on her husband.

But, it will be argued, owing to the jealous defence on the part of African husbands of their property rights, there is no such thing as joint ownership by spouses (except among the Fulani, where the *sadaaki*, the gift of the groom, is held jointly by the couple, although the wife never enjoys more than rights of usufruct with regard to the *sadaaki:* she receives the usufruct, that is to say the milk from the cows, without ever being able to dispose of the

4

capital which will later revert to her children). But a wife enjoys similar rights: she has control over goods acquired by her own labour; and wherever women choose to trade rather than till the soil, they may acquire independent control of quite large amounts of cash.

Some informants are emphatically and genuinely of the opinion that women spend their whole lives under male dominance, submitting first to the authority of their father or their mother's brother (according to the kinship system which prevails), and later to that of their husband. Moreover, these informants will add, women never attain legal independence: a woman cannot sue or be sued in her own name, and is not answerable for her actions. Her labour belongs to her husband and if she earns any money, for instance by engaging in petty trading, only with his consent can she herself enjoy the profit. Apart from her clothes, and at most a piece of jewellery, everything she has belongs to her husband and can be claimed by his heir. A man may have several legal wives and will be allowed a mistress, but a woman must remain faithful to her husband. Finally, women lead secluded lives from puberty onwards, their activities restricted to domestic tasks, this being particularly the case among Islamised peoples. If this persuasively drawn picture did indeed correspond to reality, the role of women could certainly be said to be a subservient one. In fact, however, it merely expresses a fondly entertained masculine ideal which does not tally with the realities of everyday life.

On the other hand, it would be equally erroneous to imagine that masculine dominance is entirely mythical. It must be remembered that it was nineteenth century theoreticians who evolved the idea of the matriarchy, to which some recent works still refer. A study of the facts shows that it is very rare to find political power vested in a woman. The case of the Lovedu, mentioned below by Annie Lebeuf, remains an isolated instance; and there the institution of the rainmaking sacred queen was the outcome of a revolution and of incest, and is not more than 150 years old. It is less rare to find the association of a man and a woman: the king and his mother; and sometimes power is wielded by three individuals forming a totality: the king, his mother, and his sister.

The rules of descent and of residence are basic to all forms of social structure. Descent in the female line (matrilineal) is found in a number of African societies, as in the Congo or on the west Atlantic coast. In this system the role elsewhere filled by the father usually devolves upon the mother's brother. As for residence, a young couple may settle with the husband's family (patrilocal

5

residence) or with the wife's (matrilocal residence), but it is extremely unusual to find permanent matrilocal residence, for after a longer or shorter period with his wife's kin, a husband generally succeeds in bringing his household to live with his own kinsfolk. It can readily be imagined that a system which combines matrilineal descent and patrilocal residence, with their conflicting pulls, may give rise to some tricky problems, as is the case with the Coniagui, described here by Monique Gessain. But whatever the system may be, the position of women within it is neither superior nor inferior to that of the men, but simply different, and complementary.

Judging by my own experience, which has been limited to four societies (the Dogon of the Mali, the Kissi of the Guinea forests, the coastal Baga, and the Bete of the Ivory Coast), I am inclined to think that women, what with their role as mothers and their work in the home, in their gardens, and in the market-place, have quite a wide area in which to exercise their authority. It is true that ideally a woman is expected to behave with a certain amount of diffidence, and when in public to speak less than men do, unless the subject under discussion concerns her personally, and in general to "busy herself with her household and not worry about other matters". Nevertheless she is often to be seen at the surrounding markets, and pays visits—sometimes long ones—to her mother, or one of her sisters, or, later, to a daughter married and settled elsewhere. Not only does she have full say regarding the affairs of her own household, but village women run their own associations and institutions, and often have their own cults, complementary to those of the men, so essential for group solidarity.

The influence exerted by women is due rather to their liveliness, their independent spirit, and their inexhaustible energy, than to rights recognized by custom, and the manner in which they are brought up certainly accentuates these innate qualities. In a patriarchal environment—the system most common in Africa—a small boy grows up knowing that all his life will be spent within the same family circle. His childhood home and the land he sees his elders till will one day be his own property, and after his death he will continue to haunt the places he has always known, and his descendants will pay homage at the same altar where he himself propitiated his ancestors. But a girl very soon learns that she will have to leave the house, and often the village, where she was born, and go to live among strangers with a husband who was perhaps chosen for her at the time of her birth. A married woman always has two homes and owes a dual allegiance, and if she should change husbands, this will mean another change of scene for her. The effect of this is that throughout her life she will often be fighting a lonely battle in defence of her own interests: her home and her children; and even there she has to relinquish her sons at an early age. On the other hand, whereas men never seem to conceive of ties other than those of kinship linked with common residence (so that acceptance of a stranger in their midst requires recourse to the fiction of making him a "brother" or an affine), among women the mere fact of belonging to the same sex is enough to establish an active solidarity. An appeal addressed by a woman to other women will reach far beyond the boundaries of a single village, and a movement of revolt among women will always be a serious matter, even if its immediate cause should be of minor importance.

Women are seldom to be seen taking part in public life, being absorbed in their own tasks. All the heavy work in the fields is done by the men—felling trees, burning the scrub, removing stones, erecting fences to keep out animals, making the furrows or the holes in which the women and children will place the seed. Later there will be long months when the men will drowse in the shade, while the women's work continues without respite. The whole year round they have the monotonous task of preparing the meals, and spend several hours each day fetching water, searching for firewood, pounding grain, and cooking. They too have work in the fields to do, for when the rains come, it is the women who do the hoeing of the crops, "as often as is necessary", and they later take part in the harvest. The housewife also has to provide the ingredients for the indispensable palm-oil or shea butter sauce, made with dried fish, leaves, onions, tomatoes and peppers, which serves as a relish to the daily dish of millet gruel, rice, or mashed yams or cassava. Finally, when grain stocks are exhausted during the lean weeks before the harvest, it is the women who provide food for the household by supplying it with tubers grown in the gardens they tend at the back of their houses. If foodstuffs still run short, they have to supplement them by purchases made at the market; but in order to be able to do so, almost all housewives are obliged to carry on some form of trade, often on a very small scale, and they prepare for sale pancakes, balls of crushed peanuts, salt, soap, and powdered pepper or tobacco. Attendance at the markets, which are held on fixed days in the surrounding countryside, necessitates journeys—often long ones—on foot (although nowadays they sometimes go by lorry), with a load carried on the head, not to mention the baby astride its mother's back. It is hardly surprising that fat women are

7

rarely to be seen in the African countryside. Most of the women are thin, the old ones often being mere skeletons.

This picture bears little resemblance to that presented by the kind of domestic arrangement still frequently found in Europe, in which the husband is the sole provider and the wife stays in the background with nothing to do except run the house. In Africa a married woman has an independent life of her own.

Since the arrival of the Europeans, the new modes of life introduced by them have altered the distribution of tasks in a way that has too often been disadvantageous for women. The peace imposed on societies which had either been warlike or had suffered from the fear of attack, removed one of the principal masculine tasks, which was that of the defence of the community; and while the introduction of cash crops may have provided the men with a substitute for their former warlike activities, women have found that this has only imposed new burdens on them. The worst of these is, that when the young men depart, often on a mass scale, for the plantations and the industrial centres, where they may stay for several years, only the old men and the women are left to carry out all the work in the village. In a household where the older sons have gone away, the younger ones may have to go to bed hungry because their mother, at the end of her day's work, is often too tired to light the fire and prepare supper.

The task of preparing the meals is not without its compensations. It provides women with a means of exerting pressure when necessary, as when a man is having an affair to which his wife wishes to raise objections. If he remains deaf to her first remarks, she resorts to a simple method for curing his faithlessness: one evening, the husband will find no dinner awaiting him when he comes home. Aware of his guilt, he does not dare to protest, and goes to bed with an empty stomach. The next morning, when he gets up, the same scene is repeated, without a word being said. The husband can do little about it, for if he starts shouting, his wife's complaints will raise all the women of the village against him.

Lastly, it is not necessarily the case that polygyny lowers the status of wives. Although it has been regarded as a practice which indicates a contemptuous attitude towards women, it is usually no more than the required manner of displaying wealth. A chief, or any other man in a position of power, owes it to himself to have several wives who will share the household tasks, and will provide him, not only with affines, but also with a numerous progeny. I should like to quote here an old district chief, who reckoned that he had had sixty wives during the course of his life, and who said

Introduction

with a sigh: "What a lot of trouble they could be . . ." Polygyny is less often found in actual practice than as an ideal to which everyone aspires, but it is generally realized what complications may ensue if a man has several wives in his household. Apart from the quarrels between the wives, from which the children suffer more than the husband, there are times when the co-wives come to an understanding, temporarily at least, in order to present a demand to their husband and then to make his life unbearable until he has acceded to it; or the wives of a jealous husband will sometimes conspire together so as to conceal the escapades of one or other of them. Polygyny, because of its uneven sex ratio, tends to encourage adultery, for if a wife were to insist upon remaining faithful to her husband, she might run the risk of going childless. So she may seek a lover in order to have a child by him. The arrangement will be accepted by the husband, who will be the legitimate father—for are not children the greatest wealth of all? Yet in none of these aspects lie the real defects of polygyny. The real defects lie in the absence of conjugal intimacy, in the distrust a husband feels towards his wives whom he may suspect of a tendency to be in league against him, and in the distrust between the wives themselves, or their jealousy over each other's children. Possible causes of discord are endless, and from this arises the greatest defect of all: that a young wife, already suffering from the strain of removal from familiar surroundings, will feel all the more inclined to withdraw into herself, and will develop latent feelings of diffidence, or even of hostility, towards the world at large.

*　　*　　*

The lives of women everywhere follow the same broad outlines, even if each individual life may present some deviations from the general rule.

Everywhere a girl may be betrothed as soon as she is born, and before she is weaned her parents will have received the first payment from the family of her future husband. A young girl does not, however, consider herself in any way bound, for she knows that she can refuse to marry the spouse chosen for her; whereas a boy must adopt the role of "fiancé"—one might almost say, of "suitor" —and must go courting and express his admiration not only in words but also by giving presents. "If you don't give me the head-scarf I want for next feast-day, I know plenty of other boys who will be glad to give it to me." "Girls don't realize how much fiancés have to suffer", complained a young Kissi boy. There is almost complete sexual freedom until the time comes for setting up house (or until pregnancy), so long as the proprieties are observed. The only society among those described here where this is not the case is that of the Wolof, who are wholly converted to the Muslim faith. The time when intimacy first occurs varies in each individual case, and the girl will bestow her favours when it pleases her to do so. But if she should become pregnant, her companions will make fun of her, and it may also happen that the "fiancé" will have to suffer the reproaches of the girl's parents, as well as public disapproval, for making her pregnant at too early an age, regardless of the question as to whether he is actually to blame or not. It would be a total misrepresentation of the facts to say that in Africa a young girl is sold by her parents to a husband whom she does not know and against whom she has no legal redress; taking all the circumstances into account, it would be more correct to say that she is "loaned".

When a girl reaches marriageable age she often undergoes clitoridectomy along with the companions of her age-group. They are not allowed contact with men during convalescence, and this period of seclusion, which used to be quite a long one, is spent in having their education completed by the older women, who instill into them the duties they will have to perform when they are married and the conduct proper to a good wife, and who may, incidentally, impart to some of them the art of wheedling a husband every time he seems disinclined to yield immediately to their demands. Although there is no attempt at formal education of any kind, the period of seclusion does give girls a clearer idea of their importance to society, an appreciation that it is women who have life in their safe keeping and who possess the secrets of birth. Even the most prosperous family will have its position jeopardized if it has no daughter-in-law. The lesson is not lost, and a young wife, in the belief that she is indispensable, may prove recalcitrant to the rules imposed by the male section of the village. Men have long recognized this problem, and have felt the need to counteract female anarchy by staging public demonstrations, the most spectacular of which are those in which the masks are paraded through the village. Excluded as they are from such activities, the women and children are unaware of the identity of the figures concealed by the masks and cloaks, and are persuaded to believe that these are supernatural beings who will punish any infringements of the established order. But in the myths the invention of masks is often attributed to a woman, who stole the disguises abandoned by spirits; only later did men monopolize the masks and their accompanying symbolic powers as being the sole means of asserting their authority over their wives, this assertion being essential for the maintenance of social order. An important role is still played by an old woman in many of the men's associations.

The end of the period of seclusion is celebrated by a feast to which the fiancés of the girls contribute, and it is usually fairly soon after this that they start setting up their own household, although in some societies the young couple do not start living together until after the arrival of the first child. The Dogon assured me that formerly a woman did not go to live with her husband until a third child had been born. The young girl's parents do their utmost to obtain as high a marriage payment as possible, in which endeavour the mother plays an important role, this being an undertaking in which she is in the true sense a partner with her husband. The young man, for his part, will be generous if he has the means at his disposal, since his prestige depends on it. Nevertheless, greed and prudence combined may sometimes result in the young girl's being allowed to join her husband before the last payment has been made, with the possible result that there is an indefinite postponement of settlement if the son-in-law finds himself unable to satisfy the rapacity of his parents-in-law. "The settlement of the marriage payment can drag on for ever", sighed an old woman who was telling me her life story. When I asked her if anyone had ever considered the possibility of concluding a marriage without any presents from the bridegroom, she expressed her disapproval by saying: "If the husband did not pay anything, the wife would be a whore."

When the day arrives which has at last been decided upon as the day when the young wife definitely takes up residence with her husband, a feast is given at the home of the latter. The bride, dressed in all her finery and wearing all her jewellery, is brought with great ceremony, often in a hammock such as a chief uses, and always accompanied by an orchestra. Her kinswomen and friends display the calabashes, pottery, enamel bowls, bed-clothes and provisions supplied by the bride's parents for the new household. The bridegroom's mother sings a joyful song: "I shall no longer go to fetch wood and to fetch water; I shall no longer pound the grain . . ." The "brothers" of the bridegroom let off their guns with as much noise as possible, and there are dances in which the bride's "sisters" take part, many of whom will fail to return to sleep in their own beds in the village that night. The ceremony is a purely civil one, not marked by any kind of sacrificial rite or communal repast. At the most, the young wife, in some societies, will be presented to the ancestors, since it is through her that their line is

11

to be continued. Personal status is far less affected by marriage than it is by initiation, to such an extent that it is sometimes difficult to establish the exact moment when a girl becomes a married woman: the first time the meets her fiancé? when the marriage is consummated? when she becomes pregnant? or when the last instalment of the marriage payment is made? Each and every one of these possible suggestions may, on the spur of the moment, be put forward as equally valid.

Everywhere the birth of the first child is a more important event than the setting-up of the joint household, and it is marked by the rise of the parents to a higher age-class, whereas there is very often no special term to differentiate the married from the unmarried man or woman.

Once she has come to live with her husband's family, a wife continues for a long time to be regarded as a stranger. She receives far from indulgent treatment from her husband's mother, who immediately adopts a dictatorial attitude, and may wish to revenge herself upon her daughter-in-law for the treatment she herself had once had to endure; and the young wife has little to hope for in the way of comfort from her husband, who is more likely to be feeling resentful about all the dresses and jewellery he has had to give her. Along with regrets at giving up the life she has enjoyed as a young girl, marriage brings homesickness as well, and the bride does her utmost to go home as often and for as long as possible, while her husband, who bears a grudge against her parents-in-law, is reluctant to see his wife go off on these visits. The beginning of married life is a difficult period.

Later, many couples stabilize their relationship and lead comparatively peaceful lives. However, mutual understanding is only gradually established between husband and wife, and rarely expressed. Speaking of the Fulani of Fouta Djallon, an author who knows them well writes: "What characterizes married life is the absence of common ground, of any real union between husband and wife. The wife leads her life within her husband's compound a little as though she were a tenant there; she has her own interests, her garden, her cattle; she receives visits from her relations, has a younger sister to stay, or a small brother, or a servant-girl. It is pathetic to see a man, who in principle is the owner of his wife, entering into negotiations for borrowing a stool or a calabash belonging to her . . . In short, she hardly ever enters her husband's family without the hope of being able to return home again: she is on loan to him."[6] And this is among Muslims, for whom, in principle, the wife is the chattel of her husband. But the gap

12

between husband and wife is just as great in societies which remain faithful to ancestral cults, in which the wife, by definition an outsider, does not participate.

The attitude usually maintained between husbands and wives belonging to the same village is one of mutual constraint which can easily change to aggressiveness. Normally this only finds expression in banter; but should a crisis arise, a certain amount of antagonism becomes perceptible. If a woman should happen to have a difficult confinement, her sufferings are usually regarded as a punishment inflicted by her husband's ancestors; she will be accused of adultery, and will have to confess the names of her lovers. She herself will be convinced that she is the victim of a spell cast by her husband or by her mother-in-law, who must be annoyed with her for reasons which she resigns herself to supposing must remain a mystery. The blame for any and every public calamity, whether it be a rise in infant mortality, an abnormal drought, a threatened epidemic, is laid by the men on the women and *vice versa*. The importance of this recurrent theme in social life should not be exaggerated, but it should also not be overlooked. It underlies the ritual of male initiation, which acts as a safeguard for those who have undergone it against those who have not, and thus first and foremost against women.

This general atmosphere of mistrust arises, in part at any rate, from the horror inspired by blood, and from the feeling that there are magic dangers inherent in menstruation. It is not only in Africa that witchcraft is more often practised by women than by men. Everywhere, contact with a woman who is "impure" is considered to be a defilement. A woman in this condition will avoid preparing food for her husband, and will keep away from the altars, and, among agriculturalists, from the fields; or among pastoralists, from the cattle-enclosures. Sometimes there is even a special dwelling on the outskirts of the settlement set aside for the use of menstruating women, who have to purify themselves before taking part again in communal life. Women always have a greater number of taboos which they must observe. It is generally believed that they are experts in magic, which they can easily practise by casting a spell on the food they prepare for their husbands. This fear, joined to the fact that women are indispensable for the survival of the group, explains not only many of the taboos surrounding them, but also the ambiguous relations which exist between the men and women of a community. The men put up with the presence of their wives but continue to regard them as strangers, while the women, aware of their husband's attitude, will if necessary remind the men that they cannot do without their wives. In some areas men adopt a different attitude towards women depending upon which of their acknowledged functions the women are fulfilling. According to J. Hurault, a Bamileke woman, in so far as she is a descendant of an ancestress, is respected and even feared by her maternal kin; but in her role as daughter she is handed over, exchanged, or given away by her father without consideration for anything but his own interests, and in her role as wife she is kept under strict discipline by her husband.[7]

An African woman sets greater store by her children than by her husband, for it is only by becoming a mother that she feels truly fulfilled. Annie Lebeuf refers in her essay to the role played in many African states by the mother, and sometimes by the sister, of the king, their thrones being placed side by side with the ruler's on all official occasions. In all societies, whether feudal or democratic, sons, whether princes or peasants, will always remain small boys in the eyes of their mother, and it is the mother who carries on the management of the household after the father's death, who chooses the first wife, at anyrate, for her sons, and who has most say in arranging the marriage of her daughters. This predominance of the mother, who continues to direct her children's lives even after they have grown up, is found in all African societies, including those which have become Muslim. The mother expects to be treated with respect by her children, and will not resign her position until the time arrives when her sons are themselves the fathers of families, and, her vigour now diminished with age, there appears to be no longer a role for her to play.

By a curious paradox, it is only when she passes beyond childbearing age that an African woman at last finds herself accepted by her husband's family. Africans are aware of the fact that in her later years there is little to distinguish a woman from a man, and whether she be wife of a chief or not, a woman of intelligence whose family has prospered will have earned the right to be held in general esteem—an esteem that increases in proportion to the number of her surviving children.

However, enviable as may be the fate of a matron surrounded by children and grandchildren who supply her needs just as formerly she looked after theirs, it is no more enviable than is pitiable the position of an old woman, widowed and childless, who was too old to get remarried, and who finds herself in the care of her husband's brothers and nephews. Supported out of charity, and often undernourished, her death will be felt as a relief. Perhaps no sooner is she buried than she will be declared to have been a witch,

Introduction

responsible for all the recent misfortunes suffered by the community. This provides an outlet and a relief for feelings of hostility —a last service, although an involuntary one, that a woman may render to the group of people who, all through her life, have been no more to her than relations by marriage, which is as much as to say: strangers.

*　　*　　*

What does the future offer for African women? These women who are so independent, so courageous, and so used to relying on no one but themselves? Already many of them have set up in businesses of their own. But if they are to do more than simply make money, they must be given opportunities for exercising their talent for organization, their energy, and their practical sense.

The number of openings which modern society offers them is still fairly restricted, since far fewer girls go to school than boys, while the number who become university students is infinitesimal. With the exception of midwives who have married a doctor, few women, whether teachers, nurses, dressmakers or clerks, continue working after they have married. The idea that a job might be a vocation, a life's work, rarely occurs. Most of the young African girls who take a job only do so while looking for a husband, or in order to acquire some savings so that they will have more freedom of choice of one, or because they do not wish to marry too young.

We have seen that it is traditional in Africa to regard marriage as an active association to which the woman has her daily contribution to make—an idea which is so recent in the West that it is still only accepted in some sections of society. Unaccustomed to relying on anyone but herself, the African woman will have no need to acquire a feeling of self-confidence, since she is already rarely without one. Perhaps the obstacle she will have most difficulty in surmounting is that age-old mistrust of the world in general and of her husband in particular. But I am acquainted with a sufficient number of African couples and have seen a large enough number of homes, in the best sense of the word, to be able, in this respect at least, to take an optimistic view of the future.

NOTES

[1]S. Leith-Ross, *African wo　en: a study of the Ibo of Nigeria* (Faber, 1939).
[2]Monica Hunter, *Reaction to conquest. Effects of contacts with the Europeans on the Pondo of South Africa* (O.U.P. 1936).

15

Denise Paulme

[3] Mary Smith, *Baba of Karo: a woman of the Muslim Hausa* (Faber, 1954).

[4] Camara Laye, *L'Enfant noir* (Paris, Plon, 1953). Trans. by James Kirkup, *The dark child* (Collins, 1955).

[5] See below: S. Faladé, "Women of Dakar . . ."

[6] G. Vieillard, "Notes sur les Peuls du Fouta Djallon", *Bull. de l'I.F.A.N.*, I-II (1940), 85-210.

[7] J. Hurault, *Notes sur la structure sociale des Bamiléké* (Roneo), p. 12.

CONIAGUI WOMEN
(Guinea)

Monique Gessain

THE POSITION, ROLE, FUNCTIONS and status of women were topics which did not much interest the first writers to give an account of the Coniagui and Bassari, A. Rançon (1894), A. Delacour (1912 and 1913) and H. Técher (1933) being the only ones who touched upon them; and no attempt at a more detailed study of Coniagui women was made until Maupoil's work in the field. Unfortunately Maupoil died in 1944 before having published a new edition of Delacour's work to which he had intended adding the important notes deposited in the I.F.A.N. library at Dakar, which it has been my task to study and classify.

Since 1946, a good deal of fieldwork has been done: by myself, in 1946 and 1948-49 in Guinea (and to a lesser extent in Senegal), and in 1953 and 1954 in France, among Coniagui resident there; by Robert Gessain and myself in 1955 in Guinea, and in 1955, 1957, 1958 and 1959 among Coniagui and Bassari resident in France; and by Robert Gessain in 1959 in Guinea and Senegal.

The Coniagui and Bassari consist of a small number of exogamous matrilineal groups which I shall call *anank*, the term which the Coniagui use to denote them.[1] It is through the mother that affiliation to his or her *anank* is handed down to each individual, together with the privileges attaching to membership of the *anank*; and it is also through the mother that a man receives, from his maternal uncle, those material possessions and political powers to which men alone have the right—namely, herds and chiefship.[2] Thus the kin of one individual man consists solely of his mother and grandmother,[3] his maternal aunts and grand-aunts and their daughters, and his sisters and their daughters and grand-daughters —but never of his own daughters. A man's only descendants are his sister's children (cf. Fig. 1). Marriage being virilocal, the children who will inherit a man's property may live far away from him, and

17

he will have little acquaintance with them. In contradistinction to this, a woman is kin both to her mother, and to her children, who live with her until they are married; and she has particularly close kinship bonds with her daughters, through whom the line of descent is perpetuated.

WOMAN AS THE KINSHIP LINK

In virtue of the fact that it is women alone who are the link in the line of descent and in the kinship structure, they also act in a pivotal capacity between men, although it is the men who wield power and who are the owners of wealth.

A study of the transmission both of chiefship and of the only important material possessions owned by the Coniagui—namely, their herds—provides excellent examples of this pivotal role of women. But chiefship is a question which brings into play a number of aspects which go beyond the study of women as such, and the transmission of cattle is a difficult subject to handle because of the frequency of epizootic disease. I prefer to give here two examples of the role played by women as kinship link and as pivot between men which derive from the practice of revenge—an important cog in human relations among the Coniagui and Bassari. I use the term "cog" here on purpose, since revenge in these societies is more an institution than a matter of feeling, with legal rather than psychological implications. Where others may find in it primarily the satisfaction of an impulse, the Coniagui and Bassari seem to regard it rather as a duty or an obligation.

The first example is taken from a chapter in the autobiography of a Coniagui to which the author himself has given the title: "The Coniagui are keen on revenge". The facts may be summarised as follows:

1. The sister *a* of a man A refuses to marry B who has made a marriage offer to her (cf. the upper diagrams in Fig. 2).

2. Learning that the daughter *b'* of his sister *b* associates with A, B orders his sister *b* to prohibit her daughter *b'* to continue her association with A. *b'* and her mother *b* then come one after the other to warn A and explain to him that it is impossible for him to continue having relations with *b'*. A, in his autobiography, writes thus concerning the situation: "I was not really worried, because I had no intention of setting up house with this girl . . . I had never said anything against either the girl *b'* or against B . . ."

18

Coniagui Women

And A settles the matter with *b*, who says to him: "B has forbidden *b'* to visit you because he asked for the hand of your sister *a* and was refused, and that is why he seeks revenge against you."

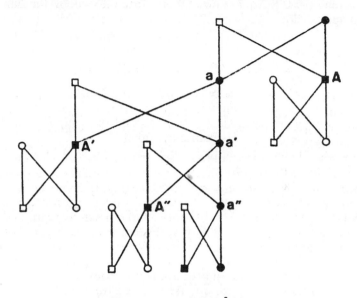

 O female   □ male   ●■ anənk **Aa**

Fig. 1.—*Kinship among the Coniagui and Bassari.*

Representing a man A and his sister *a*, both belonging to the *anənk Aa*. The *anənk* is an exogamous group (cf. p. 17) and membership of it is transmitted from mother to child, so that the only persons standing in a kinship relation to A and *a* are the children A' and *a'* of the woman *a* (who inherit from their maternal uncle A), the children A" and *a"* of the woman *a'* (who inherit from their maternal uncle A'), the children of the woman *a"* (who inherit from their maternal uncle A"), etc. . . . while excluded from kinship relations are the children of the men A, A', and A", whose inheritors are the children of their respective sisters *a*, *a'* and *a"*.

"As she repeated the words, her tears were falling down on the gown she was wearing. I thought it over for a moment and then I said to her that I was sorry about it, but it was natural that he should want his revenge even if it was my kin or rather my sister that had brought it about, and as they say: a debt is a debt, and the Coniagui repay vengeance with vengeance. Only B ought to have waited until I came to make him a marriage offer for *b'* as he had done for my sister.[4] Thank goodness I was told about it in time.

You may be sure, *b*, that I shall never speak ill of you, nor of your daughter, nor of B. I am far from feeling any grudge against your family. If you should at any time hear that I had spoken against its name, come to me immediately to demand why." And then he promptly follows this with: "But I can assure you that there will be no end to this feud. I shall in turn take my revenge even although I have suffered no wrong. Go back home now and go to sleep. Tomorrow I shall tell my kinsfolk what you have told me. It was nice of you to come . . ."

3. "The feud was not over", writes our Coniagui friend. "*b'* married a friend of mine, and there were no grounds for my harbouring a grudge against her . . . but all the same I was determined to revenge myself against B's family."

Some years passed, and then the occasion arose for his doing so.

"*a'*, my big sister, has some daughters who are nearly grown up. B has a little brother of my age—B'. One day, B' went to my sister *a'* to make a marriage offer for her eldest daughter, *a"*. My sister wrote to me to ask my advice. I replied that I did not want to hear anything more about this family or this *anank*. I would have something to say, I wrote to her, to whoever it was came to make a marriage offer for your daughter. Up until the present the fellow hasn't yet written to me, and the affair goes back now to February 1958. I am just waiting for a letter to come from him, and then it will be my turn for revenge. And that is what I mean when I say that this feud will never end, because I know that if I take my revenge, they will take theirs again later or else my family will continue to take theirs."

"Maybe my kin would be ready to forgive and forget, but I know that *a'* will want to repay vengeance with vengeance."

I have quoted this autobiographical material in some detail, because it provides an illustration of how what might be called the Coniagui vendetta is carried out in practice. It might lead one to suppose that a vendetta of this kind only arises over marriage arrangements, and is restricted to disputes between different *anank*. Such is by no means the case, however, as the second example will show. The story may be summarized as follows:

1. A, a Bassari of Senegal, enlisted in the French army. During his absence, his younger brother A' was born. A asked their common father to send A' to school. The father did not do so, for since his wife (the mother of A and A') had died, he had become very attached to his youngest son A' and did not want to part with him (cf. Fig. 2, lower diagram).

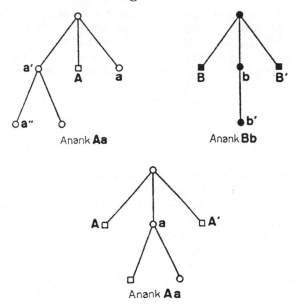

Fig. 2.

Diagrams illustrating two examples of the woman as kinship link and as pivot between men (cf. pp. 18-22).

2. When A returned home, he decided to recruit A' into the army. A', sixteen years of age, knowing not a word of French, and never having left his village, suddenly found himself recruited into the army, his brother A having succeeded in signing up for him. The father of A and A', and their sister *a* shed many tears.

3. A' decided to revenge himself for the first six months he spent in the army, which had been a terrible experience for him. In order to do so, he decided, and gave warning to his brother A and to his sister *a* about his decision, that his sister's son must go into the army and his sister's daughter must go to school.

4. My informant A' added: "Perhaps the 'repayment' (this being the actual expression used by A') will stop there, if *a*'s son decides it that way. It is up to him to leave it at that or to continue repayment through the children of his own sister."

These two concrete examples, the one Coniagui and the other Bassari, appear to me to show very well the role of women as kinship link and as pivot between men.

In the first case:

First: a woman (*a*) offends a man (B).

Second: the man (B) takes his revenge upon the brother of *a* (the man A), with the daughter of his sister (*b*) acting as pivot.

Third: the man (A) takes his revenge upon the man (B) with the child (*a'*) of his sister and the brother of B acting as pivots.

Thus the *anənk* A*a* took its revenge upon the *anənk* B*b*.

In the second case:

First: a man (A) offends a man (A').

Second: the man A' takes his revenge with the children of their common sister (*a*) acting as pivot.

Thus one man took his revenge upon another within the same *anənk* A*a*.

In both cases, a member of the same *anənk* as that to which the person giving offence belongs must pay, even if this should at the same time inconvenience members of the *anənk* of the offended person. In both cases, the person giving offence, man or woman, sets off a chain of reactions which will end in reprisals falling not on him nor on his children,[5] but on the children of his sister, who herself has not been directly involved. This comes out particularly clearly in the second case, where the woman *a* had defended her brother A' against her other brother A; but that did not prevent A' from taking revenge for the offence given to him by A on the children of *a*.

I have given these concrete examples in order to show how the fact of their being the only link in the kinship structure gives to women an important social role among the Coniagui and the Bassari.

THE POSITION OF WOMEN

The fact of being the kinship link carries with it a certain status, a certain social position, and I shall now describe the position of women among the Coniagui and Bassari by discussing the stages in a woman's life from her childhood until her death.

Childhood

It is probably when she is about four years old, the age when she first puts on an article of feminine clothing—a narrow piece of indigo blue material made of strips of cotton joined together, which she ties round her waist in imitation of her elders—that the little Coniagui girl[6] first becomes aware of the duties and privileges which will be hers as a woman. It is also at this age that the little boy begins to leave his mother's side and join company with his

Coniagui Women

father, and with the other boys of his own age, together with whom he will soon go off every day and spend long hours running about in the bush. The little girl, on the other hand, has already learnt that the women's domain is the house, the fields and the well, and that that is where she and her mother belong.

Until the time of her marriage, a girl lives in her mother's hut and helps her all day long with her work in the house and in the fields. Her mother instructs her and trains her, and it is usually she who punishes her, which may even include, on rare occasions, beating her.

The little girl becomes initiated at a very early age in the occupations which will busy her when she grows up, and in particular in the techniques practised by her mother. Thus, for instance, the daughter of a potter will amuse herself at her mother's side making little dishes and pots, copying the methods used by mother. There seems to be no line drawn between work and play, and it is with the greatest enjoyment, in company with her sisters, half-sisters, and the daughters of her father's other wives or of neighbours, that the little girl will learn to look after the babies, prepare the food, work in the fields, and fetch wood and water.

Friendship and companionship play an important part at every stage in a woman's life. Every girl usually has her special friend whose role and duties are quite specific (giving presents at the time of the excision ceremony, for instance). Like the boys, the young girls of the village are grouped together in an association of which one of them is the head.

The little girl prepares herself for her role as mother both by playing with her doll, which is usually made of cassava-flour or maize, according to the season, and by looking after her younger brother or sister. The mother often leaves one of the younger children in her care while she herself works in the fields, taking the baby with her.

She is all the more aware of her future as a wife because very often she has been betrothed at birth or since earliest childhood to a boy older than herself and sometimes to a man who greets her by the name of "wife" when he comes to see her. This adult man will speak of his betrothed, the little girl playing with her doll, with the greatest interest and tenderness, which are, however, far removed from the love relations usually associated in the West European mind with marriage. Child betrothal and in particular the presents which the little girl receives and those which her parents receive because of her, undeniably have a distinct influence on the development of a woman's personality, for from an early age she finds herself being valued for being a woman. The presents received by the young fiancée and those received by her parents because of her can therefore be regarded as expressions of feeling which help the young girl to assume her feminine role.[7]

Whether betrothed or not, and still by her mother's side learning the skills she will spend all her life in practising, the young girl will come to an age when, for several years, her life will be greatly occupied with sexual escapades. At the age of about fifteen she begins to become interested in companions of the opposite sex. Still too young to have her parents' consent, she has to enjoy herself on the sly, and resorts to all sorts of stratagems to deceive her mother and meet her admirers.

Then, around the age of eighteen, comes the time when she must undergo clitoridectomy.

Adolescence

The excision ceremony is an important occasion in the life of a young Coniagui girl. It is then that the fiancés set the seal on their approaching marriage. The young man offers presents to the girl and she plights her troth in accepting them. A Coniagui girl receives many other presents at the time of the excision ceremony, in particular from her best girl friend. The ceremony gives her an opportunity to have her beauty and her courage admired, as well as for displaying her social success and her success in affairs of the heart. For these reasons it is of great importance in the life of a Coniagui woman, quite apart from the fact that it brings an actual change in her status: before it, a Coniagui girl is merely a child; after it, she is regarded as an adult enjoying new rights and privileges. During the period of seclusion which lasts for several weeks after the ceremony, the girls probably undergo what amounts to an initiation comparable to that of the boys. It is true that this initiatory aspect of the excision ceremony is of a more secret nature and less obvious than the ceremonies by which Coniagui and Bassari boys become men. But among the Coniagui, at anyrate, where all the girls in a village who have undergone the ceremony live together for several weeks under the supervision of young women who are senior to them, it seems likely that these older women take the opportunity to transmit to their juniors those feminine secrets to which men are never admitted, and which certain old women are adept at imparting.

The few years which follow the excision ceremony and precede marriage are the happiest time in a young girl's life, according to the opinion of most Coniagui.

Coniagui Women

A. Delacour, who remains the best observer of Coniagui life, gave an excellent description of it when he wrote:

"The young girl lives with her mother up until the time when she goes to live with her husband, a step which she only takes when absolutely forced to. For, as long as she stays with her mother, she enjoys considerable freedom, and at festival times can gad about the neighbourhood as she pleases. Meanwhile her fiancé must keep dancing attendance on her for fear a rival may succeed in alienating her affections. Wishing to enjoy herself to the full, it is not until she becomes pregnant that she will finally decide to leave home. As soon as she begins living with her husband she has to take her share in the household work, and then it is goodbye to the gay life and the tom-toms, for the only festivals she will now be able to join in are those specifically for married women. She could take part in other festivals if her husband gave her permission, but in fact this seldom happens and is not considered quite proper."[8]

Between the excision ceremony and marriage Coniagui girls go from village to village and from festival to festival, sometimes even travelling beyond Coniagui territory. What characterizes this period in the life of Coniagui girls, and also the life of the young men, is the important part played in it by boy-and-girl relations, the importance of having love affairs. This seems to have escaped the earliest writers on the Coniagui, and in 1894 Rançon even wrote: "I do not believe the Coniagui ever have love affairs, in the true sense of the term." Delacour says nothing at all on the subject, but Maupoil, who made a study of the Coniagui in 1941, notes:[9]

"I have good reason to suppose that the love life of the Coniagui is rather a subtle affair. One has only to observe, in the bustle of the market or amid the silence of the bush, how a young man courts the girl of his choice, to become convinced of this.

"Repartee is an important element in striking up an acquaintance. It might even be described as a verbal duel, full of proverbs and quips. The pair both want to touch each other, and indulge in a series of fencings and parryings in the hope of attaining their desire. Each measures the quick-wittedness and intelligence of the other, as they try themselves out in that 'art of conference' in which Montaigne discovered all the elements of athletic sport. Each attempts to get the better of the other, and reputations are quickly established in a society where the idea of shrouding a love affair in secrecy, such as may be found among the bourgeoisie of Europe, is quite unknown. In less than no time the age-class of each contestant will have the latest information as to who is due for praise and who for ridicule."

"The young man often expresses his feelings by playing an instrument with the name of *usir*,* which is made from the rib of a raffia palm leaf, the skin of which is cut loose lengthwise in thin, narrow strips which are left attached to the rib at both ends and raised off the rib by pieces of twig wedged in to serve as bridges; they are played by striking them with a millet stalk.[10] One end of the *usir* is held between the lips, the mouth serving as a resonator. The instrument makes a very faint sound, which matches the rhythm of the girl's walk, especially the jogging of her breasts. The musician is rewarded with a smile.

"The young man can also make the *usir* speak a kind of musical language-without-words, making it say, for instance: 'Nǝmolo . . . Nǝmolo, come, let us not waste time, I swear to be true.'

"If the girl joins in the game, she will say coquettishly: 'You are trying to coax me, but you don't love me' etc . . .

"The best players of this instrument use it for giving the rhythm when the young men dance in the moonlight, but the *usir* is first and foremost the instrument for expressing love and desire.

"When a girl accepts an invitation to a rendez-vous, the boy, if his pleasure at her acceptance is intense enough, sometimes gives a loud shout so as to proclaim his joy. He will do this even if his companions, or those of the girl, or her fiancé, are present.

"His sweetheart will, however, set off for their tryst in secret, usually alone and at dusk. A pre-arranged sign will enable her to recognize her lover's house. Most commonly, it is a long bamboo pole . . . put in front of the door, with something stuck on top of it (a tin can, perhaps). Sometimes the young man comes to meet his sweetheart at some spot decided beforehand, but intercourse will not take place in the bush, because a girl would be afraid that an evil spirit might discover them and might cause her to become pregnant.

"In the man's house the couple are always alone, even if he has invited several girls to come during the same night. It is believed that if two girls were to share the bed of a lover at the same time, their combined potency might magnetize his and deprive him of it."

Further study of the Coniagui—and in particular a review of the autobiographies recently collected—does in fact show that during five, ten or fifteen years of their life, Coniagui adolescents, both boys and girls, are preoccupied with their love life more than with anything else, as is indicated by the following text which comes from the pen of a Coniagui boy called Sara:

*cf. C. Béart, *Jeux et jouets de l'ouest Africain* (Dakar, IFAN, 1955), II, p. 679, note 51: "Coniagui children make and use a kind of two-stringed zither by cutting loose two strips of the skin of the rib of a palm-leaf. Adults have a similar instrument (fig. 496). The upper string is used in the manner of a musical bow, the vibrations being set up by a stick, while the mouth forms a resonator which gives the tone; the lower string is stopped with the fingers of the left hand." [Trans. of excerpt from text.] The illustration 496 shows such an instrument from Yukunkun (French Guinea). [Tr. note.]

Coniagui Women

"Free at last, after 12 months confinement to barracks, in this *tyareg*,[11] and with my *usir*, this instrument of revolution! And this *usir*, playing it, ideas came to me which only my heart knew! There were these five girls in the same village at O., and all of them Catholic missionaries like me,[12] and because of my swagger clothes, they vowed each and all of them, Sara to become her fiancé. Turn and turn about they came to my house, and end up not knowing who had been the first to come! So I had been as polygamous as they. Jealous talk between them. Niena, E. and J. meeting for the first time. What heart-searchings for all of them. J. was the youngest, and she, more jealous learning suddenly her two sisters run after the same boy and after that she has made big brawl in the *tyareg*. Meanwhile Niena and E. were resigned to being co-wives, sly, trying to get the advantage, each doing her best to declare her love by giving proof of it. Eau de Cologne, handkerchief, drink, etc. . . .

"And me, in this time of danger, in terrible temptation, worried by how affectionate all these candidates were, each one for herself, the first the same as the others, announced having made my choice when very young, when I was at catechism class. With feelings for them ponderously weighed in the balance, I answer their questions with false promises waiting until my heart tells me what final decision to make. In my own mind, I have chosen Niena, the one who all this time has never made declarations of love like the others and has always seriously believed that she is not worthy of me. In secret, a marriage offer has been made on my behalf to my future father-in-law, Z., who at once, taking a favourable view, begged me not to delay the marriage for he knew how much his daughter had suffered and that she was set on the idea and afraid of losing me. Since the prospects of marrying Niena seemed bright, the whole affair got put off until the end of the year because meanwhile I had to go to X . . .

"After three months service in this new district which was strange to me, although I often had gloomy thoughts about my many future wives, gradually I got accustomed to all those smooth-tongued people in X. One day comes a reception for a young Frenchman recently posted to be head of the subdivision and he has come to be presented to M.N., the departing head of the subdivision. Here is an opportunity for Sara to forget his thoughts about Yukunkun. At eight o'clock in the evening Mr. New-head-of-the-subdivision has made friends with his secretary, Sara. In the course of a conversation about polygamy in so far as it concerns the Senegalese, was declaring that he enjoyed African fun and dancing, when along comes from I don't know where a girl called Aissata, daughter of a schoolmaster who lived in the district. Her greetings of good-evening gentlemen said very sweetly wakened us out of our stupor and made us forget our futile talk about patience in love in this bush of ours. The young French gentleman and me, have forgotten our promises to be good, and have now multiplied our questions to this quarry who has suddenly appeared just at the right moment. But now is the question: two men and one girl! My poor girl was in danger! But, remembering the official position he had come to take up, the young French gentleman was finding himself in a difficult situation, first of all not to get annoyed with the crowd that had come in his honour, and then Aissata, the young lady in danger, was all for Sara! another temptation! From that day on, she was tumbling over herself sending me cakes, dishes of rice, grilled chickens. She could not go two hours without seeing me. In the end she was very unhappy, because she saw there would be an end to it all, that we would say goodbye, and she cried bitterly. A difficult question which made me cry too! out of pity for her! because one day I told her that I was engaged and that I could not succeed in marrying her because her family are Muslims; poor girl! And such a strong character, that as soon as I said that, she vowed she would leave her family and give up her religion and follow me in this world and the next. I consoled her with false promises, because I was too much of a coward to send her away when she made her decision."

Coniagui girls enjoy a great deal of freedom, for they are allowed to have a lover in each village (and there are about 80 villages) and every fortnight may spend a couple of days or so with one of them. Should a girl want to leave home oftener, she sometimes has to deceive her mother, inventing an excuse, for instance, that a girl friend who lives in the same village as her lover needs help. She tells her mother that she will spend the night with this girl friend. She can also slip out of the hut at night after her mother has left it.[13] Usually the mother feels that it will not be any too long before her daughters will have to submit to the discipline of married life, and mother and daughters are in league against the common enemy: man. Among the Coniagui the battle between the sexes is never-ending. Every shortcoming on the part of the enemy is utilized immediately, no man ever trusts any woman, and every woman is afraid of the men while at the same time mocking at them.

When boys and girls meet, they mock at each other. If a group of girls comes up against a group of boys, the battle is even. But a group of girls will get the better of a boy on his own, although a boy will get the better of a girl in single combat.

Relations between boys and girls are further complicated by a number of taboos. Thus, a woman must never pour water over a man, never touch his big toe, nor his head (unless he has expressly asked her to cut his hair for him), nor step over his body, even at night and even if he is asleep. One of my informants told me that one night he was lying stretched out on a mat when a girl came to his hut. He pretended to be asleep, and the girl, probably afraid lest she disturb his nap, stepped over him in order to lie down on the bed on the other side of him. He did not say a word, but gave his lady-love one single, but very hard, slap (in spite of his being, by his own account, the most gentle of Coniaguis), and left. On the excuse of looking for a light for his lamp, he stayed a while in the hut of an old man. He then returned to his own hut and, without saying anything, lit his lamp before going in, stood for a moment, then entered, and—what a pleasant surprise!—found the girl waiting for him.

They greeted each other.

"Have you been here long?"

"I have just arrived," said the girl, "and found the hut empty."

"Yes . . . had to get a light for my lamp."[14]

The girl will scarcely want to boast about having been slapped, and the boy will say nothing about it. Custom has been complied with, all is well—the incident has not taken place.[15]

If the contrary had happened, what gloating there would have been the next morning among the womenfolk, and what a risk the man would have run if he had not followed the custom and if he had allowed a woman to go unpunished. But men never forget the story that is repeated to them every day of their seclusion during the initiation ceremonies, about the village head who was murdered for having said to his wives, while drinking with them the initiation beer (which is forbidden to women), that the initiation ceremonies were nothing but humbug and play-acting.

During adolescence, Coniagui girls are under the authority of both father and mother and have to get their permission in every important decision. For example, if a girl wants to go along with a young man into the Gambia, she has to get her father's consent and also that of her mother and of her mother's kin (or at least of those who are close neighbours).

But the girls know that their mothers are usually on their side, especially in the matter of putting off the moment when they will have to live with their husbands. Among the Coniagui it is often the case that a man is eager to get married soon, while the woman is in no hurry to do so.

During the privileged period which Coniagui adolescents enjoy, both boys and girls are first and foremost preoccupied with the business of attracting each other and making conquests, whatever activities they may otherwise be engaged in. Whatever they may be doing, whether taking their share in the agricultural work or making long trips to gather wild plants, exchange commodities with neighbouring peoples or earn some money, it always serves as an opportunity to wear their finest beads and show off their skill in repartee. This is what the Coniagui who speak French call "faire la jeunesse" (enjoying their youth), and they look back all their life long to this time of their youth. Many married men cherish deep down a fond memory of a dearly loved sweetheart whom they plan to visit the next time they go her way and with whom they compare all the girls they meet. It would appear, however, that they have never made any great effort to marry her . . .

In point of fact, all the narratives contributed by men which have come to hand feature a fondly cherished sweetheart with whom the man, before his marriage, had had sexual relations of varying degrees of intimacy, in some cases not having gone beyond the stage of preliminary play, while in some the woman had given birth to a child or even several children. The woman in these stories was never betrothed to the man; but then in the majority of Coniagui marriages the husband and wife have formerly been betrothed to other partners whom they did not marry; so one can only suppose, in many cases at anyrate, that if a Coniagui man has not married the beloved of his youth, it is because he did not want to. Several of the biographies and autobiographies which have been collected make this plain, so that one wonders if perhaps Coniagui men distrust the idea of marrying for love? Several of them have told me that it is better to marry a woman who loves you than a woman you are in love with . . .

Marriage

If there have been few general studies of the life of Coniagui and Bassari women, one particular aspect of it—namely, marriage and the position of the married woman—has excited the attention of all the writers concerned, who on this subject provide us with a large amount of what is unfortunately often highly contradictory information. A. Rançon (1894), writing of the Coniagui, says: "Nor is there any marriage ceremony, properly speaking. When a man wants to get married, all he does is to ask the consent of the girl's father . . . The woman is never consulted under any circumstances". And on the topic of succession to the chiefship he writes: "All this would seem to indicate that among the Coniagui the position of women is much higher than it is among the other peoples of French Sudan. This may be true of the royal family, but it did not strike me as being the case among the ordinary people", and he sums up his opinion thus: "Women . . . receive exactly the same treatment as they do among the majority of African peoples. It is to them that the most laborious tasks are relegated".[16]

But A. Rançon finds that Bassari marriage differs essentially from Coniagui marriage, because: "Marriage among the Bassari takes place without any kind of ceremony, the consent of the woman being all that is required, although that is absolutely indispensable"; and from this he draws the following conclusion: "The Bassari are perhaps the only people in the French Sudan known to me among whom the woman is consulted upon the choice of her husband. This fact would seem to prove that women here are freer than elsewhere".[17]

Forty years later (1933) H. Técher wrote of the Bassari: "The consent of the woman is necessary in principle only, the parents having the real say in the matter" . . . "In any case the fiancée is not often consulted". But then he contradicts himself immediately when he remarks: "The position of women among the Bassari is much higher than is the case among other primitive peoples. In fact, a woman is free to do as she pleases".[18]

Here again, it is A. Delacour who gives a more accurate picture of the situation: "Here, the consent of the girl is of real importance" since Coniagui and Bassari women enjoy a considerable measure of freedom in all spheres, including that of the choice of husband.[19]

Formerly, it was the mother who chose a fiancée for her son, often when he was still quite a child. Her choice generally lay with the newly-born daughter of one of her women friends. If nowadays it occurs less frequently than before that marriages arranged between the mothers shortly after the birth of the girl actually take place when the children have grown up, this nevertheless remains the traditional form of marriage, thus illustrating the important role played by the mothers in the marriage of her sons. The importance of the mother's role is further stressed by the fact that if a girl wants to marry, she must obtain the consent not only of her father, but also of her mother and of her mother's family, to wit and above all, of her maternal uncle.

Although betrothal is arranged during childhood, it is open to question and to confirmation at the time of the excision ceremonies. As it is not my purpose here to describe the marriage rites,[20] I shall confine myself to commenting on those aspects of marriage which throw light on the role of women among the Coniagui and Bassari.

Nowadays a Coniagui woman often goes to live with her husband at the time of her first pregnancy, but formerly she did not do so until she had one, two, or three children.

Once she has set up house with her husband, a married woman must, as A. Delacour says, "occupy herself entirely with her duties as wife and as mother".[21] The wives of a man owe him obedience, "but when conflict arises, they do not hesitate to return to their own families until some grounds for conciliation have been found. In any case, the husband does not usually abuse his authority".[22]

"Moreover (a married woman) is looked up to, and often has real influence on her husband, who is careful not to ill-treat her, since he knows that if his wife is not happy with him, he will be unable to force her to remain".[23]

In the marriage relation, the normal marked antagonism between the sexes is reduced. But even if a certain degree of amicability has been reached between husband and wife, the man will usually take care not to show it. The men say that women, even after they are married, try to take advantage of the least sign of weakness in their husbands, and that a husband will do well to show some severity. But married women enjoy a great deal of freedom. For instance, they can go off for several days on a visit to their family, or on an expedition into the bush with other women to gather the roots of wild plants, etc. . . .

However, in general relations between men and women improve as they get older, and a couple who have been married for many years sometimes succeed in establishing a very good relationship, full of mutual trust.

The wife must remain faithful to her husband, and this is where the life of a married woman most differs from that of an unmarried girl, who enjoys a great deal of sexual freedom.

Coniagui and Bassari men practise a mild form of polygyny, a man being, as Delacour puts it, "at liberty to marry several wives if he is clever enough to persuade several to marry him".[24]

Certain complications with regard to this have not been lacking in Coniagui households owing to the conversion to Christianity of quite a large number of Coniagui and Bassari. Sara, from whose autobiography quotations have already been given, provides an example. His girl friend Aissata came to join him at Y., where he had got married to Niena.

"She had tracked me down, and I got a bad name on her account, this girl of temptation that my heart could not forget . . .

"One day, being assigned by Mr. the Head-of-the-subdivision to make a tax register in the Bassari district—dangerous mountain country—since I was keeping Miss Aissata at my administrative quarters and now it was a question either of leaving her or of sending her back home, since she could not live there all alone, she had been to see Mr. the Head-of-the-subdivision about this and had demanded to be allowed to go along with me. What a problem! A girl in these mountains with their rough roads? Mr. the Head-of-the-subdivision wanting to refuse, Miss Aissata strengthens her case with pitiful tears saying to Mr. the Head-of-the-subdivision that she would rather die of hardship along with me than stay in a prison of anxiety in Yukunkun during my absence. Mr. the Head-of-the-subdivision after giving her a long look full of pity, grants the girl leave to go

Coniagui Women

with her husband who is due to set off shortly. In company with my little Aissata in a service vehicle which was leaving that day for N., we made the journey feeling very pleased with ourselves, during the course of which my girl with a look whispered to me to escape with her to a foreign country and take refuge there and get married privately, for her father and his kin had already forbidden our marriage because of the religious differences . . .

"At the end of 35 days, her patience exhausted, Niena the legitimate one, accompanied by her mother, sent me a message to meet her at a house belonging to a Mr. Goutinek, where a Bassari feast was being held. We left T. for I. after getting through the work very quickly so as not to keep my mother waiting who was most likely with me in mind inclined to be feeling annoyed. We got to N., where a regular feast was laid on for me, because in this village all my friends were expecting me, the kin (of my father) and village heads and notables who had all come to this place for the feast. After taking various steps for making everything all right, my mother to consult, to tell about and to present most pitifully this girl, who, because of love for me, had gone through all the hardship of this long journey with me! And Aissata too, what with all the mixed-up ideas in her mind, went on crying for a long time, and my mother was soon joining in with her tears for consolation. As for wife Niena, jealously back in position and her mind made up, very craftily, was consoling the girl telling her she would be second wife and not to have any regrets. This was a piece of pure bitchiness on her part, because before she had chased after me she had first been to lay a complaint against me with the senior Reverend Father, who very soon sent me a very severe letter.

"Three days we spent there! What a business! Sara as head of the family with two wives. Fortunately my young lady came under the category of servant to my wife and she was ready to obey her slightest command in case anyone might be watching, until soon my mother and wife decided to return to Coniagui country. On the fifty-fifth day we arrived at N., the last place on the list! And there, in the company of two young Bassari men I sent Miss Aissata back to Yukunkun promising that I would return in three days time . . ."

After six years spent in the army, Sara returned home.

"We had just begun to enjoy ourselves when along came my much-missed Aissata who had as companion her little girl, my daughter Marie, to present her to the father she has never known 'oh may God forgive me for behaving so disgracefully!'

"At the very moment when Aissata had thrown my six-year-old daughter into my arms saying: 'There is your Papa, I do not want to see you ever again, you child of a no-good man!'

"Poor Aissata then fell in a dead faint.

"Was she putting on airs or behaving in the way African women usually do? No, what she was really objecting to was me betraying her after reaching such an advanced stage in adultery. I asked her to come with me

33

somewhere outside the village so that we could be alone so that I could console her and make her forget me. She accepted in the hope of getting something out of it, her smiles came back and she began going back on old times and making them out to be a wonderful memory.

"Two hundred metres outside the village I made her sit down and began explaining about why I had never written, etc. . . . 'because your father could not stand the idea of me and so as not to put you wrong with your father, I thought it was better not to think about you any more, and of course all the more not to write to you, but believe me, I could not forget you. And now here you are, it will be very difficult for me to do as you want and take you back to Dakar, but please find another Muslim lover so that you can keep in with your father because it is nothing but the various religions that go against what everyone accepts as natural and believe me I can do nothing to help you.'

"At this, she asked me if I was trying to kill her saying things like that to her, she wept bitterly like a lost soul. I was full of moral distress. It was seven o'clock in the evening, people returning to Labe, Gaual, passed by in trucks and jeered at us. There was nothing true left to me to say and I could not console poor Aissata without adding 'I still love you', a serious matter! At that moment time held me in a prison. Finally it passed, we returned to the village where I called in to greet her mother and also her father who sulked at me with a piercing look.

"Not wanting to stay for long I asked permission to leave and set off with the girl . . . Aissata was busy over getting back her husband in spite of having given him up and I invited M. as there might be something to hope for there in one respect because the child had been brought to me to acknowledge her and declare her so that she could obtain from the office a suppletory birth certificate which she had not had 'because' she said 'you had gone off and there was no one to make the declaration for me'. So there I was not rid of her yet and the next day just as we were departing she arrived and was in tears in the truck and N. had made her go she said to say goodbye to her mother (my mother where she had stayed for eight months, when I was away, and my mother too was fond of her, as much as of Niena and the children).

"So when we were doing our official tour there was Aissata at U. being Sara's wife No. 2 and I was afraid because all the time I was trying to find a way of sending her away before we were due back at Dakar with M.H.

"I succeeded in making her go and feeling very sorry for myself hearing my mother's reproaches who said to me: 'You do not understand why this girl is crazy with distress like this and you send her away as if you were the lord of all humanity and it is not good' and it hurt me to hear and to see my mother and Aissata crying with so much overpowering affection on my account! For two whole days I could not do anything nor eat anything."

The Mother

The essential value of a woman lies in her fecundity, and it is over the question of children that tension is most often created between husband and wife, both of whom want to have as many children as possible. "How can my wife have any cause for complaint against me?" said an informant to me, a Coniagui who travelled a lot, leaving his family at home. "Every time I go home, she is pregnant within a month." Conversely, a man whose wife has borne him few children will complain about her. The loss of a child or of several children often leads to divorce among the Coniagui.

It is as a mother that a Coniagui woman plays her most important role.

Moreover, it seems to me that the term 'mother' should be taken in the widest sense, because for the Coniagui and Bassari it does not denote so much the biological mother as the relative who brings you up: mother, aunt or sister. One of our informants writes:

"My mother used to leave me sometimes with my elder sister Nyafu while she went to work in her field . . . Simply because of spending all my time with Nyafu, as soon as I was able to talk I called her Mummy and I called my real Mummy by her name: T.P.

"In 1942, when I was quite big, I used to go to the fields with Nyafu but never with my mother or with V. (his other sister) unless all the family were going together. On the way there, if a got tired, my sister would carry me on her back as she had done many a time in the past. By the age of five I could easily manage to walk the whole way with Nyafu. Sometimes I got tired, especially if I felt hungry, I did not want to walk any further. My sister would take some birds out of their nest and say to me: 'You see these little birds? We shall find some others in our field, and I shall cook them for you and you won't give any to V.' I would start walking again full of glee . . . In spite of the pleasure it gave me being with my father, I could not go a whole day without seeing Nyafu. If my mother was away for two or three weeks getting millet from the Bassari, that meant nothing to me. I was quite happy as long as Nyafu was with me."

When, after he was grown up, he wanted to go off and find work in Dakar:

"I ask my mother to let me go to Dakar and stay with my uncle Z. She was willing and so was my father but I had to beg Nyafu, who did not want me to leave her. I go on talking to her for a whole week, and my mother too tried to coax her to let me have my way. She lets me go and says to me: 'Away you go but do not forget me. You are the only boy left in the family, Sara is dead and now you want to leave us. I brought you up as if you were a motherless orphan. Now that you have grown up, it is your turn to work in the big millet fields to provide food for my children and you run away. Above all I hope that you will not get married away from home. My children will grow up while you are away and will not know

Monique Gessain

you. May God bless you, and do not forget your father nor your mother
. . .' At Dakar, he kept in touch with his sister: 'As for Nyafu, she wrote
to me every two weeks. In every letter, she said: 'If you are unhappy, you
must come back to me. I would rather you were here with me than away
living somewhere else. You know I love you like a son. All I want is your
health and happiness."

When he found work, he sent 7,500 of the 9,441 francs which he
got as wages at the end of the first month to Nyafu, who gave 2,000
to his father, 2,500 to his mother, and kept the rest, that is to say
3,000 francs, for herself.

Now his sister will not rest until she has got him betrothed to
a Coniagui girl "for fear" he says "I should marry into a different
race".

Pregnancy

There is a marked difference in attitude towards pregnancy
between girls who have not yet undergone the excision ceremony,
girls who have, and married women.

Traditionally, a girl is not supposed to have sexual relations
before she has undergone clitoridectomy. So if she should become
pregnant, she will try to induce abortion, usually with her mother's
help.

A girl who has been through the excision ceremony does not like
becoming pregnant because it hastens the day when she will have
to leave her family and go to live with her husband, to whom she
will have to be faithful. On the other hand, and for the same
reason, the future father is delighted. So some girls, if their fiancé
does not yet know about their being pregnant, will try to have an
abortion, and as often as not with their mother's complicity.

Married couples, however, once they are living together, are very
happy to find that a child is on the way. Both husband and wife
want children because children bring wealth to a family—by
helping adults in their work—and happiness. If her husband
cannot give her children, a woman will seek out other men. The
husband will not like it, but will say nothing and will be delighted
with the children. A woman who is unable to have children will
consult a healer, or offer sacrifices to the ancestors to ask for their
pardon, for childlessness is often regarded as punishment for a sin.
If a pregnant woman has a miscarriage, she will try to discover
the spirit through which someone has brought about the miscarriage. It might also have been due to an evil spell cast on the
woman by a former rejected suitor. Sometimes, as a cure for childlessness, a woman and her husband will leave the village; or the

woman will leave her husband and his village and return home to her family. There are also certain remedies, such as eating a queen ant.

A pregnant woman is much preoccupied about the sex of her future child, and there are old women who can predict this. While a woman prefers to have daughters who will perpetuate her family, help her in her work, and bring her wealth, a man is said to wish for sons (who will help him in his work and increase his possessions). An informant said to me: "A woman is proud of her sons, but loves her daughters".

The baby

As soon as a baby is born, and during the first few years of its life, mother and child live together in an atmosphere of the greatest tenderness. Night and day, the baby is never parted from its mother. It spends the day on its mother's back, wrapped in a cloth from which only its head and its feet peep out. When the mother is working, she tucks the baby's hands inside the cloth, and then frees them when it wants to play. At night it sleeps on the same bed as its mother, with perhaps a brother or sister close on its other side. The mother gives it the breast every time it cries, day or night. She enjoys nursing it and taking it about with her wherever she goes. She is very tender with it, plays with it, is the only one to understand its first attempts to talk, sings lullabyes and rocks it to sleep, sees that it keeps warm. During the period she is breast-feeding it—about two years—she has no sexual relations.

When the baby begins to crawl, it starts getting boiled rice or fonio, then millet and mashed peanuts, and it is weaned once it is able to walk. Weaning is always gradual. Often the child itself will refuse the breast, but sometimes the mother, in order to stop it from sucking, will put it to shame, saying for instance "if you go on drinking milk you won't grow up", or "you won't have any teeth", or "your teeth will decay". Usually, by the time the child can talk, it is eating the same food as the adults, and can manage to do so on its own, without help. Once the child is weaned, the mother can again have intercourse with her husband and can have another child. That is the end of the time when she and the child are never parted.

The child

Weaning inaugurates a new stage. The mother continues to spend much time with her children, taking the youngest with her wherever she goes, whether it is to work in the fields or to pay a visit to relations or friends. Young children of both sexes have their meals with the women, and are forbidden to eat anywhere else for fear of their being poisoned. If a child is hungry between mealtimes, its mother will get something for it to eat. If the family has not got enough food for everyone to eat three meals a day, an effort will be made to enable the children, at least, to keep to their three meals a day. An older child who will not eat his food is not forced to do so, and care is taken to give him what he likes. A mother never punishes her child by depriving him of food, but sometimes rewards him by giving him something to eat. As soon as a boy can eat his food unaided, he takes his meals with the men. The child is allowed a great deal of freedom to eat or run about as much as he likes.

Children play beside their mother, running about all the time, but never allowed beyond the ground belonging to the house. At night, they sleep in their mother's hut—on the same bed, when they are small. Later, the little girls, and also the older girls until they are married, sleep in the same hut, but on a different bed. The boys, from around the age of five or six, sleep at night in their father's hut or in a hut specially built for them.

When a woman is expecting another baby, she never announces the fact to her elders. The mother occupies herself with the new baby as soon as it is born, and the next youngest child is then looked after by the older daughters.

Very young children can be said to belong to the woman, for in cases of divorce or widowhood, it is always she who keeps them, and they are never sent back to the husband's family, except for short periods spent by boys with their father for circumcision and initiation ceremonies.

After the age of five or six, boys spend most of their time with their father, while girls stay with their mother and help her with her work, only leaving her when they get married.

The boys are circumcised at the age of about six or seven, and then spend the better part of their time with their boy companions. From that time on, a mother sees very little of her son, who is now looked after by his father.

Although a mother may henceforth be less directly concerned with her son, this does not weaken the bond between them, as the following excerpts from Sara's autobiography, about his childhood and adolescence, will show. He is describing the day when, according to "a decision reached by my father and not by my mother", he leaves the companions with whom he had spent the last three years and sets off for school:

Coniagui Women

"I left I., upset to be parting from my little playmates who were all in tears like me, and my mother's eyes grew big with tears which she shyly let fall in sympathy with my little comrades."

Later, he had a long and difficult journey returning home to see his parents, and writes:

"My mother, my poor mother, was so overcome that instead of embracing me she fell in a faint and cried for a long time. Instead of everyone being pleased to see me, what struck my mother was how shocked everyone was at her son surviving such an ordeal."

Later still, after another spell of absence, he again returned home:

"I got back home with my family in K. that I had left three years ago. Ho! My mother, thin with worry, was in the seventh heaven."

The relations between mothers and children may be said to be very good. Moreover, one never hears of parents complaining about their children. It is simply the normal thing to do, they feel, to bring up and support their children. But soon both boys and girls grow up, and the moment comes for the boys to be initiated and for the girls to undergo the excision ceremony, and then a new stage opens in the mother's life.

The Initiate

Initiation consists primarily in a period of seclusion spent outside the village, during which the boys are instructed by the men in the traditions of their people.

The women see the boys disappear from view. They have been told that the boys are going to die, and that it will be different people—men—who will return to the village. Let us again allow Sara to speak:

"The ghosts who returned, now men who have been initiated . . . faithfully guarded those secrets never to be revealed to those poor women, among them mothers like my mother weeping in the village for fear that their sons will be killed and changed into little tiny babies of Numba and that they will grow up again in one week to the same size as they were before."

One of the trials which initiates have to undergo is that of a severe beating. Let us once again hear Sara's comments:

"Beaten! Beaten! until they nearly died of it . . . the young men kept on beating them until I came to a brave decision . . . and I went to the representative (of the village head) and said that I would be a witness in any trial that might arise where the mother of whichever son were to be

39

killed by you would plead and that I would give the names of you all. What is needed is a French army specially formed to avenge the poor mother in your brutal customs."

This man, then, seems to have felt that the greatest victims of the brutalities perpetrated by the men at initiation ceremonies were the mothers of the initiates rather than the initiates themselves. And in point of fact, one of the aims of the initiation ceremonies seems to have been to cause disquiet among the mothers.

Thus, for example, on the eve of the ceremony a capon is brought to the village by the *falug*,[25] and shown to the mothers of the initiates. But sometimes the *falug* may fail to bring the capon to one or other of the mothers, and she weeps, in the belief that that means that her son will die shortly after returning to the village. In fact, her son is in just as good health as the other initiates. It is nothing more than a kind of joke inflicted on a mother, if, for instance, her son has shown outstanding courage. In this way, the young men seem to wreak their revenge against the son upon the mother.

The bond between mothers and sons is particularly evident during the whole period when the initiation ceremonies take place. Every year, at this time, it is forbidden for a Coniagui mother to strike any of her sons, even if he should still be quite a small boy.

The initiation ceremony completely transforms the relationship between mother and son. On return to his village, the initiate has entirely forgotten his past life and all the things and people in it, his mother in particular. The child she loved so dearly is dead, and a man has been born who will be presented to his mother at a special ceremony.

A sacrifice held on a Sunday terminates the period of seclusion spent outside the village. The next morning the initiates, their bodies greased until they shine, their heads shaved, and wearing nothing but a penis sheath, are led to the village by the *falug*.

The *falug*, holding the initiate by the waist, lead him to his mother's hut. The mother comes forward, but the initiate does not recognize her and makes as if to strike her. Scarcely has he touched her, however, than his strength fails him and he falls down and has to be lifted up again by the *falug*. One by one all the women of the family come forward if they wish, and the same scene is repeated. When the sun is high in the sky, the initates return to the hut where they have spent the initiation period, have their midday meal there, and rest. Then they return at two o'clock and pretend to beat the women until sundown. They return to the bush to have their evening meal and spend the night there. The following

Coniagui Women

morning, they appear in the village, stronger now, and armed with a stick. They strike the women on the back, in the same manner as the previous day. It is obligatory to strike their mothers, while with the others it is optional. They gradually feel their strength returning with every day that passes, they become freer with their hands, begin to be able to speak again, draw the bow, wash themselves in the river, and they strike every woman they meet. At the end of several days they no longer have the right to beat any woman except those belonging to their own family, and they may now speak to all the others.

Each kinswoman offers beer to the initiate. From the moment she has done so, the initiate stops striking her and calls her "my mother", *nəma*. But he will continue to beat his own mother and his closest kin (aunts and maternal grandmother), because they are not allowed to offer beer to the initiate until several months have passed.

During the dry season that follows (December-April), each mother prepares beer and food for the ceremony known as the salutation ceremony.

The women to be presented to the young initiate squat on a mat in front of his mother's hut. The village head presents the mother to her boy: "Here she is, she is now your mother. Whatever she may want, you must do for her. She has made beer to wash you with. All these people present are your kin, you may ask them for food whenever you are in need."

Then the mother sprinkles beer over her son with her hand, and next on the other boys. All of them writhe about as if the beer had burnt them. Then the woman goes back into her hut, and the boys return to the bush.

In the evening, the boys bring the mother some wood, saying: "There, my mother. We have heard that you have offered a sacrifice, we have come to greet you." "It has not done you any harm?" "No." The boys are given food and drink, and then bring back the empty calabashes and say to the woman: "We have drunk enough, now we want to go to bed with you."

"Go and sleep at the *tyareg* and come back tomorrow."

"No, we want to go to bed with you."

They lie down on the ground outside her hut. When they have settled down there, the woman calls for the *dyarar*[26] who lead the boys away.

The next morning, the boys come back to make their salutes to the woman.

"Have you slept well?"

"Yes."

The woman brings them food and beer.

Once this ceremony is over, the boy is no longer allowed to beat his mother, and he may now speak to her. But the new initiates have quite forgotten their past life. No allusion will ever be made to it, either by themselves, or even by others in their presence.

With regard to the relationship between mother and son during these rites for ending the initiation period, it is perhaps permissible to suggest that the incestuous proposal and the fact that the son is obliged to beat his mother may be interpreted as providing an opportunity for the son to give socially accepted expression to the ambivalence of his feelings towards his mother. The rite marks the end of such feelings and establishes a new emotional relationship between mother and son.

The change in their relationship brought about by initiation is marked by a change in the form of address the son uses. Before being initiated, he calls his mother *ama*, which might be translated as Mummy; while afterwards, he calls her *nəma*, for which the translation would be "mother". (The word *nəma* seems to be etymologically related to the word meaning old woman).

Adult men and women

Children have it instilled into them that they must retain feelings of gratitude to their parents and give them food when they themselves have plenty. Both men and women are usually polite and respectful to their father and mother. But, as A. Rançon was the first to remark, "the mother is more respected than the father".[27] Indeed, all adults, both men and women, retain a close tie with their mother. This can be seen in individual attitudes as well as in traditional rites.

It is particularly noticeable with married women, who cannot be said to have left their own families when they get married. The mother maintains her authority over her daughters throughout her life, and the Coniagui say that after a woman is married she must obey both her mother and her husband. If a woman lives far away from her mother, she probably visits her for two or three days every month. But the bonds between mother and son are just as strong.

Thus the young *dyarar* who is building his hut in the *tyareg* must take the roof, before putting it on the hut, to show to the village head. But before taking it to the village head, he must first take it to his mother. And even when he is living in the *tyareg*, his mother will still exercise her rights as a mother over him. For instance, if a woman finds that her son is in the habit of rising too late for getting to work in time, she may go to his hut to wake him up in the morning.

A number of texts have been collected which show the warmth of affection between mother and son:

"My mother had just recovered from a bad fever caused by not having heard from me for so long . . ." "My mother, poor dear, fell ill two days before we were due to depart . . ." A village head going off to fight against another village loaded his rifle and then "said his last goodbyes to his mother".

Conversely, the Coniagui expect a mother to defend her son even at the risk of herself being exposed to danger. Speaking of a mother who had taken her son's part against the district chief and had in consequence suffered a severe beating, a man writes: "It was thus that poor Y. bravely carried out her duty towards her son". But the son ought to have come to the help of his mother: "This showed his cowardice, his lack of feeling, to see his mother there groaning and not hurl himself into the fray".

Furthermore, a Coniagui man will, throughout his life, consider his mother to be the only woman he can trust, really the only woman who does not share the faults of her sex. The ideal woman, it would appear, is the mother.

*   *   *

In conclusion, I should like to consider whether, among the Coniagui and Bassari, it is not in the period of early childhood, when mother and child are never separated, that the close bonds I have tried to describe are established. I shall quote a last extract from the autobiography of a young Coniagui as a contribution towards the discussion of this question:

"Not having my father with me, I was brought up and carried about by my mother during the time when my father was doing his military service in 1924. Three and a half years old, but still carried astride my mother's back, we set off every evening to go eight kilometres into the country east of Yukunkun. When night had fallen, as we went through the plain interplanted with Palmyra palms, I would hear eerie sounds of hammering that haunted the plain. It was the toddy tappers, who used to spend the whole evening working at the top of Palmyra palms that had been badly damaged, from which the toddy was flowing, or *bandji* as it is called locally in French West Africa.

"These eerie noises gave my mother an excuse to frighten me into being quiet, saying that it was sorcerers and I must not cry any more. I stopped crying and went to sleep on her back, carried there in addition to the heavy load of foodstuffs which she carried on her head.

"We always arrived about eight o'clock. The time when the crops were

Monique Gessain

growing passed. The good weather came. Then it was the grain harvest. I remember during this time how often I enjoyed seeing the great carpet of yellowish green bordered by the bush where gay flights of birds of all kinds would fly in and out among the scrub, and how my mother had a boy to keep watch in her field of fonio and scare away the birds that I loved to watch. When this boy used his catapult to chase them away, I used to cry and used to take a small catapult and loose it off in the opposite direction, and one day it happened that a stone hit my mother on the chest and she fainted. But how she loved me! So much, that she used to spoil me. She protested against the threatened revenge of my brother S. who died in 1945. What I remember about this time is how spoilt I was by my mother."

BIBLIOGRAPHY

DELACOUR, A., "Les Tenda (Coniagui, Bassari, Badyaranké) de la Guinée française", *Revue d'Ethnographie et de Sociologie* (Paris, 1912), pp. 287-96 and 370-81; (1913), pp. 31-52 and 105-53, 2 maps and 10 photographs.

GESSAIN, M., *see* Lestrange, M. de.

LESTRANGE, M. de, "Pour une méthode socio-démographique. Étude du mariage chez les Coniagui et les Bassari", *Journ. de la Soc. des Africanistes*, XXI (1951), pp. 97-109

— , *Les Coniagui et les Bassari*, Institut International Africain, Presses Universitaires de France, 1955, 86 pp., ill., map.

RANÇON, DR. A., *Dans la Haute-Gambie, voyage d'exploration scientifique 1891-1892*, Annales de l'Institut colonial de Marseille, 1ʳᵉ série, II, 2ᵉ année, Paris, Soc. d'Éditions scientifiques, 1894, 1 vol., 8vo, 592 pp.

RICHARDS, I. A., "Some types of family structure amongst the Central Bantu" pp. 207-51 in A. R. Radcliffe Brown and Daryll Forde, *African systems of kinship and marriage*, published for the International African Institute by the Oxford University Press, 1950.

TÉCHER, H., "Coutumes des Tenda", *Bull. du Com. d'Et. Hist. et Scient. de de l'A.O.F.*, XVI, No. 4 (Oct.-Dec. 1933), pp. 630-66, 1 map, 7 photographs.

NOTES

[1] For a fuller description of Coniagui and Bassari kinship, see M. de Lestrange, 1951 and 1955.

[2] Without entering into comparative studies with which the present essay is not concerned, it may be remarked that the Coniagui-Bassari system is similar to that of the Bantu of Central Africa (from the central districts of the Belgian Congo to the north-eastern plateau of Northern Rhodesia and the highlands of Nyasaland) described by A. I. Richards, 1950.

[3] Theoretically also the mother of his grandmother, etc. . . . . But in practice it is rare to find generation depth of this extent in kinship sentiments and customs.

Coniagui Women

[4] Would the affair really have ended if B had expected A to come and make him a marriage offer for b'? I think this is unlikely, but shall not discuss the question here.

[5] If the person giving offence is a woman, reprisals might fall on her own children, but this was not the case in either of the examples cited here.

[6] The stages in the life of a Bassari woman differ appreciably from those in the life of a Coniagui woman. The Bassari woman is excised at an earlier age and with less ceremonial, she marries earlier, is divorced oftener, etc. . . . I have thought it preferable to describe here in greater detail the life of Coniagui women, about which I have more information, rather than to keep making comparisons between the lives of Coniagui and Bassari women.

[7] The way in which Coniagui and Bassari children are brought up results in there being a deep differentiation between feminine and masculine roles, which undoubtedly facilitates social adaptation among adults. Hence it seems to me that the abandonment of certain traditions runs the risk of interfering with this adaptation, so essential for the fecundity and for the efficiency of their social system.

[8] A. Delacour, p. 46.

[9] As Maupoil's notes have not been published, I shall quote them in full.

[10] The Instrument in question is a bar zither. (M.G.).

[11] The *tyareg* is in the centre of the village, and it is both the dwelling of the village head and the place where young adults who are bachelors live.

[12] That is to say, Catholics, as about one in ten of all Coniagui are.

[13] Each Coniagui man owns a one-roomed hut where he sleeps, and each woman two huts at least, in one of which she does the cooking, while in the other she sleeps with her daughters and the younger children. At night, when she wants to be with her husband, she leaves them there and goes to his hut, which is a short distance away from the women's huts.

[14] Biographies are very valuable sources for the kind of information provided by the above story, as are also long and repeated interrogations of the same informant, particularly when they are more in the nature of a conversation than of a questionnaire. It is possible in this way to collect a number of significant details concerning personal relations.

[15] A schematic outline of an incident of this kind runs somewhat as follows: an uninitiated person (a woman or a child) transgresses a taboo concerning an initiate; the latter strikes the guilty person a single blow without giving a word of explanation, and then goes; he returns after having passed some time with an old man. The incident has never been mentioned. This recalls another instance of breaking a taboo which was told me: a small boy when washing his hands inadvertently let a few drops of water fall on two men; without a word, they struck him, got up, and went into the bush; their father would go and look for them later and bring them back to the village. This incident coincides in every detail with the first one, except that the small boy who was at fault would have his mistake explained to him several years later, when he was initiated, while to a woman the men never explain anything.

[16] A Rançon, pp. 331, 333 and 337.

[17] A. Rançon, pp. 340 and 341.

[18] H. Técher, pp. 638 and 640.

[19] A. Delacour, p. 50.

[20] Cf. M. de Lestrange, 1955.

[21] A. Delacour, p. 46.

[22] A. Delacour, p. 373.

[23]A. Delacour, p. 46.

[24]A. Delacour, p. 46.

[25]*Falug:* young men who took part in the previous initiation ceremony.

[26]*Dyarar:* the young bachelors belonging to the age-class immediately senior to that of the *falug*. Their huts are grouped round the village head's in the *tyareg*.

[27]A. Rançon, p. 327.

THE POSITION OF WOMEN IN A PASTORAL SOCIETY

(The Fulani WoDaaBe, Nomads of the Niger)

Marguerite Dupire

INTRODUCTION

A.—THE REPUTATION OF BORORO WOMEN

IN THE SAHEL* the nomadic zone of the Niger where the Bororo[1] live—the reputation enjoyed by Bororo women is rather a peculiar one. To put it bluntly, they have a bad reputation. But how could it be otherwise when one considers that the judgments pronounced upon them are made by peoples practising sedentary agriculture, who view the nomadic life with just as much contempt as is felt by the muscular, highly-strung Bororo for the comparatively easy life led by sedentary farmers? There is a total lack of mutual comprehension between the two groups. While the Bororo appear to the Muslim agriculturalists as homeless wanderers living on the fringe of normal society, to the nomads the farmers are miserable scratchers in the earth, devoid of ideals.

The dress, behaviour and customs of the nomads form a subject of mockery and of jokes of a more or less disparaging nature. The bang of hair on the forehead worn by the young girls? The Fulani of the Book will say it is arranged thus to prevent them from praying, Muslim prayer being accompanied by prostrations in which the forehead touches the ground. The married women? Nothing but concubines, since the bridewealth[2] they receive from their husbands is a mere pretence. Bororo mothers? The most

*cf. D. Stenning, *Savannah Nomads* (O.U.P., 1959), p. 6 [Translator's note.]

47

inhuman imaginable, because when they marry for a second or third time, they leave all the children who have passed the weaning stage with their father. There is hardly a single aspect of Bororo customs which has not been regarded as inhuman and anti-social by their neighbours.

This is the normal attitude of agriculturalists towards nomads, and the old Hausa woman from the province of Zaria, who told her life-story to Mary Smith,[3] several times reveals her dislike and lack of understanding of the behaviour of the Fulani pastoralists.

The insulting term "bush bitch" by which the farming peoples, when they are angry, refer to a nomad woman, is due, they say, to the way she behaves, to her loose habits, and her inability to adapt to a regular life. As incapable of remaining with one husband as of staying in her camp for more than a few days at a time—a vagabond—she represents the very image of the bad housewife, and "bush woman" is, in their language, the equivalent of our "street-walker".

The flighty character attributed to them is something of which the parties concerned are themselves perfectly well aware, and an old woman, commenting on it, said: "Bororo women are not like other women, they want to move around, they go off and leave their husbands. That is why, when I was young, they were not even allowed to have possession of their bridewealth, because they might have taken it with them and left their husband a ruined man."

Yet this woman of the bush is proud and does not make use of her freedom in order to prostitute herself. How many men would be able to boast of having received her favours? The only evidence with regard to this is a remark made by a Bororo in his fifties: "All my life I have never succeeded in possessing the women I really desired". To judge from the kind of set expression, haughty and distant, often seen on the women's faces, one would guess that the mystery it conceals is no easy one to pierce, and that this mask they wear is one way, not only of concealing their inmost thoughts, but also of preserving the independence they value so highly.

Again according to people of other societies, who find in it a matter of amusement, women occupy too prominent a place in Bororo society. Are not the dances held during the winter season absurdly effeminate?—that *gereol* in which, for days on end, the men, simply to please the women, teeter about on their toes, their faces painted, and their heads surrounded with the elegant if not exactly virile adornment of ostrich feathers? Or again it is said that the Bororo talk about women too much, are forever chasing after them and trying to please them—not manly behaviour at all. Such is the negative of a picture which will have to be developed before its positive can appear.

B.—SEPARATION OF THE SEXES

In Bororo beliefs, the sexes are opposite and complementary, but belong to one and the same human category which is totally different from, and excludes, all other categories. Here it should be briefly mentioned that in the Fulani language masculine and feminine genders do not exist, but nouns are arranged in a number of classes which indisputably indicate a manner of conceiving the universe which is both qualitative (classes of plants, trees, insects, birds, antelopes and the like, liquids, bounded objects) and geometrical or quantitative (plurals, length and duration, small quantities, parts of a whole, diminutives, augmentatives). Among these classes, the ones which appear to us Europeans as the strangest are probably the most important, or at least were so for a pastoralist society.

The first of these is the human class, to which belong both sexes of human beings and a certain number of abstract nouns. With domestic animals, however, males and females belong to different categories (class *ndi* comprising most male domestic animals, castrated and uncastrated; class *nge*, cows). The term used as the generic term for the species is sometimes the one that designates the female of the species (as in the case of the goat, the ass, the cow, the sheep) and sometimes the male (the dog, the horse), the reason for this probably being the importance ascribed, in the cases where the female term is employed, to the producer of milk, an important feature in the pastoral economy.

The second important class presents a most fascinating riddle to which so far no answer has been found. This is the class *nge*, which includes, as well as the cow (female and generic), also fire and sun. Although no discoverable common element exists between these three things, one must suppose that whatever people it was (the Fulani?) that originally invented this class must have done so in virtue of some essential value shared by all the things assigned to it, and this might also mean that a ritual meaning was attached to them.

Thus, linguistically speaking, while the class of things human is asexual, with domestic animals the males belong to a different class from the females. But there are constant similarities and

Marguerite Dupire

interrelations between the three orders of animate objects, human, animal and vegetable, all of which depend, for the maintenance of the species, on the same basic principle—prolificacy. Procreative power is thought of as being transferable from one order to the other, evidence for this belief being provided by numerous magic recipes, particuarly those concerning the increase of the herd. However, although stress on this common factor is carried to great lengths in the universe of magic, where like is called upon to produce like in a different but parallel order (without any conscious appeal to a superior power), that does not mean that the human order is regarded as sharing anything except this one common factor with the other two orders. Thus the human species, male and female, is on a different level from the animal and vegetable kingdoms.

If we leave linguistics and the philosophical concepts they imply and turn to every day life, we find that it is characterized by a cleavage between the sexes, whose contrasted roles are expressed either directly, by the activities each engage in and by the behaviour manifested, or symbolically, by the difference between the male and the female manner of arranging material objects, or by the ritual distribution of meat at ceremonies, to mention only the more obvious instances.

Man and woman complete each other like the prow and poop of a ship, the west and east of a line on the horizon, the head and hindquarters of an animal, the blood and the milk of a living creature. The man precedes and the woman follows, as is indicated by the word for woman, *debbo*, from the root *rew*, to follow. In contrast to what has often been observed in societies of hunters or farmers, it is the man, the herdsman, who, when camp is struck, goes on ahead, with his herd following him, to spy out the grazing lands in advance, while the women, in Indian file behind the pack oxen which are in their charge, follow at the tail-end of the procession, carrying on their heads the household calabashes filled with goods. If the pack ox is primarily a pack animal for the women which a man would scorn to ride, a woman for her part never uses a camel saddle, for when she rides with her husband she sits behind him, astride against the hump.

Within the camp, the arrangement of the women's huts, of the cattle enclosures, and of all material objects always follows the principle of sex differentiation. When the members of an extended family live together, the eldest of the heads of the component individual families—the father or the eldest brother—takes up the position furthest to the south, with his juniors following in order of seniority. But within each separate polygynous group, each man's wives will arrange their huts in hierarchical order in the opposite direction, that is, from north to south. The eastern part of the camp is the women's domain, and the western the men's. Behind each hut (to the east of it), the woman washes her cooking utensils, and also herself. Here she can be metaphorically protected from view, if not actually so, since the hut is no more than a simple screen of thorn, unroofed. This is also the place where she will be buried. The man, on the other hand, does his work on the other side of the hut, for the cattle corral is to the west, near the entrance to the hut, and it is in this corral, or a little beyond it, that his grave will be dug. Because they come under the sphere of masculine activities, the calves are tethered in a row running in the masculine direction, from south to north, arranged according to age, from the oldest to the youngest; while the calabashes belonging to the women are arranged on a raised table in order of decreasing size

The woman's grave

Place where the woman washes herself

HUT

Calabashes arranged in the feminine direction according to size

NORTH

WOMEN
MEN

calf rope

Calves tethered in the masculine direction according to age

cattle corral

corral fire

Man's grave

running in the feminine direction from north to south. In the foreground, then, are the men and the goods that belong specifically to them, while behind are the women with their property arranged in a hierarchy like the men's and according to the same principle, the essential difference between them being expressed by an inversion of orientation: to the women belong the east, and the direction north-south; to the men, the west, and the direction south-north.

In all ceremonies in which the women take part along with the men, they have a customary right to certain portions of the meat. Normally the portions are distributed to groups, according to age-grade, and there are only two occasions when an individual receives a portion: at a betrothal ceremony, when the wife of the paternal uncle of the fiancé (this uncle having directed the distribution of the animal offered up by his brother) and a cross-cousin of the fiancée each receives an individual portion; and at a ceremony for naming a child, when the mother receives a portion of the sacrificial animal. When specially reserved parts such as these, as well as portions assigned to men who have played certain designated roles in the ceremony, have been set aside, the following groups receive collective portions: adults (*ndotti'en*: old men and adult men who have reached the age when they can direct public affairs), young men, young girls, married women and their children, old women. This distribution underlines differences in sex, age, and role, and does so not only quantatively, but also qualitatively, because a particular portion of the animal is assigned to each of these groups in accordance with the idea that certain qualities are shared in magical participation by the human and the bovine species. According to this principle, women have a prior claim not only to the intestines (*reedu*, the belly, comprising the first stomach, the uterus, and the large intestines), which are regarded as the seat of procreation, but also to the hind quarters, including the hinder end of the vertebral column: "Is it not natural that the women should have the hindquarters? Is it not they who follow the men?" So, whether it be the assignment of hindquarters "because they follow" or of the intestines because of their procreative capacities, the distribution of meat to women differentiates not only between age-grades, but also between social roles. Just as the portion assigned to married women is in contrast to that assigned to adult men, so that assigned to young girls is in contrast to that assigned to young men: they receive the heart, the centre of the feelings, while the young men receive the *biol*, a piece of the breast regarded as the organ of potency. The group of senior members on either side

Women in a Pastoral Society

(maternal and paternal) of the family each receives one of the two sides of free ribs. As for the cross cousins of the fiancée, young or old they all fight tooth and nail, along with the full cousins who have cut up the animal, for the half of the skin which is their due and from which each individual attempts to cut off a piece to make sandals from. Neither age nor sex counts, and a brutal free-for-all momentarily abolishes all the usual rules of the code of politeness. A young man will jostle his mother-in-law, who may be a cross-cousin with the same rights as he has, and will only say with a laugh: "Too bad! It is my mother-in-law", knowing that she will make a scene when she gets home because he has prevented her from bringing back anything from the slaughter. Everything will calm down later, but on this unique occasion, and in public, the differences of role and of sex are abolished.

At these ceremonies which bring together the kin on both sides as well as the neighbours, the distribution of meat seems to express symbolically a recognition of the various social roles. The women figure as companions of the men, whom they have to follow; as mothers, whose warm flow of affection makes them the paramount representatives of that "kinship through the milk" that characterizes uterine descent; as old women, who have the right to certain special marks of respect; and as cross cousins—and in this capacity they have to compete on the same level as their masculine counterparts, beyond all the rules of kinship, sex, age and status which ordinarily regulate social relations.

SOCIAL STATUS

A.—UPBRINGING

Sex differentiation appears very early in the ways in which babies are looked after. While a girl is washed in warm water during the first four months, this treatment only lasts for three months for a boy; and certain amulets worn by babies differ according to sex, those worn by boys being for virility, and by girls for fertility. The mother wants her new-born child to come up to the racial standards of ideal physical beauty, and that demands special care while the body is still supple. The daily beauty treatment consists of pressing the nose of the baby between thumb and index finger so as to lengthen its line from the forehead downwards and make it thinner. The limbs are also gently stretched, and the head is squeezed between the palms in both fronto-occipital and parietal directions so as to obtain the rounded, globular skull which is the ideal striven after. Among the pet-names, often quite absurd, which grandparents sometimes give their grandchildren, are found expressions such as "big head" or "colocynth head". In spite of this beauty treatment designed to attain an anthropological characteristic which may have been lost through cross-breeding, the Bororo remain on the whole dolicephalic, and it is rare to find anyone who can boast of a small round skull.

During the first years of its life very little attempt is made to discipline the baby, and its early upbringing allows it a great deal of freedom. The child is given suck by its mother or mother-substitute whenever it wants, and neither weaning nor the birth of another child results in a psychological trauma. The mother avoids giving the child any emotional shock or causing any jealous reactions by abruptly rejecting it. If, on the birth of a second child, the older one, who now has to be weaned, shows any signs of resistance to the weaning process, she will offer it her second breast while she is giving suck to the new-born child. Tiny children are without exception always treated with gentleness, affection and patience, and both men and women, young or old, will immediately leave any task, however absorbing, to look after a baby that is crying.

The first lessons in social behaviour are taught by the method of reciprocity, "an eye for an eye". A child who persists in hitting his brother is given a gentle slap on the arm; but if he gives signs, by indulging in whims and tantrums, of becoming difficult or spoilt, he will calmly be excluded from society by dumping him like a parcel outside the circle of women and children. It is taken for granted that the mother and all the other women of the camp will together give a child this early training based on patience and reciprocity.

At a very early age a little girl begins playing games which are a direct imitation of the work done by women. She joins in some games with her brothers—mostly games entailing some form of physical exercise, such as leap-frog, chasing each other over the sand, making miniature wells in the *gulbi* during the winter season —but she leaves them to "play at herds" while she models small pots or carries around on her back a doll made from a narrow-necked gourd or simply consisting of a stool, until soon the doll will be exchanged for her own small brother. As soon as she can stand up straight, she is put in the middle of a circle of women dancers, and the old women clap their hands and admire her for being so grown-up if her chubby little body manages to keep in

Women in a Pastoral Society

time with the rhythm while she maintains a precarious balance. By three or four she is already quite a coquette, admires herself in a pool or turns round to watch her shadow when her hair is done in the style worn by the older girls; and she becomes skilful, like her mother, at polishing up her metal bracelets by rubbing them with sand. At two or three, the lobes of her ears are pierced, six holes in the right ear and seven in the left. The rings which are placed in them are scarcely more than a centimetre in diameter and allow for her becoming progressively accustomed to wearing ever heavier rings, which will not, however, replace the previous one until the holes have become large enough.

The stages in the upbringing of a little girl, unlike that of a boy, continue smoothly without a break. While a boy receives a profound emotional shock at about the age of six, a girl has no such experience until she is married at fourteen or fifteen. By slow degrees her play activities become the tasks it will be her duty to perform. At six or seven she begins fetching water from the well, on foot, or perched on a donkey; or stick in hand she helps to keep the beasts in order that are brought there to be watered. Under the guidance and supervision of her mother, she pounds grain, weaves winnowing-fans and mats, decorates and mends calabashes, sews, until these activities gradually become the tasks that have to be done. And just as she becomes aware, at a very tender age, of her responsibilities as an elder sister by carrying a small brother on her back, looking after him and defending him, so she also learns to look after the house in her mother's absence.

When children are four or five years old, a beginning is made to teach them the essential rules of the socio-moral code, the *mboDangaku*. Thus a little girl learns, among other things, that sexual play between brothers and sisters is forbidden, that she must never look her fiancé (for she is already betrothed) in the face nor go to visit him, nor even mention the name of her future parents-in-law, and that respect must be shown to all old people. Her elders show her, by force of example, in which circumstances she is expected to display modesty of behaviour and in which others she is free to behave as she likes.

Nor is her mental education neglected. It is given to her by her mother, who answers all her questions, gives her practical training in the use of customary equipment, and teaches her how to count by means of notches cut on a bed-pole.

During these short childhood years spent in the paternal camp, the little girl learns to fill the two essential roles which her family expect of her: that of daughter and that of sister. Her relationship with her father is much less spontaneous and less affectionate than that with her mother. She actually sees very little of him, but she knows that she owes him absolute obedience. It is he, together with her mother, who has chosen a husband for her, often at the time of her birth, and she is not allowed to have any opinion in the matter. However, in practice, the father is not any more tyrannical towards her than he is towards his sons, and as often as not one is struck by his weakness and his difficulty in making his children obey him. Either at the naming ceremony, or just before his daughter goes to live with her husband, the father will present her with at least one heifer from his herd. Later he will avoid close physical contact with her, and once she is married, he cannot enter her house without a feeling of shame. But this attitude of restraint will be compensated for by the interest, affection and generosity he will display to his grandchildren, which are indirectly intended for her.

The relationship between mother and daughter does not undergo these changes during the course of the years. The mother always remains her daughter's counsellor, especially during the first years of her marriage and at the time of her first confinement. A daughter may want to let her mother have one of her own daughters as a household help, either as soon as the child is born, if it is the first girl to be born, or later when the mother is getting too old to manage all the household tasks by herself. However, once the children are married, a mother relies more on her sons than on her daughters, and this is certainly one of the reasons why a woman desires so much to have sons.

The relationship between brothers and sisters is determined and influenced by two main factors: kinship (as siblings or half-siblings) and seniority. There is much more affection, and a greater obligation to give mutual help, between full brothers and sisters than between mere consanguines. The fact of being born of the same mother, of having been brought up by her in the same hut and of having shared in the affection of the same maternal kin, reinforces considerably the relations resulting from mere consanguinity. These shades of difference in emotional attachment between brothers are important, and it is almost always brothers sharing the same father and mother who stick together and help each other in later life. In the same way, the bond between brothers and sisters who are all children of the same mother overrides any conflict of interests which may arise from sharing agnatic rights of inheritance. A woman would be ashamed to claim, in accordance with Muslim law, her share of the paternal inheritance if this had been assigned to a full brother, but if it were only a half-brother in question, her scruples would disappear, and in some cases she might pursue her own interests even if this meant disturbing the harmony of the consanguineous family.

Seniority, on the other hand, is an important hierarchical factor which affects all the members of one single generation alike, including cousins and parallel cousins, who have perhaps all been brought up together in the camp of their paternal grandfather if the pattern of common residence of the extended family has been followed, which was formerly the norm but is less frequent nowadays. All refer to each other as senior and junior, these terms deriving, in the case of parallel cousins, from the order of birth of their respective fathers. The eldest brother will eventually have to fill the role of father towards his brothers and sisters—a role which becomes important as far as the sisters are concerned in the event of their returning to the paternal camp after being divorced or widowed, as is customary if they have no married children to go to. The same attitude of restraint as obtained between father and married daughter will then be repeated between eldest brother and younger sister. It is similarly forbidden for the eldest brother to enter the hut of this younger sister, who may be classed together with the wives of his brothers; according to the institution of the junior levirate, these wives are prohibited from becoming secondary wives of the eldest brother. Thus between eldest brother and younger married sister affectionate relations are qualified firstly by the role of representative of authority played by the eldest brother, and secondly by the attitude of avoidance which he must adopt. Brothers and sisters being co-inheritors of the same paternal inheritance and also sexually taboo to each other, it can easily be understood that relations between them, however fond they may be of each other, can never be as free from constraint as those which exist between parallel cousins and, to an even greater extent, between cross cousins. Jokes are out of place between brothers and sisters once they are past childhood days, particularly jokes made by the older ones, who must adopt a more formal attitude towards their juniors.

The period preceding puberty is undoubtedly one of the happiest times in the life of a woman, in spite of the many household tasks that devolve upon a young girl. She is no more than nine or ten years old when she begins to take part in dances, where she and her companions meet young men and married men. Although she only plays a minor role in the men's dances, she is nevertheless the source of inspiration for songs which combine praises for the beauty of the women and of the cows belonging to the lineage segment. Her charms may be perpetuated in some monotonous little song, or she will achieve celebrity under some charming sobriquet (*moosaiDo*, 'she who smiles', *liccel*, 'little branch') given to her by her male companions. She may be dumpy, chubby and awkward, but she knows of other ways of attracting men and becoming their special 'little frog' (*paaBel*). She has every freedom, since no value is attached to virginity, and it is an understood thing that girls will have had plenty of experience before marrying. There may be times when a girl finds herself alone with an older boy and is too inexperienced to defend herself against his importunities, but no one will be worried if she is heard weeping in the night. The adults will simply say: "The children were playing yesterday evening".

Girls become wiser as they grow older, and when it comes to the time for holding the most important dances of all (*yake* and *gereol*), it is they who do the choosing as they advance in couples towards the line of boys to select the one each has picked out for his particular gracefulness and beauty. The men will take the initiative again when everyday life is resumed, but meanwhile, during these celebrations, the *sukaaBe* (bachelors, and married men up to the age of thirty-five to forty) under their group-leader the *samri* on the one hand, and on the other, the *surbaaBe* (young girls and childless married women) led by the *lame*, are performing a collective rite which is a duty that is expected of them. But when, late in the evening, the dancing is over and both groups have departed to their huts to take their rest, couples will form and, shouldering a rolled-up mat, will disappear into the cool, damp night of the winter season.

A young girl learns to assert herself, and will refuse an invitation which has the rowdy backing of the whole male group—for at this early stage affairs are a matter of group experience, into which jealousy does not enter at all, couples forming and unforming themselves without any restrictions. These 'games' may be accompanied by feelings which are expressed in the discreet language of song, or by the exchange of small presents, the most common being a ring given by the girl to her lover, which he fixes to the ear of his favourite heifer. When the dancing has ended and the dancers have dispersed, rings such as these, or little scraps of material, can be found hung upon the scrub in the bush, now silent and deserted—mute witnesses that lovers have passed that way. Having complete sexual freedom at this period of her life, under the one condition that certain partners must be avoided, a young girl feels no shame in expressing her feelings and is full of initiative and audacity. This liberty contrasts strangely with the extreme modesty that has been inculcated into her since early childhood concerning anything to do with her marriage. The very mention of marriage makes her run away or hang her head in shame, and she absents herself as soon as her fiancé is mentioned, being forbidden to speak his name. So she is very little acquainted with the life companion destined for her by her family, although she is not in the least embarrassed to talk about her lovers either to her girl friends or in public, and will say to anyone who cares to listen: "I like X, and I shall go to his camp because I want to live with him". These pre-marital relationships do not usually last very long, because the girl knows that she is destined to marry her fiancé. She knows that she cannot attain a status equivalent to that of *koowaaDo* except by going through the traditional form of marriage. It is only after marriage that a young woman may attempt to free herself from a union which has not been one of her own choosing.

B.—MARRIAGE
AND THE NEW SOCIAL ROLES INVOLVED

Marriage brings to a young girl a double break with her former life. She has to renounce the sexual escapades and the love affairs she has hitherto been free to enjoy, and she has to leave her natal family, this separation being one which may be accentuated by having to live some distance away. On the other hand, she has been preparing since her fourteenth year for the role of mistress of the house which she will have to fill. But this change in her life, even if it has been led up to gradually, is nevertheless so great that it often creates serious difficulties in adaptation.

The most striking feature of Bororo marriage institutions is the co-existence of two types of marriage which give institutionalized expression to two tendencies always at war in any social system, the one being exclusively socio-centric, and the other wholly egocentric. The traditional marriage arranged by the families (*koobgal*) entirely disregards the personal feelings of the individuals concerned. The other type of marriage flouts outrageously all the principles of social reciprocity, being an individual contract sanctioned by a simplified ceremony borrowed from the ritual of traditional marriage. Since girls are always betrothed, and divorce by mutual consent does not exist, in the great majority of cases this second form of marriage involves married women.

Marguerite Dupire

A young girl remains apparently indifferent towards the arrangements made for her marriage, which have begun very early in her life, often as soon as she is born. Her attitude towards the whole affair is essentially a passive one and consists of negative taboos. The parents who make the arrangement for the marriage of their children are either consanguineous brothers, or a brother and sister. The verbal promise, which does not yet bind the parties, is accompanied by the gift of a necklace, which the mother of the boy places round the neck of his young fiancée. The father of the fiancé then sacrifices three cows, in a ceremony consisting of either two or three stages held during the times when the members of the lineage segment meet together in the winter season. This public sanction of the contract is the vital one, for from the moment of the first sacrifice the two families are solemnly and irremediably committed, and the family of the fiancée is not obliged to pay compensation even if she should die, refuse to marry, or be abandoned. The girl takes no part in this. Not only is neither she nor her fiancé allowed to eat the sacrificial meat, lest she run the risk of having "a trembling of the head in her old age", but she may not even be present. This rule also applies to the representatives of the two families directly concerned, and their place must be taken on this occasion by their closest kin. At the time of the first sacrifice, the betrothed pair learn not to speak each other's names. They call each other husband and wife, and already enjoy certain reciprocal rights conferred by marriage. The last sacrifice is accompanied by the public presentation of a gift[4] to the family of the fiancée, generally consisting of a cow and its calf, a heifer, and a bull-calf. The father of the young man, and the brothers and sometimes also the parallel cousins of the father, collect their herds together for the occasion and drive them to the hut where the women representing the young girl are waiting. The entirely theoretical discussion which takes place is essentially an affair between women, although the mother of the girl, out of modesty, does not interfere in these material details. But the valuation of the animals sacrificed is the men's concern—that is to say, the concern primarily of the paternal uncles of the fiancée. The maternal and paternal aunts of the girl are always eager to defend her interests and always maintain that the beasts offered up are not worthy of her. These animals are not removed from the herd of the young man (or rather of his father, since the two are not yet separate), and we shall see later what their real significance is for the bride, who on this occasion accepts them symbolically. The role of the fathers is stressed in the short song that sums up this ceremony: "He has married, he has married (that is, given in marriage), he whose daughter has been wed is happy". It is not forgotten, however, to make an appeal for fecundity to bless the future couple by enacting a short symbolical scene as epilogue.

After this, the young fiancée takes up her daily life again, with its many strenuous tasks, but also with its leisure hours for dancing and meeting other young people. As soon as menstruation occurs, the period of preparation for the marriage can begin, so long as the fiancé has completed the sacrifice of the three bulls and presented the gift of cattle. The fiancée is then obliged to observe a period of seclusion—the *puDol*—which lasts in some groups for three months and in others for five months and ten days. During this time she is cut off from masculine company, which has hitherto been completely open to her. She may not lift her eyes in the direction of a young man, nor reply to one if spoken to, nor show herself in public, nor, obviously, have sexual relations. A special hair style marks this period.[5] On his side, the fiancé must give presents to the parents of his fiancée. If these are three gowns, they are later given to the young woman; but among certain groups in the east the gifts consist of a heifer to the father of the fiancée and a sheep to the mother, and these remain the property of the parents.

The period of seclusion ended, one of the brothers of the fiancé, sometimes accompanied by a paternal aunt, goes to fetch the girl, who is hiding in the bush. Her parents, according to the ritual, refuse to be separated from her, but let her go at the second attempt made to take her and without receiving any further prestation. Bearing the gowns given by her fiancé, a pair of sandals and her jewellery, she accompanies her brother-in-law on foot and goes to her mother-in-law, to whom she presents a calabash filled with couscous as a gift from her family. No hut has been prepared for her, and she has to spend the first night alone, sleeping under a tree near the camp, on a mat lent by her mother-in-law. Custom underlines the distressing character of this separation from her family. Not only do they put up a struggle against letting her go, but the day following this first night, during which the marriage has not been consummated, the young woman takes flight and returns to her parents, where she stays for a week before once more going to her husband's.

It is difficult to know what young wives feel about the first months of married life, but judging from the eagerness with which they look forward to their first confinement, it would seem that they do not regard them exactly as a honeymoon. The young wife is no more than a stranger in the family of her husband, and entirely dependent on them. She herself has as yet no hearth of her own, no house, no furniture, no cows to milk. She sleeps under a tree with her husband on a mat lent by her mother-in-law, whose pestle she uses to pound the food which she prepares for him; and she drinks the milk of her husband's cows but is not yet allowed to do the milking herself. This period of probation, during which she is merely an apprentice—she is only 14 to 17 years old—has the advantage of not suddenly loading her down with the cares and duties of a married woman. With the authorization of her husband, she returns to visit her parents, and it is permissible for her to take part in public dances, which brings her into the company of the young men she used to meet so freely. Strict conjugal fidelity is not yet demanded of her, and the fact that at this stage of her life she is still called *surbaajo* (girl) shows that she is not yet a wife in the full sense of the word. Many young wives become anxious if after two or three years of marriage there are still no signs of pregnancy. But their position as wives will be established in just the same way as with those who have become mothers. However the fear of remaining permanently childless almost always results in a woman's leaving her husband and seeking a union which will provide open confirmation of the status of womanhood which she has attained.

Towards the fifth month of her pregnancy a wife obtains her husband's permission to go to her parents. He gives her three gowns and a pair of sandals, which is his contribution towards his wife's support during the whole period when she is, as it is said, *boofiiDo* 'she who hatches'. This period of between two and three years comprises the completion of the pregnancy, confinement, suckling, and weaning, all of which form part of one continuous social process which takes place, in the case of the first-born, in the bosom of the young wife's own family. The husband assumes an attitude of indifference, but the event which is taking place is of capital importance to him, because it will give him not only an heir, but also his independence, for it is usually after the birth of his first child that he leaves his father's household and sets up his own with his own herd. The same taboos which kept him apart from his fiancée now separate him from his wife during her pregnancy and maternity. He would feel ashamed to go and visit her, but he makes enquiries about her and sends her millet and salt, and, after the confinement, a handsome gift which is intended as compensation to the wife's family for expenses incurred in supplying her with food, and which is enjoyed by all the members of the camp where the confinement took place.

This period is one of peaceful seclusion for the young wife,

Women in a Pastoral Society

during which she can relax after the difficulties of her first experiences in living with her husband's family. She is fussed over and petted by her mother and by the other women in the camp, and shares with the old women the right to have a little hut of her own, which is roofed, but simple, and just big enough to contain a bed. There she rests with her baby, screened from inquisitive eyes. She may not, in fact, be seen in public nor be seen by men. The birth takes place in her father's camp under the direction of the midwives there, and the young mother is given free rein to cry out when the labour pains come on, although at later confinements this would be considered a sign of cowardice. The mother breast-feeds her infant, but her own milk is supplemented by that of all the nursing mothers in the camp and by an additional supply of cow's milk. She follows all the advice that is given to her, which is of a character that is magical as much as physiological. After the confinement, she is given a purgative gruel "to get rid of the bad blood", and she then continues to purge herself with Bilma salt, and takes a stew of haricots mixed with the leaves of the milk-yielding plant *agoahe* in order to increase her supply of milk. If the birth has taken place in the winter season, when food is abundant and the diet rich, she is recommended not to eat too much butter, meat, couscous or cassava, or else the baby will suffer from her milk being too rich. The young mother is not required to do any work and is free to spend all her time with her baby in her little hut, and begins to feel an interest in it which, however, she may not display in public. An attitude of the utmost reserve must be maintained by both parents towards the first-born child, and relations between them are regulated by strict taboos. All public manifestations of affection between a mother and her first-born are considered out of place, but this in no way means that the baby is deprived of affection. On the contrary, brought up as it is in the mother's family camp, it risks becoming a spoilt child. It occupies a privileged position from the moment of its birth, and that more ceremonious affair, the naming ceremony, is the occasion for the annual gathering of the lineage segment.

It is not until about two years have passed and the baby has been weaned that the husband sends one of his brothers, bearing two gowns, to fetch his wife. This return of the wife—now a mother —to her husband's family is known as *Bantol* and is of a victorious and triumphant nature. She is no longer timid and empty-handed, for, as well as the child, she has brought with her the dowry contributed by her parents (calabashes, mats, gowns, bed) which will now enable her to set up her own independent household for the first time. Her mother or her mother-in-law will give her that curious article of feminine luggage, the *kaakol*, which is treasured as much for its aesthetic as for its economic value, and which will adorn the back of one of the pack oxen each time camp is moved. Both dowry and *kaakol* are symbols of her new status. A hut of thorn awaits her, built by the women of her husband's camp, with the rope for her calf fixed at the entrance. As soon as she has her own household and her economic independence she becomes a woman in the full sense of the word—a *kaabo debbo*. This very important change in status is marked in some lineages by a small ceremony at which the two families exchange presents of food-stuffs, known as the *worso naatal suudu* (ceremony for the entry into the hut). This event marks the beginning of the young couple's independence and the completion of the marriage transactions. The fact that the couple have called each other husband and wife since the sacrifice of cattle, that the right to repudiate has already become legally valid, and that no further prestation has been made by the husband between the first period of cohabitation with his wife and the birth of his child, indicates how extremely prolonged the whole marriage procedure is, and it should be emphasized that, with all its various stages, it is a very gradual process for the woman.

Now a new stage opens in the life of the young mother. She no longer joins in the games and dances of the adolescents, and new duties towards her husband—including conjugal fidelity—and towards her children will tie her to her own household. She is now assured of economic security for herself and her children and has attained a social status which it would be impossible to acquire otherwise.

It now remains to consider the new roles which the young wife is called upon to play towards her natal family, her husband and her husband's family, and her own offspring.

1. *Relations between husband and wife*

Marriage does little to modify the attitude towards each other which betrothal has enjoined upon a couple since childhood. Coldness persists between husband and wife as it does between a father and his eldest son, although relations between affines gradually lose their restraint.

Since division of labour separates the sexes, husband and wife each pursue their separate tasks during the day. The husband eats with the men of the camp, his wife with the women and children, and each goes his or her separate way to the well or to the market. It is quite out of place for a wife to appear during the day by her husband's side, or to show any affection for him in public. On returning from a journey, a man will meet with the other men of the camp under a tree, but will be in no hurry to go and greet his wife, and she for her part would be ashamed to admit that she looked forward to her husband's return. This lack of any expression of affection does not imply a lack of interest, but the sociomoral code demands a lifelong attitude of restraint between husband and wife, in utter contrast to the freedom with which, as we have seen, lovers express their feelings for each other, even if this is always done with moderation.

A woman has claim to her marriage rights only so long as her husband is alive or so long as she remains with him. As soon as she leaves him or is repudiated she must relinquish the *sadaaki*, and on his death she inherits nothing from him. As a widow she regains her freedom, and her consent is required for marriage with a younger brother of her husband. Apart from the customary obligations, it is rare to find any 'extras' entering into the marriage relationship. Once a husband has given his wife a *sadaaki* and a certain number of cows for milking, he will make no further gifts of cattle to her whatever happens. The very idea would raise in a Bororo woman an incredulous smile, for it is in her eyes inconceivable. Would it not be to the detriment of the future capital of her children to expect any such haphazard gestures of generosity from her husband? She derives far less emotional security and stability from her marriage relationship, strictly regulated by custom as it is, than she does from the relations she enjoys after marriage with her own family and later with her children, and there is less spontaneity, unselfishness and generosity in this relationship than in any other. What it demands above all is mutual forbearance, for there are frequent occasions when domestic harmony may be disturbed.

The misunderstandings that arise between husband and wife are consequent upon the conditions of nomadic life and upon the very structure of the traditional form of marriage, which, in Bororo society, is patrilocal both in theory and in practice. There is never any question but that the wife must live in her husband's camp, which sometimes adjoins her own father's camp if she and her husband are parallel cousins. But a concession is made whereby she is not forced to go with her husband if the search for grazing land takes him to a distant region. The wish to avoid this acts as a subsidiary reason for arranging marriages between families that camp round the same wells, and hence belong to the same lineage segment; and the simplest solution, which avoids the separation of husband and wife and also enables the husband to keep an eye on the cattle belonging to his wife and on their common property, is to betroth the children of two consanguineous brothers, the betrothed children thus being paternal parallel cousins. However it sometimes happens that one of the families leaves the area after the first sacrifices have been made and the first prestations handed over. Almost invariably this results in breaking off the marriage. If the same thing should happen after several years of marriage, the wife will in most cases leave her husband, without this being held as a grievance against her, since, according to Bororo custom, she is considered to have sufficient reason for doing so. The husband then loses all his rights over his wife and is not reimbursed for any expenditure incurred, but, as in cases when the wife has been abandoned, he retains the *sadaaki* which is their common property, and keeps all children past the weaning stage.

Polygyny may encounter various difficulties which will interfere with its smooth functioning. It is necessary because of the customs regulating the first marriage and the sexual relations between the married couple, but less so than in many agriculturalist societies. It can in any case only be practised on a very small scale owing to problems of a demographic and ideological nature (the difficulty of obtaining women from outside the group and the antipathy towards giving daughters to strangers). But while it may be more or less a necessity for the men, Bororo women for their part are almost always stout defenders of monogamy. In contrast to what happens in a society of agriculturalists, where the various wives of one husband can be of help to each other in their work, with nomad pastoralists women's tasks are individual ones, and any curtailment of them which results from sharing out the economic benefits of the herd among the members of a polygynous household entails a serious financial loss. A polygynous household might be thought to have the obvious advantage of enabling co-wives to help each other in looking after the babies, preparing the food, or milking, but in practice it is more often the sisters-in-law who live next to each other or the mother-in-law who perform these services in a Fulani camp. Usually the co-wives do not get on well together, although there are exceptions of course, particularly in the case of women who are themselves childless and who become attached to the children of a co-wife. But if a woman wants to leave the camp and pay a visit to her own family, she can do so with an easy mind without having to have a co-wife to leave in charge: any other woman in the camp will do as well.

It is, however, above all the economic disadvantages of polygyny that prejudice women against it. What happens is, that after each new marriage the husband redistributes a certain number of his milch cows (the *birnaaji*) between his wives, although of course the *sadaaki* animals always remain in the care of each particular wife concerned. Thus each wife has her share in the dairy products that much reduced by the inclusion of the new wife in the redistribution. If the WoDaaBe of this area possessed large herds requiring a considerable number of women workers, this division of labour could be regarded as a necessary one. But their herds are mostly small ones ranging from eight to 100 head of cattle (the average for the Nguigmi region being 42 head, 12 of them being milch cows), and a herd of 100 head is considered to be a sign of great wealth. In most cases, the wives in a polygynous household could undertake the milking of a larger number of cows than those actually assigned to them, and would derive a definite economic gain from doing so. Thus in this society co-wives are rivals not only in so far as sex and emotions are concerned, but also in the economic sense. It is therefore understandable that they should be so bitter about defending their rights and so lacking in compassion when one of them, less lucky than the others, finds her supplies of milk diminished. Moreover, the husband is not usually greatly concerned to maintain the elementary rules of justice and equity so essential to polygyny, and this provokes justifiable jealousy between the wives and leads to the break-up of marriages.

The chief wife, due to the fact that the *koohgal* form of marriage that unites her and her husband has a higher social standing, and also because she often enjoys the confidence of the master of the house, derives a certain prestige from her position. But her supremacy is not nearly so great as it is among sedentary peoples, and she has almost no control whatsoever over her co-wives. Less importance is attached by WoDaaBe women to being the chief wife than to being the favourite wife of a husband chosen by themselves, with whom they are united by the secondary form of marriage known as *teegal* which has an inferior social standing. Thus polygyny, here, is far removed from the usual picture found in other parts of Africa, and it does not come up to the ideal as expressed by the men any more than it does to that cherished by the women. A man attaches more importance to making a conquest, so long as it can be publicly confirmed by a marriage of however short a duration, than to the actual size of his harem; and a woman, for her part, prefers to be the last in the line, provided she is married to the man of her choice, rather than be the frustrated chief wife of a husband imposed on her by her family. These individualistic and

Marguerite Dupire

anarchical tendencies are typical of this society of nomads. In practice, polgyny comes down to being a series of consecutive marriages, and expresses an unsuccessful search for equilibrium in marriage relations, and for a form of marriage liberated from too heavy a burden of social restraint.

Both men and women can dissolve their marriages and contract others with the greatest of ease. Divorce in the strict sense of the word does not exist. A husband has the right to repudiate his wife even before cohabiting with her, and a wife will leave her husband when she is tired of him although she has no legal right to do so unless her family have left the region and she finds herself separated from her husband. This breaking of the marriage contract, even when it is purely a matter of individual choice, is not accompanied by any restitution (of the bulls sacrificed or the presents given). But whichever of the spouses is responsible for breaking the contract, the husband keeps the *sadaaki*, even if his wife has not borne him any children or if she has removed all her personal possessions. This is a victory for individualism which summarily destroys the results of all the efforts made by the two families. When his wife leaves him, a man, helped by his brothers, will normally attempt to achieve compensation by physical force, or even by armed force if necessary. The runaway wife almost always goes straight to a lover who will later enter into the secondary, *teegal*, form of a marriage with her.

Current practice regarding such separations is actually equivalent to the force of law, so that women enjoy a wide freedom of choice such as is totally prohibited to them in their first marriage. Cases in which the wife leaves the husband occur, in fact, more often than cases of repudiation. In one segment of the Jijiru, among 46 women of all ages, 25 per cent had left their husbands, and only ten per cent had been repudiated. The chiefs try to mitigate as best they can the bad effects such broken marriages have on the solidarity of a lineage segment by forbidding the re-marriage of runaway wives within the lineage. Fifty years ago, when the Bororo were still in Nigeria, abduction could not be regularized by sacrificing a head of cattle as it can nowadays. If the man who had committed it was seized and brought before the senior chief, he had to return the woman to her husband, or keep her only on the condition that he re-imbursed the first husband for the animals he had sacrificed, and himself sacrificed one to sanction the new marriage. This was in effect divorce with the husband's consent. There is another practice, whereby two chiefs who want to prevent abductions of this kind from occurring between members of their segments swear an oath on an upturned calabash. This had efficacious results, and continues to be adopted up until the present. Abductions are very rare in lineages linked by such an oath, but frequently occur within a single lineage in spite of all the efforts made by chiefs and elders. The proliferation and subsequent regularization of these secondary marriages provide evidence of the freedom with which Bororo women can dispose of their persons once they have escaped from the subjection of a first marriage made without their consent. It is almost always the woman who instigate these marriages by abduction. There is no question of free love or of concubinage. The *toginDo* or Don Juan of the Bororo, however great his charm and his sex appeal, must also show himself capable of keeping and of supporting the women whose conquest he has made. He must therefore steer his love affairs to a conclusion in marriage, sacrifice an animal in the presence of the men of his camp in order to legalize the union, and live with the woman for a short time at least, keeping her in his own household for all to see. As for the woman, this secondary form of marriage enables her to benefit from the cattle belonging to her lover, and provides a social father for her children. Needless to say, this anarchical practice provokes conflicts which are sometimes violent, and causes splits within the patrilineage. Women play a leading part in this struggle for the liberty of the individual, and their desire for independence constantly threatens the socio-political equilibrium of the society.

This secondary form of marriage, contracted as it is between consenting adults, is nevertheless as unstable as the other. What are the reasons for this? In the first place, the absence of social controls, and in the second, the fact that owing to the scarcity of women, there is always open competition. If the marriage does not satisfy her, the wife can easily try another, or return to her own family where she will find the necessary emotional security which she has failed to find in marriage. This general picture of marriage relations between men and women must not, however, be allowed to obscure the variations which occur. Out of six households which I was able to observe fairly closely, having spent a whole winter season with them moving from one pasturage to another, I found that four of them showed the usual persistently unstable character, while the two others provided striking examples of marital equilibrium. The first of these two households was monogamous, and the wife had been betrothed at a very early age in place of her deceased elder sister.[6] Neither the difference in age between the couple (the wife being 12 to 15 years younger than her husband) nor the childlessness of the wife had affected the good relations between them, which had continued to be exactly as they were from the beginning. Each of them had adopted a child, and now that the husband had become old and rheumatic, his wife did not hesitate to take on the masculine tasks, and she cultivated the small field which the man could no longer dig himself. Her independence was as great as her devotion. With the kind of enterprise which is rare in this society, she had herself, out of her own savings, bought a heifer at the market, and also exploited commercially a herd of small livestock. The husband only smiled when people made fun of them saying "it was the woman who wore the *dedo*" (leather breeches worn by men), for he respected his wife's intelligence as much as her courage and fidelity.

The second of these trouble-free households was polygynous. The chief wife was a distant cousin of her husband. They had known and loved each other since their youth, having lived in neighbouring camps, but the girl had had to go some distance away to the husband to whom she had been betrothed since childhood. She did not stay there more than a year, and then became, by *teegal* marriage, the first wife of her cousin, who, an orphan and with slender means, had been unable to contract the traditional *koobgal* marriage. The second wife, a Fulani woman who been repudiated, was married to him at about the same time as the first. A fine person and very intelligent, she had won the sympathy of the first wife who, still childless after seven years of marriage, adopted the little girl of the second wife. There was complete harmony between them, and they had apparently only had one quarrel during the seven years they had lived together. Although the first wife, who was more unstable, sometimes tried to play the usual game of running off to her own family, her husband had always been able to persuade her to return to him. The harmony that reigned in this household must be attributed to the compatability of its three members, and even more to the character of the husband, who was fair-minded, generous and conciliatory. It must be stressed that, in the open-air conditions of Bororo life, strict privacy in domestic life is impossible, and compatibility between n people is more than ever necessary if polygyny is to work, especially as some of them, the co-wives, have not chosen to live with each other and often have more than one reason to be jealous of each other and to hate each other. The rough conditions attendant upon nomad life increase the difficulties normally experienced in the functioning of polygyny and in the achievement of a stable marriage.

Women in a Pastoral Society

2. The married woman and her husband's family

Relations between daughter-in-law and mother-in-law are particularly delicate during the early stages of a marriage because of the mutual attachment that binds mother and son. We have seen how, at the beginning of her marriage and before the birth of her first child, the new wife is entirely under the thumb of her mother-in-law, who remains in charge of her son's cows. These rights are not handed over entirely until after the birth of the first child. It is only then that the mother-in-law authorizes the young wife to have her own hut and to instal herself there with the articles given as dowry by her own parents, and, most important of all, to milk the cows from her son's herd. When the wife has had several children she can get on to more familiar terms with her mother-in-law, although she must continue to use the polite form of address, and it would still be incorrect to speak loudly, sing or shout in her presence, and shameful to spend a night with her husband at her hut. But the daughter-in-law may now eat with her mother-in-law and behave less timidly to her. They avoid all physical contact however, and should the daughter-in-law have her hair dressed by her mother-in-law, she would not lay her head on her knees, but on a stool.

Any expression of affection between them is made indirectly. When the children get bigger they will be bearers of small gifts between their mother and grandmother. In the latter's old age, the daughter-in-law will let her have one of her daughters as a permanent household help.

Towards her father-in-law a woman always maintains a more respectful distance, never speaking to him directly, unless he is a paternal uncle with whom she has always shared the same camp, in which case the rules of etiquette are less strict.

If the camp is one belonging to an extended family, she will constantly have occasion to meet her husband's brothers, towards whom her attitude varies according to whether they are senior brothers or junior. The former are theoretically in line of succession to their father as head of the camp, so their sisters-in-law must treat them with respect and would not dare to enter the hut if any of them should be present. She has, on the other hand, a joking relationship with her husband's younger brothers, and they call each other "old fellow" and "my wife". This attitude accords with the custom of the junior levirate, which is always practised.

The wives of her husband's brothers are the *fecciraaBe*, literally "those who share". This expression corresponds to a social reality, for they do in fact share the same conditions, all being strangers living in the camp of the extended family of their husbands. As no jealousy or rivalry enters into their relations, they usually co-operate with each other in a friendly way. A woman will much sooner ask a *fecciraao* to look after her children for her than ask a co-wife to do so.

Thus, deferent towards her husband's parents and her elder brothers, a woman is on equal terms often of an affectionate and friendly nature with her sisters-in-law, and has a joking relationship with her younger brothers-in-law. But she will not have a permanently subordinate position in these surroundings to which her marriage has brought her. Once the first years of adaptation are over, her status as wife and as mother will give her a place in the life of the camp which can become extremely influential.

3. *The married woman and her children*

The reason why the birth of the first child is awaited with such eagerness is that having a child is what gives a married woman her purpose in life. Some childless women learn with the years to make the best of things by adopting a daughter or two daughters, but not before having tried out all the traditional remedies, consulted the baobab of Dakoro, or even married several husbands in the hope of having a child. A man who has learnt by experience that he is impotent will provide himself with an heir by "surrendering his mat" and his wife to a temporary substitute whose sole function in such a case is a biological one. To her children, the mother is the chief representative of the uterine kin who are related "through the milk" and whose characteristic feelings towards each other are those of devotion and affection. It is she who brings up her sons during their early years and who remains the counsellor of her married daughters. She never gives any open signs of her affection for them, because it is not customary in this society to give overt expression to feelings, and any public exhibition of affection towards her eldest son would be particularly shameful.

The instability of a wife's position might be thought to be detrimental to her children, for if she leaves her husband she is obliged to let him keep her sons at least. But even so, such children are not entirely cut off from their mother and their mother's family, and later in life mother and sons will come together again. The youngest son is very often the favourite, and the most devoted to his mother because he is the last to leave the family camp and is there to look after her at the time when she is getting on in years. She in turn surrounds him with affection and showers him with small presents.

Women in a Pastoral Society

Everything that a woman possesses is designated for her children, and just as the father distributes his cattle to his sons during his lifetime, so the mother shares out her *sadaaki* among them, only keeping the few milch cows that are necessary for her own subsistence. She often has to play the part of peacemaker, either between father and sons, or on occasions when her sons seek vengeance by force of arms. When fighting with sticks breaks out, it is the mothers who can be seen intervening between the assailants.

After the father's death the children of each wife gather round their mother again, their solidarity including the duty of mutual aid as well as of revenge. Segmentation within a patrilineage often occurs at the "hut" level—that is to say, between groups of half-brothers. Each new segment bears the name of the eldest of the group of full brothers composing it, but the hierarchy between these segments is that of the various wives whose sons form the segments, the *suudu maundu*—the 'big hut'—consisting of the offspring of the chief wife.

It is on her sons rather than on her husband that a woman depends for support in her old age. When she is too old to be of further use in her husband's camp, she goes to live with one of her married sons, who will spare her some milk from one of his animals. It sometimes even happens that a wife who has been repudiated or separated will return to her former husband's camp to live with her sons. There is no more serious accusation than that of ingratitude towards one's mother.

4. The married woman and her natal family

A woman always and above all remains a member of her own paternal and maternal families, even when she has passed from living under her father's to living under her husband's authority. When she arrives to live with her husband, she changes neither her name nor the branding mark on her animals, which is that of her father. Even the rights which a husband acquires over his wife on marriage are restricted, either actually or symbolically, by the ascendancy which her natal family retains over her.

The first proof of this is that a husband finds it impossible to lay any claim to his wife if she has gone with her kin to another locality. Then there is the custom by which a woman's first child is born, and brought up until weaned, at the camp of its maternal grandparents. There is no doubt as to the practical advantages of this custom, since it gives the young mother her apprenticeship in motherhood. But it is difficult to see where the practical advantages lie in the habit which the maternal grandparents have of keeping their daughter's eldest son until the time of his marriage. It is true that this arrangement is in no way obligatory, for if the boy's father is short of labour and wants to have his son with him, he can usually obtain his father-in-law's consent; and, in practice, there are certain psychological advantages for the boy, for with his mother's family he grows up in a more affectionate and less tense atmosphere than he would experience, as eldest son, in his father's camp.

A maternal aunt is regarded as a second mother, but because of the operation of the principle of patrilocal residence, she rarely has the opportunity of being wet-nurse to her sister's children, nor does she ever become their stepmother, for the sororate, said to have existed formerly, is now prohibited. Moreover, marriage with the daughter of a maternal aunt is regarded as incestuous. Her role is in fact much less important than that of the male members of the mother's family, which is natural in a society where rights are transmitted through men.

The maternal kin, as a group, provides the necessary affection, generosity and trustworthiness which is lacking in the paternal kinship group; but as well as this distinction between them, there is a linkage between the two groups consisting of a series of minor claims made upon each other, which are perhaps symbolic rather than essential, but significant none the less. It is the wife's father who, in the early stages of her marriage, lays claim to her first male child. But when this child has reached marriageable age, he has, as nephew, the right to lay claim to a portion of the property belonging to his mother's brother and to his mother's brother's sons, along with the right to lay claim to this maternal uncle's daughter. Thus the marriage of a woman establishes between three generations of the two families involved certain reciprocal relations for exchange of services, of property, and sometimes, but not necessarily, of women.

It is always her natal family that a woman relies upon, until such time as her sons are married. She often leaves the small live-stock which are her personal property with her father, not trusting her husband to look after them. She frequently visits her family, and returns to it when unhappy, widowed, divorced, or when suffering from a long illness, to find the support she has need of. The husband is well aware of this constant admonitory threat which hangs over him. The supervision from a distance which his wife's kin continue to exercise over her own well-being and that of her livestock is reason enough to induce him to treat her according to the rules of customary law.

Women in a Pastoral Society

ECONOMIC STATUS

A.—DIVISION OF LABOUR

The characteristic association: man-cattle, as against woman-household, is a feature that has already been stressed. The basis of the differences in rights between the sexes must be sought in a division of labour which has the characteristic features common to most cattle-keeping peoples, in Africa at least.[7] To look after the humped cattle, which are only semi-domesticated, demands activities of which a woman is physically incapable. It would be beyond a woman's strength to draw water for the herd in the dry season, to go on long marches to reconnoitre for grazing-lands, to protect the herd against wild animals and thieves, to hold her own with a buyer at the market, to castrate bulls, or to train the pack oxen. This hard, dangerous life, full of uncertainty and of prolonged absences from the camp, would be incompatible with the duties of motherhood, which require a more sedentary and more regular life.

Thus among the activities required for the care of the herd, only those that are compatible with staying at home are assigned to her: those of milking and of making butter. She also looks after the minor ailments of the animals under her care, and has a direct interest in doing so; but for anything requiring more forceful treatment (blood-letting, yoking . . .) she passes all responsibility over to the head cattlekeeper. Among the Bororo it is inconceivable that a woman should be *jom-na'i*, master of the herd.

It should be noted that this division of labour is not in any way a hard and fast affair. Apart from the period of married life preceding the birth of the first child and the month or two following upon each time she gives birth, there is no period in a woman's life when she may not do the milking. However, although the reason why Bororo men do not undertake this task is because they have never learnt to do so, should the necessity arise, they would not hesitate to assume this feminine role. Thus it is the very conditions of existence that have determined cultural choice. This is proved by the fact that among the semi-nomad Fulani of the Niger it is the men who practise the technique of milking, while the women are unversed in it. The reason why, in this society, it is the herdsmen who have learnt how to milk, is because they spend half the year, parted from the women, looking after the cattle in the

75

bush at some distance from the village. The few milch cows left behind in the village are milked by the older men, while the butter is churned by the women.[8] It is obvious therefore how much these habits, which sometimes persist long after there has been a change in the mode of life, are functional in origin, and not based on any magico-philosophical concepts of irreducible differences between the sexes. In any case, a man sometimes has to intervene when things go wrong with the milking, for if the cow is restive, or if her milk does not flow after the first calving, she has, in the first case, to be controlled by tying her up, or, in the second, to be treated by blowing air into the vagina or, in the last resort, by appealing to a specialist in incantations.

Women also do the milking of the smaller livestock, and here their responsibilities have a wider range (including looking after the animals and negotiating sales), due to the fact that these smaller animals are more amenable to treatment which requires less physical strength. Normally, small flocks of sheep and goats belong to women rather than to men. Being a form of capital that is easily convertible, they provide women with the same kind of "savings bank" as castrated cattle do for men.

Women also undertake all the tasks concerned with the house. As soon as the head of a camp has decided upon the place where they will stay for several days or several weeks, it is the women who build the huts from the thorn branches they have gathered, while their husbands busy themselves with tethering their calves and taking the herd to graze. It is also they who decorate the calabashes, fabricate the mats made out of bark, weave the winnowing fans. They look after the fires belonging to the hut, while the men look after those for the cattle—a task which requires knowledge of the magic talismans associated with it. The women plait the light ropes that are all that is required for their own use, while the men plait the heavy ones needed for drawing water or for tethering the calves; but it is the men who collect the bark used in making them. Helped by her children, the mistress of the house fetches water from the well for domestic purposes, while it is the man's job to draw water for watering the livestock. At the market which both attend, the wife sells her milk and her butter, while the husband buys salt, millet when necessary, and tobacco, sugar and tea for himself, as well as haggling over prices for the sale of cattle.

Both men and women know how to ply a needle for sewing or repairing their own clothes. Nor do men despise doing some cooking, although they usually leave this task to the women. When a man is on his own, or when he is taking part in a ceremony, he cooks meat by grilling it on a skewer, while women boil it in one of the pots they have made.[9]

In this allocation of work between the sexes there is no idea whatsoever of inferiority of status being associated with those tasks normally assigned to women. But it is obvious that in a pastoralist society, in which it is the man who undertakes the heavy work and the responsibilities involved in looking after the cattle, that he, as master of the herd, will achieve social and economic superiority over the woman, whose tasks are confined to managing household affairs and looking after her sheep and goats.

The few fields cultivated by some families at the beginning of the winter season do not employ more than one or two men; and as soon as the crops are sown, these men hasten to rejoin the other members of the camp who are on the move with their herds. Here again it is considerations of a practical order which determine the arrangement, and this is particularly the case with the WoDaaBe, among whom the men are responsible for providing the supply of millet for the family, while the women supply the milk. The Bororo, however, are not unaware of the magical associations which link woman with the fertility of the soil, for one of their recipes for the fertility of the herd includes some seeds from a field belonging to a female sedentary farmer, which are called *umma* (meaning "arise"! in their language).

In the Niger region, WoDaaBe women do not either spin cotton or know how to make cheese, in contrast to their Fulani sisters belonging to tribes that practice sedentary farming.

From this picture it can be seen that upon women fall the less strenuous tasks, but also those which are the most monotonous and which take up the most time. In the dry seasons, they often walk a distance of 20 to 30 kilometres to sell one or two litres of milk in the village. It is the woman who is the first to get up in the morning, at dawn, to pound the grain, when the air is still chilly. But her night will have been undisturbed, unless her baby has wakened her; whereas her husband may have had to stay up half the night getting his herd watered; or he may have had to get up in the middle of the night because a jackal was prowling round the camp.

B.—PROPERTY BELONGING TO WOMEN

From their earliest years, children enjoy undisputed rights of possession over their personal belongings. No mother will give away or exchange her little girl's doll without first asking her permission. With stock, however, the situation is different, for, although both boys and girls are indeed the owners of the cattle given to them by their father, mother, or other relatives, and refer to them in the possessive, yet they have no active control over this property so long as they remain members of the paternal household. The father looks after the cattle, while the mother does the milking and uses the dairy products to supply the needs of the household. If the father's herd is failing to produce enough to support the family, the children cannot raise any objection if the cattle-keeper finds himself forced to sell one of their animals which had been given to them in front of witnesses. It will be accepted philosophically as "God's will", in the same way as nobody will be held responsible for the good or ill luck that may attend the first heifers given to them by their parents. At birth and as the children grow up, portions of the herd are allotted to them which cannot then be re-allotted or compensated for (in principle, at least). These allotted portions remain under the exclusive control of the father until his children marry, or more precisely, until they leave the paternal camp. This economic dependence acts as a stimulus to married sons to set up on their own as soon as possible. When a daughter gets married, the care of her cattle passes from her father to her husband, who is then responsible for their well-being in the interests of his wife and her children. That women consider this question of control to be a delicate one is proved by the fact that young wives are in the habit of leaving their stock with their father until they can feel sure of the integrity of their husbands, preferring to be temporarily deprived of the dairy products of their herd. Some of them even leave them there for good. When the husband becomes cattle-keeper, he keeps his wife's animals along with his own, but is aware that they do not belong to him.

If a woman wants to sell one of her animals, she must first ask the consent of her husband, and he in turn, should he find himself in difficulties, may not sell one of his wife's animals without her consent. Any sharp practice concerning the cattle will immediately bring complaints on the part of the wife and departure to her family. But if husband and wife get on well together and the husband has shown himself to be trustworthy, his wife is not likely to refuse him one of her animals in order to pay tax or, as is more often the case, to make up the *sadaaki* to be given by one of their sons to his fiancée. In such an event, the combined wealth of husband and wife provides for the maintenance or for the future of their children, thus playing the normal role for which the double contribution of cattle was intended.

Women in a Pastoral Society

Astonishing though it may seem, a wife maintains a much stricter supervision over the *sadaaki*, of which she is only co-owner with her husband, than she does over her own stock given to her by her family. To a woman, keeping the *sadaaki* intact is equivalent to preserving a tangible symbol of her matrimonial rights while also safeguarding the future of her children. For this reason, it is the most socially sacrosanct part of the herd, and the one which must remain the last to be depleted. A wife will as little pardon her husband for having misappropriated their *sadaaki*, especially if he has done so for the children of another wife, as she will be willing to distribute it during her lifetime among her children when they get married. This prevents further quarrels with her husband on the subject without entirely depriving her of her rights to the dairy products, for a mother can easily go to live with one of her sons. Thus a married woman as often as not prefers to hand over her stock to her family or to her children rather than to her husband.

A second way in which women play an important role in the transmission of cattle derives from the manner in which the herd belonging to the father of the family is divided out.

To his chief wife a husband entrusts, in addition to the *sadaaki*, a certain number of milch cows (*darnaaji*), the milk of which will belong to her personally, and which immediately become part of the stock which her children alone will inherit together with the dairy rights. His other wives, with whom he is united by the *teegal* form of marriage, do not receive any *sadaaki*, but he assigns to them a certain number of animals (*senndereeji*) on a scale comparable, in so far as is possible, with the combined *sadaaki* and *darnaaji* of the chief wife. In addition to those cows which have been divided out, the head of the family may possess others which he can entrust to anyone he pleases for varying lengths of time. He is free to dispose of these animals and their progeny as he wishes. Along with the steers and bulls which do not come from the *sadaaki* or *darnaaji* they will form part of the common inheritance of all his children.

This manner of dividing out the herd accentuates the economic basis of the group of full brothers, who share common interests with their mother. Their calves are tethered in front of their hut, and the children get to know them and are aware that they can be certain of inheriting some of them, to the exclusion of their half-brothers and sisters. They understand, too, that the well-being of the animals depends on the care their mother bestows on them and on her firmness in preventing any depredations. In this way, the mother, without herself being its source, is the channel through

Marguerite Dupire

which a large part of the father's stock is transferred to his children. A woman enjoys much greater economic independence with regard to the small livestock which she acquires out of her personal savings. She can in fact do what she likes with it. She is free to a considerable degree to put to use the results of her labours. The milk from her cows belongs to her, but out of the income derived from this she must contribute towards the household needs. In principle, the husband is responsible for expenditure required for the cattle (natron, taxes . . .), and for clothing and the supply of millet, while the woman's share of the budget covers expenditure on daily requirements such as cereals, cooking salt, and condiments (which are however a luxury). But actually, in the dry season it is customary to barter milk for millet, and during the winter season the WoDaaBe do not eat cereals. There remains the difficult period before the harvest, at the end of the dry season, when the milk yield is low and there is no surplus for exchange. The husband is then often obliged to sell one of his sheep, or even a bullock, although this is an extreme measure to which he is loth to resort. It is in fact also in the wife's interests to safeguard the family capital, and in the dry season it is much more sensible to exchange milk, which is scarce, for millet, than to sell a skinny animal at a low price. Milk and butter are the basis of the household economy. Particularly during the winter season, the women manage to accumulate large quantities of butter stored in calabashes, which, already rancid, is sold in the villages on return from winter quarters. This provides pocket money for buying, for themselves and their children, extra gowns, trinkets, and even sheep. It is astonishing what a Bororo woman manages to do with the small savings from the "butter money", which gradually mount up. During the worst time of the year, four cows give a daily yield of a pat of butter weighing about 250 grammes (costing 15 C.F.A. francs in 1951). This butter is exchanged in the villages or sold on the market, and the women spend quite a lot of their time on these petty commercial transactions.

They may also mend calabashes for village women, or, when food is very scarce, offer to pound grain for a slight payment in cereals or bran. But a young and active Bororo woman will avoid such menial tasks. Similarly, it is only young men who have no cattle of their own who will offer themselves as herdsmen in a locality where they are not known, where they will be less likely to feel ashamed. None of the other articles which women make, such as mats, winnowing fans or ropes, are saleable.

Occupied as she is with her house and her children, a woman

Category of cattle	Description and source	Looked after by . . .	Alienation rights held by . . .	Rights to use the milk held by . . .	Inheritance rights held by
birnaaji	Stock held by the head of the family. Acquired through inheritance, gifts, purchases, or *nannga na'i* loans . . .	Father of the family.	Father of the family.	*All the wives alike* as required.	The children of all the wives.
darnaaji	Portion of the stock of the head of the family entrusted to the chief wife, *koowaaDo* (same sources as *birnaaji*).	Father of the family.	Father of the family.	*Only* the wife to whom they have been entrusted.	Only the children of the wife who has rights to the milk.
sadaaki (Western Niger region).	Stock given to the *koowaaDo* wife.	Father of the family even after divorce or repudiation.	*Husband or wife* with the consent of spouse.	*Only* the wife who is co-owner.	Only the children of the wife who is co-owner.
sadaaki (Islamized Eastern Niger region).	Stock given to the *koowaaDo* wife.	Father of the family except in cases of repudiation.	*Husband or wife* with the consent of spouse.	*Only* the wife who is co-owner.	Only the children of the wife who is co-owner.
sennudereeji	Portion of the stock of the head of the family entrusted to secondary wives (in place of *sadaaki* and *darnaaji*).	Father of the family.	Father of the family.	*Only* the wife to whom they have been entrusted.	Only the children of the wife who has rights to the milk.
sukaaji of the children.	Gifts received by the children.	Father during their minority, sons after setting up households, husband of married daughters.	Father of the family during their minority, sons on coming of age.	Usually *the wife who is the mother of the children who own the stock.*	This is an inheritance in advance of each child in question.
sukaaji of the wives.	Gifts received by each wife from her family.	Father of the family.	*The wife with the consent of her husband.*	*Only* the wife who is the owner	Only the children of the wife who is the owner.

81

is nevertheless just as much sentimentally attached to the cattle as the men are. In her earliest years she was accustomed to stroke gently the ears or the vagina of the cow her mother was milking. She has to keep constant watch over the calves entrusted to her, and like her husband and her children, she knows the history of every single animal. When she has to part with a cow that is ill or too old and that has to be killed, it is like parting from a human being, and her sorrow speaks volumes for the attachment she feels for these companions in good times and bad.

It goes without saying that for men as for women the expression *miin-jei*, "I possess", covers various methods of appropriation entailing varying rights: of alienation, of administration, of usufruct. A woman will say of the pack ox that forms part of her *sadaaki* "my pack ox", and it is true that she has exclusive use of it so long as she remains with her husband; but she can neither sell it without her husband's consent, nor take it with her should her marriage be dissolved (this at least is the case among the WoDaaBe groups of the western Niger region).

If a woman's rights over the large livestock are restricted owing to the fact that she is considered incapable of looking after it, those of a married man over the herd of which he is nominally "master" are no less so, (1) by his wife's co-ownership of the *sadaaki*, (2) by each wife's ownership of the cattle given to her by her family, (3) by the wives' exclusive rights over the milk of certain animals, (4) by his children's rights of ownership and of inheritance over the stock divided out during his lifetime.

A glance at the above table in which the various types of ownership are listed will show that a wife not only has exclusive rights to the use of the milk from the animals in one category or another (*darnaaji* and *sadaaki* for the chief wife, *senndereeji* for the others, as well as the *sukaaji* of their children and their own *sukaaji*), but also enjoys co-ownership of her *sadaaki* with her husband and exclusive rights of ownership over the animals given to her by her family, although the care of them is entrusted to her husband, the master of the herd. The restrictions on the rights of the father of the family over his cattle are connected with his children's future. As for the wives, their rights to the use of the milk and the co-ownership of the *sadaaki* act as a guarantee for the services they render their husband.

These rights of ownership, co-ownership or merely of use of the milk which a wife enjoys over certain animals are connected with the fact that the capital which these animals represent is inalterably destined to be transmitted to her own children (table col. 6). A mother not only transmits to her children life and "milk", but also channels to them the cattle belonging to their father, simply in virtue of being married to him.

The ownership of all other goods belonging to husband and wife (clothes, furniture and other articles) remains completely separate throughout their married life. When a wife leaves her husband or is repudiated by him, she leaves the hut, people say, with "nothing but the dust" in it, and perhaps also the old blackened cooking pot which would be too cumbersome to take away. She removes all her possessions, including her own livestock and the dowry given to her by her parents. But the presents given to her by her husband's family are left behind: the *sadaaki* and the furniture lent to her by her mother-in-law. Clothes, furniture, and other articles down to sewing needles, are individually acquired either by the husband or by the wife. Marriage does not entail any sharing of such belongings by the couple.

Thus the only rights of ownership that marriage brings to a woman are her rights of co-ownership or of usufruct in cattle belonging to her husband, while her husband only has the use of his wife's possessions (dowry and stock) for as long as she remains with him. Whatever the reasons for the dissolution of a marriage (separation, repudiation, death), the sharing of goods in common ceases with the physical separation of the couple.

The belongings over which a woman possesses permanent rights of alienation or usufruct are, in fact, not those which come from her husband, but those which come from her own family or which have been acquired as a result of her own work under her husband's roof: the gifts of cattle and the dowry given to her by her parents, and the livestock bought with her "butter money".

She is, however, complete mistress of those belongings which do not fall within the large number of restricted categories. But a BoDaaDo woman possesses little enough stock: a few cattle calved by the heifer given to her by her parents, supposing it has survived, and a small flock of goats and sheep. It is usually childless women that have the flocks of sheep, because otherwise a married woman finds that most of her slender income goes on necessary household expenses. Among the WoDaaBe there are no much-sought-after widows whose personally owned cattle and *sadaaki* make them wealthy, such as can be found among the sedentary Fulani, because when a husband dies it is the children and not the wife who inherit the stock. I only came across one widow possessing a small herd of cattle, who was married to an old man without any property at all, and lazy into the bargain. This man who allowed himself to be kept by his wife soon became the laughing-stock of his neighbours. The widow lived with her son, the future inheritor, who threatened to go away, taking the herd with him, if she did not get rid of her good-for-nothing spouse. Even if a widow has no son, her property is controlled by the consanguineous kin who will inherit it, directly if she has made a leviratic marriage with her husband's brother, indirectly if she has opted for some other arrangement.

The Bororo maintain that women are thus incapacitated both because of their lack of physical strength and because of their marital instability. But it is clear that the situation arises from the very nature of the structure of inheritance in this thoroughly patrilineal society.

Since among pastoralists women are usually not owners of capital, that is to say, of cattle, which belong to the men, their economic position would appear to be less favourable than it is in some agriculturalist societies in Africa. There it is land, inalienable in the traditional context, that represents capital, but capital that is less valuable because it is neither mobile nor easily convertible. Hence the position of the women, who are the direct producers, should be, by comparison, higher in relation to the men of the lineage, who own the land that they cultivate. But this would appear to be too summary a generalization, because in some pastoralist societies women do have the right to manage the herd. J. H. Driberg reports that among the Lango a man may not dispose of his property without the permission of his wife, who is co-owner of the property which the children will inherit. She even has sole rights of administration over the property of her husband during the minority of the inheritors. In this society a woman also enjoys far greater political rights than is the case with a BoDaaDo woman, for the widow of a village head may even govern a village during the minority of her son. Thus there is considerable variation in the economic and legal rights of women in African pastoralist societies, whether of Nilotics, Nilo-Hamitics, or Fulani, in spite of the fact that in all of them it is the men who deal with the cattle.

The prestige which her wealth confers upon a woman is similar to that which a man derives from his cattle. At the ceremonies that take place when the lineage segment gathers together in the winter season, the heads of families who are celebrating the marriage of a son parade the herds of the extended family to display in public how many of them there are, and how strong and beautiful they are. The women have their own display, exhibiting their possessions in their huts: calabashes and polished-up spoons from their dowry stores, gourds and countless straw hats from the *kaakol* bags. Not a single article of personal belongings but is shown off to the best advantage, painted red or white, ornamented with metal that flashes in the sun. The whole display bears witness for all to see of feminine wealth, which gives personal prestige to the woman who owns it.

POLITICAL AND LEGAL STATUS

Bororo folklore and oral traditions do not feature any feminine figure comparable to that of Kahena. The typical BoDaaDo woman was neither Amazon nor leader of men, but appears in the legends as mother or as wife, guardian of the physical and moral heritage of the race. Censured if she contaminates the purity of the blood by union with a negro slave, she is the subject of compassion should a narcissistic instinct unconsciously make her feel attracted towards her own image sexually reversed—that of her brother or her son. The Bororo woman of the legends, where she plays the role of erring wife or of incestuous mother or sister, represents the eternal quest in this society for equilibrium between the two poles of endogamy and exogamy.

In the legal, political and religious spheres a woman is regarded as a minor. The social roles which confer status on her, whether in terms of kinship, seniority, or even personal achievement, have no political implications.

At ceremonies, the senior matron present always receives an extra portion of meat, but her role is in no way comparable with that of the patriarch, who officiates at each sacrifice and always takes the place of honour. The *lame* or *lamiDo reuBe*, who is selected for her personal qualities to be leader of the group of young girls, plays a subordinate role to that of the *samri*, head of the young men, who has himself chosen her. If any litigation should arise, she cannot lay any complaint before the head of the lineage segment except through his intermediation, he being responsible for both groups. It sometimes happens that the head of the segment exercises pressure to have one of his relations, especially his sister, appointed to this honorific position, without this in any way enlarging the scope of her activities.

The roles played by certain women in the ceremony of enthronement of a chief are connected with aspects of a primarily magico-biological nature. This ceremony, as well as being an affirmation of the status of the new chief, is also a rite of passage and of fertility, as its name implies: *lottingal laamu,* the cleansing of the chiefship. Although women are allowed to be present at the public part of the ceremony, none of them is allowed to enter the south door of the great hut where the chief spends his retreat, permission to do so being granted only to men of equal or superior status to his. A woman plays the obviously important role of being the officiant who bathes the chief and robes him, pronouncing the ritual words. This woman need not be related to the chief. All that is required of her is that she should know the ritual and have both parents living—a condition which emphasizes the magical associations characteristic of fertility rites. These are in fact numerous in this ceremony, and it is a function of this kind that is performed by the first wife of the chief in the concluding rite. When the chief emerges in procession from the great hut where he has been secluded for the past seven days, cut off from the presence of women, his first wife follows the procession and throws after it a mixture of haricots and millet seeds which have been previously moistened. Thus the power of the chief is associated with a rite of the sowing of seed and of fertility. The procession then goes to the hut of the chief's mother and to those of his wives. None of the parts played by women in this ceremony has any political significance. Just as with the care of the cattle, public affairs among the WoDaaBe are entirely in the hands of the adult men and of the head of the lineage segment.

As regards inheritance, women unquestionably have much fewer rights than is the case in the other two large nomad groups bordering with the Fulani, the Tubu and the Tuareg. Only a few segments of the WoDaaBe in the Eastern Niger region are beginning to follow, up to a point, the Muslim law of inheritance,[10] which differs from their former practice of following Bororo customary law based on agnatic principles. Although a woman has the same rights as a man to give away, exchange or sell her own household belongings and her small livestock, her cattle, as I have shown, remains under the control of "her master" and of his lineage. Naturally her rights of inheritance of cattle are limited, for to allow women to inherit them would be detrimental to the male members of the lineage, brothers or sons. Thus in theory the entire inheritance goes to male agnates, women of the same degree of kinship not partaking in it at all except for a minute portion which is not even formulated with any precision. In fact, among the non-Muslim WoDaaBe, if any part of the cattle inheritance is allotted to women, this is considered as a mere concession on the part of the male inheritors towards their kinswomen of the same degree of kinship. The unequal distribution of the father's herd among

Women in a Pastoral Society

his children has already been noted, the sons receiving the major portion, and the daughters usually no more than a heifer each.

In this agnatic system, neither the daughter, mother, sister, nor wife, has any real rights over the cattle. Nevertheless, in practice daughters do inherit a few animals on their father's death if he has left a large enough number of them, and on condition that such a distribution is not against the interests of the sons. But some WoDaaBe of the Ader do not allow daughters to inherit anything at all at the death of their father "because they marry elsewhere". A sister may inherit in the same way as a brother, but neither father nor mother may inherit from their children, for inheritance does not go backwards.

Whatever their degree of kinship may be with the deceased, women never take precedence over male inheritors in the order of succession. An only daughter has no more chance of inheriting from her father than she would if she had any brothers, for it is the brothers of the deceased who inherit if there are no sons.

On the death of their husband, widows recover possession of the cattle that belong to them personally. Their *sadaaki* is divided out among their sons, if that has not already been done by the widow in question; and each widow receives, as a token part of the inheritance of her husband, a single animal, this marking the termination of the mourning period, for which reason it is called *suddorge*. This animal is not regarded as her due, but as a gift made to her by the inheritors, although custom demands that it should be made.

The same male priority is found in the inheritance of the livestock that is the personal property of women. Sons, whether legitimate or illegitimate, get preference over daughters, who receive an even smaller share than they do of the cattle inherited from the father. When a woman dies childless, the principle of separate ownership of property is strictly applied: anything that came from her own family is either returned to her parents who gave it to her or given to her brothers, while the *sadaaki* which came from her husband remains in his family. There is no uterine inheritance except of the mother's property. The only exception to this is that in a few groups there is a right of primogeniture through the mother which gives priority of inheritance of the father's property; that is to say, that the eldest sons of all the wives come first in the order of succession before any of their younger brothers, and receive a larger share of the inheritance.

A woman's personal belongings, her clothes and her jewellery, go to her daughters in order of birth, or, if she has no daughters, to her sisters or other female members of her lineage.

Marguerite Dupire

A woman can never be the recognized administrator of her children's property during their minority, and no wills are made by women any more than by men, although gifts made during a woman's lifetime are permitted by the lineage so long as they are not prejudicial to the legitimate heirs.

She has the same right as her husband to adopt daughters if she herself is childless, but adoption among the WoDaaBe carries very limited rights, and adopted children are never included in the order of succession to the property of their adoptive parents. This is a matter in which the individual rights of both sexes are directly determined by patrilineage membership.

Since women only play a secondary role in looking after the herd, it is not surprising that the magic recipes for the fertility of the herd are transmitted through the men, while a mother passes on to her daughters the secret of the amulets used in their own special activities (for fertility, for abundance of milk, for casting spells, for protection against sorcery).

No women are healers by profession, but some of them know the secrets of the magic spitting which is supposed to protect against, or cure, certain ailments (snake bite, for instance; but the spells for protection against attack by hyenas or jackals are only known by men). They pass them on to those kinsmen or kinswomen who show a special gift for such things. The profession of healer is said to be hereditary through either the paternal or the maternal side of the family. It is a gift which, although hereditary, also requires an apprenticeship, and it is believed that the remedies were originally inspired by spirits.

Both men and women can be sorcerers, and it often happens that aged parents are accused by their children of having caused the death of one of their grandchildren or caused an epidemic in the herd by casting spells on the tracks of the cattle. Whenever an old man (or woman) is found living alone in the camp off a little water and milk, it is usually because he has been abandoned by his offspring in the belief that he is a sorcerer. From this it can be seen that sorcery is something that directly affects close kin in both ascending and descending generations. Its effects operate within the group of potential heirs, and express the tensions resulting from the sharing of property and of inheritance rights in common. The sedentary peoples draw false conclusions about such occurrences, and say that the Bororo abandon their parents and leave them to die alone.

CONCLUSION

What means does the Bororo woman have at her disposal for defending her rights? She can always rely on the support of her own family, but individualism is such a marked feature of this society that when a married woman wants to express her dissatisfaction, she does so by a passive refusal to obey or by threats to leave or by temporary flight. The dispute may be settled later, and if the husband is shown to have infringed her wife's rights he has to offer certain compensations before she will return to him.

Women are far from feeling passive about their rights.

I have been present at stormy discussions in the camps, when a group of women have called upon the men to express their opinions on problems concerning the right of a wife to leave her husband if he beats her, or her right to dispose of her own cattle or sell them at the market. It does sometimes happen that enterprising women themselves look after their cattle, but such cases are exceptional, and a woman who wears the trousers is a cause of amusement.

Labouret[19] has reported mass attacks by Fulani women in the eastern territories of West Africa, conducted as a demonstration against men repudiating their partners without valid customary reasons for doing so. Such feminist leagues do not exist among the Bororo of the Niger, the women there being too preoccupied with their own petty personal problems, although opportunities to discuss their common interests do occur when they meet together at the market.

However women are very much at the centre of the problems which are rapidly contributing to the inevitable transition from traditional customs to Islamization. The sedentary Fulani make fun of these backward nomads: the Bororo woman does not pray, she has no *sadaaki* that really belongs to her, she cannot inherit.

Laws of inheritance are changing, although not without resistance, among the wealthiest segments of the WoDaaBe in the eastern Niger region which have most come under the influence of Mohammedanism. Significantly enough, the right which these more advanced people have found easiest to accept is that of a woman to inherit in the line of paternal descent. The positions adopted are obviously compromises, because primogeniture is retained as a factor in the order of succession, and the girls' share is still less than half that of the boys'. The practical application of the somewhat imprecise rules clearly indicates a desire to avoid

Marguerite Dupire

dispersal of the patrimony among inheritors of differing degrees of kinship, which would be the inevitable outcome of the application of Muslim law. However, indirect consanguineous heirs who see their share of the inheritance going to the daughters of the deceased usually do their best to oust them, arguing from custom.

Although the right of female inheritance in the direct line is becoming recognized, there is no recognition of the right of a spouse to inherit. Neither the widower nor the widow may inherit from the other, the widow contenting herself as in the past with the *suddorge* cow allowed to her by the inheritors.

Among the Uda'en, nomadic sheep-owning Fulani, priority is given to female heirs in the direct line (daughters, sisters) over male collaterals (brothers, nephews, parallel cousins). An only daughter inherits the whole flock, and if there are several of them, they receive a larger share than that allowed by Malikite law, thus detracting from the share received by the brothers of the deceased.

The varying adaptations to change in the law of inheritance are all orientated towards one and the same end: avoidance of the dispersal of the family patrimony, the very nature of which should exclude transmission through females. It is easy to understand the mechanism operating within the social structure. Property owned by women is not lost to the lineage if a woman, as is current practice, is given in marriage to the son of her paternal uncle. In spite of the refusal on the part of the older generation to allow women to be introduced into the order of succession, women are progressively acquiring more and more extended rights, and first and foremost in virtue of membership of their patrilineage.

Although development along these lines is already an accepted fact, since in the eastern territories women dare to lay claim to their share according to Muslim law before Muslim tribunals, it is difficult to foresee what use they will make of this economic emancipation and what changes this will bring to the social structure. What is actually happening is, that it is the men, influenced by the prestige of Mohammedanism, who are providing the initiative for the emancipation of Bororo women, and this emancipation can only be conceived in terms of the society into which women are being integrated. Do those who consider themselves to be "emancipated" think any differently? What comes to mind as some sort of vague comparative evidence are memories of several examples of women among the sedentary Fulani who had escaped from traditional surroundings and who, after a long period of enjoying complete sexual and economic freedom, had returned, towards the end of their lives, to customary paths. The attraction of having possessions in the European style had not at all obliterated their appreciation of the values they had inherited, and they had converted their capital into cattle. Then, with all the wealth of a herd which they had acquired entirely by their own initiative, the only way they could conceive of making use of it was within that very pattern of kinship which they had apparently—but only apparently—rejected. By adopting girls and boys of their lineage, by giving dowries to the former and by enriching the latter, by distributing their possessions to their paternal and maternal kin, they chose to re-integrate themselves into the society which had given them birth.

This classic theme, common to all human societies, would seem to prove that individual success, however emancipated the persons concerned may be, can only be expressed by them in terms of what is already known.

NOTES

[1] The name commonly given, in the eastern regions of West Africa, to the Pastoral Fulani, among whom the WoDaaBe form one of the largest groups.

[2] "Bridewealth" has been used here to translate the French word *dot* (since English Social Anthropologists do not use the word "dowry" in this sense), about which the author has the following note: "Here, as in the translation [into French] of the Koran by M. Savary (1948, ch. IV, Les femmes), the word *dot* signifies the Mohammedan institution of the *sadaaki*."

[3] M. Smith, *Baba of Karo* (1952), ch. 8: ". . . Fulani have no human feeling" Baba affirms, giving examples in illustration.

[4] This gift, known as *sadaaki* or *hakkundeeji* (the cows between . . . the husband and the wife), is, among the WoDaaBe, no more than the ceding of rights of usufruct by the husband to his wife, and of future rights of ownership to her children. This means that it is not at all the same thing as *sadaaki* in Malikite law.

[5] Among both sedentary and nomadic Fulani the various stages of masculine and, in particular, of feminine life are marked by changes in hair styles. Among the WoDaaBe, the hair styles which indicate the main stages in a woman's life are as follows:

durol yesool:	worn by little girls.
durol cakaol:	worn normally by young girls and married women.
durol bedyeli puDaaDo:	worn during the last week of the period of seclusion before marriage.
durol tyeli:	worn by the mother during the three weeks following upon the naming ceremony of her new-born child.
durol pila dorungol:	worn by the young mother during the week following her return to her husband with her new-born child.
durol chuddito:	worn by a widow during her five months' period of seclusion.
durol bedyeli:	worn by a widow during the last week of the mourning period.

Marguerite Dupire

[6]This is the only form of the sororate allowed by custom: marriage with the sister of a fiancée who has died previous to co-habitation.

[7]J. H. Driberg, "The status of women among the Nilotics and Nilo-Hamitics", *Africa*, V, 5, 1932.

[8]J. H. Driberg, *op. cit.*: among the Nilotics, the milking is done by the men, but by the women among the Nilo-Hamitics.

[9]Driberg (*op. cit.*) has already recorded this difference.

[10]As these observations were made in 1951, the rapid developments now taking place may have advanced a stage further.

[11]H. Labouret, "Situation matérielle, morale et coutumière de la femme dans l'ouest africain", *Africa*, V, 13, No. 2, 1940, p. 105.

THE ROLE OF WOMEN
IN THE POLITICAL
ORGANIZATION OF
AFRICAN SOCIETIES

Annie M. D. Lebeuf

BY A HABIT OF THOUGHT deeply rooted in the Western mind, women are relegated to the sphere of domestic tasks and private life, and men alone are considered equal to the task of shouldering the burden of public affairs. This anti-feminist attitude, which has prevented political equality between the sexes from being established in our country until quite recently (and even so, the equality is more *de jure* than *de facto*), should not allow us to prejudge the manner in which activities are shared between men and women in other cultures, more particularly, so far as we are concerned, in those of Africa. And we are entitled to ask ourselves if it is not an attitude of this kind that is at the bottom of many erroneous ideas about the very real authority exercised by women in African political systems; and whether it has not contributed, to a certain extent, to the initiation of policies which deprive women of responsibilities that used to be theirs.

The role of women in political organization may be defined in terms of their participation, direct or indirect, in the activities of government, or, in societies without a State, in the activities of groups or sub-groups which exercise authority.

To facilitate analysis, the very large number of African political systems has been assigned to two main categories of societies:[1] on the one hand, societies in which there is an organized State with centralized authority and administrative machinery, and in which an economy based on the profit motive has created social classes between which there is an unequal distribution of wealth and differences in status; on the other, societies in which the political structure is more or less fused with kinship organization, kinship ties being the basis of social relations. In the case of the latter, authority rests with the heads of lineages and of families, who act in concert with the various social segments based principally upon age-sets and ritual functions.

Thus African societies offer a large variety of types of political organization, from monarchy—very rarely of the absolute variety —to democracy, from the administration of a vast State to that of a single village. In some places, hierarchical systems have been reconstructed, on a very much reduced scale, following upon the collapse of great kingdoms, whereas in others large populations are divided up into smaller political units coterminous with lineages or with clans, each one independent of the other.

Everywhere the political picture is a complex one. It seldom appears in a political guise as such, being more often manifested in terms of social institutions in which the political element is merged with functions of another kind, social, economic, or ritual—thus providing multiple opportunities to individuals and to groups for participation in the general life of the community.

Everywhere, too, the functioning of these institutions has been abruptly disturbed by the imposition of the colonial system. Even if earlier forms of social organization still, in most places, underlie the new system imposed upon them, they have nevertheless been profoundly altered for the worse, and have rapidly been reduced to a level upon which they no longer answer the needs they were designed to fulfil and the demands which are made on them.

Women have suffered from this even more than men, for, having had their role in earlier forms of organization, they now find themselves systematically excluded from any participation in the new set-up which has been hastily formulated by the intruding colonial powers. Completely swept aside by this new development, they found that both the material and the psychological basis upon which their authority had rested had crumbled, and that gradually their privileges were disappearing. This state of affairs leads to the necessity of entering into a certain amount of historical reconstruction if we are to attempt to form a picture of what their former position was.

On turning towards the past, it is noticeable that exploits performed by women are a preponderant feature in African legends and historical traditions, and justification for this is provided by local chronicles and the accounts of early travellers.

In the Niger and Chad regions and in Hausa territory, women

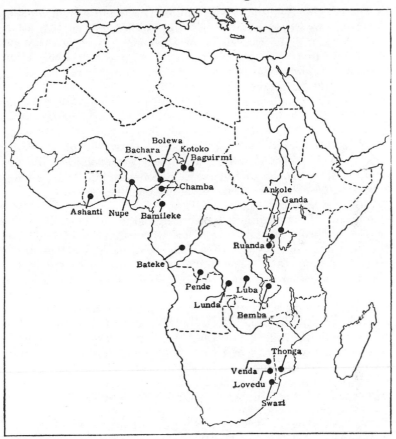

founded cities, led migrations, conquered kingdoms. Songhai groups still remember the names of celebrated ancestresses who governed them:[2] in Katsina, Queen Amina became famous during the first half of the fifteenth century through her widespread conquests. She extended her influence as far as the Nupe, built many cities, received tribute from powerful chiefs, and is still held to have been responsible for introducing the kola nut to the region.[3] In a neighbouring state, south of Zaria, another woman called Bazao-Turunku appears in the tradition at the head of a group of warriors who established themselves in a town, the ruins of which are still extant.[4] In the myths concerning the establishment of the So in North Cameroon it was also often a woman who chose the site of a city, held the insignia of power, or governed a district.[5]

Annie M. D. Lebeuf

The Lango,[6] a Nilotic tribe, recount tales about the feats of arms performed by women; and long before we heard of the exploits of the "Amazons" of the kings of Dahomey, Gezo, Glegle and Behanzin,[7] there were written accounts celebrating the courage of the female legions who fought in the armies of Monomotapa and reporting the privileges they enjoyed.[8]

In West Africa, among the Ashanti and other Akan-speaking peoples, oral tradition frequently tells of women founding small states such as Mampong, Wenchi, Juaben.[9] And if, in this area, the rule of matrilineal descent provides a possible explanation for this, no such interpretation comes into play in explaining the fact that, on the west coast and in the Cameroons and the Congo, many groups, although patrilinear, yet trace their genealogies back to eponymous ancestresses.[10]

In many of the traditions concerning the founding of kingdoms there is a constantly recurring theme with variations of a woman, the queen or the daughter of a chief, who marries a stranger to whom she hands over the insignia of the power invested in her. There is the Queen of Daura who, according to the Kano chronicle, married Abayejidu, the progenitor of the Hausa kings, after he had killed the sacred serpent.[11] Or the hunter Kongolo marrying the woman who governed the country where he founded the first Luba kingdom, while the second kingdom had similar origins in the marriage of a stranger to the Ndalamba Bulanda, the king's own sister.[12] In the high Kasai the Lunda trace back their dynasty to Lueji, the daughter of a local chief, who, before marrying a man from the north, the hunter Ilunga Kibinda, promised him that he would be ruler of the region.[13]

The early travellers have also left us accounts of the role played by women in such matters. Ibn Batuta[14] tells of the intrigues carried on by the women of the Melle court and describes Queen Kassa, wife of Mansa Suleyman, as taking part with him in the government. Then in the sixteenth, seventeenth and eighteenth centuries various authors[15] mention with astonishment the prerogatives and privileges of Wolof, Serer, Vili or Bakongo princesses such as may still sometimes be found in our own times.

This hasty survey should provide sufficient examples to show that when Africans turn to their past they do not forget the part played by women in it, but on the contrary assign to them a place that in many respects is theirs no longer. Moreover, it should also show that there are no valid historical grounds for explaining the present lack of interest in political matters so often found among African women as being a heritage of the past.

Women in Political Organization

Most of the traditional social systems, viewed from the political angle, provide scope for women to play their part, although their participation may assume different forms. The opportunities open to them differ enormously according to whether the form of government in question is one based on relations between social classes, or one based on kinship relations. Further, various other aspects of the society, such as the system of descent, the mode of life, the economic structure, the ritual pattern, may provide limiting or favourable factors with regard to their rights and obligations, which again may vary, within the same community, according to the position held in the family system, or to seniority, or to general activities.

None of these criteria taken in isolation permits making any valid classification by means of which it would be possible to define the corresponding feminine roles. With such knowledge as is at present available, it seems preferable to start off by examining the various forms which feminine authority assumes as observed in specific examples, whether these be cases where women have effective exercise of power, or where they fulfil functions, either individually or collectively, which are associated either directly or indirectly with the structure of power.

It seldom occurs that a woman is invested with supreme sovereignty, occupying an isolated position at the summit of the social hierarchy; but on the other hand, in most of the monarchical systems there are either one or two women of the highest rank who participate in the exercise of power and who occupy a position on a par with that of the king or complementary to it.

The example provided by the tribes inhabiting the North-Eastern Transvaal, the Lovedu[16] and their neighbours, who grant to women sole exercise of supreme power, is unique. This cultural trait distinguishes them from the Sotho tribes with whom they are linked in other ways. It seems to have been introduced about 150 years ago by the last Lovedu king, Mugodo, whose predecessors, since the foundation of the kingdom in the sixteenth century by a small group of Karanga immigrants inheriting the traditions of Monomotapa, had always been men. During the past century three women have reigned. The first, Mujaji I, was Mugodo's daughter, and after a time of great trouble and misfortune, she came to the throne at her father's wish, after having consented to commit incest with him.[17] At her death, her place was taken by her daughter, Mujaji II, who died in 1894 and was succeeded by Mujaji III, the daughter of her "sister" and "principal spouse".

The kingdom has about 40,000 inhabitants, who practise agriculture, whose rule of descent is patrilineal, with patrilocal residence, and among whom the legal status of women is, in general, comparatively high, although it is a function of their position in the kinship system, their rights as elder sister or father's sister being greater than the rights enjoyed by wives as such.

From the administrative point of view, the kingdom consists of a confederation of districts governed by district heads—either men or women—who have great local autonomy but who recognize the superior authority of the government at the capital, where the queen, to whom they are linked by a complex system of reciprocal ties, has her seat.

The prestige of the queen rests primarily upon the supernatural power with which she is invested—the power to "make rain", and to make it for her own people and prevent it from falling upon their enemies.[18] Any failure on her part to carry out this essential task entails the risk of deposition, and since men depend on her performance of it for their wealth and security as plants and animals do for their growth and fertility, it is to her very person that all are linked, and it is her personal behaviour that guarantees the cyclic regularity of the seasons. The belief in the queen's power and the sacred duties demanded of her mean that she is bound in a network of obligations and ritual prohibitions of so rigorous a nature that they even include putting a term to the length of her reign, which must end by ritual suicide at the end of the fourth *vudiga*, an initiation ceremony held every ten years or so.[19]

In return for the security and prosperity which she ensures, nobles, local chiefs and sometimes foreign chiefs send their daughters and their sisters to be her "wives".[20] She does not have the right to be officially married to a man, although she may have children whose father will be chosen from among her close kin, but she is obliged to keep a "harem".

Through her "wives" she stands in the relationship of *tsetse*, "fiancé" or "son-in-law", to a great many of her subjects, and this affinal link creates mutual obligations between them that reinforce other relationships.

Sometimes some of the wives have children, who are regarded as belonging to the queen and may eventually become claimants to the throne. Further, the queen may marry some of her wives to men chosen by her, thus extending the network of affinal relationships, which carries on into the subsequent generation through her right to demand in return one of the daughters of these marriages, in accordance with the prevailing rules of kinship. She thus directs this system to political ends, seeking always to exert her influence in the direction of peace, conciliation and harmony.[21]

Women in Political Organization

In her capacity as head of the judicial system, she is assisted by the "mothers of the kingdom" who represent the various districts and are appointed by the queen to act as her intermediaries with the people of the district.[22] Her authority is not supported by any military organization, but relies essentially on her divine nature.

As a result of the fame of Mujaji I, which spread as far as the Swazi and the Zulu, the first queens appeared in the neighbouring Khaha and Mamaila tribes, an example later to be followed by the Letswalo (or Narene) and the Mahlo.[23]

A much more frequent occurrence is that in which a woman exercises joint sovereignty, and in many states the monarchy consists either of a couple—the king and a woman of rank; or a triad—the king and two women. I prefer, for the moment, not to give these women any precise title in case this should impute to them a role which is not borne out by the facts. In order to give an exact translation of an African title, it is first of all necessary to know precisely how it is interpreted by the people concerned. Now as often as not these women were called Queen-Mothers or Queens, even when the king was neither son nor husband, and what confronts us here is a complex system of correspondences in which symbol and reality interpenetrate yet do not coincide.

In the Ruanda of former times "it may be said", writes J. Maquet,[24] "that the royal power was invested in two persons equally, without any differentiation in duties or privileges". The *Umu-Gabe-Kazi*, who was the mother of the *Mwami*, shared with him all the responsibilities of power. If she died before the king, she was replaced by another woman; if the contrary happened, she retired.[25]

Among the Swazi[26] the *Indlovukati*, mother of the king, is, along with her son, at the head of the political hierarchy. They each have their own residence in separate villages, their own court, their own officials. Their relations are regulated by a series of obligations. Together they control the age classes, allocate land, dispense justice, preside over religious ceremonies. They assist each other in all these activities, but not so much, it would appear, by sharing the same prerogatives, as by wielding power separately, but in such a way as to complement or balance each other in all the various spheres in which they operate.

In legal matters, for instance, the king alone could pronounce the death sentence, but in the highest court where such cases were discussed with him, the counsellors of the *Indlovukati* could appear, and men sentenced to death could take refuge in her hut. In the same way, the king controls the entire army, but the commander-in-chief resides with his own regiments in the capital of the queen-mother, while she has regiments under the leadership of princes at the capital of the king. In ritual matters, she takes part with the king in rain-making rites and in the ancestral cult; she is the custodian of the regalia, but they are not effective without the co-operation of the king.

She is the Elephant, the Earth, the Beautiful, the Mother of the Country; the king is the Lion, the Sun, the Great Wild Animal.[27]

Among the Lunda, a matrilineal tribe ruled over by a patrilineal aristocracy, the *Mwata Yamvo* has by his side the *Lukonkeketha*, a woman chosen by his four chief dignitaries, who must be a kins-woman of his, and who was originally his classificatory sister. She takes part in all matters concerning the administration. She has her own court, her own officials, and collects her own taxes. She may marry, but her husband does not apparently fill any definite role. She is regarded as the mother of the kingdom.[28]

Among the Bamileke[29] in South Cameroon, the *Mafo*, mother of the *Fong*, is regarded by the whole tribe as being equivalent to the chief himself. She partakes of his divine nature, and at her death she is accorded the same rites. She does not, however, share all responsibilities with her son, although she exercises authority in some spheres in which the *Fong* does not intervene. She has her own residence, and her own estates, which do not come under the control of her son, and over which he has no rights of jurisdiction and thus they are a place of refuge. She directs all feminine activities, thereby controlling the agricultural work of the whole community. Dressed in masculine attire, she takes part in the deliberations of the *kamvə*, the administrative council, where she takes precedence over the chief himself. She presides over all the women's secret societies and belongs to those of the men unless they are of a military nature. Her status is completely different from that of any other woman, and she has her own property, may undertake commercial transactions as she thinks fit, may choose a husband, has the right to commit adultery, and in general enjoys complete freedom and immunity. All her children belong to her and not to their father, which is contrary to the accepted rule of descent.[30]

In the Benue region, one of the most important officials among the Chamba of Donga is the *Mala*,[31] the paternal aunt, or elder sister, or daughter of the paternal aunt, of the king or *Gara*. She rules over all the women, and her duties correspond to those of the *Angwu Tsi* of the Jukun.[32] She has judicial functions and intercedes with the *Gara* for all those who have incurred his displeasure. She also exercises important religious functions, being in charge of the strictly female cult, the *Vonkima*, while in addition she takes part along with the king in the ancestral cult. When the king is away, she presides at all the rites performed for his safety and for the success of his mission. She can be married, but her husband remains a comparatively unimportant person.[33] At her death, she is buried with the same rites as those accorded to chiefs.[34]

In the kingdoms of the west which are characterized by matrilineal descent, one of the Akan peoples, the Ashanti, have an *Ohemaa*, the name given to "the chief's female counterpart".[35] She is the senior female of the royal lineage, either the mother or the classificatory sister of the *Ohene*, and as joint ruler she holds prerogatives far greater than those of any man.

She inhabits a different palace from that of the king, and like the mother of the Swazi king, maintains a court and numerous functionaries. She directs and supervises all feminine matters, concerning herself with marriages, births, and children's education, settling disputes in cases of adultery or divorce, and, most important of all, presiding at the initiation ceremonies held for girls when they have reached puberty, and at the rites performed by women for ending periods of drought. Being the custodian of the consecrated stools of her predecessors, she shares in the royal ancestral cult and participates with the king in certain rites.[36]

She enjoys great prestige as a genealogist, responsible for maintaining traditions and preserving customs. When a new king is to be elected she is consulted and has to decide the legitimacy of the rights of the various claimants. At the nomination of the new king, she has to present him to the people, and takes part in the enthronement ceremonies. Throughout her life she remains the only person in the kingdom who may give him advice, guide him, and criticize him to his face, even in public.

In time of war, when the king is absent, it is she who takes his place.[37] In spiritual matters, she incarnates the feminine, and in particular the mother,[38] aspect of Nyame, the Supreme Being, while the king represents the masculine aspect.[39] She is the moon, while the king is the sun.

In the royal family of the Bemba (in North-Eastern Rhodesia) the *Candamukulu*, who is either the mother or the oldest uterine relative of the king, also plays an important role. She takes part in tribal councils and herself governs several villages.[40] Like the *Mafo* of the Bamileke she enjoys great sexual freedom. The same pattern is found among the Bushongo of the Kasai. Among the

Annie M. D. Lebeuf

Loango, the *Makunda* formerly held a similar position as joint ruler with the Vili king.

In these various matrilineal systems, although the female element as such acquires greater significance than in the systems mentioned earlier, yet the functions of those women who are, so to speak, the symbolic representatives of the matrilineal principle, do not exceed the functions fulfilled by women in the general division of labour between the sexes that is found in the societies in question, where the role of women does not impinge upon purely masculine activities any more than it does in societies where patrilineal descent is the rule.

In the examples that follow, a third figure appears—again that of a woman—at the head of the government. This tripartite rule does not essentially differ from the systems described in the foregoing examples, for it would be impossible to maintain that the specific functions allotted to the third figure are not already latent within these other systems.

In the region of the Great Lakes the title of Kabaka is borne by three people: the king, his mother (*Namasole*), and one of his classificatory sisters, the *Lubuga*, who is at the same time his official spouse. She is enthroned along with him and must remain childless.[41] Their offices are superior to those of the twelve principal chiefs of the kingdom.[42] They have separate residences from that of the king, and own estates in each district from which they receive taxes in addition to receiving their portion of the taxes collected by the king.[43] Their ritual functions are important, and the *Lubuga*, after the king's death, becomes the guardian of his tomb, where she keeps up his cult and pronounces oracles.[44]

In Kitara the mother of the claimant to the throne is involved in his activities even before he mounts the throne, and takes part in the struggle against his brothers from which he has to emerge the victor in order to become king. As soon as he is nominated, his mother takes the official title of *Nyina Mukuma* and receives special insignia. She is supposed to lead a chaste life, and must never see her son again, although they keep in contact through certain functionaries who act as intermediaries. She has her own court and her own estates, with power of life and death over the people on them. But her primary importance lies in her custodianship of the royal crown which by implication gives her a protective role over the whole kingdom. When she dies she is replaced by a woman of her own clan.[45] A similar position is held by the *Mugole wa Muchwa*, a half-sister of the king chosen by him to be his only official wife,[46] who, as in Ganda, must not have any children. She enjoys prero-

Women in Political Organization

gatives similar to those of the queen-mother, having her own court, her own estates, and the power of life and death over her own people. When the king dies she retires to an estate that is given to her.

In the same way, the monarchy in Ankole consists of three persons: the king or *Mugabe*, his mother, and one of his classificatory sisters who, however, is not, as elsewhere, his wife, and who is free to marry and have children. At one time they all three enjoyed equal status.

Neither of the women has a special title, and they are simply called *nyinya omugabe*, king's mother, and *omunyana omugabe*, king's sister.[47] The mother of the *Mugabe* has her own residence and estates. The king visits her as often as he wishes. If she falls seriously ill, he administers the ritual poison and chooses another maternal kinswoman to be her successor.

Both he and the king's sister have their herds, their armies and their officials, and formerly they levied the *ekyitoro* tribute on Bahima cattle, as well as receiving a share of cattle taken in raids.[48] The king's mother also has judicial and administrative functions, sits beside the *Mugabe* at all judicial cases, and decides on questions of war and peace. No man may be executed without her consent. It is she who receives foreign ambassadors before they are presented to the king. With the king's sister, she has direct say in the choice of the prime minister, the *Enganzi*.[49] Her function is eminently that of protector, as with the queen-mother of Kitara. By performing the appropriate rites, she protects the king against maleficent spirits and fends off the vengeance of slain victims. She takes part with him in the ritual connected with the worship of the ancestors, and at the new moon makes offerings on the altar in her own dwelling that is consecrated to them.[50]

The *omunyana omugabe* performs a special function of a purificatory nature at the enthronement ceremony, and she is in charge of her brother's health. If she falls seriously ill, she is not given the royal poison.[51] In general, both women are closely linked with all rites performed to ensure the prosperity of the kingdom.

Among the Bateke it is also a triad that rules: the king, *Ma Onko*, and two women, the *Wanfitere* and the *Ngasa*. Their functions, although essential, are predominantly spiritual and ritual rather than political, or at least this is so nowadays, when the political aspect suffers from the confusion resulting from the process of emancipation from European rule at present taking place in this district.

The title of *Wanfitere* implies that this is a hereditary office transmitted to women within one particular family according to the rules of patrilineal descent observed by the whole Bateke tribe. The primary function of the woman who holds it is to initiate the king and his wife, the *Ngasa*, and the importance of her role is most marked during the period which extends from the death of the king to the enthronement of his successor, a period which may last for years. She is, during this time, the sole custodian of the regalia, and owing to this her power is greater than that of the heir, whom she has officially chosen with the help of the chief officials of the dead king. She maintains this position of authority until the day when she allows the heir and his wife to take over from her, after they have gone through a series of tests to which she submits them and which they must pass successfully. These tests take place during the coronation ceremonies for which she herself has fixed the date and which she directs. As soon as the coronation rites are over, she chooses from within her own family a senior woman who, on behalf of the new king, will manipulate the sacred objects, look after his fire, and do the cooking for him and for the queen—to which end she has been cultivating a field specially reserved for this purpose—and who will agree to renouncing all sexual relations.[52]

The *Ngasa* also belongs to one particular family. She may have been the king's wife before his nomination and have had children by him, but as soon as she has been enthroned and has received her official title, she must have no more children. She rules over the entire female population and directs the agricultural work that is their principal occupation. Her life is intimately bound up with that of the *Onko* with whom she shares the same dwelling and whom she assists at religious ceremonies. Formerly, if she was the first to die, the king was put to death, but now he is merely dismissed from office. If she survives him, she loses her position and goes into retirement, although still surrounded with special marks of esteem.

The Bateke interpret the functions of these women as a projection in the physical world of mythological events, thus conjoining the monarchical system with the cosmic order. In their view, the world was created by a hermaphrodite spirit, the *Nkwembali*,[53] and arranged by it into a fixed number of species in a fixed hierarchy, at the summit of which is placed a pair of individuals who are unique of their kind, and to whom it is permitted to recover the knowledge and power originally possessed by the primordial twins but subsequently lost by them. The *Wanfitere*, commonly called "mother of the kingdom", is an embodiment of this spirit, and the rites during the crucial period of the enthronement of the king and queen are a re-enactment of the drama of the loss and recovery of knowledge, after which she enables them to acquire the power of the primordial twins whose substitutes they have become.

In the countries that have adopted Mohammedanism in Nigeria and the Chad, these feminine roles have lost much of their earlier importance and are more in the nature of survivals.

At the Nupe court (Nigeria) the Fulani have retained the two former titles of *Nimwoye* and *Sagi*, which are bestowed on the king's mother, paternal aunt, sister or daughter. They must be women of about 40-50 years, and they take part in the king's council. Although they have lost most of their political prerogatives, they still have great moral authority. They live in the *Etsu's* house and used to have their own estates, officials and regiments. They still settle quarrels between women, especially women of noble families, and officially represent the court at certain ceremonies.[54]

Among the Bolewa (Kanuri), the Kotoko and the Bagirmians, the king is assisted by two women: the *Magira* or *Magara* and the *Gimsu* or *Gumsu*. The first of these is the mother or the classificatory sister of the king.[55] She lives in a part of the royal capital specially assigned to her, has her court, her officials, and her estates over which she has jurisdiction. She levies taxes, and her domain is regarded as a place of refuge. Her principal functions, as with the *Gumsu*, are concerned with women's activities. At her death she is replaced by another woman of her family. It should be noted that in Bagirmi a man may be appointed *Magira* in the same way as a woman, fulfilling the same functions and wearing female clothes for the ceremonies.[56]

Upon the election of the king, the title of *Gumsu* is conferred on one of his wives chosen from among those who have not borne him a son.[57] Among the Kotoko of the Chari delta, it is the daughter of the chief official of the kingdom, the *Iba*, chief of the land, on whom the title is bestowed. In distinction to the other royal wives, she must never have any children, and she does not live in the same part of the palace as they do. She lives in the southern part of the building, according to a strict system of correspondence between functions and spatial directions. Along with the *Magira* she rules over the women of the kingdom, and she helps to choose some of the officials, in particular the army leaders whom she appoints personally, having chosen them from among the officials attached to her own house. She plays an important part in the septennial ceremonies for ensuring the perpetuation of the kingdom. She is associated with the morning star, the mother of all the stars, and is regarded by the people as the mythical mother of all the nobles.

Annie M. D. Lebeuf

In general, her power is such that it provides a constant counterbalance to that of the king, the entire political system being conceived as a delicate balance between masculine and feminine, right and left, north and south, that must be maintained in the power-relations of individuals, in all their activities, and even in their spatial location.[58]

In all the political systems which have either one or two women at the top of the hierarchy, these women belong to a very restricted group drawn from a social class which already confers on them, even before they occupy their special roles, rights and privileges which are in marked contrast to those of the rest of the female population. The woman who fills the chief role always belongs to the generation senior to that of the king, and her position in the royal lineage, whatever it may be, is just as important as the kinship relation between her and the king. In general, she is regarded as his "mother", and acts as guide, protector, or initiator. Almost everywhere, it is she who has to choose the woman who will play the second role in sharing power with the king. This second woman, either a classificatory sister of the king or the daughter of some powerful family in the kingdom, is, with the exception of the sister of the *Mugabe* of Ankole, his official "wife". But as wife she has a completely different status from that of the other wives, which places her on an entirely different level. Emphasis is everywhere laid on the importance of both these roles, closely linked with the king as they are, either through his life, or in the period from the opening of his reign until the enthronement of his successor. When the women who fill them die, they are replaced by another member of their family, except in the case of the *Ngasa*, whose death entails that of the king.

In general, the relations between the two queens and the king, whether he be their son, their brother or their spouse, are of an exceptional nature, quite without parallel in the ordinary course of life. Thus to understand the association of all three, it is necessary not only to determine the position they occupy in relation to each other, but also to see this within the whole pattern of the royal lineage system.

We have seen that queens may take their full share in the responsibilities of power, either by performing the same functions as the king, or by carrying out tasks which are complementary to his; or they may have a restricted field in which they operate, although this in no way impairs their authority.

There is no doubt, however, that it is in the moral and ritual spheres that their importance lies. Or at any rate it is here that we

Women in Political Organization

can most easily observe the importance of their role, for these are the spheres that have suffered least from the recent political upheavals, since the spiritual values on which institutions are based long outlast the institutions themselves. But it would be wrong to view the queens' participation in state affairs from this angle alone and make them out to be nothing more than performers of sacred rites. If this function now eclipses all their other functions, this is because of the collapse of the system as a whole; and it may well be the case that this aspect of the queens' role has acquired increased significance because of the restrictions placed upon their judicial and administrative activities.

In political systems such as these, characterized as they are by a pronounced hierarchical structure, most women who either belong to, or have affinal ties with, the royal lineage, enjoy various prerogatives which often have political implications. They are frequently given positions of territorial authority, having one or several villages under their control or full powers over a district, in which latter case succession in the female line may be involved, as with the Bemba.[59] The rights usually assigned to them place them apart from the rest of the female population, and enable their behaviour to approximate more closely to that of the male sex than to that of their own.

They enjoy greater freedom and authority in matrilineal than in patrilineal societies, but here, too, their position is similar, although the rule of patrilineal descent imposes restrictions of varying severity on rights acquired through marriage. In the kingdoms situated in the region of the Great Lakes,[60] the daughters of the king are prohibited by their very rank not only from having an official husband, but also from bearing children; and should a Shilluk princess, bound by the same rules, dare to infringe them, she is liable to be put to death on giving birth to a child.[61] This, however, is an extreme case. Most tribes have been able to arrive at a compromise, and, as in the case of the Bagirmians or the Bamileke,[62] either recognize the children of princesses as belonging to the king, whoever their father may have been, or, as with the Nupe,[63] confer a status upon the members of the aristocracy which is transmissible through women as much as through men, both to their husbands and to their descendants.

Many chiefs are able to strengthen their position by arranging diplomatic marriages for the women of the royal lineage, thus helping to seal alliances with foreign tribes and provide ambassadors with special privileges; and even if a chief's wives have little

107

to do with state affairs, they can nevertheless act as guarantee for alliances that have been formed. Thus marriage among African chiefs can play the same sort of role as it did for the monarchs of our own *ancien régime.*

In Bagirmi, for instance, the *Maiarami*, daughters of the king, were married to the most important nobles of the kingdom and held a position of absolute authority over them.[64] If a noble happened already to have a wife, he was obliged to divorce her, as polygyny was forbidden.

It was by means of similar systems of marriage alliances, in which kinship and political ties are intertwined, that many royal families were able to establish their authority and extend it over tribes which had originally been strangers to them. We have seen how the Lovedu queen used a system of this kind. The Swazi royal family provide another interesting example. All the king's wives were chosen from different clans, whose members thus acquired affinal ties with the reigning family, while the king gave his female relatives in marriage to important chiefs, even foreign ones. Because of their origin, these women held special positions in the households of their husbands, and were the potential mothers of their heirs.[65]

It is a fairly widespread practice for members of a group to present one or two of their daughters to the king of another group as a mark of allegiance. The small kingdom of Ngoio was where the Vili king's chief wife came from,[66] and the four oldest Maba families provided the Sultan of Wadai with his chief wives, while it was the Buffalo clan that supplied the wife of the Kabaka who bore the title of *Nanzigu.*[67] Among the Ngoni, a quarrel between the chief and his wife was enough to create a state crisis.[68]

It sometimes happens in systems of this kind that a power structure similar to that of the central government is found at the district level, with a woman giving full assistance to the local chief in his duties, or with female officials helping him in his decisions.

Among the Ashanti the head of each village has at his side a senior woman (*obaa panin*) chosen by him and his elders to direct the affairs of the community.[69] The Kotoko afford another example, every town having two *Mra Saba*, whose role among the local women is similar to that of the *Magira* and the *Gumsu* among the women of the capital. They are appointed by the members of their own sex, one for the northern districts and one for the southern, to direct their work and leisure activities, to settle quarrels, and to look after their interests. These women also take the lead in certain fishing expeditions in which they are the only women to take part along with the men.[70] In the same way, at Bida, among the Nupe, the *Sonya* organizes the women of low birth as the *Nimwoye* and the *Sagi* do for the women of the aristocracy. She is elected by the married women of the town, who treat her with great respect, and her rank is confirmed by the *Etsu*. She organizes all the work that is done collectively and supervises the market. Formerly she levied a due on all commercial transactions, a portion of which she returned to the queen. [71]

Again, in every village a woman is elected by her companions to fulfil similar tasks, and given the title of *Sagi* originally reserved for one of the two leading female figures in the kingdom. This title seems to have replaced an earlier one, that of *Lelu*, which used to be conferred on the woman who was believed to be the most powerful witch in the village and who, by thus being used officially in the service of the village, could be of benefit to it. [72]

In societies where the political system is based on kinship organization, the opportunities open to women for participation in public affairs are no longer so clear cut, but extend to a larger number of them. In a few isolated cases women are found at the head of a community, but it is mainly indirectly, by the tasks which they perform and by their preponderant role in spiritual matters, that they are able to exert a profound influence on the life of the community.

Those cases in which women do act as village heads or local chiefs, or are at the head of a larger unit corresponding to the lineage or the clan, are found among tribes of great apparent diversity, and scattered over a wide area, always excepting those which have adopted Islam, where women are usually precluded from taking part in activities regulated by the precepts of the official religion.

When women exercise functions of this kind, it is generally because they have inherited them. In the absence of a male heir, many groups permit a woman to inherit the functions of her father or her husband. A more rare occurrence is when chiefs, during their lifetime, designate a sister or a daughter to succeed them rather than a son. She is then invested with the same powers and occupies the same position as if she were a man. She presides over religious ceremonies to which formerly she was not admitted, and may even be leader of the hunt and on occasion war leader. [73] Masculine behaviour of this kind extends even to matrilineal societies such as the Lovale, for instance. [74] In patrilineal societies women who fill such roles are not, as a rule, permitted to have an official husband, the status conferred upon them being incompatible with the normal relations between husband and wife; but they may have children, which will belong to their own family, the father losing all rights over them.[75] In some tribes, such as the Venda, a woman who has inherited the headship of a village or even a chiefdom is allowed to marry if she wishes, in which case her husband maintains his rights over his children, who cannot then claim succession to their mother. But she is also entitled to divorce, whereupon she will make an official marriage with another woman whose bridewealth she herself pays. She chooses one of her kin to be father of this woman's children, who will be regarded as her own children. The father will have no rights over them, and one of them, either male or female, will be chosen as successor.[76] We have already seen that the Lovedu queen proceeds in a similar fashion.

Also among the Venda, as with the Mboshi (Congo), the Luba (Katanga) and the Mende (Sierra Leone) and other tribes, certain groups, in contradistinction to the usual tribal practice, are reported as having a woman as hereditary chief. Apparently the explanation of this institution, as given by the groups concerned, is, that the spirit of a female ancestor is believed to reside in the place where the woman is chief. The Bachama (Northern Nigeria) give a similar explanation for the fact that the town of Njimoso is always governed by a woman, her main responsibility being the maintenance of the cult of the local tutelary deity.[77] The Chamba Tsugu town of Debbo apparently follows the same pattern.

Among the Luba there is a district in the neighbourhood of Kamina which is governed by the *Mwadi*, two women who at every new moon are always possessed by the spirit of a former ruler. In the days when the kingdom still existed they had been closely associated with him, their special function having been to supply the paramount chief, the *Mulopwe*, with his supply of kaolin for ritual purposes.[78] This duty shows what an important position they must have held, for the transfer of kaolin always implies that the giver is the superior of the receiver.[79]

Thus we see that on kinship or ritual grounds women may fulfil functions normally performed by men.

The frequency with which cases of this kind occur varies greatly from region to region. It does not seem to have anything to do with the rule of descent obtaining or with the position of women in the community; but possibly occurrences tend to increase in certain circumstances where economic and historical factors play a determining role, as for instance among the Mende. There, the number of women in positions of authority increased in consequence of the troubles arising from the British occupation, having

Women in Political Organization

been put forward by the people so as to obviate reprisals. The fact that the conquerors had a woman—Queen Victoria—as sovereign may also have been a contributing factor.[80]

Some tribes have special institutions that enable women to play an important part in the accession of a chief (whether standing in a kinship relation to him or not), and in supervising women's activities and controlling relations between villages.

Such is "the wife of the district" among the Tonga, a Bantu tribe of the South-East. The title arises because the woman who holds it has become a wife of the chief owing to the marriage payment having been made by his subjects in the hope that she will be the mother of his heir. She organizes the women of the community, particularly in their agricultural work, and performs the rites for the women's cults.[81] Between the Kwilu and the Kasai, the Pende, Bunda, Dinga and Lele have an institution called the *hohombe* or *ngalababola*, usually translated: "wife of the village", which, until recently,[82] gave the women concerned a position of paramount importance. The "wife of the village" was not in any sense a prostitute. She was of high rank, enjoyed certain privileges, and both she and her children held a special status. There were various ways in which she might come to hold the position. She might be directly chosen by the villagers, either after having been captured by them from a neighbouring group, or, on the other hand, after she had come to them seeking sanctuary; or she might be the daughter or relative of a chief chosen by him at the time of her birth to occupy the position, when the time came, in a neighbouring village.

For some time after she had taken up her duties she did not do any of the work usually done by women, but took part in all male activities, even hunting. She then took a small number of husbands and went to live beyond the boundaries of the village, and was then at the disposal of all its inhabitants. Her children were regarded as "the children of the village". The villagers as a group supplied her sons with the amount required for the payment of bridewealth. The bride-price asked for by her daughters was much higher than average, and to become a "son-in-law of the village" meant acquiring a position of influence and bearing insignia similar to those of a chief.

These relations were stabilized by a rule of succession whereby the father of every family has the right to his daughter's daughter, either for himself, or to give in marriage to his brother, nephew, or grandnephew. This system, as applied to "the wife of the

Annie M. D. Lebeuf

village", meant that a daughter borne by her daughter would take the place of her (i.e. the daughter's daughter's) maternal grandmother, and that the "son-in-law" of the village (the daughter's daughter's father) would in turn lay claim to her daughter, either to marry her or give her in marriage to one of his close kin.

Most of the local chiefs made use of this institution to strengthen their position, giving their own daughters to whatever villages they chose, thereby placing the inhabitants in the relation of son-in-law to them, while themselves standing in the relation of son-in-law to these villages in the following generation.

Although it is a well-known fact that in most tribes women are organized into age-classes or associations of a ritual or initiatory character, extraordinarily little is generally known about the actual activities of such groups.

To each age-class belong duties, collective tasks and ritual obligations, but everywhere age brings increasing authority, and an old person of either sex is always treated with respect and asked for advice. Very often women past child-bearing age become elders, and take part in their discussions.

Sometimes there are mixed associations such as the *Butwa* of certain Lunda groups for instance, in which old people of both sexes, the *Mangulu*, are included in the highest grades, and thus enjoy direct participation in all public affairs.[83] But more often the women's organizations are parallel to those of the men and each operates within its own sphere.

Associations such as the *Nimm* of the Ekoi of Southern Nigeria, or the *Akejuju* of their neighbours, the Bini, give women powers which are in some respects greater than those of the men, who dread the effects that might result.[84] Among the Ube, Gere and Wobe on the Ivory Coast the village head is obliged to consult the leader of the association of women initiates, mainly concerning the agricultural work.[85]

The *Sande* society has considerable influence among the Mende, representing for the women what the *Poro* is for the men, an initiation group that bears entire responsibility for education and for general behaviour. Its leader, the *Majo*, is in a position to exercise a direct influence over the attitude of the men towards its members.[86] Also among the Mende are found the *Njayei* and *Humɔi* societies, formed to look after the mentally sick and to ensure the fertility of the soil by adopting the appropriate procedures, and they are at the service of every community. These women have techniques both for promoting the development of the personality

Women in Political Organization

and for encouraging self-confidence. Chiefs often ask them for advice, and they take part in the election of candidates for office.[87] Their leaders bear hereditary titles and sometimes acquire such a high standing locally that the English, when the protectorate treaties were being signed, often mistook them for political chiefs.[88]

While it is a general tendency for women to form groups for the purpose of carrying out their various activities, in wealthy and populous areas like Southern Nigeria, such groups, owing to the importance of women in commerce and agriculture, have become powerful organizations which have been in existence for a long time.

An example of a complex system of groups of this kind is provided by the Yoruba. Its development was partly due to the existence of large towns, and its objectives are mutual aid, defence of common interests, and the organization of markets, for the attainment of which women in every town have formed producers', sellers', and buyers' associations. The Oyo associations are called *Egbe Iyalode* (literally: association of the *Iyalode*), the *Iyalode* being the title of the leader of these associations; and they are consulted by the political authorities. An *Iyalode* is often an important figure. The *Iyalode* of Ibadan, for instance, was a member of the Council of State down to 1914.[89]

Ibo villages all have their women's councils, and in large towns each district nominates its own spokeswoman, these together forming the council. There is no hierarchy between the various councils, but their members maintain permanent relations with each other as between one urban or village area and another. Each council is presided over by a woman elected, not on account of her seniority or wealth, but because of her personality and experience. These councils are responsible for everything concerning agriculture and the interests of women in general. They fix the timetable for all the important agricultural tasks, look after the protection of crops, and regulate all the ceremonies involved. If anyone, man or woman, contravenes any of their decisions, they can take sanctions against them, and they have great authority in judicial matters. When the interests of a woman have to be defended, the council meet to discuss the matter with her family, or, if she is married, with her husband's family.[90]

Although their powers are not so great as they used to be, their strength and cohesion can be measured by the widespread nature of the movement for the assertion of their rights which they organized in 1929, which was known as "the Aba Riots" or "the war of the women". Following upon a rumour that the government was on the point of introducing a tax on women's property, they started making demonstrations which broke out first in Aba and then spread through the two provinces of Owerri and Calabar, mobilizing more than two million people, very few of whom seem to have been men.[91] The rapidity with which the trouble spread and the gravity of the situation which resulted illustrate the tremendous strength of the women's organizations.

African women have a tradition of practical participation in public affairs. Among many peoples the very conceptions on which power is based associate them closely with the exercise of power, and although it is usually men who are called upon to rule, the norms which regulate the position of individuals within a community often permit a woman, under special circumstances, to take the place of a man. In general, the profound philosophical ideas which underlie the assignment of separate tasks to men and women stress the complementary rather than the separate nature of these tasks. Neither the division of labour nor the nature of the tasks accomplished implies any superiority of the one over the other, and there is almost always compensation in some other direction for the actual inequalities which result from such a division.

BIBLIOGRAPHY

APTHORPE, R., "Rhodesia and Nyasaland", in *Women's role in the development of tropical and sub-tropical countries*, Report of the 31st meeting of the INCIDI held in Brussels, 1958 (Brussels, 1959), pp. 158-73.

BARNES, J. A., "The village headman in British Central Africa", *Africa*, XIX (1949), 89-106.

BINET, J., "Condition des femmes dans la région cacaoyère du Cameroun", *Cah. Internationaux de Sociologie*, XX (Paris, 1956), 109-23.

BUSIA, K. A., *The position of the chief in the modern political system of Ashanti*, O.U.P., 1951, 233 pp.

DELAROZIERE, R., "Les institutions politiques et sociales des populations dites Bamiléké", *Etudes Camerounaises*, Nos. 25-26 and 27-28 (Duala, IFAN, 1949), 5-68 and 127-75.

DRIBERG, J. H., "The status of women among the Nilotics and Nilo-Hamitics", *Africa*, IV (1932), 404-21.

EVEN, A., "Le caractère sacré des chefs chez les Babamba et les Mindossi d'Okondja (Moyen-Congo)", *Journal de la Société des Africanistes*, VI (Paris 1936), 187-95.

FORDE, D., "The Yoruba-speaking peoples of South Western Nigeria", *Ethno-*

graphic Survey of Africa, Part 4, Western Africa, O.U.P. for Int. Af. Inst., 1951, 102 pp. map, bibl.

FORTES, M., "Kinship and marriage among the Ashanti", in A. R. Radcliffe-Brown and D. Forde, African systems of kinship and marriage, O.U.P. for Int. Af. Inst., 1950, 399 pp.

FORTES, M. and EVANS-PRITCHARD, E. E., African Political Systems, O.U.P, 1940, 302 pp.

GRÉVISSE, F., "Les traditions historiques des Basanga et de leurs voisins", Bull. du CEPSI, II (Elisabethville, 1946-47), 50-84, maps.

GRIAULE, M. and LEBEUF, J. P., "Fouilles dans la région du Tchad", Journal de la Société des Africanistes, XXI (Paris, 1951), 1-95, pl.

HEUSCH, L. de, Essai sur le symbolisme de l'inceste royal en Afrique, Brussels, Institut de Sociologie Solvay, 1958, 266 pp.

HOLAS, B., "L'évolution du schéma initiatique chez les femmes oubi", Africa, XXVII (1957), 241-50.

IBN BATUTA: Voyages d'Ibn Batouta, tr. C. Defrémery and B. R. Sanguinetti, Paris, Société Asiatique, Imprimerie Nationale, 1914-26, 5 vol. [Ibn Batuta, travels in Asia and Africa (1325-1354), tr. H. A. R. Gibb, Routledge, 1929, 398 pp. ill.]

JOHNSON, S., The history of the Yoruba from the earliest times to the beginning of the British Protectorate, Routledge, 1921, 55 + 684 pp. ill. map.

JUNOD, H. A., Mœurs et coutumes des Bantous, Paris, Payot, 1936, 2 vol. 513, 580 pp.

KRIGE, E. J., "The place of the North-Eastern Transvaal Sotho in the Bantu complex", Africa, XI (1938), 265-93.

KRIGE, E. J. and J. D., The realm of a rain-queen, a study of the pattern of Lovedu society, O.U.P., 1943, 335 pp.

KUPER, H., An African aristocracy: rank among the Swazi, O.U.P., 1947, 251 pp.

LEBEUF, A. M. D., see Masson Detourbet, A.

LE HÉRISSÉ, A., L'Ancien royaume du Dahomey, Paris, Larose, 1911, 376 pp. ill. maps.

LEITH-ROSS, S., African women: a study of the Ibo of Nigeria, Faber, 1939, 367 pp. ill. maps.

LEO AFRICANUS: Léon L'Africain, Description de l'Afrique, new ed. tr. from the Italian by A. Épaulard, Th. Monod, H. Lothe and R. Mauny, Paris, Adrien-Maisonneuve, 1956, 2 vol. ill. maps. [Leo Africanus: the History and Descriptions of Africa and of the Notable Things therein contained, done into English in the Year 1600 by John Pory, ed. and selected R. Brown, Hakluyt Society, 1896, 3 vols.]

LESTRADE, G. P., "Some notes on the political organisation of the Venda speaking tribes", Africa, III (1930), 306-22.

LITTLE, K., "The changing position of women in the Sierra Leone Protectorate", Africa, XVIII (1948), 1-17.

— , The Mende of Sierra Leone, Routledge & Kegan Paul, 1951, 307 pp.

MACLEOD, O., Chiefs and cities of Central Africa, across Lake Chad by way of

Annie M. D. Lebeuf

British, French and German territories, Edinburgh, Blackwood, 1912, 322 pp. ill. map.

MAQUET, J. J., "Le systéme des relations sociales dans le Ruanda ancien", *Annales du Musée royal du Congo Belge*, series in 8vo, *Sciences de l'homme, Ethnologie*, No. 1, Tervuren, 1954, 221 pp. ill. maps.

MASSON DETOURBET, A., "L'organisation politique du royaume Lagouané (Nord-Cameroun)", *Journal de la Société des Africanistes*, XXIII (Paris, 1953), 7-34.

MEEK, C. K., *A Sudanese kingdom, an ethnographical study of the Jukun-speaking peoples of Nigeria*, Kegan Paul, 1931, 548 pp. ill. maps.

—, *Tribal studies in Northern Nigeria*, Kegan Paul, 1931, 2 vols., 582, 633 pp.

MEYEROWITZ, E. L. R., *The sacred state of Akan*, Faber and Faber, 1951, 222 pp. ill.

MWAMBA, R., *Le royaume balouba*, unpublished typescript.

NADEL, S. F., "Witchcraft and anti-witchcraft in Nupe society", *Africa*, VIII (1935), 423-47.

—, *A black Byzantium, the kingdom of Nupe in Nigeria*, O.U.P., 1942, 420 pp.

OBERG, K., "The kingdom of Ankole in Uganda", in M. Fortes and E. E. Evan-Pritchard, *African Political Systems*, O.U.P., 1940.

PALMER, H. R., "The Kano chronicle", *Journal of the Royal Anthropological Inst.*, XXXVIII (1908), 58-98, ill.

—, "History of Katsina", *Journal of the African Society*, XXVI (1926-27), 216-36.

PIGAFETTA, F., *Relatione del reame di Congo e della circonvicine per Filippo Pigafetta*, Rome, 1591; Eng. tr. by Margarite Hutchinson, John Murray, 1881, xxi + 174 pp. map.

PROYART, ABBÉ, *Histoire de Loango, KaKongo et autres royaumes d'Afrique*, Paris, C. P. Berton et N. Crapart, 1776, 393 pp., map.

RICHARDS, A. I., "Mother-right among the central Bantu", in *Essays presented to Seligman* (Kegan Paul, 1934), pp. 267-79.

—, "The political system of the Bemba tribes, North-Eastern Rhodesia", in M. M. Fortes and E. E. Evans-Pritchard, *African political systems*, pp. 83-120.

ROSCOE, J., *The Baganda. An account of their native customs and beliefs*, Macmillan, 1911, 547 pp. ill. maps.

—, *The Bakitara or Banyoro*, C.U.P., 1923, 370 pp. ill. map.

—, *The Banyankole*, C.U.P., 1923, 176 pp. ill. map.

ROUCH, J., *Les Songhay*, Paris, P.U.F., 1954, 100 pp. map.

SELIGMAN, C. G., "Some aspects of the Hamitic problem in the Anglo-Egyptian Sudan", *Jour. of the Roy. Anthrop. Inst.*, XLIII (1913), 593-705.

SLASKI, J., "Peoples of the lower Luapula valley", *Ethnographic Survey of Africa*, Part II, *East Central Africa* (1950), 77-95, map.

TALBOT, P. A., *In the shadow of the bush*, Heinemann, 1912, 500 pp. ill. map.

—, *The peoples of Southern Nigeria*, O.U.P., 1926, 4 vol. ill. maps.

TEW, M., "A form of polyandry among the Lele of the Kasai", *Africa*, XXI (1951), 1-12.

116

Women in Political Organization

THEUWS, T., "Textes luba (Katanga)", *Bull. du C.E.P.S.I.* XXVII (Elisabethville, 1954), 153 pp.

VERBEKE, F., "Le Bulopwe et le Kutomboke par le sang humain chez les Baluba Shankai", *Bull. des Juridictions Indigènes et du Droit coutumier congolais,* II (Elisabethville, 1937), 52-61.

VERHULPEN, E., *Baluba et Balubaïsés du Katanga,* Antwerp, 1936, 534 pp.

NOTES

[1]M. Fortes and E. E. Evans-Pritchard, *African political systems,* pp. 5ff.
[2]J. Rouch, p. 36.
[3]H. R. Palmer (1926-27), pp. 218-19.
[4]*Léon l'Africain,* II, p. 477, note 92.
[5]M. Griaule and J. P. Lebeuf, pp. 5-6.
[6]J. H. Driberg, pp. 404-21.
[7]A. Le Hérissé, p. 68.
[8]F. Pigafetta.
[9]K. A. Busia, p. 20.
[10]K. Little (1951), p. 196; J. Binet, p. 119 and elsewhere.
[11]H. R. Palmer (1908), p. 61.
[12] R. Mwamba; E. Verhulpen.
[13]F. Grévisse, pp. 50-84.
[14]Ibn Batuta, *Voyages d'Ibn Batouta,* IV, p. 417.
[15]Pigafetta, Proyart, Dapper and others.
[16]Krige, E. J. und J. D.
[17]Krige, *op. cit.* pp. 9-10.
[18]Krige, *op. cit.* p. 271.
[19]Krige, *op. cit.* pp. 114, 166.
[20]Krige, *op. cit.* pp. 165, 173-5.
[21]Krige, *op. cit.* p. 185.
[22]Krige, *op. cit.* pp. 197-8.
[23]Krige, *op. cit.* pp. 310-11, and E. J. Krige, pp. 265-93.
[24]J. J. Maquet, p. 47.
[25]Maquet, *op. cit.* p. 148.
[26]H. Kuper, pp. 54-8.
[27]Kuper, *op. cit.* p. 70.
[28]J. Slaski; Irstam considers that she is both queen and queenmother; L. de Heusch (p. 121) regards her as representing the ideal, but forbidden, incestuous spouse.
[29]In spite of the fact that the Bamileke do not belong to a single, centralized State but to a confederation of several states, I have nevertheless cited them as an example because of the extremely hierarchical structure of each of these states.
[30]R. Delarozière, pp. 46ff.
[31]C. K. Meek, *A Sudanese kingdom . . .,* p. 340.
[32]C. K. Meek, *Tribal studies . . .,* Vol. 1, pp. 335, 346.
[33]Meek, *Tribal Studies,* Vol. I, p. 335.
[34]Meek, *Tribal studies,* Vol. I, p. 336.
[35]M. Fortes (1950), p. 264.
[36]M. Fortes (1950), p. 257.
[37]E. L. R. Meyerowitz, p. 42.

Annie M. D. Lebeuf

[38]Meyerowitz, pp. 37ff.

[39]M. Fortes (1950), p. 264.

[40]A. I. Richards (1940), p. 93; and (1934), p. 271.

[41]J. Roscoe (1911), p. 84.

[42]Roscoe, *op. cit.* p. 236.

[43]Roscoe, *op. cit.* pp. 203, 245.

[44]Roscoe, *op. cit.* pp. 283-4.

[45]J. Roscoe, *The Bakitara*, pp. 145-9.

[46]Roscoe, *op. cit.* pp. 136-45, 149-55.

[47]K. Oberg, p. 160.

[48]J. Roscoe, *The Banyankole*, pp. 59, 60.

[49]K. Oberg, pp. 138-9.

[50]K. Oberg, pp. 125, 160.

[51]J. Roscoe, *The Banyankole*, p. 61.

[52]The last woman to be given this title, who was known as Queen Ngalifuru, reigned over the Bateke plateaux between 1892 (the date of the death of the *Onko* by the side of whom she held this position) and 1956, when she passed away, having been the chief authority recognized by the French administration; it was she to whom her unfortunate subjects owe the schools and dispensaries that have been established. Her role was reinforced by the fact that she never allowed the regalia to be taken from her, so that none of the numerous kings who succeeded were able to survive after their enthronement. The *Onko* at present on the throne refused to allow her to enthrone him, fearing to suffer the fate of his predecessors, and he contents himself with exercising very much reduced powers.

[53]This name is also given to the chief emblem of royalty, which is always considered to belong to the *Wanfitere*, even when held by the *Onko*.

[54]S. F. Nadel (1942), p. 147.

[55]Among the Kotoko, until fairly recent times, the title of *Magira* was never borne by the king's mother, since she was ritually put to death by her son on the day of his enthronement; cf. M. Griaule and J. P. Lebeuf, p. 22. This practice is also found among the Yoruba; cf. S. Johnson, pp. 46-8, according to L. de Heusch, p. 125.

[56]O. Macleod, p. 160.

[57]Meek, *Tribal studies*, Vol. II, p. 292.

[58]A. Masson Detourbet, pp. 15, 32.

[59]A. I. Richards (1934), p. 271.

[60]J. Roscoe, *The Bakitara*, pp. 169, 171, 175; *The Baganda*, pp. 8, 85.

[61]C. G. Seligman, pp. 652-3.

[62]Delarozière, pp. 48ff.

[63]S. F. Nadel (1942), pp. 149-50.

[64]O. MacLeod, pp. 177-8.

[65]H. Kuper, pp. 58-9.

[66]Proyart, p. 60.

[67]J. Roscoe, (1911), p. 155.

[68]J. A. Barnes, pp. 89-106.

[69]M. Fortes (1950), p. 256.

[70]Masson Detourbet, p. 30. Their role during these fishing expeditions may be similar to that played by certain women among the Sorko fishermen in the Niamey region mentioned by J. Rouch, p. 48.

[71]S. F. Nadel (1942), pp. 147-8.

[72]S. F. Nadel (1935), pp. 423-47.

[73]A. Even, pp. 187-95.

Women in Political Organization

[74]R. Apthorpe.

[75]K. Little, (1951), pp. 195-6.

[76]G. P. Lestrade, p. 315.

[77]Meek, *Tribal studies*, Vol. I, p. 5.

[78]F. Verberke, pp. 52ff.

[79]The handing-over of kaolin by the supreme chief to his subordinates was a significant act indicating the participation of his vassals in maintaining the vital forces of their sovereign, the founder of the dynasty, (cf. T. Theuws).

[80]K. Little (1951), pp. 177, 196.

[81]H. A. Junod, pp. 355-7, 391.

[82]This institution was prohibited by a decree promulgated by the Belgian Government on 31 January 1947, being regarded as "the practice of polyandry", (cf. M. Tew).

[83]J. Slaski, p. 88.

[84]P. A. Talbot (1926); and (1912), pp. 94ff.

[85]B. Holas, pp. 241-50.

[86]K. Little (1951), p. 126.

[87]K. Little (1951), p. 250; (1948), pp. 1-17.

[88]K. Little (1951), pp. 196, 249-50.

[89]D. Forde, p. 17.

[90]S. Leith-Ross, pp. 105-10.

[91]S. Leith-Ross, pp. 23-39.

NZAKARA WOMEN
(Central African Republic)

Anne Laurentin

INTRODUCTION

I PRESENT HERE FIVE BIOGRAPHIES taken from a col-
lection amounting to nearly three hundred. The subjects of these
biographies are five women belonging to different social classes and
different generations, and the choice was made in the hope that
together they will provide a brief general survey of the life of
Nzakara women since the end of the last century and a conspectus
of the changes that have taken place in their social position during
this period.

It can be seen, from the life histories of these five women, that
the period falls into three stages. The first is that of the Nzakara
kingdom ruled over by the Sultan. With its downfall came the
arrival of the Europeans and the profound social and political
changes that this brought about. Finally we come to the present
day, with its developments taking place far more rapidly than is
realized by women of the previous generation who considered
themselves to be emancipated.

I collected the texts about the older generation by listening to
old women who, with all the wisdom of their experience, would
recall their memories of the past as they sat of an evening peeling
peanuts by the light of a wood fire. The last surviving witnesses of
a time gone by—the time "before the Whites"—and the last heirs
of an oral tradition which is dying, their desire to perpetuate the
past made them choose their words with eagerness and care. I have
endeavoured to interpret them as faithfully as possible. As for the
younger women, they came to me asking me, as a doctor, to cure
them. Feeling that the inability to bear children from which all of
them were suffering was the result of previous happenings, they
were anxious to tell me about their lives as accurately as possible

so as to ensure recovery. I have made every effort not to falsify such vivid and moving personal accounts.

* * *

The first biography has as its subject Natélégé, one of the nobly-born wives of the great Sultan Bangassou who died in 1907. She was born about 1855 and died about 1900, and was probably the most famous woman, celebrated by poets and storytellers, of the period "before the Whites". But she is not merely a legendary figure, for the few remaining older people who had witnessed the last years of her life were able to give an accurate enough picture of the part she played in the events narrated. Hence it is a true portrait of her that appears in this biography, a portrait as seen, and depicted to me, by Sultan Bangassou's sister Dekateyo, by Nasinga and some other wives of the Sultan, and by her niece Nakindi.

Each of the other four women told me her own story. They were quite uninhibited about it, and since my meetings with them took place in their own village, I was able to get comments from their husbands, relations and neighbours about what they told me concerning their youth, marriages, divorces, and everything that had happened to them. From all this evidence emerge four portraits of women differing both in age and in character.

They represent two generations: the two older ones, Kafi and Songombi, are among the last surviving witnesses of former days and of the arrival of the French, and they grew up in a time of great upheaval in the political, economic and social spheres. Between them and the young women of today, such as Nakpangi and Nabate, a great gap yawns, created by the transformation that has taken place in the position of women.

The changes that have been wrought in the last fifty years have broken down the barrier of class distinctions, and have, say the men, given women a feverish desire for independence. It was possible to observe the effects of the levelling process by comparing the accounts of the older with those of the younger women. With the two older ones, membership of their patrilineage had, by imposing upon them the privileges of aristocracy or the duties of slavery, to a large extent determined the possibilities open to them.

Does this mean that their lives were completely pre-determined? Hardly, for some women's lives did not follow the pattern supposedly prescribed by the social category to which they belonged, and I have purposely chosen two examples to demonstrate this, those of Kafi and of Songombi. While Natélégé, the Bandia

Nzakara Women

aristocrat, was a powerful woman-chief, her descendant, the sentimental Songombi, is a solitary waif under the care of relatives. What was lacking that prevented her from repeating the brilliant career of her ancestress? Again, Songombi, as aristocrat, provides a contrast to Kafi, the old slave woman. But their life stories immediately raise the question as to whether there is not much more than a mere difference in social class at the root of this contrast.

Finally, the stories of the two youngest, Nakpangi and Nabate, show the gulf that divides the two generations. While their elders still live according to the tenets of an outworn tradition, they, like all the young people, have come under the influence of a foreign civilization, and, to the dismay of their relatives, neglect the duties which were supposed to ensure the bearing of children.

* * *

The Nzakara had consisted, for a hundred years or more, of small separate units of varying tribal origin, all subjected to the authority of one dominant clan, the Vu-Kpata, and dispersed over the forest lands of the Mbomu in the eastern part of Ubangi. Situated at a crossroads of the slave trade, they had as neighbours the Zande to the east and the Banda to the west.

A handful of men from the N'dendi country in the south (north of the present Belgian Congo) began, about 200 years ago, to conquer the country. The Ubangi river did not constitute a barrier, but was more a route of communication than a natural frontier. Only the forest, in the north, and the guerillas inhabiting it, put a stop to their progress, which, but for the arrival of the Europeans, might have been no more than temporary. They became assimilated to the country they had conquered and took possession of its language, its customs and its women. These were the Bandia.[1]

This Bandia "kingdom", before it split into three separate parts often at enmity with each other, was vast. The senior branch of the lineage was established in the Zande country, the next in seniority governed an area of the N'dendi country, and in the north the junior branch ruled over a number of tribes that had been under the suzerainty of the dominant Vu-Kpata clan in an area lying on both sides of the Ubangi river. The whole territory had as yet no other name but that describing its geographical position: the *Bolo*, the "country beyond". This word was also applied to its inhabitants, thus distinguishing them on the one hand from foreigners and from the slaves of the conquerors, and on the other—and more importantly—from the family of the victorious Bandia: the *Benge*, the "chiefs".

It is a curious fact that it was not until the arrival of the Europeans with their Banda guards that the Banda expression: *N'sa ka la?* was first of all used by the French in reports and on maps, and then adopted by the people themselves, with the result that it is now the expression used to designate their cultural unity. Whatever clan they may belong to, all declare themselves to be Nzakala (or Nzakara).

A word should be said about the epic feat of the Bandia in establishing their conquest. Briefly, there can be said to be two reasons that made this possible. The Sultan distributed to his sons and nephews villages for them to govern and troops to support their authority; their loyalty was guaranteed by "the inviolability of the blood".[2] Secondly, the conquest was secured by making use of the technique of hunting in groups that had been practised in the region, and transposing it into military terms.

Tales, legends and myths still survive that relate the power of "the first man" (the first of the Bandia lineage) to the discovery of the hunting net:

"Of old, when men went hunting they all fell upon the quarry, cut it up on the spot, and divided the spoils, with no other claim to partake in the feast but that of individual strength and cunning. Then a man who was found in the forest, Kole,[3] was brought among them. Kole was their servant, but he was ingenious: he invented the net . . . From the first day when they did it this way, everything was different. He who had put people on the track of the quarry had a right to the head and the feet;[4] with them he made a big dish of food and summoned all the people of the village to share it. He was a *benge*—a chief; he had summoned the *bolo*—the peasants—to the hunt and, in giving them this food, had manifested the true ways of a chief."

It is thus to the inventor of the net, the heroic founder of the technique of encirclement and of group action in the hunt, that tales such as this ascribe the beginnings of the rule of law and of a social hierarchy which would bring some harmony to their rude way of life.

Formerly, tracking down men was for the Nzakara exactly the same as tracking down big game. The same word was used for both, the same amulets, the same technique of encirclement. The trophies of the chase, men, elephants or buffaloes, all met the same fate: if dead, they were eaten; if alive, they became the property of the chief who divided them out among the hunters according to their deserts.

This conception which the Nzakara have as to the origin of

their society amounts to being two or three hundred years of their history in a nutshell. It provides them with an explanation for their social hierarchy which was as follows:

First, the *benge*, the chiefs by right of lineage descent, that is, the sons of the inventor of the net, the Bandia; alongside of them, yet subordinate, are ranked the war-leaders, who have a right to a portion of the booty and share it out of their own free will with the *bolo;*

then, the *bolo:* the peasants, the common people;

lastly, the slaves, mere chattels acquired.

Yes, life was hard in this society. Tales and legends tell of the times when a man had to kill his father, mother and brothers in order to survive. "It was before Kole", say the storytellers. On the other hand, the older people who lived through the last days of the hegemony of the Sultans say emphatically that the young people of today are mere weaklings.

The position of women in such a rigidly stratified society depended upon their rank. All the daughters of Bandia fathers, whatever their mother's lineage, were princesses. Women of the autochthonous subjugated tribes either had the rank of *bolo*—that is to say, commoner—which was theirs if their paternal clan had taken part in the wars of conquest, or else they were mere *kangabaso*, slaves of war, like their fathers before them. Although the distinctions of rank no longer exist, Nzakara still remain very much aware of these former differences.

Bandia women—the aristocrats—enjoyed special rights from their childhood onwards. The blood which flowed in their veins was that of the inventor of the net, of the great conquerors, of all their paternal ancestors. Up until a few years ago, every Bandia woman worthy of her name could still recite her genealogy right back to Kole, the founder. They knew that their ancestors, worshipped in the great collective cult, kept a watchful eye on them and on the marriages they made, and for this reason marriage was always a great event for them. It was arranged, when they reached marriageable age, according to the law of exchange; this exchange made their "worth as princesses" felt, to adopt the expression used by the older people. The man who received one of them as wife gave, as bride price, the currency in use at the time: several strips of iron,[5] chests of cloth, servants and servant-girls. The woman arrived at her husband's house accompanied by the slaves who would serve her. It was up to her lineage to see that this was done in style. The ancestors were notified of the event, and received their share of the *ma*ⁿ*la*.[6] With very few exceptions, all the older Bandia women had gone through this form of marriage. However, it sometimes happened that a junior member of the lineage found himself obliged to give one of his daughters to a senior member, either as payment of tax or rent, or in exchange for a woman he had earlier received in marriage from him. Girls married in this fashion more nearly approached the rank of the common people. The proportion of such marriages increased towards the border areas of the kingdom. The women, however, retained their freedom as an "aristocrat" in their private life, and some of them became chiefs.

What was the position of the girls of the subject peoples who were the original inhabitants? They grew up in the village of a chief who held the right to dispose of them in marriage. This form of marriage was known as *ti-gbenge*.[7] It offered three possibilities:

The *ti-gbenge:* the chief made one of his subjects his own wife.
The *ma'on:* the chief used his "chiefly right" and gave one of his subjects to another chief, or to a subject who was thus rendered beholden and had to reciprocate with an equivalent or greater amount.
The *bosi*[8] *ma'on:* the daughter of a woman given in *ma'on* was handed over to the chief's family by her mother's husband. Sometimes, if the chief was powerful or demanding, a man had to hand over all his daughters to him in exchange for the wife he had received.

As for the slaves, they had no hope whatsoever of settling the debt of which they themselves were the permanent repayment.

It is not difficult to imagine how each category of women was affected by this system:

—the Bandia, as daughters of "the blood of chiefs", enjoyed a freedom that was inconceivable for the others. It should be stressed once again that this was because they had the "blood of their ancestors" in their veins. To realize how real a factor this is, one has only to hear, as is still possible today, the father or the uncle of one of these wom ˑ ʻefending his own "blood" in marriage negotiations or divorce proceedings, with all the fervour of one who feels that "he who spills the blood of one spills the blood of all". Thus under the old régime these women could act with the greatest impunity, particularly when they married a man of the common people with an inferior social status to theirs. They even had the right to take a male concubine, whose function was rather to satisfy their desires than to fill the role of husband. We can see something of this free way of life in the biography of Songombi, the old Bandia woman born at the time when the first French military missions arrived upon the scene.

The privileges were naturally accompanied by rites and ceremonies. When a Bandia girl moved to another clan, this had to be announced to the whole lineage, including the ancestors who kept watch over the village. They partook in receiving the bridewealth given for their daughter, which gave the contract a religious sanction.

A Bandia woman's fertility was a matter which concerned her husband's clan, and it also depended upon her own ancestors. Hence the importance of religious ceremonies such as the presentation of the bride to the ancestors, or the "placation of their wrath" when they have been angered. Such rites were not performed for slaves, who did not come under the care of the ancestors, but they were carried out for some women of the subjugated tribes, either members of the former dominant clan, the Vu-Kpata, or of one of the clans that had been awarded the honours due to warriors.

Some Bandia women exploited their position in order to assert their authority, and, like Natélégé, acquired a powerful influence, becoming authentic heads of villages or even district chiefs.

In the border areas, insecurity, raids from neighbouring tribes, and the burden of tribute that had to be paid to the Sultan, made life precarious for the local Bandia chiefs. A nobly-born woman married to one of these border chiefs found her marital privileges curtailed, and this curtailment of her rights was sanctioned by the combined views of the elders and the diviners: the childlessness of Bandia women was due to the wrath of the ancestors, who were angry because their female descendants had not been given enough bridewealth, and angry, too, because the mothers of the brides had not received their share. This explained misfortunes such as the death of their children, or epidemics in the villages. In this same border region, where unfavourable conditions still prevail today, although the last diviner is dead, yet the memory of his explanations still remains, and an obscure resentment persists against those who, a hundred years ago, roused the wrath of the dead and caused it to fall upon the living of today.

—The women of the commoner class, the *bolo*, were perhaps the most numerous group. When the early inhabitants were subjugated by the Bandia, they supplied them with warriors for their conquests and wives for their chiefs. The chiefs adopted the language and the domestic habits of their subjects and wives. The women lived at the chief's court, "in the hand of the chief", who either took them for his own use, or used them as a form of currency. But some of the clans acquired definite privileges when one of the clansmen, as a reward for war services, was appointed to be a chief by the Sultan. Daughters of such a clan were then exchanged in the same way as nobly-born women, and, like Bandia women, enjoyed the protection of the clan's heroic dead, now elevated to the dignity of being ancestors. They were presented to the ancestral spirits of their husband's clan, and a portion of the bridewealth was offered to the ancestors of the bride's lineage. They no longer were the property of a chief, but a daughter of the blood of their fathers. Rare at first, instances of this increased with the increasing prosperity of the Nzakara kingdom. The respect accorded to a wife of this type grew greater the more children she had, or if her cooking was of such a high standard that the food she offered to her husband's guests was such as to make him a *benge*, a chief. In the Biblical sense, they really were "stout women".

—Finally, the slavewomen were, in this warlike society, the sign of their master's wealth. When the "women's courtyard" got depleted, the chiefs lost no time in organizing an expedition for the purpose of procuring new slave-girls.

There were three possible destinies for these women:

1. Some were sold to the slave trade.

2. Others stayed in the chief's house and were servant-girls, known as *dimbi*, to nobly-born wives. They were allowed as unofficial husband a slave from the farm village. Their children belonged to the chief, the sons becoming soldiers or farm slaves, thus supplying the man-power for the requirements of the economy. Military requirements absorbed many able-bodied men in the prime of life—Sultan Bangassou kept up a permanent army. The daughters of these slave marriages provided the chief with a form of currency: when they were given in *ma'on* to another chief, this had to be repaid by providing a wife for the chief in return. This system guaranteed the continuation of the practice of exogamy which was customary among all the tribes subjected to the Bandia, although among the Bandia themselves consanguineous marriages were a frequent occurrence.

3. A slave-girl could be given, as a slave, to another chief. These gifts were made according to the law of exchange. They were never in the nature of free gifts, but involved long negotiations, for the gift to be made in return must be worthy of the position

and rank of the first donor. A powerful chief who gave a slave-girl to one of his subjects (*ma'on*) had the right to demand in return not only one of her daughters, but all of them.

The future of a slave-girl was unpredictable. Her fate depended upon "reasons of State".

The vicissitudes of a slave-girl's life are still fresh in people's memory. In the biography of Natélégé as in that of Kafi, who was one of them, we hear how some slave-girls ran away, to return later to their former master. An incident of this kind may not throw much light on the complexity of the whole system of exchange, but it does at least show the psychological climate experienced by those who were the counters in the game. Whatever her final fate might be, a slave-girl never possessed anything; not even her fiancé, if he also was a slave, belonged to her; she did not even own the clothes she wore or the mat she slept on. Everything belonged to her master. We may be astonished at the way these slave-women passively accepted their fate. But it was impossible for them to imagine any other kind of existence, even when some of them were lucky enough to find themselves in a comparatively stable position in the household of a chief, and were able, like Kafi, to rise to the rank of a wife who had borne children and had become the mother of a chief, and thus finally attain the rank of honoured matron for whom water is fetched in her old age.

Their only defence against adversity was to appeal to the spirits of their native land, which proliferated in the very places where they were most oppressed. They knew about the magic properties of plants, and could concoct poisons, medicines, and love-philtres. Those people who still retain such secrets have more often learnt them from old women than from old men. The prestige enjoyed by women who know magic secrets does not alter the scorn in which the race of slaves is held. Some of them manage nevertheless to find a social niche for themselves as repositories of village customs.

*　　*　　*

The position of women has been transformed during the past 20 years. The levelling down of class distinctions began with the decline of chiefship resultant upon the chiefs' being deprived of their principal means of support: the trophies of war or of the hunt, and slaves and wives procured on the cheap by waging war.

It continued as a result of an administrative measure that was carried through relentlessly: every man was obliged, whatever his clan, and even if his rank was that of noble or of chief, to pay

Anne Laurentin

bridewealth in order to obtain a wife, whether the woman were slave or free. The chiefs put up a resistance for 15 years, but both commoners and slaves won their case in every dispute brought before the government authorities. Faced with the choice of paying or going to prison, the chiefs had to give in.

Remembrance of "the good old days" is accompanied by nostalgic regrets on the part of older men and sons of chiefs. However, the former state of affairs still has its repercussions on the present. Among old and young alike there is a profoundly anti-feminist spirit, which stems from a feeling of impotence upon realizing that women will refuse to return to the state of dependence they knew a century ago. The old people lay the blame for the fall in the birth rate on the women, who, they say, gad about too much and are too fond of pleasure. Yet no husband will bring an accusation against his own wife. The accusation is a general one, the result of a change in the whole fabric of society.

This change is especially evident in the story of Nabate, the youngest of the five women whose stories are told, but not the only one of her kind.

The First Period

NATÉLÉGÉ, PRINCESS AND PIONEER

Natélégé, grand-daughter of the great conqueror Mbilinga, was by birth a noble princess, but only entered history upon her marriage with her cousin Bangassou, the Sultan of the Nzakara. Two generations are spanned by the period since her death.[9]

In a country where it is the father alone who is the source of all wisdom and knowledge, who would dare to tell of the childhood days of a woman whose father was not present at the time? Besides, is it permissible for anyone to speak of events which occurred before he was born? Only the old people, nowadays, have fragmentary memories of them. Her junior co-wives have not forgotten Natélégé. Her niece, Nakindi, who spent her childhood days at the Sultan's court, can bring back memories of it with an intuitive sense developed by 30 years of study and practice in the divinatory arts. Natélégé is no more dead than the great chiefs are. Invoked by Nakindi, her "spirit" still returns today to give judgments in disputes as in the days of her power, to bestow fertility, and to punish the guilty.

130

Nzakara Women

She was one of the first wives of her cousin Nzongo, the future Sultan Bangassou, "he who treated as one chief to another with the great white chiefs". She became the *dekana*[10] of a harem which is reckoned to have had more than 300 women in it.

The history of this woman who, on the eve of her country's expansion, was able to carve out for herself a man's career and who became a chief, is a strange one. The first woman-chief, she surpassed all those who followed in her footsteps. The magnificent funeral ceremonies held in her honour were the last to be performed according to the traditional rites.

She is spoken of with a sigh, as when remembering times that will not occur again. "Was it because of the fear she inspired, or because of her goodness, that she attained such a high degree of power? What does it matter: she was a chief." Such a vindication throws light on the warlike nature of a society in which weakness could not be tolerated or power would crumble, nor kindness indulged in or authority would be held in contempt.

Let us hear what Nakindi has to say:

Natélégé entered the household of the young prince Bangassou, son of the Sultan Mbali, in the manner possible only for a young noblewoman. Mbali had sent in exchange for his son's bride several bundles of iron bars, which the smiths would render useful by turning them into lances, weapons of war or of the chase, spades and hoes. Natélégé's family had received some young boys, and several young girls who were the *mbalaba*,[11] the women "of the exchange". For her part, Natélégé arrived at her bridegroom's court like a princess, accompanied by her servants and servant-girls. No commoner could have come anywhere near her in rank, and hers demanded a number of women in *mbalaba*,[11] in exchange, for the young bride. She went to live with her husband at "Hyo" on the banks of the river Ubangi. Bangassou's father, after having sent him on several distant expeditions, had set him up as ruler of the northern part of the kingdom.

Natélégé was installed with her servants in two round huts in the women's courtyard, at the far end of the enclosure. At the other end the troops were mustered. Near them, the young pages, future soldiers and nation-wide messengers, occupied two "pavilions" that flanked the entrance to the chief's courtyard, in the centre of which the chief had his hut. This being the dwelling of the master and husband, it was the largest building. It was surrounded by vast granaries which were stacked with millet and sesame after each harvest, and which also served as storehouses for the elephant and buffalo meat brought back from the chase. All this meat had to be smoked in order to preserve it. This meant a great deal of work. The way of the chief is really the way in which he divides out food for everyone. Further away, beyond the enclosure, stretched the groups of farmers' and fishermen's huts.[12] Natélégé soon became one of the favourite wives of Bangassou. Most of the others at that time were only concubines or slaves, given by Mbali to his son as reward for his military expeditions. She, as chief wife, was entrusted with distributing the foodstuffs to her co-wives. Natélégé had a born gift for making herself obeyed, and was good at dividing out the food fairly. When Bangassou had to go away for military reasons, he could rely on her.

Accomplished as she was as a wife, Natélégé however remained childless. It was in vain that she had taken the medicines of the *ba-do-ndoli*.[13] So a diviner was consulted on her behalf. Bangassou had several, given to him by his father Mbali; and he had also sent for experts from Zande country, in the south-eastern part of the kingdom. These men had learnt a subtler art than any known to Bangassou's own subjects, who only knew about the tarantula (*mbili*). The Sultan also kept great dancers, who danced the *nganga*, and were clever at foreseeing events in the flames of a fire. One of them, Tya'igui, saw in the fire a spell[14] from which the young wife must be delivered. He predicted the birth of a child who would one day be a great chief and he gave Natélégé some plants. Shortly after, she became pregnant and gave birth to a son, Gambo, he who later governed the Uango district.[15]

To help Natélégé, one of her younger sisters was sent for, as was customary. Nalogo was a lively, blossoming child. She proudly carried the baby on her hips. The months passed by, she became a woman. When Bangassou saw her thus, she pleased him and he took her for his wife. There were long discussions over the bridewealth, but that was no affair of Nalogo's. She had had ambitious dreams, and already she saw herself being an important wife like her older sister.

Natélégé remained in retirement, as all young mothers do so long as their child is not yet able to walk. She could not go near her husband without harming her son's health.[16] But she saw to it that the great hut of Bangassou sheltered three or four women every night. More than that, she had learnt the art of serving her husband by enlarging his household. On the first visits which she had paid to her own family, she had brought back young girls who had become his wives. The power of Bangassou was growing. He always returned victorious both from the hunt and from his wars.

Nzakara Women

He worked hard for it too on important occasions; not content to send the *tyango*, the body of warriors bearing the banner and the name of a noble prince, he himself went with them and supervised the tactics in battle as well as ensuring that customs were duly observed.

With all the men away, Natélégé became more than ever the grand stewardess. Her tasks became ever heavier as the number of wives and of subjects increased. Her son Gambo would soon leave her with all her time at her own disposal, for like every other boy, noble or commoner, he would enter the ranks of the army as a page.

Yes, the Sultan's household became immense. He had ousted his brothers and added their subjects to his own. Neighbours had come and put themselves under his rule, preferring his protection to war. For all this population, enormous granaries were required, "bigger than the cotton warehouses today". In them were piled up ivory tusks, smoked meat, and the trinkets and gems that the women loved to adorn themselves with and that the Arabs brought in exchange for more substantial commodities—slaves. Natélégé supervised the baskets of foodstuffs which each *dekana* took away for the group of women under her—for there were a number of *dekana*, each one looking after ten women. Then, going over to the other side of the enclosure, Natélégé made a count of the soldiers. She was a careful housewife, and Bangassou could be proud of her. In her idle moments, she reckoned the portions to be distributed and adjusted them according to rank with such authority that there was no occasion for grumbling.

She kept the peace between the various groups. She also kept watch over the comings and goings of the wives as they moved about fetching water from the spring or bringing firewood to the kitchen. The men who kept the huts in repair would prowl around the enclosure. Thus it often happened that the wives had adulterous affairs, but those who took their pleasure in this way were so cunning at becoming lovers that it required a very sharp watch to find them out. Meetings took place in the bush, or in a hut under cover of the dark, and with the complicity of a co-wife who hoped for the same favours herself. All these clandestine goings-on could easily enough escape Natélégé's watchful eye, for her many duties often took her away. But Nalogo, Natélégé's rival, took a passionate interest in them, hoping in this way to attract to herself the favours of her husband. She knew the tricks the young pages got up to as they moved freely about the courtyard where the soldiers were and near that of the wives, performing services for both, being

Anne Laurentin

useful go-betweens for arranging a meeting or for carrying the meal prepared for a lover by his mistress in exchange for his services. One evening, Nalogo caught two pages who were leaving the women's courtyard with a dish in their hands. She asked them: Where had they come from? And thus learnt the names of the wives.[17]

Two pairs of lovers had been found out that evening, and Nalogo herself brought the matter before Bangassou. One of the lovers strenuously denied the charge. Bangassou sent for one of his court *ba-sa-iwa*, those who consult the oracle and test the words of the accused by the poison of the *benge*. The man fell down in convulsions and died. "O you who denied having touched a woman, would you have us forget that woman is a river? What man approaches without drinking?"

The other lover was seized by the executioner who, holding him down by the hair of his head, cut off his head with a single stroke of the axe and threw it away. Such was the treatment of criminals. The poets might well sing of the misfortunes of disobedient subjects: "One who lives at the court of a chief does not survive infidelity".

Accusations of adultery, such as this, often created trouble in a chief's household. Soldiers from the village of Gagbu had several times been accused, and when brought to the Sultan's court were maltreated by the bazingers[18] detailed to bring them before Bangassou. One day it was the bazingers who returned with a chain round their neck, like prisoners. The Gagbu chief followed soon after with his soldiers. He threw the arms he had taken from the bazingers at the Sultan's feet, who told him to approach and said: "It is you, the Chief, who fights me and makes my soldiers prisoners?"

"Yes!" replied Gagbu proudly, "Your bazingers have done nothing but create trouble in my village. I have made your men prisoners and confiscated their arms. Here they are. If you have a war, O Bangassou, will it be those women who will go out to fight, those women on account of whom you have maltreated my warriors?"

Everyone present was tense with apprehension, but Bangassou held out his hand to his officer and did not allow any more "discussions" about adultery in the village.

Yes, these trials over adultery were a plague.

Natélégé listened to the complaints of the wives: Nalogo spoke too much; she betrayed her friends so that Bangassou might listen to her and be pleased. Natélégé might well scold her, but Nalogo held her head high. Was she not now as powerful as her elder sister? She, too, had several households of women under her and a group of servants in the village of Sawala. Natélégé was never beaten. She had a discussion with Bangassou and the chiefs. Did not the Sultan get from Natélégé everything a chief could desire? She looked after his nocturnal pleasures, and, knowing his ardour, had supplied him with numerous wives; during the day, did he not always have wives by his side who prepared and looked after his pipe, who brought him *nzaba* leaves[19] before his meals? She was a model housekeeper, and settled all disputes among the servants. Her words were wise and her management successful. That day Natélégé received two *tyango*. These corps of troops were officially known as *Vu-Natélégé;*[20] everyone would thus know who their commander was. They joined the group of farmers and servants she ruled over several kilometres from Hyo. But she did not content herself with honours, for she knew that a real chief is one who commands and distributes. Gambo, her son, also had troops under his command. She buckled on the barkskin gown and the liana headdress of a warrior and the bracelet of a prince and went off at their head, by the side of Bangassou. The hunt was successful and Natélégé's bravery acclaimed. Bangassou handed her her share: five elephants, the booty of a troop commander. She could now herself fill her granaries in her village.

Some time later, Bangassou sent his sons and several corps of troops to fight against the country of the Langba. Everyone had been awaiting this military expedition. The *tyango Vu-Natélégé* took part in it and Natélégé went with her men. She had her own diviner and her war fetishes. The expedition was successful. Natélégé distinguished herself by her bravery. She had killed several of the enemy with her own hands; she obtained new slaves. No one was astonished to see her depart for new wars, but Nalogo's jealousy was growing: she had been supplanted.

Not long after that, the Whites arrived. Two of them had already visited the kingdom, but these ones came with a paper to sign and with presents: rifles, gunpowder, as much as a chief could want in his wildest dreams. The rifles were of a very different type from the old muskets. To demonstrate how powerful they were, the white chief had a kid placed at a distance of a 100 metres, held at the end of a rope; he killed it dead. Amazement filled the court. Bangassou took aim. At the second shot, the kid fell. Natélégé took a shot at the target, her hand stayed steady and the kid dropped down. When the arms were divided out Bangassou gave her some rifles and some ammunition for herself and for her troops. Now

Anne Laurentin

Natélégé could walk around proudly with a well-filled cartridge-pouch as a belt.

Nalogo's jealousy was beyond all bounds. One morning when Natélégé was in the Sultan's hut, she threw a burning torch into the hut where they were in consultation. The roof took fire. The Sultan's anger was terrible and the author of the crime was quickly found. He had her placed near the gateway; she was tied up so tightly that the blood flowed from her feet and hands. Consternation reigned among her friends, the co-wives. The event caused such stupefaction that it was heard of far and wide. Chiefs and relatives came running. Bangassou wanted to have the criminal executed that very evening. How to change the Sultan's decision? Throughout the day the wives came to place at his feet fowls, their bead necklaces; the men (Nalogo's servants), knives and lances; her relations and familiars, kids, *gbogbo*.[21] By the end of the day the ground was strewn with innumerable objects for Nalogo's ransom, the price of her life. Nalogo was let off; she ended her days in exile, in the village that Bangassou had once given her.

As for Natélégé, she continued her ascent to power. As commander of a troop and as head of a village she got her share of the booty; the number of her subjects and slaves increased. She no longer gave her body in service to her husband, but she continued to add to his power. She spent more and more of her time at her village, some minutes' walk from the Sultan's court. There she settled disputes. She was feared like a chief.

One day, returning from the hunt, she fell ill. Everyone at Bangassou's court got alarmed; her co-wives surrounded her hut; those who knew the properties of plants wanted to bring her remedies. Bangassou, when he was brought the news, told the diviners and dancers to consult the omens about her. They were unfavourable. Everyone, moreover, was soon able to see that it was *zikposi* she was suffering from.[22] The dreadful pustules spread over her body, her back began to be eaten away by them; the healers brought their plant, but when the pustules were pierced, it only left an open sore, her nose was apallingly marked. She was isolated in a *ngbango*.[23] But everyone knows that when the sores reach the heart, the patient dies, and that is what happened.

Bangassou had a great *gaza*[24] brought and ordered the funeral ceremonies to be performed. He was sore at heart. All the people at the court were weeping and dancing. Natélégé's body was placed in the drum and brought solemnly to Kelebili, the place of the tomb of the Sultans themselves (the only woman to be given such honours). Many men were killed to accompany her after death and some women were strangled; slaves were thrown on her *gaza*. It was the burial of a great chief. The period of mourning lasted for a long time. On her estates and in her villages her subjects were determined to conduct the mourning rites with all solemnity. There too men were buried, and women as well, in her honour. Today, singers praise her bravery in war, women recall her life story, the elders say: "If the Whites had not been there, Natélégé would be upon the altar of the ancestors". Magicians evoke her spirit to cure the sick and interpret events. Women who bear her name owe their fertility to her power. Her example opened the way to rulership for other noblewomen. Three are still heads of villages: Nzapa, Nagonzi and Golossende.

Second period: Colonization

1. THE BEGINNINGS OF COLONIZATION

KAFI, THE OLD SLAVE-WOMAN

Kafi is one of the very old women in the village—she is seventy-two.[25] She is known by all as a wise woman, and is sought out whenever a woman falls ill; she knows about the magic properties of plants and about healing ointments; she can tell what food should not be eaten. Water is brought to her from the spring as though she were a noblewoman. Her son, who is village head, keeps the thatching on her hut in repair. Yet nothing in Kafi's childhood days could have led her to expect an old age like this, for Kafi was a slave.

She was born in the country of the Langba, a country neighbouring upon the Nzakara kingdom. Her first childhood memory is of a long journey carried on the back of her uncles.[26] Nzakara troops, armed with lances, had once again crossed the river which formed the frontier and pillaged Langba villages. The bedtime stories of Kafi's childhood were all about the sudden attack on the village which had been secretly surrounded, the attempts to flee, the cries of people surprised in the middle of preparing the evening meal and the death of those who had fought with their lances to defend the entrance to their huts. "Your father had gone to gather taros;[27] we saw him, dead, in the middle of his field. Your mother died after the journey was over, together with the daughter she gave birth to, stillborn. The Whites had not yet arrived."

"When we arrived at Chief Ngbangbali's,[28] the courtyard[29] was

137

full of women. On the side opposite to them were the men and the peasants. Those who had been troublesome had a cangue round their necks. We waited to know what would be done to us."

Kafi stayed for some time at Ngbangbali's court, he having kept one half of the *kanga-baso*[30] and sent his cousin, the Sultan Bangassou,[31] the other half. Thus a large number of men and women slaves went off to the commander of all the armies, for the Sultan did not treat the respect due to him as a light matter; his messengers were quickfooted and had sharp eyes and ears.

Kafi does not remember the journey to Bangassou's court, but she does remember being taken to Yongozo, one of the Sultan's chief wives, and of the royal race. Yongozo's manner of welcome was to make the child lie on the ground, whereupon she put her foot upon the child's back and said, as she did to all the girls brought to her: "You are my slave". Then she showed her what her work would be.

Kafi's youth passed without incident. She fetched water for Yongozo and pounded her millet. She enjoyed working. Yongozo did not beat her much. Often she took her to the distribution of food presided over by the *dekana* Nalogo, one of the most important of the chief wives of the Sultan. Kafi would return with a huge load on her head, booty from a big hunt or a raid.

These expeditions required a large number of men. The Sultan kept a permanent force of men under arms, but the women saw little of them, because the soldier's camp[32] was on the other side of the stream in a separate enclosure. However, everyone in the women's courtyard knew what was going on there, for they could hear the bustle of preparations being made for an expedition, the shouts and the drums. Those wives who had one of these warriors as a lover knew the purpose of the dances, and could explain it to the others.

Kafi took little part in the women's gossip; she was still no more than a child, and was much more interested in the food she got to eat. Once a day she waited in a small hut that served as kitchen to be given a plain stew of maize or cassava which was the slave's diet. Seated round a great pot, the women ate hurriedly so as to get enough before the pot was empty. Kafi never had a taste of elephant or of buffalo, but had to content herself with bearing dishes of these meats, carried on her head, to Yongozo. Sometimes she had to help with smoking the meat over the embers of a fire, turning it over and over until it was quite dry and blackened. What a good smell that was! But the noblewomen kept it on the wood blocks that formed their larder under the roof of their straw huts.

Nzakara Women

Kafi would never have dared to touch it. Only Nandu and Nganzi who, like Yongozo, were of the noble blood of chiefs, had the right to eat it. It was not food for slaves, and punishments were severe. One day one of her young companions, a Mbangi[33] slave, Da Yongozo,[34] was caught with a piece of elephant fat in her hand. Several times she had hidden a piece in the mat which she unrolled at night in the kitchen to sleep on. Kafi had even shared a few mouthfuls with her in secret. But Da Yongozo's little store had been discovered: someone must have talked. She was taken to the Chief's courtyard and disappeared for a while. When she came back, she had one hand missing. Nobly-born wives did not like having thieves at the court of Bangassou.

As for Kafi, she never spoke a word to the great ladies and her companions respected her.

Sometimes, in fun, she was called *Bosi Ndogo*, daughter of the lizard, or *Da Singba*, Singba's woman. One day she asked an old woman to explain these names to her, and the old woman referred to things of which she had been quite ignorant up till then, and which explained why she had come to Bangassou's court:

"Singba is the lizard and you have acted as his daughter." The old woman laughed. It was a riddle which Kafi only fully understood later. "Singba was a troop commander; he was a subject of Ngbangbali, my first master. One day when he was at Bangassou's court he was caught with one of the Sultan's wives. The lovers were brought to trial. Singba had merited the death penalty, but in recognition of his high feats of arms, the Sultan allowed him to pay ransom for his life by giving him a daughter. Singba had no daughter. He promised to bring one; a noble kinsman of Nbgangbali stood as guarantor. Singba was able to return to his chief and ask him for a woman;[35] he promised, in return, to give him the first daughter born to him. Ngbangbali agreed. Thus it was that I was brought to Bangassou's court. Does not the lizard leave his tail in the hands of his would-be capturer? Singba had given his daughter (or rather the woman exchanged for his daughter) as the price for his life."

Kafi grew up and her breasts began to form, this being the important event in her life that enabled her to date her departure from Bangassou's court. This happened very simply: A man had come to the Sultan's court. She was called for, and she left hand-in-hand with the man who took her away; he told her that she need not be afraid to come with him; she would be his wife. And in fact he had bought her by laying at the Sultan's feet the price of Singba's adultery with the wife of Bangassou: four kids and some beads.[36]

Kafi walked for two days; the man was one of the nephews of Ngbangbali, his name was Nyaⁿlikawo, she would be his second wife.[37]

How different everything was from the Sultan's court! The Chief's court seemed very small to her. Already by the first evening she had made the acquaintance of all the women. Some of them recognized her; they looked at her, astonished to see this lovely young girl whom they had seen as a child at the court of Ngbangbali.[38]

Kafi shared the hut of Migozo, the chief wife; she obeyed her orders; however Migozo was not a princess, but a simple commoner. She had grown up in the court of Nyaⁿlikawo's father where she had been from the time she was five years old, and where her mother had been born. One day the Chief had given her mother in marriage to one of his subjects and had commanded the young husband to give in exchange the daughters borne to him by this wife. Thus it was that Migozo had been taken back when she was still a child by Nyaⁿlikawo's father; she had been a servant-girl while awaiting the time when she would become one of his wives.

It was here that Kafi began her life as a wife. On becoming pregnant, she was entitled to have more to eat than she had had at Bangassou's court. Several times after a hunt she was given a piece of roasted meat. Her happiness as a young wife made her forget all the brilliant entertainments she had witnessed at Bangassou's court. On the evenings when they were held, huge numbers of men had danced the *mbaka*, the war-dance on feast-days, while the servant-girls prepared the great bowls of food for the feast. The Sultan enjoyed celebrations. When the fun was at its height, his intimates or his wives would make him join in the dancing. What excitement and what shouts of joy there were then! His wives would come to stick into his carefully barbered beard the most highly prized of tokens: the little hairpins that the women used for dressing their hair. So many people dancing, singing, playing the *gaza*,[39] it was only at Bangassou's court that such sights could be seen. The sound of the rejoicings could be heard far and wide[40] among all his subjects and even among his neighbours. They all knew that he was a great chief. The feasts at Nyaⁿlikawo's were on a more modest scale.

But Kafi was a wife favoured to enjoy the pleasures which the night had to offer. Those around her could soon see the signs of her coming motherhood. This child would be the first in the household of the young chief.

As soon as it began to move, the old women gave her advice.

She must devote herself entirely to the child, and once it had begun to stir, if only "to make more room for itself", her husband must no longer have anything to do with her.[41] She must also learn what things her child liked and what things it rejected.[42]

Changes were taking place in the kingdom. The Sultan's son was now reigning; mystery surrounded the disappearance of his father. All the women knew was, that the Sultan with his halo of glory had joined "the ancestors". The Whites had come and were taking men to make them work; many fled to the forest.

Kafi gave birth to a daughter. Nyanlikawo was disappointed, he would have liked to have a son; Lamada, one of the old midwives who had helped at the confinement, said without making any bones about it that he ought to be thankful to have a daughter to exchange or to endower! Lamada was older than Kafi, but, like her, a slave, although in spite of that her skill in helping young mothers had given her a reputation. She used plenty of "free" language when she was engaged upon her tasks.

The newborn baby was a fine child, and knew how to use her lungs. All the village women came with their babies to see it and encourage it to grow up well. Some of them stayed in the doorway, because it is not good if a woman who has spent the night with her husband comes into contact with a newborn child and its mother. It could cause her death.

Kafi felt safe with Lamada. Lamada saw to everything: she had put a wreath of lianas round the neck of the baby so that it should not move; she had slid a ring round one leg and a bracelet round one wrist, so that its limbs might grow and become strong. On the eighth day the umbilical cord broke off; she cut this lifeline into small pieces and collected them together in a flask of oil so that the life-force in them should not be quenched and should continue to supply the child with vitality. Then Kafi could emerge from the hut. Already an aunt of Nyanlikawo had given her little daughter her name: Dadua.

Nyanlikawo bore the young princess[43] to the sanctuary of the ancestors and made an offering of a fowl. The little Dadua (woman of Dua) had now entered upon her life.

Kafi and her daughter were now the centre of admiration for the whole village; they hardly ever went out of the enclosure of the Chief's court, but wherever the child was to be found, there was a circle of women round her.

Next it was the turn of Migozo, the chief wife, to conceive. Two new wives then came to join them; they were to fulfil the duties of a wife which were now prohibited to Migozo and to Kafi.[44] But when the day of the confinement came, the child gave one gasp and died.

This was not the only misfortune. Shortly afterwards, Kafi herself fell ill. Lovely and strong as she was, she was nevertheless shaking with fever. Her baby was pining away, and Nyaⁿlikawo became anxious. His father's diviner came and consulted the oracle. He discovered the workings of a sorceress: Da Mbagi, wife of the Water Spirit. It was she who had cast a spell on the wives of Nyaⁿlikawo. This did not surprise the villagers. Da Mbagi was old and went round the huts begging. She had come several times asking for salt or cassava from two wives who had chased off the importunate creature. Da Mbagi was feared by everyone. In her youth she had killed a young mother by her powers of sorcery.[45] Her father had been put to death and his entrails publicly exposed so that everyone could see the white organ in which his power lay. A person was born a sorcerer and the organ of sorcery grew as he grew. Da Mbagi, when she was still a young woman, had had two fingers cut off after she had cast the spell on the young mother. The two wives had been very foolish to refuse the old woman's demands and send her packing. Nyaⁿlikawo's father commanded Da Mbagi to stop casting her spell.[46] Soon after, Kafi got up from her sick bed; the child recovered at the same time as her mother.[47]

Soon the child began to make her first attempts at walking. Kafi, anxious for the health of her daughter, did not resume married life until the child could run about all by herself in the courtyard. Then she could leave her child with Migozo or with another woman on the evenings when she was summoned to her husband's hut for the night. She became pregnant again, and this second pregnancy created a certain amount of jealousy.

When Kemba, the third wife, had her first child, Kafi came to her hut and helped the midwife to deliver the child. Their mothers were of the same lineage, so she knew what customs should be followed for the confinement.[48]

Kemba gave birth to a fine boy, and Nyaⁿlikawo was delighted. He longed for a court full of children. But for this he needed many wives, as his father had had. He had just acquired a very young one, Dangba, and was negotiating an exchange that was to bring him his sixth wife, Salingbi.

The women's courtyard was in a great state of excitement that year. Not long after Kemba had done so, Kafi also gave birth to a boy, which was given the name of his grandfather. Then there was the arrival of the two new wives, as well as two more births, and on top of that a slave-woman came back who had taken flight from the husband she had recently married. She was a woman of the Togbo tribe, a former prisoner of war. She arrived one evening, thin and in a bad state; her body and her shoulders were covered with the visible marks of blows she had received. She threw herself at the feet of the Chief, who scolded her; she begged to stay. There were long discussions about it between the men at the court. A messenger came and the Togbo woman departed. She came back about a year later. She stayed for a few days. She was put in Kafi's hut. She looked after the children as if she were their mother. Kafi knew that there was a great "palaver" going on about her. Nyanlikawo asked her one evening if the slave worked satisfactorily for her. Yes, she replied, wondering if the Togbo woman was going to stay in the women's courtyard. She was so helpful that they were glad to have her. Her former unofficial husband had come to see her again. She could sing. Things continued thus until Kafi had her third baby; a few days before that, the woman left, tied up with a rope. Kafi could not ask Nyanlikawo why the slave had had to go, it would not have been correct for a young wife to do so, he would have replied: "Mind your own business, *Langba*!"[49] Sometimes she talked it over with the other women.

One day, Kafi heard talk about the Togbo slave when she was serving food to Nyanlikawo; it was after the harvest feast when every lineage brings its ancestors what is due to them. That evening there were two cousins belonging to another lineage[50] who had come to claim some women, and the negotiations were under way. Kafi heard them talking about the great annual harvest feast, about the good omens and about the people who had taken part in it. They announced with pride that their ancestors had two new wives dedicated to them;[51] one of them was called Da Mbilinga,[52] and this was the Togbo woman. So this was what had happened to the slave! She had become one of those women like the two wives-of-the-ancestors that Nyanlikawo had whom she knew.[53] The men of the village with whom they shared their hut were only temporary husbands. Their real husband was the ancestor whose dwelling they had to look after. They lived on the margins of society. Natives of the country of Langba, they too had been brought back with returning military expeditions. Kafi asked no questions, but came back to the women's hut and told Migozo and Kemba what she had heard. Then they spoke no more about it. Da Mbilinga was far away, beyond their day-to-day preoccupations. Cultivating their small field, fetching water from the well, preparing the meals, feeding the children, their thoughts were absorbed by the round of everyday life.

Kafi's life as the wife of a chief went on. Her two youngest children—she had four at this time—died of *manda vulu*.[54] Many children and many people died that year.[55] The women discussed it with strangers who brought news about the men who had gone away to work in the rubber camps for the Whites. The men were excited over all this news, and the death of Kafi's children did not cause so much consternation in the village as there had been at the time when she was ill. But she kept thinking: Might not the children have been poisoned by Salingbi, the childless wife who did not like her? Kafi had caught her one day scolding her son Nombazu because he had touched a bundle of wood she had just set down. Kafi had intervened, but the other woman had answered back and had threatened to strike her. An elder who had been sitting not far off making baskets had come up at the sound of the quarrel. He was an uncle of Salingbi; he had given her a good scolding: "Did you come to the house of Nyanlikawo with this child that you start fighting about him? Is it you that brought him here?" Ever since that day, this co-wife had avoided Kafi and eyed her askance. Might she not have poisoned the two children with the plants she had brought from her father's house? Now Kafi only had two children left.

It was shortly after Kafi gave birth to another son that Nyanlikawo lost his father. It was a great chief died when he died. Unfortunately it was no longer possible to have such splendid funeral ceremonies as before. When the Whites heard about men and women being placed on the grave of a dead chief, there were trials and chiefs in prison! The diviner announced that the mourning period should not last too long.[56] The dead man left a large estate: women and goods. Dividing it out was a laborious business; the chiefs and elders had many meetings. Five women came, when the mourning period was over, to add to the numbers in the women's courtyard of Nyanlikawo. Two of them were old women of the royal lineage. There were quarrels between them and the wives of their son-in-law. The chief wife could not settle the differences between them, and Kafi, as had happened in the past, often had to be the arbitrator accepted by both sides. Her words were wise, and then did she not have three children, as many as all the other wives put together?

Kafi later had two more children. The second youngest was born in the village built[57] by order of the Whites alongside the newly constructed road. Nyanlikawo was often away during this time. He was now chief in place of his father and went to the big town on business. He was often called upon to contribute to the work on the road. He had to see about a case concerning a young wife who had taken flight after a quarrel with the two elderly inherited wives. Nyanlikawo was no longer free to do what he liked with his own men. He had to reckon with orders given by the Whites, that was a fact. Kafi could guess at what was going on, now that she had had experience of life. She would soon be thirty and she was her husband's favourite wife, because he was proud that she had borne him so many children. But one evening he summoned her to his hut before her last baby, Nalungo, had reached the stage of being able to walk. Kafi wanted to get out of it: the child would come to harm if she resumed married life again so soon. But what can a wife do if the master insists? Nyanlikawo refused to change his mind and Kafi had to obey, and began taking her turn again in the Chief's hut.

After that Kafi began her seventh pregnancy. But Nalungo, her youngest daughter, had an attack of *maya'o*[58] shortly before the confinement. She died of it. As for the baby, it only lived for three days. Kafi's sorrow was unbounded. She wore mourning, and when the mourning period was over, she refused to take her place again in her husband's hut. She felt quite certain that the death of her two babies was due to the premature demands her husband had made upon her. She persisted in her resolve right up to the death of her husband. Thus she became an old woman.[59] Her daughter was married to the head of a neighbouring village; her eldest son, who had been to school, went to the town and got married there. The youngest was already a man when his father died; he was a "cotton boy" and received money every month. He was rich. He took the place of his father and became head of the village. Kafi stayed with him; she had her own house, kept in repair by the bazingers of her son,[60] behind the house of the head man.

So it is that Kafi, former slave, is now the respected mother of a village head. Nobody ever bought a piece of elephant-flesh for her, to ensure a successful confinement;[61] she was never presented to the noble ancestors as her children were. But still, she has her hut and can be sure of getting enough to eat, and she is a woman respected for her wisdom, for she has learnt so much in the course of her life and from being the mother of so many children! Kafi never thinks of her native land, the country of the Langba, from which war once tore her away so abruptly. This is her children's country; she has lived here as wife and as mother; she knows its customs so well that she is a *yagba-ni*, a "great lady". It is here that she will die.

Anne Laurentin

2. COLONIZATION

SONGOMBI, THE WAIF PRINCESS

It would be impossible not to pick out Songombi[62] from amongst a group of women; her slow, supple walk and her proud bearing reveal her noble ancestry: she is a true princess. Facial expression is a language more natural to her than words. She is a solitary, holding soliloquy with herself, "silently turning over everything in her heart", as the Hebrew expression has it.

She has a frightened look in her eyes, but she maintains a bold, haughty attitude to other people. Ever since she was a child she has been treated by the Nzakara of her village as the daughter of the Chief, as someone free to act as she pleases. Her father Ganda, son of the great conqueror Gbandi, had his own soldiers, farmers and slaves; his concession was full of women he had received in virtue both of being the son of his father and of being a military commander.

Songombi lived in her mother's hut in the women's courtyard. They had servant-girls to fetch the water and the firewood. Songombi ate the meat killed at the hunt that was reserved for those of noble birth. She had access to the public courthouse of the village where the elders met for their debates, in which they settled disputes and discussed the marriage payments of her seniors. Yes, she was a true Bandia woman. There are some women, just as there are some ants, who are superior to others, and the former can be recognized by their adornments[63] just as the latter can by the style of the ant-heap.[64]

How could she possibly feel identified in any way with the women at the court who were commoners, or slaves sent to her father as part of his chiefly rights or as ransoms of war or of adultery. Songombi could see what sort of women they were as soon as they arrived at Ganda's court. Their clothing was scanty, they were given the food assigned to inferior beings, and they slept on the floors of the kitchens. They did the household tasks, at the beck and call of the nobly-born wives. Sometimes one of these slaves was commanded by the chief wife to go at night to the Chief's hut along with three or four other women; but one day they would leave this court, taken away by a man, either a chief or a commoner, to whom the chief had given them in exchange for another woman, or as a reward for services rendered. They were the property of their chief, a docile and mobile form of currency;

their own private joys and sorrows depended upon a network of decisions that were unpredictable and beyond their control. But their comings and goings provided plenty of distraction in the women's courtyard.

As for Songombi, her future prospects were a very different matter. She could imagine it all in the light of what happened to her seniors among the women of the royal lineage. There would be a whole series of events in connection with her marriage: her future husband would come and would admire her beauty. He would be her *bakole*, her betrothed of the blood royal, and he would seal their betrothal by giving a present to her mother and by paying visits to her. Witnesses to the contract would come to discuss the marriage payment in public. All this would serve to enhance the marriage market value of the young princess. On the departure of Nzapa,[65] an older kinswoman, from her father's household, there had been an evening of dancing. The next day she had departed, chaperoned by two experienced older women, and taking with her her slave-girl, loaded with baskets. And then her first visit, after her marriage! Songombi had hastened to come and admire the clothes given to her by her husband and the presents for her "mothers".[66] All the women were saying: "Look what her husband has given her". Everyone envied her. Hers was the destiny of a woman of wealth, of a woman of noble birth, of a woman in whose veins ran the very same blood as ran in the veins of the great chiefs of bygone days, now the ancestors worshipped at the lineage shrine. They, too, were watching over the return of their daughter.

All events of this kind were the subject of excited comment in the women's courtyard. Many of the things that were said were too complicated for Songombi to understand, and there were some things that the older women talked of in veiled terms. But everything she saw made a deep impression on her.

Songombi was ten years old when her father died. He was given a grand funeral. The *gaza* sounded, the mourners and the musicians filled the chief's court. The singers sang praises of his merits. There was no eating—nothing but dancing. In the women's courtyard a preoccupation of another kind held precedence over the preparations for the feast to come. The dancing girls had gathered round one of the huts to "honour" the two wives who had been chosen to follow the chief into the grave. Dressed in their best, with all their bracelets on, they received all the women of the village who had come to visit them, passing by in procession with cries and exclamations: they were beautiful, they were true wives! All the women envied their fate. By their side were old women who exhorted them to follow their husband and serve him well. Songombi listened to their replies: "They were happy to follow their husband and to live with him for ever; they were pleased with the celebrations made for them." No, they did not mourn their fate.

Songombi did not accompany the wives in the procession to their husband's grave, but for long after she followed them in spirit. The expression "faithful wife" was no longer an abstract term for her.

Ganda's death was to bring great changes in Songombi's life. Her father had really belonged to the older generation typified by Gbandi, the great conqueror of the time "before the Whites". But while Bangassou, who was his nephew, although senior to him in age, was a great Sultan when the Whites arrived upon the scene, his successor Labasso no longer enjoyed undisputed political power. He none the less still retained his authority in all family affairs. He arranged the matter of the succession to his deceased great-uncle, and authorized the diviners to fix the length of the period of mourning. Ganda's wives, kept in seclusion during this period, were inherited by the descendants of Gbandi, the distribution being effected according to rights of seniority. Songombi, who was approaching young womanhood at the time when the mourning period ended, went to live at the court of her uncle Labasso. She had no brothers, and her only consanguine uncle was at Bangi, so there was no one who had direct charge of the question of the marriage payment to be made for her and no one to defend her rights in the system of exchange by means of which men acquired their wives. This meant that the freedom she enjoyed already as a Bandia woman was transformed into the most complete independence.

She moved around freely in this new household, but her memories of this time in her life are hazy. All she does remember is that her uncle Labasso, being blind, was unable to have much control over the women at his court. There was much more latitude in the supervision kept over them than had been the case in former generations.[67]

But time passes quickly. Songombi was 16 when Labasso died, to be succeeded by Kelenga.[68] The death of her uncle made no difference to her carefree life of a woman sure of having her appetites satisfied, both sexual and otherwise.

She did not trouble to find out much about her rights and obligations and the reasons for them. Daily life taught her what was required of her in order to get along as best she could, and from listening to conversations between the women she learnt what was essential without having to make any special enquiries. The essential thing was, that a woman must every day prepare a meal for her man so that he should be well fed, while the man must provide her with the nourishment without which her breasts would sag, her skin dry up, and her vitality wane, so that she would no longer be able to bear any children. She could see what happened to women who no longer had any men; they became old women. There were men at the chief's court who, by pleasuring her, had provided her with the requisite nourishment and vitality. There was no need for her to hide herself away from them, because she belonged to nobody, and there was no one who would start a dispute with her lovers. Nor had she any need to seek them out, for as soon as men saw her they admired her beauty, and, aware of the freedom she enjoyed, knew they could approach her with impunity.[69]

One of Kelenga's slaves attracted her, and she got into the habit of meeting him every night, preferring him to the others. But her friend was sent to Uango to serve under a Bandia commander. She would never see him again. It was then that she met Bilima, who was to become the "man in her life". She got on better with him than with anyone else. "She loved him with her whole heart." She became pregnant. All the women in her hut and around the court gave her advice:

"Do not eat the meat of a female animal that is with child, or the spirit of fertility will kill your child, and might even turn on you; be careful about eating red meat: it has blood in it, your child might fall in the blood.* Avoid animals that are harmful to man, especially snakes of all kinds. As for fish, choose carefully which ones you eat; the *nzambo* with the bulging eyes breathes too heavily, your child would not be able to stand it."

She had heard this kind of thing said in her childhood, but had paid no attention, since it did not concern her then. And she had seen children die gasping for breath like the *nzambo;*[70] she had seen the little son of Nalogo, the woman in the hut next to hers, who had been flourishing up until the time when he began to walk, suddenly lose all his strength in a few days. His mother, weeping, had said that she had not been with a man since the day the child was born; but it was in vain that she took the bottle with his *nagili* in it, in which the very substance of his life was kept,[71] and rubbed him with it—it did not help; his limbs wasted away until he could not even stand up on his mother's knee. He lay on his mat, looking every day more and more like a little snake, and then

*See note 95.

149

he was gone. Songombi would be careful not to eat any *sumba*,[72] that born thief that might steal her child; if it took the baby into its hole, the baby would become a *sumba*.

One day Songombi was sick. Two old women—the ones who looked after mothers and their babies—came to see her and find out the cause of her sickness. What was the food that the child was rejecting? Songombi had eaten a salad made of cooked *bang-bangzia*[73] leaves, which are so watery a vegetable that the liquid oozes out on to the plate it is served on. "You should not eat it, Songombi", said the midwives, "the water of the man makes the child grow, nourishing it every night, and now the water of the bangbanzia disagrees with that of Bilima, your husband, and that is why your child rejects it; you must not give it any more of it. Be careful, Songombi, your mother did not teach you anything, you were too young when she left you, that is why you are ignorant. Listen to us, there are things you must know about: never cross a stream, neither a small one nor a big one, neither on foot nor in a canoe, or your child will be taken away by the water spirits." This rather surprised her, as she had never heard any Bandia woman mention it; but she did remember that some women would never cross a stream, and that if, when they were near the banks of one, their foot should touch the footprint of a hippopotamus or other water-animal, they would have to purify themselves. Some Bandia women had adopted this taboo, for women follow the customs of their mothers, whatever clan they themselves may belong to.

The day of the birth arrived, and the labour did not last long. When the baby saw the arms of the good midwife stretched out to receive it and encourage it to come, it immediately emerged from its mother's womb. But Songombi's baby had a nose that was raw and bleeding, and sores round its lips, and a few minutes later it gave a gasp and died.

Why had it died? The old women wondered if Songombi had had lovers, which would have disturbed the growth of the baby. But no! The baby was well-formed, fully developed—it could not have been that. Songombi was worried. She heard people talking about the anger of the ancestors without understanding what they meant; and then it all became a thing of the past. She recovered, and no one round her mentioned the death of the child any more. It would have belonged to her alone; it was not Bilima's child, because he had made no marriage payment for her; it was not her own family's child, because no one had received any marriage payment for her. She continued to live with the other women, joining her husband at night, and giving him his meals or sending them to him by a servant-girl as every self-respecting woman must do.

Some time later Songombi became pregnant again, but the child fell in the blood when it was scarcely even formed. Songombi felt very sad; she was full of thoughts that went round and round in her head: Why had this child died? What was she to do? She knew that the ba-sa-iwa, the diviners, could explain the hidden causes of events. But who would consult them for her? Who cared whether her children lived or not? Her children were the children of a "free" woman,[74] and the person who should go on her behalf to the diviner had been taken away by the Whites, so who would pay the diviner for her? Very well then, she would go herself. She took the small amount of money she had been able to save, and Bilima gave her a present for the journey and left her to set off for Mbilingi, the village where the Bandia ancestors resided. In this village there lived a man of the noble lineage of the Vu-Gbelu, called Ndunga,[75] who was, of course, a relative of hers. This man enjoyed a considerable reputation: he had learnt from the Zande the art of divining the hidden causes of events by means of the dance of the Nganga and by consulting the oracle. Songombi told Ndunga about the death of her two children. Ndunga took some so[76] powder in order to consult the oracle and got ready to ask it questions. At the first mention of the word "ancestors" the powder flew away: the reply was in the affirmative. It was they who had killed the children. Songombi, full of anxiety and astonishment, listened to the questions Ndunga put to them to find out the reasons for their anger; she was not aware of having done anything to bring their curse upon her.

"No marriage payment has been made for you?"

"No. I am and remain a daughter of the Bandia, and Bilima is my fiancé, but he has never made any marriage payment for me."

"And your mother?"

Thus the dialogue between Songombi and Ndunga went on, with the diviner patiently trying to find out if any departure from custom had occurred such as might have angered the ancestors; and what Songombi heard was the very voice of the oracle, speaking through the mouth of Ndunga. The consultation revealed that Songombi had transgressed by failing to comply with a custom about which she had been, until then, completely ignorant: she had not offered food to the ancestors in order to ensure their granting her fertility, and the ancestor Mbilinga, her great grandfather, was angry about this. Songombi had not known; she had, until then, thought that serving the ancestral spirits was a duty reserved for men, since women—except the women consecrated to the ancestors —never went near their dwelling.[77] Ndunga made scathing comments about flighty women and told her that Mbilinga was awaiting his offering of food. Two days later, aided by a more experienced cousin called Naketo, the daughter of Mada Gbandi, Songombi prepared the *miya*, a dish concocted of fish which she herself had caught in a stream, made up with sesame. They brought the dish to the guardian and handed it over to him in front of his hut together with a small offering for himself. Ndunga would take the offering to the ancestors and would invoke the power of Mbilinga while placing it in one of the fertility jars at the foot of the altar.

Songombi accepted the words of the oracle, but from this memorable day on, her naturally carefree spirit was clouded over by disturbing thoughts which were never again to leave her: misfortunes occurred, and there was nothing one could do to prevent them.[78] Expecting now, but expecting in vain to become pregnant again, she kept feeling amazed that fertility had not been granted her. Would the anger of the ancestors go on for ever against a woman for whom no marriage payment had been made? Had she infringed a taboo? Would Ndunga allow the curse to go on hovering over her because she had not had enough money to pay him with? She could only draw her own conclusions. Later, women who had attended Protestant baptismal classes would tell her that it was Nzapa[79] who did not want her to have a child, and Nzapa was to become for her the final explanation—another of the many explanations that women have to accept without knowing the reason why.

Songombi, now older and wiser, returned to Bilimi. He was worried by what she told him. The publicity she would receive from having consulted the oracle would draw the attention of the Bandia upon Songombi, and one or other of them might suddenly claim rights over this woman of noble birth. He, unable to escape from his former status of slave, was in danger of becoming involved in the misfortunes that might subsequently fall upon this "great lady". He had it drummed into him that his former status was in no way cancelled by the fact that, since the accession of Bazanga, he had been given the position of a "capita", which meant that he was overseer of a group of workers, whose job it was to make sure that the quality of rubber collected was up to the standard required by the Whites. Some elders came to see him: he must make a marriage payment for Songombi. He promised to take the matter into consideration, but his new job entailed moving about a great deal, and Songombi left the hut she shared in the women's courtyard and followed him to the new workers' village. If it had not been for this, the question of the marriage payment would have been settled. Songombi found that Bilimi no longer behaved to her in the same way as "before". But times change and so do people. It is in youth that with us (as with many other people) happiness is to be found.

Bilima's job took him to the Belgian Congo, in the vicinity of Mondo. Songombi settled there; but the memory of unhappy events stayed with her. No children for her. Who was it that was hindering her from becoming pregnant? Bilima decided to come to her aid. Full of the dignity of his new position, he was going to act like the leader he had become; he was going to put an end to the curse. He took his lance and made his departure in secret along the road which led to the ancestral shrine. Songombi thought: "He is going to fight them!" When he got to the edge of the enclosure he stuck his lance in the ground and pronounced the ritual words:

"O you who are harming the fertility of my wife, stop harming her, I command you by the power of my words."

It was a "vow". It had the intangible efficacity of the words uttered by chiefs, as mighty as the strength that lay in their arms, enough to make slaves and enemies tremble.

Bilima returned. Yes, he had defeated the ancestors. And life went back to normal.

Songombi was often left alone, and what can a lone woman do with herself? "She plunges about like a carp, she flies around like a bird. To keep her, take your bow when she is in the hollow of a rock[80] or perched on the top of a tree and draw (to pin her there)!" Songombi was a bird. Among the men in the village who desired her she had a regular lover who was a son of Wuza.[81] Songombi once more became pregnant. When she again had a miscarriage, no one could be in any doubt as to the cause: the child had been sacrificed to the struggle between the two men. Songombi was free, as a Bandia woman, to have a lover; but as a mother, she must only allow one father to nourish her child, or else she was in danger of killing it. She fell seriously ill. A debilitating fever and fits of trembling kept her confined to bed. It was a month before she was able to get up again, and even then she was still very weak. Was Bilima angry about the devotion of the son of Wuza? Was he afraid of the powerful spells of Yanda? Whatever the reason, he brought a case before the judge at Mondo, accusing the man of having killed his son during his wife's pregnancy "because of his *Yongo Boli*" (adulterous affair), and of having put the young mother in mortal danger. The case being presented in this way, there could be no question as to the guilt of the lover, and the judge sentenced him to pay 100 francs damages and costs, which, in 1935, was equivalent to quite a large marriage payment.

Songombi slowly recovered and continued her life with Bilimi, but before very long, on going one day to dig up *gbobi*[82] at the edge of the forest, she got bitten by a snake. Her leg swelled up and went black. She nearly died, and the attentions of several *ba dondoli* were required to save her from death. Bilimi was worried. This was the second time that Songombi had been in danger of dying. Bilimi's brother came, still somewhat heated after the dispute with the son of Wuza. During Songombi's illness he had already brought home to him the trouble he was likely to have if Songombi should die in his house—a noblewoman, a woman who did not belong to him. "She is a princess. It will cost you too much if she dies in your house."

So Bilimi decided to send Songombi away, and told her his decision. Songombi understood the point of what the two brothers were saying. She felt sad about Bilimi—she would have liked to stay with him for the rest of her life; she wanted him. She knew that the brother's advice went against their feelings for each other, but, Bandia woman as she was, she had to submit to a decision of this kind. Songombi would be alone now, an unmarried woman of 40, still exceptionally young-looking and attractive.

She returned to her family, staying with the head of the village of Balama who was a cousin of hers. Was she not related to all the heads of villages? There was no more collecting of rubber now, everyone was cultivating "government" cotton, women as well as men. Songombi took her place among the village head's family, shared a hut with two other women, was given her own field to cultivate. A farmer, Sayo, saw her and was struck by her. He stayed for two or three days, and said he would come back. It was out of the question for Songombi to go away with him. She was a great lady and Sayo had a wife for whom he had given marriage payment, a simple village woman. For two years the man returned for a few days every week, bringing presents, money, cloth; but Songombi longed for the old days. Now the men laughed at her in the fields and in the village. They knocked at her door, stayed for one night, and then went off. And Sayo got tired of her. He brought no more presents. She became annoyed. He left her, after giving her a last "present". Ageing now, Songombi is in need of gowns, of money to buy food at the market, and she gets tired cultivating her field. It is a small field of cotton that she works in, but what man other than a fiancé will clear it of weeds for her? She will have to ask help from the head of the family, and Songombi does not like doing that; she prefers to wait for things to be done for her, as used to happen when she was young. She goes to and fro between the village and the town, to the market, visiting cousins and nephews, for all the village heads belong to the Bandia family as she does. The "fiancés" are becoming tiresome; even the presents they leave her when they say goodbye do not please her any more. They are typical of Nzakara, vulgar people who even as far as that is concerned do not treat her as a princess should be treated. They try to make bargains with her, she can hear them laughing at her outside her hut. So then she will go off to pay a visit to a relative. It was at Nandu's, who is slightly older than she is, that I first saw her. Nandu is one of the village midwives. Her household is well provided for, for families bring presents after the birth of a child, and children when they grow up bring her the basket, filled with supplies, that have contained their belongings since the day they were born, as a way of expressing their gratitude to the good midwife. There is always something to eat at Nandu's and water is brought to the door of her hut. Songombi has just seen her cousin, Nzapa, passing proudly by on her young husband's arm. She was showing herself off as a properly married woman, and although the young man may repudiate her later, today he is preening himself like a young cock, proud of all the experience he is acquiring by knowing this fine lady.

Yes, the young people do nothing but laugh. And what nourishment will laughing bring?

Songombi's destiny will not be the same as that of either of her two blood relations, Nandu and Nzapa. She goes every day to fetch her own water and search for firewood. "You see, I have no children with whom I can end my days in peace and who will fetch my water for me." She busies herself with a little gardening and with going to the market. She does not enquire into the cause of things: that is the diviner's job. But, when the day seems long and the walk home tiring, all Songombi need do is to start thinking of the past, and a light comes into her eyes as she remembers the days of her youth.

Third period

WOMEN OF TODAY

NAKPANGI

Nakpangi, now a young woman of 26, was born at Ligandunga, in the north.

Anne Laurentin

It has long been a primitive part of the country. "In the old days", before the Whites, it was a frontier post to which the Sultan had sent his nephew to be in command of the troops. There was a constant need to be on the defence against neighbouring tribes, and to make war, not only to obtain supplies of ivory, but even more to obtain supplies of women for the Sultan's messengers to collect. The taxes imposed by the Sultan scarcely allowed any great accumulation of wealth on the part of the chiefs, and they had to make stern use of their authority in order to be able to maintain a number of women at their own courts. For, at times when the cattle were lean, their own supply of women sometimes had to be drawn upon in order to send the Sultan his quota, or to pacify warriors with claims to make by presenting them with a gift of women. Memories are still preserved of murderous brawls over wives being claimed, snatched or coveted. Life was hard; but it had to be lived.

Nakpangi has had no experience of the epic days of old. At the time when she was born, war was a thing of the past in her village. Women were bought with money and were no longer a currency to be fought for or exchanged. But she used to listen with passionate interest to the stories of the past, and they remain vivid for her today.

She was a lively child, full of curiosity. She used to follow her mother and her aunts to the spring. Behind the hut, a track made a straight line through the forest. The women would descend the hill carrying a light pot on their heads, and go down to the stream, where they would bathe, chat, draw water. The track fascinated her. Near where it began she could descry the little straw house that was looked after by a Togbo woman for her Gassuluma.[83] She knew that the woman was old, but she was not looked up to in the same way as were certain women of noble birth, respected for their wisdom, for this woman was a former slave. She did not own enough cloth to hide her ungainly body, and the gown she wore was too short, so that her great frog's belly hung down over it. It made Nakpangi laugh to see her; but she hid when imitating the way she leant upon her stick, for when the old woman raised her head you could see two bright eyes that made you feel afraid. One day, this woman paid a visit to her mother, and told her that she ought to invoke her Gassuluma, for if she did he would give her more children, the father of the house would kill plenty of game, the sick would have the spell on them cast off and would recover. But her mother had not given her anything to eat. Some evenings the woman would start dancing: you could see her making frantic movements as her Gassuluma took possession of her, and she spoke in a hoarse voice. The men would listen to her words, even although they made jokes about her in the daytime. Nakpangi had seen women following her along the entry to the track. They left money and a bowl of peanut paste at the little house, placing them on the very plate from which Gassuluma himself would eat. Sometimes Nakpangi would come with some other children to play round this hut. They would creep forward quietly towards it and then run away, afraid of being caught by the guardian spirit.

Quite different from this were the big dances that were held, further away, round Mada's little hut. There, in a great clearing in the bush, the whole village would assemble round a fire. There was dancing, and *Soko*[84] was invoked and a good kill requested; and the next day the men would set off shouldering their great nets, with their dogs following, bells jingling round their necks. This was a great day. Her mother and the co-wife would clear the scrub from their "garden" in order to while away the time, and then would prepare a dish of millet or of cassava as they did every day. While waiting for the messenger to come with the first news, they would forestall him with boastful guesses about the bag that would be brought back. The village would be quite empty, and then all of a sudden a man would arrive, the bells of the dogs and men's voices would be heard. There would be tremendous celebrations if they had brought back an antelope, some wild pigs, or even some pidgeons and rats—the guardian spirit of the hunt had favoured them. In the evening, after everyone had retired to his hut, how good it was to lie by her mother's side; and she snuggled up to her as she heard vague noises, cracklings, heavy breathings round the hut, in case the sorcerer or his spell might find her out.

During the day there were two poles of attraction: the road, and the Chief's court. Strangers would go through the village, either on their way to the town of Bakuma, or else bringing back news from there. The Chief's house overlooked the road. From his official residence he could spy out arrivals and challenge passers-by, adding some amusing remarks to the traditional "good-day". It would make Nakpangi laugh. She was often in his courtyard, without feeling any shyness about being there, and saw the visitors that came. There were always children about, and two of them, one of whom was a nephew of the Chief called Sango, were only there on a visit. They spoke about the town and about school, and played at making drawings on the earth of the courtyard with the other boys. This was not a game that girls took part in, so she watched them from a distance. Nakpangi could also see her father, seated on a chair beside the Chief; he was one of his intimates, but not a member of his family.

The day came when her mother told her that she must stay by her side, fetching water and helping with the cooking, and must not play with the other children any more. Her breasts were filling out, and the men of the village said that she was a fine young woman. She knew that this was true, and she laughed. Her mother told her that she must behave herself with the boys, and must not go around with them. A woman's life was beginning for her. She had already seen men coming to the village asking for a bride from one of their relatives. And sometimes they came to take back a woman, as had happened with the co-wife of her father. Two relatives of this woman had come to the Chief's court at a time when she was away visiting relatives in a nearby village. Later her father had gone off too—men's affairs always meant that they had to move about all the time. On his return, she had heard that he had been to see the "district chief". He had been to see him several times,[85] but the woman had never returned. After this she knew that women do not belong to their huts as trees do to the forest: they can go away to other houses.

Nakpangi was an adolescent when the district chief paid a visit to the village. He was a son of the great Sultan. His visit was an event for everyone. He had come to announce the amount of tax to be paid, to make claims for his own share, and to carry out government orders regarding cotton crops and roads. There were few young people in the village, but all of them instinctively crowded around for this great occasion; and Nakpangi was not one to stay hanging around in the background. The man was a fine fellow. He had a hat, and many clothes which covered him up completely like the Whites. He looked at them all and asked them to come nearer. They laughed without quite knowing why. One day, Nakpangi's father told her that this *benge*[86] wanted to have her as his wife. Her mother showed her the gown and the little hair comb that they had received from him. The gown was new—she would keep it for special occasions. As for the comb, she had hidden it between two bundles of the thatch. Now Nakpangi was a *nakobe*, a woman specially reserved for this chief. She had seen the pledges of her marriage, and the little comb would remain hidden in the thatch as long as the two families were *kobe*.[87] Now that her family was connected with the chiefs—that is to say, with royalty—Nakpangi felt proud yet disturbed. She knew already that she, too, would have to leave the house; yet in spite of the fact that she knew she would be going to the house of a chief, and that it would be a great house with many wives and plenty of food, the strangeness of it all left her with a queer feeling of sadness when she thought about it.

But soon she was to experience a still greater upset: her mother died, and after that her father moved from their house to a "business house" in Uango, a much bigger town than their neighbouring one had been. To get there required a walk of several days, with their baggage and poultry carried on their heads. They went through village after village, and everywhere people asked if they were going far, and if so, why? At last they arrived. Uango was a big town. Nakpangi would see no more the path to the spring, and the forest that had lain at the edge of the village. Her father's new house was small. But there were so many people, all strangers . . . She was happy; her father allowed her more freedom. Had she not become a woman? She "knew about life", for, just before their departure, the Chief had met her one day on the way to the stream, and he had gently taken her aside and taught her what it was to be a woman. In Uango she could talk freely about these things to her father's oldest daughter, Nataki.

Nataki[88] had left home several years before to marry a man belonging to a village some distance away. She told Nakpangi about her brief marriage: how her father had come to seek her out there; how he had brought her before the chief who, sitting in judgment, had said: Why had the husband not given his sister as a wife?[89] The husband had promised to do so. The father, for his part, had given his daughter, and now the husband had refused to give him a wife in exchange. The chief[90] had scolded[91] her father. He said that since the Whites had come, women were no longer exchanged; now everyone had to pay. If he wanted this wife, he must have money to pay for her.

Nakpangi began to realize that money was needed for everything. It was needed if one wanted to buy cloth or the various articles displayed in the shops which she gazed at in vain. Her father brought money from Ligandunga, when he came back from his journeys to the "district". After the co-wife had gone, he brought back some because the woman would not come back any more.[92] He had visited the diviner several times, and was full of grumbles when he did so. All these things were tied up with each other. She felt rather sad when listening to Nataki's tales, but Nataki herself was never sad. She made a joke of it all: "It's much better not to have a husband who grumbles at you every time you go about with the boys!" Nakpangi got on well with her. It was fun to go together to the spring, to receive compliments from the men for their good looks on the way, to steal off into the bush with one of them, and come back to the spring laughing merrily like two good girls. For a while, the "present"[93] received was kept hidden, until one day one went walking through the village with a fine red handkerchief carefully arranged round one's head.

But that did not last long. The district chief sent his messenger. As Nakpangi was a real woman now, her father could not keep her any longer. She took the road back to the village accompanied by two of her aunts loaded with baskets of poultry and of smoked game, and took with her some plates and a brand new gown which her father had taken from one of the shelves in the shop, so that she should look her best in her husband's house. Everyone who saw her passing by along the road knew that this was no woman of low birth going to seek her husband. Her aunts told her that she must be good once she was with her husband and not go running after other men, or her husband would scold her, and a well-born woman does not behave like that.

Her husband was a chief. He owned a big square hut which was where he lived. She had to wait for him to call her to his hut and must always be ready to go. The women told her the story of Nalogo, who is now dead, the one who hid herself from her husband, one evening, in order to go and meet her lover; her husband had known about it. It had been a big affair because her husband was a chief, and the lover had been brought to trial and executed. Nakpangi knew this story. The *kundi* players[94] used to sing about the plaints of the lover and the cruelty of the chief. Everyone knew that lovers were always reproaching women for not being a Nalogo; but now she listened to the counsels of wisdom and was moved thinking about her new duties.

Nakpangi does not remember very much about the district chief's house. The first few days were full of excitement with the arrival of the three travellers. A week later the aunts set off on their return journey, with a handsome present and provisions for the road. Each of them had the right to be given a gown—it was really worth while acting as companion to the wife of a chief, because chiefs give such handsome presents. Nakpangi shared a hut belonging to one of the wives, who was the mother of a young baby. She did not yet have her own place.

Nakpangi became pregnant, and the co-wife told her not to eat either monkey or red meat. But this woman was a Langba, a slave; how could she know the customs of Nakpangi's mother? There was no woman in the village belonging to her mother's family, and she did not know who to talk to about it. The child "fell in the blood".[95] Yet she had followed all the advice given to her. The

Nzakara Women

ancestors of her husband had been called upon to bless her with fertility. She remembered this ceremony. It was shortly after she had entered the chief's household. The chief wife had told her to prepare a meal, for the time had come for her to be presented to the ancestors, so that she should not be a slave. She had caught several fish and had cooked them with sesame. An old man, seated next to her husband, was looking at her. She had seen him several times in the village, but had taken him for an ordinary farmer; she did not know that he was the custodian of the altar. A maternal cousin had been chosen to accompany her. The men all rose at the same time as her husband, and she followed them, with beating heart, to a dense thicket. The men entered into the presence of the ancestors, while she waited at the edge of the grove. They invoked the ancestors in a loud voice, and then came out again and returned to her. She had to confess the names of the lovers she had had before coming to live with her husband, for that might anger the ancestors. The chief wife had already explained about it to her, and she was prepared for it. She had searched her memory for the faces of the men and for their names; one by one she named them to her cousin; when she could not remember any more, she told him the names of their clans: Banda, Ngezo, etc. . . . . The cousin repeated the names to the old man who, at each name, broke a wooden stick. By the time he was finished, he had quite a large bundle in his hands. Then she handed over the food she had prepared to the men, who disappeared into the sacred grove. On their return, they assured her that the ancestors had accepted her as the wife of their son, and that they would protect her. The old custodian had added with a smile: "If you don't run after other fellows, no harm will come to you!"

And yet, harm had come: her baby had died when it was scarcely formed in her, with tiny feet and tiny hands. This child had begun to grow from the time she had been with her husband, this child that had been waiting so many years within her belly! She lay on her bed and wept. The chief wife came and rubbed her with plants she had prepared. Very soon she was able to get up again and eat.

Shortly after this, she returned to her family on her first visit. Her father said that the death had made a bad impression on them, that it had "insulted" his brothers; she was to go with him up the hill to the big white houses of the governor. It was the first time she had been there. The men on duty smiled at her and said a few words, and she felt less frightened. They were taken into a very big room. The walls were white: it was the house of the White Man.

Her father was very cross. Then the governor was cross too. The interpreter slowly and faithfully explained the big questions of the White Man: he wanted to know if she had been happy down there and if the baby had died down there. The next time, two of her father's brothers went with them. Her husband, the district chief, was there, but she knew that her father did not want her to return to him. At the governor's, she understood well enough the complaints of her uncles that they had not received their presents and they objected to being insulted, and the claims of her father and of her husband and the discussion about the death of the child and other difficult matters. The governor had said that Nakpangi was too young and that she should return to her father.[96] Her father had paid back 22,000 francs: 18,000 francs for the marriage payment and 4,000 francs for the case. Her husband had taken the money, he had a down-hearted look, although from time to time his eyes flashed with anger in a way that was familiar to her. She returned home feeling sad. But she was a topic of conversation in the shop, and that made her forget about things. And then, being a free woman, she could pay visits to her family in various villages. But when she was at home, her father did not like it if she joked with a man. He was more severe than anyone else, he really was.

Nataki, whom she had taken up with again, took her to the mission. They learnt songs and did dressmaking with good cloth. Her father had had to give way to her when she wanted to go to the mission like the other women. Down there, the Sisters told stories about Nzapa,[97] about the sky being full of white angels, about the devil. They said that they must not go with men, that they would catch illnesses; and sometimes they scolded them, saying that they must not go and see guardian spirits and make offerings to them; and they told stories about other women with quite a new slant to them. They also said that God was good, that it was He who would give them children, and that they must not believe in sorcerers and other magicians, even if they threatened them with death, for they only said that to get money.

One day Nakpangi met Sango again—a boy from her village, belonging to the chief's family. They had played together at Ligandunga. She was amazed: "You are dressed like the Whites, Sango! You have got their clothes on!"[98] They spoke together for a while. She liked Sango. His ways were different from the village people's.[99] He was a chauffeur and actually drove the *kutu*[100] belonging to the Whites.

Sango was a great man; she would very much like him to be her husband. Even when they were children he had said to her: "You are my *ba^nlum'e*".[101] She met Sango again at the mission. She had had her hair done by Nataki, and had put on her best gown for his benefit. He would go and speak to her father about the marriage payment, because he earned a lot of money. Sango spoke well. He said nice things: that he had set his heart on her, that he would love her always; and he had shown her the banknotes he had in his pocket, lots of banknotes. And he did come to her father's house, and waited, leaning with his elbows on the wooden counter as if he had come to buy something, and then they went into the hut. She had hidden herself, but her aunt and her father's new wife brought the news: the two women were to receive a kid and a gown to celebrate the betrothal. Sango told her that he was going to buy the marriage paper at the governor's. One evening he brought a lance and a hunting net. It was funny to see Sango carrying these things dressed in his White's clothing. It was evening. He brought them to her father, and it was then that she learnt that this was the *ma^nla-za^nla*,[102] the present for her father's ancestors. They would have to be taken to her uncle, the custodian, who lived a day's walk away. It was agreed that Sango would take them in the governor's car the next time he took him to Bangassu.[103] She would not be there to see this done; it is not a matter for women.

When the Sisters learnt that Sango was going to take Nakpangi, they asked if he had learnt the "book"[104] from the Fathers. She replied that Sango had learnt the *Nzapa ti Madame*.[105] She was advised to take him to the Fathers and not to go, like those who did not know about Nzapa, to the "devils", even for her marriage. She spoke about it to Nataki, who explained to her that she must not take food to Sango's ancestors as she had done at her first marriage. Nzapa would not be pleased, and would punish her, and not give her any children.

And so Nakpangi was once again going to leave her father's house. Sango had rented a small hut at Uango. He had bought a lot of things, among them a bed with a mattress and a mosquito net . . . The aunt who came with them gave cries of astonishment at that! It was not a long journey like for the first marriage, and this time she would feel no anxiety when she arrived, for she loved Sango with all her heart, she knew how to make well-cooked meals for him, and she would have a small field for growing cassava near by. She would go in the White Man's car and Sango would give her presents.

It was two years later that Nakpangi and Sango came to live at Bangassu. Sango was out of work, "the White Man had gone", but there was still money in the house. He was waiting for new Whites to arrive in the town and would then offer his services, like so many others. Sango had built a small house. The head of the ward was a member of his family, like all the other heads. He had found a field for them where they could grow government cotton, and where Nakpangi would plant cassava, taros and peanuts. Sango did not give her much money for buying food, and anyway it was pleasant to earn a little money by selling a few things at the market. She brought back huge bundles of firewood—more than was needed for the cooking—when she returned from the field. They had many neighbours, as in Uango, and Nakpangi learnt all about this one and that one when they talked together in the courtyard.

They live a peaceful life, the eventless life of happy people. The only thing that troubles them is that Nakpangi has no children. A neighbour had had one after being given injections. Nakpangi went to the hospital so that she, too, could have the injection that gave children, but they gave her "quinine".[106] They had told her to bring Sango, but he was away at the time, and then there was the cotton harvest. The neighbours often mentioned *Sa gbeya*, the little beast in women's insides that bites, gnaws, scratches and cries out. One woman had given her some herbs for a small payment. Since then, she has not gone to the ancestors any more, nor to any guardian spirits where many people leave so much money. But nothing does any good.

Nakpangi is respected in the district. In a few years she will no doubt have become a *Yagba-ni*, a woman "remarkable" for the wise advice she gives.

NABATE, WIFE OF THE ANCESTORS

Nabate lives in a small hamlet belonging to the village of Z., which is on the Great East road leading to French Sudan.[107]

On the first day of my visit to the village, Nabate came, like the other women, to the door of the stranger's hut to see her and receive her medicines.[108] But, apart from this first meeting, there was nothing by which to distinguish her from the crowd sitting about in small groups. She did not speak, did not complain of anything, and did not come again. I had scarcely noticed her quiet smile, and I should have remained ignorant about her history, the troubles with her fiancé and the curse of the ancestors cast on her children, if it had not been unveiled for me by chance one day when I went off looking for oranges.

A man who was working on the road invited me in to his hut.

He was an "elder". The courtyard of his house was screened from inquisitive eyes by a hedge of trees. The house, a square one, flanked by two round huts, occupied the centre of the courtyard, like the house of a chief of former times, surrounded by his women. I was too recent a visitor to this part of the world to be able to assess to what degree this man's ways were a survival of the past.

Kpata, for that was his name, received me in the manner of a host anxious to comply with custom. He had come to this district as a young man to help his older brother Zallo[109] in his duties as chief. Now he had two elderly wives, who were sitting some distance away shelling peanuts. The older one was a wife he had inherited from Zallo, the other he had obtained by means of exchange. Beside them there worked a young woman, Nabate, who was the latter's niece, and whose mother Nagala had run away a long time ago.

Kpata told me right away the story of Nabate to explain the presence of this niece, not directly related to him, in his house.[110]

Nagala had been a slave of Zallo's whom he had given as concubine[111] to a man of the same tribe as hers, called Duguma, who was also a slave. Duguma's sister was one of Zallo's slave-wives.[112] Since then, many things had happened to the woman I had just seen in Kpata's courtyard. It was the commands of the Whites that really changed things. It was the time when they decreed that all wives, even if they were slaves, must have bridewealth paid for them. So Duguma came to claim bridewealth for his sister from Zallo. The case lasted so long that Zallo died before the dispute was settled. Kpata, the elder I had met, inherited this wife from his older brother. After that it was from him that Duguma claimed an additional sum for the marriage payment, for his claims grew in keeping with the monetary inflation. Kpata paid him 300 francs, but that still did not put an end to the affair, for Duguma now demanded, according to the new customs, to be paid for his sister's three children who had died in Zallo's house. He rested his claim on the revelations of the diviners of his lineage, who said that the three children had been killed by the ancestors in anger that their daughter had had no bridewealth.[113] This case kept dragging on, because the judge was always calling upon new witnesses.

When the suit was dismissed, Duguma, who was at the same time indicted for a recent adultery offence, fled to the other side of the river.[114] There he fell ill. Meanwhile his slave-wife Nagala found herself abandoned, and pregnant. She took refuge in Kpata's house, one of his wives—Duguma's sister—being the only relative she had. Kpata welcomed her, and so it was that the little Nabate was born there.

But he was worried, for Duguma, ill and exiled on the other side of the river, might bring a case about Nagala and her child. Kpata, carrying Nabate in his arms, went across the river. The other man met him with reproaches. Thoroughly disgruntled since his brothers had failed to support him in his case, he told Kpata a dream he had had about Nabate:

"The great ancestor Gambo appeared to me in my sleep. He wanted his daughter Nabate to be consecrated as one of his wives. The illness which he sent me was a sign of his intention. That is why she will be called Da Gambo."[115]

Who can question the words of the ancestors? They have power over life and death, over illness and fertility. If Nabate was not offered to Gambo according to his command, Duguma might die beneath their anger, and most probably Kpata as well. So the two men went at once to Gambo's shrine which was not far from the village. They placed Nabate on the altar and presented her to Gambo with the correct ritual invocations. To seal the agreement, they had brought a chicken. From then on, Nabate was the legitimate spouse of Gambo and must be so for the rest of her life. No man could claim her from the ancestor, and in any case, she could not have bridewealth paid for her.

"Ah!" concluded Kpata, "it served the brothers right for not having helped Nabate's father out of his difficulties nor succoured him in his premature old age. They will never receive any bridewealth when the girl gets married."

Nabate was brought up in Kpata's house by her mother and her two aunts. The only child in the house, she became very spoilt. She grew up full of vigour,[116] because Kpata, respectful of custom, made sure that Nabate carried out the duties of a Da Gambo, the spouse of Gambo. Several times during her childhood he presented an offering for her on Gambo's altar on the first day of the new moon.

When Nabate was four, her mother ran away with a fiancé. She was not bound in any way to Kpata's household, since he had given no bridewealth for her. Nabate lived with her two aunts, and Kpata loved her like a daughter. When she began to shows signs of approaching marriageable age, Kpata took her to the village of Gbanga, a day's journey away. There was a centre of the Gambo cult there, presided over by his chief wife, a woman who got possessed by Gambo. When the fit came upon her it shook her violently and threw her down upon the ground; then she transmitted the words of the great ancestor. Many people came to listen to the words of Gambo or to make a vow at his altar so as to have one of their wishes fulfilled. Round the house of this Da Gambo were several huts for the other wives of Gambo and for the guards, the "bazingers",[117] of Gambo. All the wives were under the authority of the chief wife, the great Da Gambo, as in the court-yard of a chief in the old days. The young ones, such as Nabate, learnt there their duties as a wife and as a woman. She had to stay there for several years.

Nabate met there another young girl of the same age, Datingi, who was also a Da Gambo. They went through their lengthy period of apprenticeship together in the courtyard of Da Gambo No. 1. They listened to the invocations she made in the name of the visitors, and the judgments she pronounced in the name of her spouse. They accompanied her to put offerings on the altar at each new moon. Nabate could not help feeling afraid when she approached the shrine. She listened with respect to the invocations addressed to her spouse to obtain his favour. Everything which at first seemed new and strange became familiar.

She also learnt from the lips of Da Gambo about her future duties as a woman. Soon she would be of an age to "learn about life". The first eight days of each moon would be kept entirely for her ancestral spouse; she would bring him his food just as any woman does for her husband.

She also saw every day the other wives of Gambo, older than she, and one day she would be like them. She too would have her ba^{n}lum'e.[118] A young woman requires the presence of a man. She might accept anyone she liked, but he would not be her husband because he would not give any bridewealth for her. Her husband was Gambo. She was attractive, and would soon find a ba^{n}lum'e among the young men of the village who were still too young to be able to pay bridewealth for a wife.

This was what happened when she came back to Kpata's house. Meso, a young bazinger of the chief, saw her on her return, now a woman, and met her several times on the tracks through the bush leading to the fields or to the spring. This was a well-known place for meetings between the young people. Nabate was slow and slack in her work in the fields, but she was passionate. They were happy with each other. She became pregnant several months after they met.

This event was to change Nabate's life. Until then, she had always lived in Kpata's house but had never been visited by Meso there, as it was always easy to find a meeting place. Kpata knew that she was supplying the meals for a fiancé and knew it was Meso. He was not very pleased about it, and even thought that Meso was a young man of common ancestry, who had no respect for old people or for tradition. But what could he do? Nabate was free. But when he saw that she was pregnant, he for the first time had his say: Meso must take Nabate to live with him during her pregnancy. Was he not the father who supplied the nourishment for Gambo's child? He must continue to see to it that the baby grew properly until the time came when it began moving in its mother's womb; she must sleep with him so that he could nourish her;[119] and he must not forget to take a chicken and offer it to Gambo so that he would grant fertility to Nabate. Meso took Nabate into his hut, but gave a disguised refusal about performing his duties to Gambo: "I have no money to buy a chicken; I have no time to go to Gambo's." Nabate listened, silent as always. What could she do about it if he refused to go to Gambo's? He would go later. That calmed Kpata a little. Nabate lived from one day to the next, working in the fields, cooking for her unofficial husband, who became fickle.

But when the child was born, it was dead. Kpata was full of sorrow. Why had Meso not made the offering to Gambo?

Nabate stayed in the hut of her *ba*^{n}*lum'e* and soon became pregnant again. She knew now that Meso would never go to Gambo's. Since the discussion they had had before, Kpata had recalled to Meso his duties and had scolded him; Meso had replied that he did not give a damn; he would take Nabate to the town so that she could receive the injection that gives children. Nabate left to stay with Meso's sister who lived in the town. It was the first time she had been there. Everything was new to her. Nabate accompanied the woman to market and helped her with the cooking. Sometimes Meso came on a visit. She seldom went to the hospital, but when the pains began the family took her there. The child was born, and cried. But Nabate felt uneasy and lost in these new surroundings, among these women who kept grumbling at her to keep quiet. The placenta of the newborn baby had been thrown away,[120] she did not know where. But when she saw that they were throwing away the umbilical cord on the eighth day, when the baby became detached from it, she asked that it should be kept. The frail little creature was given injections. Yes, she felt uneasy. One evening she wrapped the baby in a gown and ran away. She disappeared into the bush behind the hospital and went back to Meso and his sister.

But two days later the baby began gasping for breath. Its breathing was so difficult that you could sense what a fragile hold it had on life. She would have to return to the hospital. Nabate and Meso were scolded. They were told that it would be their fault if the baby died. Meso, in spite of protestations, was pushed out. Nabate stayed on by herself. By the evening, the baby was dead.

When Meso came back to fetch Nabate he was scolded again, which he did not like. He was told to bring Nabate back for injections if they wanted to have a child.[121] She received two, and then did not come back: there was the small cotton-field to cultivate, and the usual round of work to be done every day. So the time passed until once again Nabate became pregnant. She was in good health. She had never been back at Gambo's shrine and scarcely ever bothered about her duties towards her real husband. The village midwife openly disapproved of Nabate and her unofficial husband. As for Meso, he objected more and more to having reproaches cast at him, and got angry when the midwife took him to task or when at night Nabate grumbled because he had been with other women. As soon as the baby was born he would leave her, and he made no secret about it.

The baby was born. It was dead, its face already wounded in its mother's womb.[122] Once again Gambo had revealed himself. Nabate was no longer astonished. Kpata dug a second grave beside the one where Nabate's first baby was buried.[123]

Meso left Nabate. But he had no money to pay bridewealth for a wife. Six months later he had another "wife of the ancestors" in his house, the young Datingi whom Nabate had known during her stay at the Da Gambo centre at Gbanga.

Nabate returned to Kpata, but she was soon sought out by Samba, another young "bazinger" of the chief.[124] Samba was full of fun, and always ready to amuse himself. He got on well with Nabate who could cook well and who also enjoyed joking and amusing herself.

When a new pregnancy began, there was a certain amount of excitement over it in the village. Everyone knew that Nabate's children had been killed by Gambo and that Samba had not, any more than Meso, taken a chicken to Gambo to ask him to look with favour on Nabate's having a child. Would this child be alive? Or would Gambo act in Samba's time as he had done in Meso's?

The child was stillborn;[125] and the year following came another, also stillborn. Kpata was in despair: "What is to be done? If Samba is playing the fool, that is his affair. But if only he would understand about Gambo and take him an offering which would reestablish Nabate's good name in the eyes of her ancestral spouse, the children would live. What else can be done, you can't bring a case against the dead . . ."

Anne Laurentin

This was the story Kpata told me; it was only later that Meso and Samba added theirs. Nabate herself never said much. Her smile was always ambiguous. She knew that she was not the same as other women and kept herself to herself; she was hardly ever seen in the village. Either she would be out in the fields or at the stacks, or else in Samba's hut. The matter seemed to be shelved. It was only upon the insistence of the nurse that Kpata came one day to my hut with a request: he wanted Nabate to come and receive the injections which give children.

"But why does she not come herself?" An evasive gesture from Kpata, then a sigh, then: "She did come once . . ."

Nabate did not like waiting among all the other women, so she had never come back. Kpata brought her, and as usual, she stayed apart from the others. When called in, she answered questions with that extraordinary "Mmmuh" which, with a scarcely perceptible shade of difference in intonation, means either yes or no. The new pregnancy was several months gone. Treatment was urgent. (There is an idea of the Whites for you!) With her usual smile she agreed to take the treatment. Every time I came to the village she kept her word, arrived, seated herself behind the hut, away from everyone, not saying a word, and after the treatment left immediately. Kpata prowled round discreetly, hoping for information. Then I went away.

By the time I returned, a month later, the next treatment was due. As usual, I was going past Kpata's courtyard when he stopped me: he wanted to speak about Samba, it was important. Samba was still playing the fool, he had not gone to take a chicken to Gambo. The child would die. I must speak to Samba and persuade him to do his duty. Samba smiled at me, but at the mention of his duty as a father, he was evasive:

"Yes, it is the fiancé of Nabate who should take the chicken to Gambo. But I haven't any money to buy it."

"And if you were given a chicken?"

"I haven't got the time, I work all day, and then there is no boat to cross the river with. And then, I am tired, and it is a long walk."

No, Samba would not go. He had other things to think about. He agreed that no one else but he could take the chicken to Gambo. No one could take his place. Nabate least of all. If Gambo saw her in her present state, he could not help thinking of the insult inflicted on him by his wife in accepting the help of Samba; she would die of it! But who was Gambo? Had he ever allowed Nabate to have a child that lived? The "old man" annoyed him the way he went on about these things. He, Samba, had his own affairs to see to.

Nzakara Women

Nabate was not present, but when he returned home in the evening she had had wind of the conversation. She spoke up energetically for her child. Samba got annoyed:
"What right has a woman for whom no bridewealth has been paid to quarrel with me? Am I not free to do as I choose?"
"You make presents to your fiancées while I do the cooking for you! The wife of Mbalazime is strutting about wearing the head scarf you gave her!"[126]
Then Samba got really angry. There were too many people out to annoy him. Nabate got beaten so badly that she fell to the ground. The neighbours were alarmed.

The midwife came. There was a regular council of old women held. What was to be done? Nabate could not be left in Samba's hands. The child would suffer from the beating it had been given inside its mother.

The midwife was astute, and she had no illusions about the difficult position of unmarried women. Her views were quite definite: certainly, Nabate had no more need of Samba for her child. Once a child begins to move, it can make room for itself without any help by turning over and over; so it did not need Samba. But if Nabate returned to Kpata, men would come and see her; they would knock at the door as men always do for these women! What would happen then? The nourishment of the two fathers would mix in the child. That would be unlucky for the child. So Nabate must stay with Samba.

It was a difficult decision. Kpata submitted it to the judgment of the village head. The midwife and a couple came as witnesses. Samba, bazinger to the chief, was beating Nabate and endangering her child's life. The village head immediately called up his guard. There was to be no playing about with discipline when a young mother was in question:
"Listen carefully, Samba. If I hear a single word of your beating Nabate, if one evening I should hear that you have so much as given her one single blow, or that you have ever refused, one single night, to let her into your hut, you will be taken to the big town by two guards and thrown into prison." Samba put up no defence, he held his head down and smiled with an air of embarrassment. The judge was extremely astute. He knew that the child when it was born would not belong to Samba; it was not his because he had not paid bridewealth for this woman. It was also impossible for him to buy the child because its father was Gambo. The judge had made a good assessment of the only sanction possible. Samba went home without saying a word. The midwife, a neighbour of Nabate's,

171

was told to keep an eye on her. Da Gambo, all smiles, was now eager to come to take the injections which give children. The midwife accompanied her.

Two months passed. On the evening when I returned to the village there was a knock at the door of my hut. It was a messenger, almost invisible in the darkness. "Come quickly, Nabate's child saw you passing, it is coming." It came so quickly, in fact, at the "call of the good midwife" that I arrived only just in time to deliver it by the light of a wood fire. It was a fine girl crying lustily. It was almost completely dark in the round hut. One saw vague silhouettes of women who were moving about, slowly performing their habitual tasks. The little cries of the child became deafening in this conspiratorial atmosphere. The midwife seemed a trifle embarrassed to know what and what not to do in the presence of this White. Anxious not to upset them, I sat on the bed beside three old women with smiles on their faces.[127] Outside the hut there were relations standing gossiping. Then, since the baby had been born and was alive, the young mothers brought their babies, as was the custom. Dawn came. What name should be given to the child? That was for Kpata to decide. But he was not there.

On the eighth day, Nabate emerged from her hut with her daughter. Kpata announced publicly the name of the baby: she would be called Da Gambo, the wife of Gambo, like her mother. As soon as she was born, he had gone himself to make the offering to Gambo. That was why we had not seen him. So now the child was consecrated. However, that day Kpata came to ask me to let it have my name and surname, which would be the name it would be known by ordinarily.

I was in some difficulty to know how to interpret the meaning of this. Several times I had spoken about the future of this child, about the role of Gambo, and about the injections. Were they not more powerful than the bad luck that Gambo had sent? If the child had been born alive in spite of the fact that the ancestor, the father of the child, had not received anything to appease his wrath, might that not mean that he had lost interest in the child? However, in reply to the question as to whether Nabate's daughter would be able to have bridewealth paid for her later, Kpata replied: "Not all the daughters of the wives of ancestors need to become wives of ancestors." But Kpata's logic differed from mine. The daughter and the grand-daughter were not one identical person. If Nabate had another daughter, she would most likely not be a wife of the ancestors, but this one, the eldest, must be consecrated.

Nabate expressed no opinion in the matter. She had never

expressed one, for she had never had any rights in this village, except that of taking any unofficial husband that happened to turn up. But now she had changed completely: she was a mother. She would come and sit in public on the tree trunk that served as bench for the villagers, with her child in her arms.

She will nurse it so well that the little Da Gambo will be the finest baby in the village. She will protect it against any harm. Smiling, she will run out on to the road to show off the baby, and then a mournful look will come over her face if she discovers a minute bruise or gets alarmed by a speck of vomit. She is in the habit of speaking with authority to the other women in the village about women's affairs: about cooking, or work in the fields or in the house.

Radiant, Nabate has now attained the status of being a mother; but she remains the humble wife of the ancestors, the woman who will never have any bridewealth.

NOTES

[1]Ur Abandia (ABandya).

[2]See *Vie de Bangassou*. This biography features numerous stories which show that respect for the blood was reciprocal in the sense that it reinforced the respect of his juniors towards the supreme chief, the Sultan, while at the same time it obliged the Sultan to protect his vassal brothers.

[3]*Kole*, the name of a barely edible fruit.

[4]Choice portions reserved for chiefs.

[5]*Ma^nla*: iron forged from local ore.

[6]*Ma^nla-za^nla*[7] the price of the *ma^nla*.

[7]*Ti* = to take; *benge* = chief.

[8]*Bosi* = child.

[9]Natélégé was born about 1860 and died about 1908, approximately ten years after the arrival of the first French Mission.

[10]Term reserved for the chief wife, the one in command of the others. To be a *dekana* it was generally necessary to be of noble birth and to have received bridewealth. Chiefs with a large harem had several *dekana*, about one for every ten wives.

[11]*Mbalaba* = exchange.

[12]There were no villages until about 1924, when the government regrouped families along the newly constructed roads. Until then, people lived in isolation in hamlets scattered through the forest.

[13]Healers.

[14]I was not able to obtain any details about the person responsible for this spell, nor about the motives for casting it.

[15]To the west of Hyo.

[16]The taboo on sexual intercourse which young mothers must observe until their children have learnt to walk is still rigorously maintained.

[17]No one would blame the wives: however great a risk they might run in sending such meals, no woman worthy of the name would omit this attention conferred upon her valiant lover.

[18]A name of foreign origin given to the soldiers of the court.

[19]Large flexible leaves used as towels.

[20]*Vu* means sons of, descendants of, and also "dependants of".

[21]A very simple form of lance which could serve as currency.

[22]Smallpox.

[23]Huts made of leaves set in the forest at some distance from the villages.

[24]A dance drum.

[25]She was born in 1886, before the arrival of the Whites. She was 21 years old at the time of the death of Sultan Bangassou.

[26]A three-days march.

[27]An edible tuber.

[28]Ngbangbali was a cousin of the Sultan. His chiefdom was close to the frontier; he made several expeditions to Langba country, bringing back from each of them several hundred prisoners.

[29]The courts of chiefs were fenced round with palisades; all the women and wives of the chief and their servant girls resided within this enclosure.

[30]Prisoners of war (*Kanga* = prisoner, *baso* = lance, war).

[31]All the "Bandia" such as Ngbangbali were of the lineage of the Sultan and on this account were given command of a military chiefdom.

[32]There is no distinction in the language between the hunt and war. The Sultan's soldiers were at the same time huntsmen.

[33]Mbangi country was another "hunting ground" of the Sultan; a few years later one of their chiefs came to conclude a treaty of alliance with Bangassou to put an end to pillaging and raids for slaves. He had to present the Sultan with a large number of women, servants and soldiers. The women were regarded as slaves.

[34]Woman of Yongozo, that is to say, belonging to her.

[35]Another woman who had lived at Ngbangbali's court reports that the "brothers" of Ngbangbali often came to request him for wives, because he was a big chief, the eldest of his lineage. He gave women to his subjects as reward for feats of arms, or to a younger kinsman to help him to establish his authority in a minor chiefdom; a man thus remunerated would later have to give a woman, or the daughters of the woman received, in return.

[36]It is not clear why it was Nyanlikawo who bought back Kafi, since he does not seem to have had any special right over this particular slave; had his uncle arranged that she should be his future wife, or did he have rights over the daughter of Singba? Singba could have bought back Kafi from the Sultan; people close to Kafi say that Singba transferred this right to a kinsman of Ngbangbali, because, for reasons unknown, he did not want to buy back this woman. Kafi herself gave me to understand that her marriage with the young chief was "a love match". Had the beauty of the young slave attracted Nyanlikawo upon seeing her at the court when he was on a visit to the Sultan? Either of these hypotheses is plausible.

[37]The order in which wives are purchased gives a certain precedence but does not cancel social class; Kafi retained her status as slave.

[38]Kafi had bloomed with health all her life, a striking attribute at a time when deformities could not be hidden under clothes. Both men and women wore a gown of bark-cloth. The nobles were adorned with tattooing. As for clothes, they are nothing but a mask to hide bodily ills!

[39]A large drum reserved for chiefs.

Nzakara Women

[40]"Far and wide" is one of the greatest indications of the power of a chief.

[41]This is the reason for the taboo on sexual intercourse which obtains during the last four months of pregnancy.

[42]Some Nzakara think that vomiting is a sign that the child refuses the food taken.

[43]Being the daughter of a prince, the child belonged to her father's lineage.

[44]Nyanlikawo would be deprived of his two wives for two years, for the taboo on sexual intercourse which women must observe from the fifth month of their pregnancy until the weaning of the child was scrupulously carried out throughout the country, and still is.

[45]Sorcery is inherited from the father by either sons or daughters; a sorcerer can be recognized by an organic peculiarity (a particular formation of the epiploon) which the father transmits to his children. The power of a sorcerer, diviner, or magician can be judged by its effects; but formerly there was no hesitation in verifying the authentic presence of the magic organ by performing a public autopsy.

[46]During the course of a special ceremony: *de dembila*.

[47]I would attribute the temporary wasting away of the baby to the fever which sapped the mother's strength and dried up her milk. They attributed it to a spell being cast simultaneously on mother and child. Events, here, do not contradict their assumption . . .

[48]All customs concerning women are transmitted through the maternal lineage. When one considers that a woman follows maternal traditions for all customs concerning confinement although bearing the name of her father's clan, it is clear that any attempt to classify these customs by clans is impossible; it is also obvious that a woman will be guided by her mother or by a woman of her mother's clan.

[49]*Langba* = race of slaves; here it means slave.

[50]Of nobles, of Bandia.

[51]See the fifth autobiography: Nabate. From the time of the Bandia conquerors, women consecrated to the cult of the ancestors were always slaves, by decree of earlier diviners.

[52]Mbilinga was one of the first conquerors of the country of the Nzakara. His name is also found in the story of Songombi.

[53]Nyanlikawo, son of the senior member of a Bandia lineage, maintained near his village the shrine of the lineage ancestors: a hut containing the representations and paraphernalia.

[54]Stomach ulcer, dysentery.

[55]Endemic diseases of this kind still frequently occur, whether caused by bacilli or by parasites; bilharziosis in particular.

[56]The dead man might be offended by the modest funeral accorded to him. It was necessary to escape his anger, which would be fierce during the mourning period.

[57]About 1926.

[58]A serious pulmonary complaint accompanied by fever.

[59]The Nzakara believe that a woman who no longer has a husband immediately becomes old.

[60]Village heads still retain one or two young men who serve as labourers and messengers. They take the place formerly occupied by soldiers.

[61]A custom reserved for nobles, for Bandia.

[62]Songombi was eleven at the time of Bangassou's death.

[63]Only the nobles were tattooed.

175

[64]A comparison commonly made. The Nzakara can distinguish a large variety of ants as much by the shape and location of the ant heaps as by the shape, form, wings and taste of the insect.

[65]Nzapa = God; a name given on account of some event attributed, under the influence of the Protestant Mission, to God.

[66]The woman's mother and her paternal aunts.

[67]There had already been a change in the system of supervision during the time of the preceding Sultan, the great Sultan Bangassou, enriched by the slave-trade and by the support of the Europeans; the security of his position, enjoying as he did a sovereignty which no neighbour could dispute, favoured a degree of personal liberty at his court far greater than that enjoyed by his other subjects at frontier posts, who were poor and in a permanent state of anxiety concerning the peace and security of their villages.

[68]1917.

[69]The story of Songombi can only be explained in the light of the demographic state of the country, with its rapidly falling birth rate, accounting for the extinction of many lineages. It was from the effects of this that this woman who had neither brother nor full paternal uncle suffered.

[70]Dyspnoea; probably a severe bronchial pneumonia.

[71]In order to make Songombi's meaning clear, I must give a brief explanation: when, at birth, the umbilical cord of the newly born infant is cut so as to separate it from the placenta, this is cutting "the child's vital substance". The cord is preserved in oil so that the child can be rubbed with the very same thing that had made it grow in its mother's womb. It is an irreplaceable "fortifier".

[72]A kind of weasel.

[73]*Bangbanzia* = cassava.

[74]In contradistinction to a woman whose husband has paid bridewealth for her, and whose children belong to the father; whereas the children of a "free woman" belong to the mother and the mother's family.

[75]Ndunga is still alive and lives at Kpinga.

[76]A red powder used in all religious ceremonies.

[77]The dwelling of the ancestors of a lineage is closed in by a dense thicket set in the centre of a grove at some distance from the village; there is only one for each lineage. It is taboo to women from the day "when they are of an age to go with men", except for fertility ceremonies.

[78]When Songombi was asked why women could not present themselves to the ancestral spirits without incurring their wrath, she gave an astonished smile at such a question; but of course the presence of married women annoyed the ancestral spirits; they were the *tita*, the grandfathers, but they were also jealous and dictatorial chiefs (these ambivalent functions being accepted by her although remaining unexplained in her mind). This interpretation does not tally exactly with another view which regards the ancestral spirits as having become possessed of demoniacal powers, resulting from being defrauded of their goods and functions by their children. This interpretation is made in the light of the attitudes of living chiefs.

[79]God, in the vernacular known as Sango.

[80]Poetic language stigmatizing the inconstancy of women. A rock, to these people, is a clear image of a woman's sexual relations with a man.

[81]An initiate of the cult of a spirit of the forest called Yanda.

[82]Tubers resembling taros or potatoes.

[83]The name of a spirit of Togbo origin (of the Banda tribe) introduced into the country of the Nzakara about fifty years ago.

Nzakara Women

[84]The guardian spirit of the hunt.

[85]These journeys were necessitated by the length of time the divorce case lasted.

[86]Chief.

[87]Affines.

[88]She had kept to the name given to her by an old woman when she was a child: thin-legged woman.

[89]In customary law, there was a form of marriage whereby two men of different clans exchanged daughters or sisters. It would seem that here the man had tried to argue from this former custom in order to obtain a woman to whom he had no claim—either because she had been promised to someone else, or because he had not wanted to pay the bridewealth demanded.

[90]This refers to the arbiter in village disputes.

[91]"Scolded" simply means that there was a great deal of noise.

[92]When the divorce had been granted, he had been given back the bridewealth he had paid for this woman.

[93]A present of this kind from a man is in the nature of a "thank you" present.

[94]Poets who recounted events past and present to the accompaniment of a stringed instrument, the *kundi Nzakara*.

[95]Literal translation of the word for abortion or miscarriage.

[96]The explanations given here are difficult to understand in view of the large amount of the marriage payment. Normally a marriage payment is about 5,000 francs. It would seem that the real cause of the dispute was concealed, consciously or otherwise, by both parties to it. I have kept to Nakpangi's version of it: the district-chief had been accused of not having given the *ma^nla-za^nia*, the present for the ancestral spirits, to the uncle who was the custodian of the shrine. This uncle was a diviner, and, according to him, the omission had brought down the anger of the ancestors on Nakpangi, which explained her miscarriage. The sentence of the "governor", the head of the district and judge, was, that the girl was too young. Yet she was nubile. Did he think the husband too old, or had the dissembling by the defendants made it difficult to give judgment?

[97]God in the language known as Sango, the vernacular used by missionaries.

[98]Sango, who worked as a chauffeur, received a wage which enabled him to buy a European suit with long trousers that "hid" his legs.

[99]A deprecatory term; the ways of villagers are contrasted with those of chiefs.

[100]The Sango word for motor car.

[101]Fiancée.

[102]Price.

[103]The custodian makes an offering to the ancestors of this present which is marriage payment for their daughter, and he then takes possession of it and can do as he likes with it, having no obligation to pay it back if the woman gets divorced.

[104]The catechism.

[105]God of Madame. "Madame" was the first Protestant missionary to come to the country before 1920.

[106]In tablet form.

[107]This area is part of the eastern kingdom conquered by the Bandia who became assimilated to the Zande.

[108]I used to hold clinics for the sick people of the village every time I paid a visit there, and on the day of my arrival all the people who were well would come rushing to attend as much out of curiosity as politeness. The story of Nabate was obtained in a different way from the others. She herself seldom spoke, and events in which I took part contribute largely to this account, which is a "reconstruction" of the life of Nabate.

Anne Laurentin

[109]The head of a sub-lineage promoted by the Whites to supervise the harvesting of the rubber crop.

[110]Nabate belongs to a different lineage from Kpata's. Kpata, being related to her on the maternal side, had no rights of adoption.

[111]As one might expect, marriage between two slaves did not involve any contract. From time to time a chief might take a slave away from her unofficial husband in order to effect an exchange of women with another chief, or to bestow a wife upon a son or a nephew, or even upon one of his dependents.

[112]Zallo had received Duguma and his sister from a neighbouring chief in exchange for a case of cloth. Slaves lived outside the chief's enclosure, in the "village"; slave-wives lived in the chief's court along with the other wives.

[113]According to custom, the children of a woman for whom no bridewealth had been paid, that is, who had been born during her period of concubinage, should be accepted by the husband in addition to his making marriage payment. Duguma's claims on the dead children of his sister indicates what changes had taken place: formerly, only noble lineages had "ancestors".

[114]In crossing the river, Duguma also crossed the frontier between Ubangi-Chari and the Belgian Congo.

[115]Wife of Gambo. It was the custom for slave-wives to bear the name of their chief, their master. The wives of the ancestors were almost all recruited from slaves for prudent customary reasons which will be discussed in a later publication. But this mention of the past enables me to convey why the title DA GAMBO is slightly contemptuous: it consecrates the woman as slave-wife of the ancestor.

[116]Health is regarded as a favour granted to those who bow to the will of the ancestral spirits and carry out the rites of their cult.

[117]Soldiers.

[118]A male concubine, a lover; one who lives with a woman without having paid.

[119]In the wider sense as understood by the Nzakara: Physical and sexual nourishment.

[120]A precise ritual governs everything concerning mother and child during the first eight days after birth.

[121]At the hospital it was simply antibiotic treatment that was envisaged.

[122]Nabate specified peri-nasal and buccal lesions of a syphilitic character.

[123]The baby that died in hospital was buried in the family burial-ground in the town.

[124]In this country suffering from a rapidly declining birth-rate, young girls are scarce, and some are sought after by middle-aged men.

[125]The fourth.

[126]Such presents leave no room for doubt: they are proof positive of relations as between a lover and his *baⁿlum'e*.

[127]The birth of a live child was a mysterious and striking event, and everyone felt that hovering over it was the great shadow of Gambo. The child was alive, but what interpretation did the villagers put upon this fact? And who will be held responsible for its death if it should die before it is weaned? The course of events will bring clarification as to their attitude.

WOMEN OF BURUNDI: A STUDY OF SOCIAL VALUES*†

Ethel M. Albert

SUCCESS IN REALIZING the central values of Rundi society is, for men and women alike, dependent on inherited caste position, intelligence and "luck".[1] In this feudal, patriarchal society, the central values are political power and authority; wealth—especially cows and lands and, today, money and the goods and services it can purchase; respect and love from one's dependants; and elegance of appearance, manners and material possessions. What is needed before all else for obtaining the good things of life, the Rundi say, is the favour of *Imana*, the Supreme Being or Providence. Divine favour is also requisite to the realization of such other important values as numerous children, protection against one's many enemies, and the retention of goods already obtained. The chief terrestrial asset for realizing values is position in the social hierarchy.[2] The likelihood of happiness is greatest for the *mwami*, the king, and for the men and women of the royal and princely patrilineages. Opportunity and hope diminish progressively with decreasing status in the hierarchy, through the patrilineages of the Tutsi herders, the Hutu farmers and serfs, and, at the bottom, the Twa, potters and pariahs.

Women, in so markedly patriarchal and patrilineal a society as

*Author's translation.

†The research upon which this paper is based was supported by a Fellowship from the Ford Foundation, African Program (1955-1957). The field work was done between March, 1956 and July, 1957. Thanks are due also to I.R.S.A.C. (Instut pour la Recherche Scientifique en Afrique Centrale) for having granted me the privileges of *Chercheur Associé*. Changes since the period of the research render the present tense historical.

179

that of Burundi, are by definition socially inferior to men. Political power, judicial rights, inheritance of cows and lands, and, indeed, the right to independent action outside the walls of the house, are traditionally accorded to men only.[3] Yet, in point of fact, there are women who enjoy considerable authority and who own or control cows, lands and other forms of wealth. What a Rundikazi—a woman of Burundi—cannot do as a woman, she manages very well to do as a Rundi. The life-history of an individual is limited but not fully determined by the formal structures of the society. The dynamics of the social system make provision for political and economic mobility by which all but the most wretched Rundi know how to profit.

The social status of a Rundi is established by the caste and class inherited from the father. A woman is inferior to the men of her own social level and to her husband, but not to men of lower castes and classes than her own. The opportunities of a princess or of a woman of the aristocracy to acquire wealth are fewer than her father's or brother's but much greater than those of an ordinary herder or, certainly, of a poor farmer or serf. Moreover, women use the same techniques that make it possible for some farmers to own herds of cattle, or for some ordinary herders to become wealthier than some nobles. To advance from his official inherited status as far as possible towards happiness, a Rundi needs the favour of a superior in the social hierarchy. All good things come from the superior. The greater the power of the superior—whether the feudal master, the father, or the husband—the greater the ambition of the inferior—whether a herder, a serf or a woman. For the latter, it is sometimes enough to have a father who is impulsive and generous, or a husband who is docile or too stupid to distinguish the truth from a lie or true affection from flattery. Women attain their goals by means of men. There are always a good many of them available for use in projects both large and small.

Although caste and character rather than the simple fact of being male or female determine the lot of a Rundi, the mode of life and the behaviour patterns of women are decidedly different from those of men. Unlike a man, a Rundikazi in public does not speak, nor does she look you in the eyes. To each question, she answers: *Ndabizi?*—How should I know? In public, she lets it be thought that she knows nothing about politics, or where her husband is today, or even the wedding date of her daughter. She is the modest and obedient wife of her husband, the mother of her children, the conscientious mistress of her house, who is always working. Whatever she does, she does within the limits of her various feminine roles. However, the obligations of motherhood, of the household and of wifehood hardly prevent a woman from participating in other activities. Indeed, in Burundi, everyone is busy with politics —the large scale politics of the kingdom for the *abakuru*, the great ones, and the petty politics of daily life for the *abatoyi*, the humble folk. Women are not less interested in it than men, nor peasants less than princes. A peasant widow plays politics to obtain a length of cotton cloth or to protect against her enemies her rights to her little plot of cultivable land. A princess plays politics to obtain jewellery and cows and to decide a princely succession. A woman is sometimes driven by ambition for the sake of her son; sometimes it is to her advantage to help her husband; sometimes she enters the game entirely in her own interest. Peasant or princess, if a Rundikazi understands and desires happiness, if she knows how to dominate men in all subtlety, if she is clever and courageous, she may even defeat her own father or husband in the political game. The ambition of a Rundi or Rundikazi of inferior birth is seriously limited by the restrictive rules of the caste system. However, the ambition of a woman as such encounters only the sometimes purely apparent obstacle of a patriarchal, patrilineal system in which all the legitimate titles to wealth and power are for men.[4] Women who are ambitious and intelligent do not seem to be at a disadvantage in having to function in politics by indirect means and in secret. These are, in any case, the preferred methods of men in the delicate business of increasing power and wealth.

Thus, in Burundi as elsewhere, one finds charming but formidable matriarchs who have considerable authority and who are perhaps more intimidating than the harshest of patriarchs. On the other hand, most of the women of Burundi never even approach realization of the central values of the society. They must work to the limit of their strength so that they will not die of hunger. This is because most Rundi are of the inferior castes, where men and women share the wretchedness of the poor. It would be vain to try to calculate the difference between the misery of a man and that of a woman, if both of them are of inferior birth, without relatives or a feudal protector, old, weak and not very bright.

Neither a Rundikazi who wields great political influence nor a man of low caste who has more political power and wealth than his social superior is regarded as an outlaw. On the contrary, they are looked upon as clever and lucky. The social structure of Burundi, like that of other societies, does not describe behaviour. It only serves as a guide. A society would be crushed by the weight of its own rules, if each infraction were punished strictly according to prescribed sanctions and if all the formal norms were always respected. To be a part of a society is to know which of its rules prescribe or prohibit absolutely or conditionally; whether a particular action which is not forbidden is nevertheless something that is simply "not done"; whether human beings, always imperfect, must in any particular case actually be punished or whether the offence should blinked. Exceptions to the formal rules are not haphazard. Rather, they are ordered by what may be called implicit norms, or secondary or functional norms. These are as well known and as well established as norms which are explicit and formal. Taken together, the explicit, primary norms and the implicit, secondary norms form the "active norms" of the society. By means of secondary norms, society can come to terms with the social and psychological impossibility of a perfect correspondence between the formal norms of the social structure, invented by men in the interest of social order, and the actions of men confronted by the empirical realities of human existence.

Each society has its own calculus of values by which it establishes its active norms, the norms to be respected verbally but understood to be neither practical nor practised, and the rules of punishment which are to be taken seriously. It will not be possible to understand the life of the women of Burundi without knowing both the formal norms of the social structure and the secondary, functional norms. The life of a Rundikazi is made up of various elements. To reconstruct it, we shall begin with a description of women as members of Rundi society, of which they form an integral part. We shall then describe women in the specifically feminine roles, and we shall conclude with an account of the devices used by women to realize the values of their patriarchal society.

* * *

The Rundi describe their society as a hierarchy ordered by *Imana*, the Supreme Being, who is at its summit. Among human beings, it is the *mwami*, the king, who is superior to all. In the past, there was also Kiranga, the legendary head of a possession cult. He was said to be of approximately the same rank as the *mwami*.[5] Immediately below the king are the *baganwa*, the princes—four generations of the descendents of a king. The *mwami* and the *baganwa* are the rulers of the Rundi. In the traditional system, the power of the *mwami* was defined by his inheritence of absolute royal power and of the entire country, together with all its goods, as his private property. No Rundi had rights, power, lands, or cows, except as the *mwami* granted. He distributed his lands and cows and administrative power to those of his brothers and parallel cousins who were on his side in the political battles. These *baganwa*, today called "chiefs", become the vassals of the *mwami*. The *baganwa* distributed the lands and cows they received to *batware*, captains, today called "sub-chiefs", who became their vassals and who in turn procured vassals for themselves by giving to their inferiors small plots of land and a cow here and there. Changes resulting from European influence are gradually eliminating the feudal characteristics of the social system. However, the principle and the order of the hierarchy have so far remained unchanged.

Below the princes in the hierarchy are the *abafasoni*, nobles, those who were once princes but who at the fifth generation are so no longer and who will one day be numbered among the commoners. To describe the commoners, it is necessary to take account of the three *aboko*, castes—the Tutsi, the Hutu and the Twa.[6] The Tutsi are by far of the highest rank among the commoners. Although they make up only ten per cent of the population, they are the masters of the Hutu, who make up more than 85 per cent of the population. It is believed that the Tutsi are of Hamitic or Nilo-Hamitic origin, whereas the Hutu are clearly a part of the Bantu hoe-culture, characteristic of East and Central Africa.[7] Burundi is beyond doubt a "cattle-complex" country. The Tutsi are herders, and nobody debates the superiority of the herders. It is said that the Tutsi, once formidable warriors, on their arrival in the country about three centuries ago, had no need to conquer the Hutu by using their spears. The Hutu to this day willingly become the serfs of the herders in order to receive cows from them. Between the princes and the Tutsi, there is very little difference in rank. Between the rank of the Tutsi and that of the Hutu, there is a very great difference. The Tutsi and the Tutsikazi disdain the Hutu and the Hutukazi, considering them their born servants. Nevertheless, the princes or the king sometimes appoint Hutu to be *batware*. A Hutu thus honoured is the political superior of the Tutsi under his authority. This circumstance in no way modifies his social inferiority. On the contrary, it exacerbates race prejudice. No social mechanism can change the caste in which an individual is born. The Tutsi do not drink with the Hutu, even when they become administrators, for one does not drink with one's social inferiors. The next downward step in the hierarchy takes us to the bottom of the social ladder and almost outside the society to the

Ethel M. Albert

Twa. A pygmoid people, the Twa constitute less than 1·5 per cent of the population. Potters and hunters in the process of becoming farmers, the Twa are pariahs, excluded almost completely from social relations with all the other Rundi and detested by them.[8] With ill grace, the Rundi grant that the Twakazi are excellent dancers and that people need the pots that they make.

It is by now evident that the Rundi are somewhat sensitive to differences of rank, but we have by no means exhausted the social distinctions they make. Within each caste there are *abaryango*, patrilineages (literally, "doors"), which are arranged in hierarchical order, more or less as social classes. Distinctions are made among patrilineages which are called very good, good, neither good nor bad, and bad. Thus, a Tutsi of a very good patrilineage is the social superior of a Tutsi in a patrilineage that is merely good or neither good nor bad. The former expects to receive a dowry of at least four cows for his daughter, whereas the others must be satisfied with one. Hutu or Hutukazi of good patrilineages are clearly superior to the other Hutu, and a well-born Twa looks upon the other Twa as his social inferiors. Men and women together at the higher levels are superior to those, both men and women, of the inferior levels, although within each class, the men are superior to the women, and, as a general rule, the older are superior to the younger. Taken altogether, to the childless youngest daughter of one of the bad patrilineages of the Twa, every Rundi without exception is the superior, and every Rundi is inferior to the *mwami*.

Although a woman's caste remains unchanged throughout her life, her definitive place in society is determined by her marriage. In general, fathers seek spouses for their children from their own caste and class. However, the *mwami* and the more important *baganwa* take their wives from among a dozen of the very good Tutsi patrilineages. The Tutsikazi of these patrilineages, through such marriages, move up in the social hierarchy. They will be the mothers of princes. The one who becomes the *mwamikazi*, the queen-mother, will be the most important woman in the country, the superior of most Rundi men. She will receive substantial presents and much respect, and she will have considerable influence in the affairs of the kingdom. After death, she will have special funeral rites and will be buried in a cemetery reserved for the remains of the queen-mothers. Although almost any woman of a very good Tutsi patrilineage may be called a *mwamikazi*, it is only a figurative way of saying that she is well born. The status of women born in the royal and princely patrilineages is somewhat ambiguous. They will be married by Tutsi of the patrilineages that supply wives to the *mwami* and the *baganwa* or by a cross-cousin. (The traditional Rundi rule favouring cross-cousin marriage is being abandoned by all classes of the population as the influence of Christianity increases).

No other women than those of the very good Tutsi patrilineages can rise socially by means of marriage. The marriage rule for all men except the king and the princes requires that a man marry a woman of the same rank as his own or of a higher rank. A woman cannot be declassed, and caste rules are not relevant. If a Rundi male should marry a woman of inferior rank—the very idea makes men tremble with disgust—he would immediately have to be declassed to the rank of his wife.[9] There are occasionally informal sexual unions between Tutsi and Hutukazi. A natural child born of such a union would not be formally acknowledged by his father, although he might provide a cow for his son and a Hutu husband for the mother of his child.

The Tutsi, it is said, give a dowry of cows, the Hutu a dowry of hoes. However, the Hutu who are liked by princes and become *batware* can give cows. A poverty stricken herder may give his daughter in marriage to a wealthy Hutu. Because it is always the father who determines the caste and patrilineage of children, a Tutsikazi may find herself the mother of Hutu children. She will be humiliated by the necessity to obey a social inferior and she will be disdained by the Tutsi and the more fortunate Tutsikazi. On the other hand, poverty is shameful and painful. Moreover, a Tutsikazi will probably be treated better by a Hutu than by a Tutsi husband. Always a Hutu, the husband nevertheless enjoys a certain prestige when he has a wife of superior status. He expects many children from her—it is said that Tutsikazi are more fertile than Hutukazi —and his children will have the good manners and intelligence of a Tutsi, his sons will know how to get rich and thereby acquire Tutsi wives.

For each caste, there are stereotypes of physical type and character. Great height, thinness, and an extraordinarily narrow skull are typical of the Tutsi, and great height, generous fleshy covering and a light skin of Tutsikazi.[10] A Hutu five feet tall will not be likely to make a mistake about his inferiority in the presence of a Tutsi of six and one-half or seven feet tall, nor is a Twakazi of four feet eight inches in height who is dancing for a six-foot tall Tutsikazi likely to forget her place in the social scale. Among the Tutsi, the women seem to be much fleshier and somewhat shorter than the men. The Hutukazi and the Twakazi, however, seem to be taller and more substantially constructed than the men of the same caste. There are some short Tutsi and some tall Hutu. This makes no difference, for physical indices are not needed to distinguish Tutsi from Hutu. Recognition is based on their manner, their way of speaking, and their behaviour. Everybody agrees that the Tutsi and the Tutsikazi are born more intelligent—or, at least, cleverer—than the Hutu. This can be seen, it is said, because the Tutsi make the Hutu work for them without necessarily giving anything in return. There is general agreement that the Tutsi have a pronounced tendency to avarice and that old Tutsikazi are the worst misers in the world. Further, the Tutsi are most accomplished rhetoricians. The Hutu mutter and the Hutukazi lisp, and they are incapable of a good lie or of an elegant impromptu oration which seem second nature to Tutsi. Here, however, a contrast must be noted between Tutsi men and women: the boys are taught to speak well, the girls to be silent except to offer polite, evasive phrases.

It is believed that the Tutsi are physically and psychologically more delicate than the Hutu. They are not made, as the Hutu are, to work in the fields, to carry heavy burdens on their heads, to eat the solid, heavy food of the farmers. The Hutu pity the Tutsi when the latter are obliged by the government to do manual labour. True delicacy is shown by the *imfura*, literally the first born, more generally any person of very high birth, whose character and conduct constitute the model of nobility. The *imfura*, it is said, are so delicate that they take only liquid nourishment, especially milk and beer. All the Rundi know perfectly well that the Tutsi and their wives eat beef, cereals and vegetables. They are, however, so much taken by the myth of a liquid diet for superiors that even those who have been servants in the homes of Europeans—by definition, superiors—insist that the European diet is "liquid", that it does not give the strength needed for manual labour. Otherwise stated, persons of superior status do not work; their inferiors work for them. Elegance and dignity are joined together in everything that relates to the *imfura*. They wear beautiful clothing and much jewellery; they walk slowly and in front of others, or they are carried in a litter (although today the well-to-do prefer to travel by automobile); they speak softly, they never show their emotions; they are always discreet, they never discuss important matters in public. In fact, the dignity of well-born Tutsi and Tutsikazi seems sometimes to be primarily a frightening coldness and reserve. To respect the *imfura* and to fear them amounts to much the same thing.

It is necessary to stay in Burundi for a long time to see behind the stereotypes of the castes. In brief, it is assumed that the Tutsi

Women of Burundi: A Study of Social Values

and Tutsikazi are tall, dignified and elegant; they know how to give the impression of great control, of intelligence and of refinement. Hutu and Hutukazi are plainly farmers, short and sturdy, clumsy, made for work, and they seem to be vulgar, stupid, incapable of controlling their emotions or of speaking well. Nothing has so far been said of the poor Twa: like the Rundi, we have forgotten them. The Twa, pariahs, are, say the Rundi, without shame. They eat anything, they employ bad language. It is necessary to pay them for the pots their women make, for no Rundi will participate in economic exchanges of gifts and services or in social relations with them. We shall see further on that the stereotypes of superiors and inferiors according to caste can be used also in describing all other superior-inferior relationships.

To complete the description of the hierarchical order of Rundi society, it is necessary to include the kinship system. The familial hierarchy has the same pattern as the social hierarchy. All benefactors are called *umuvyeyi*, parent. The *mwami* is like a benevolent father, it is said, who likes the Rundi, his children. The nursing mother is the symbol of feminine generosity. The best way to thank a benefactress is by means of the formula: I am a nursing child at your generous breasts, or alternatively: you are to me as a freshened cow. The herders sometimes argue about the relative superiority of women and cows; both sources of milk appear to have their partisans.

Whatever the position of an individual in the social hierarchy, he will also have his place in the familial hierarchy. The head of a patrilineage, prince or pariah, is at the summit of the familial hierarchy. He is the *mukuru*, the highest, the oldest by rank, though not necessarily by chronological age. He speaks first, he drinks first, he must be respected and obeyed by his brothers, his sons, and the women of the patrilineage. The household consisting of a man and his wife and children is the smallest independent unit of Rundi society. There, the father of the family is *nyene rugo*, the master of his household. His children and his wife—if he is polygamous, his wives—owe him respect and obedience. Addressed in the familiar by his superiors, the father of the family addresses his inferiors in the familiar, in his capacity as a patriarch of almost absolute power. His wife kneels before him when she offers him his gourd of beer, and his child kneels before him to receive his blessing. (The Old Testament comes inevitably to mind at the sight.) Sons receive a part of their father's property as their inheritance not later than the time they receive a wife but are all their lives subjugated to their father's authority. The father chooses one of his sons as his heritor. The mother chooses one of her daughters as her heritor, to whom she will leave her clothing, her baskets and her pot of perfumed butter. Daughters inherit nothing from their father. Sooner or later, they leave his property to go to live with their husbands. Nevertheless, when a woman says, "my home", she is referring to her father's kraal. All her life she is, like her brothers, under her father's authority. After marriage she must also obey her husband, but her father will always have the greater authority over her. She herself is the superior of her younger sisters, of her children, and if there are any, of the inferiors, servants and serfs of her husband.

The inferiority of women as women is only a special case of the general form of inferiority in Rundi society. However, both men and women have multiple roles in society. As a result, the superiority and inferiority of an individual are relative, rather than absolute, except for the *mwami* at the top of the hierarchy and the poor little Twakazi at the bottom. It has already been indicated that a social superior is sometimes inferior in the hierarchy of politics and economics. Also, the eldest brother may be the inferior of the youngest, in the likely event that the latter is chosen as the father's heritor. A Tutsikazi, the social inferior of her father and husband (provided the latter is not a Hutu), is nevertheless the superior of all the Hutu and Twa, of her children and those Tutsi who are the inferiors of her husband. Each Rundi must learn his place in relation to that of every other, calculate the distance and direction of the relationship, and find his way as well as he can through the social labyrinth.

Despite the striking simplicity of its structure, the social hierarchy of Burundi allows for mobility and for some very complex variations in conduct. There is incontestable evidence of both constant efforts of men and women to improve their positions in society and of the associated phenomena of social instability and of fierce competition among the inferiors of a given superior. One may risk the generalization that the norms and rules dictated by the social structure will not survive a conflict with the values of wealth and power. One may say also that the greater the wealth and power of the superior, the more acute the rivalry and the more bitter the struggles among his inferiors. Thus, quarrels among Hutu, who are usually very poor, are rarely more than noisy spats quickly forgotten, while the silent hatreds of the Tutsi, born of the desire to own cows, sometimes explode in murder and fratricide. Quarrels among sisters, who inherit nothing of value, are rarely as bitter or prolonged as quarrels among brothers. On the other hand,

Women of Burundi: A Study of Social Values

rivalry among a man's plural wives and among sisters-in-law constitutes a serious domestic problem. Moreover, there are persistent rumours which have never been effectively squelched that the late queen-mother arranged for the death of her son, the former *mwami*, for political reasons. Maternal tenderness and friendship cannot stand up against the pressures of economic and political self-interest. Moreover, instability is a result, probably an inevitable one, of the very wide powers of superiors over their inferiors.

Ubukuru, superiority or seniority, is everywhere of the same pattern—in the relationship between the *mwami* and his subjects, between parents and children, between Tutsi and Hutu, between husband and wife. The superior is active, the inferior passive. The superior commands, the other obeys. Out of respect, the inferior waits while the superior drinks first, eats first, walks ahead of him. If there are burdens to carry, it is the inferior who carries them— the Hutu for his Tutsi master, the wife for her husband, the children for their mother. A powerful taboo forbids a Hutu to look on while a prince or a Tutsi eats or drinks. There is no comparable taboo in domestic life, but the husband usually eats alone, or he may invite his wife to join him. Children, always inferiors, always eat afterwards and apart.

The concept of *ubukuru* as chronological seniority is relevant to changes in social role according to age. The changes of social status for women, from child and adolescent to wife and mother, then to mother-in-law and grandmother, constitute a progression towards independence, power and the other attributes of superiority. For men, there is a progression of approximately the same kind. The boy during childhood and adolescence is of no importance; at marriage, a man is superior to his wife and children, but he remains subordinated to the authority of his father and the lineage chief; if he is clever and wealthy enough to pay for the beer for the ceremony, he will be initiated when he is about forty-five years old, as an *umushingantahe*, a mature man qualified to serve as a judge and councillor. In his old age, when he has become feeble, a man is obliged to retire from active participation in important matters. The principle of increase of power with age is valid throughout the life-span for women. Nevertheless, superiority is not determined by chronological age but by social role.

To ask for a gift, say the Rundi, is to honour; to give a gift is to like. It is the superior who gives, the inferior who asks. In order to receive, it is necessary to obey, but everything depends on the will and the affection of the superior. He will give if he wants to; if not

189

he will not give; and if he wishes, he will take back what he has already given in order to give it to someone he likes better. An inferior, whether it be the serf of a Tutsi or a wife in relation to her husband, can protest only in vain that he has worked hard, that he has always been docile and obedient, that he has always liked and respected his superior. There are no formal sanctions against a superior who accepts services and goods from his inferior and gives him nothing in return. However, there are more subtle measures to be taken against him. An inferior, if he has any alternative open to him, will abandon an ungenerous superior.

Sometimes a Tutsi deserts a prince who has not given him cows or a subchiefdom, in order to enter service with one who is more generous and powerful. A son may leave the property of his father if he is not satisfied with his heritage and will enter service with a stranger who promises to give him lands and cows. A woman will return to her father's home if her husband mistreats her, and ask her father to find her a better husband. When those who are dissatisfied complain publicly about ungenerous superiors, they will have difficulty in replacing the inferiors who desert them. However, if one does not find another superior with whom to take refuge, it is necessary to stay with the bad one and to resign oneself to unhappiness, sometimes to hunger, sometimes to death. For, physical violence is the privilege of the superior. It is up to him to instruct and correct his inferiors by words and blows. Or, if he is in a bad humour, his inferiors are always around, and he can take out his displeasure on them. Children expect to be beaten by their parents, serfs and servants by their master and mistress, and a woman, even an *imfura*, considers it quite normal for her husband to beat her, especially if she has been difficult or if he has had a good deal to drink. According to the ideal, a superior is always benevolent, generous, wise and just. Beating does not suggest a lack of affection. If the superior does not give presents to his inferior, then it is known that he does not like him.

In principle, *umutima*, sentiment (literally, "the heart"), is always combined with the material value of a gift. *Urukundo*, love or affection, rather than law or rights, explains the gifts of superiors and the services rendered by inferiors. It is possible that the Rundi insist so much upon the importance of sentiment and love because they have so little of them. However this may be, there is no doubting their joy and sense of well-being when they receive even the smallest present. However, they mistrust *urukundo:* love can change to hate very quickly, they say. Inferiors are always afraid that the superior will stop liking them or will send them packing or will take back the cow he has given. In turn, superiors consider defection and disloyalty as the worst of crimes. Even if a servant is insolent and lazy, he will be well taken care of if he always tells his master whatever news and rumours he has heard about him. A woman who is disagreeable, lazy or even sterile will not be chased from the household if she is clever in helping her husband with his business and if she never speaks ill of him. An individual may have confidence only in his blood-friend, male or female. However, occasionally, true friendship ties a vassal to his chief or a *mwami-kazi* to her confidential servant. In these secure and friendly relationships, the principals tell each other their troubles, give each other advice, and remain loyal to each other forever. It is a matter for much discussion when a husband and wife stay together for 20 years, both married and mutually affectionate. However, neighbours, acquaintances, relatives, and spouses, it is said, do not remain friendly for a very long time. Several months, at most two or three years, suffice to create reasons for hatred, jealousy, vengeance, burning a house, calumny, fights, and visits to the witch to obtain poison.

The maximum of instability is associated with the role of the *abatoni*, the favourites. Fierce rivalry is considered normal among inferiors of the same rank—the men of the princely courts, brothers, plural wives, the servants of the Tutsi. The favourite son or wife is envied by his or her peers and must expect quarrels, poison and calumny. Because a superior may easily change his mind about a favourite, someone else will wait hopefully to take his place, In fact, happiness—many children, a good harvest, a cow which gives much milk, a present large or small—is the mark of the favourites of *Imana* and of human beings. One has received, one is liked by a superior, one is hated by all those who have not received. By this syllogism, it is logical for a rich Tutsi to be jealous both of a poor Hutukazi who has just received from her son-in-law a length of cheap cotton cloth and of a rich Tutsi who has just received another cow. To receive and be liked are identical. Together, they constitute the core of the well-being of inferiors.

Although *ubgenge*, intelligence, is normally accounted an attribute of superiors, it is well understood that inferiors have great need of it. The superior must be intelligent in order to exercise his authority, to judge well of his inferiors, to know the right moment to give and to take back. The *ubgenge* of an inferior has obviously to be of another kind. His goal is to make his superior like him. He must therefore understand his character, his moods, his fears, his desires. He must learn how to flatter him and to seem always loyal and devoted. The *umutoni* is before all else an informer. It is the way to show his interest in the well-being of his superior. It is for this that he is favoured and given gifts. Men who are poor or women who are by law without property, if they know how to play the role of the inferior effectively, can become rich, have their advice heeded, and find life most agreeable.

Attitudes and behaviour change according to role. Everyone has his turn as an inferior, if not to a human being, then to *Imana*. Adult Rundi have their turn as superiors to their children and to various others according to their rank. There is an astonishing ease and rapidity of psychological change according to the situation. The very man who explains to you today that he has sent his wife back home because she did not work enough, will tell you tomorrow that he was dismissed by his master for no other reason than that his enemies calumniated him—he does not see that he has been disobedient or lazy. A woman who has just served her husband his dinner from a humble, kneeling position, on leaving the house, gives haughty, authoritative commands to the men who work for her. Like any other superior, a woman as the mistress of her house, as a mother, and as an elder sister, commands and punishes. She is respected, she chooses her favourites, and her inferiors ask her for presents. When her role is that of an inferior, she must be obedient, she must work, she must ask for presents, she tries to win the affection of her superior, and she is jealous of those who receive presents.

The Rundi conception of the innate differences between men and women is as well-defined as their conception of the innate differences among the various castes and of much the same content. Both Tutsi and Hutu and men and women agree on the stereotypic differences of physique and of psychology between the two sexes. To begin with, it is believed that women are better suited by nature than men for manual labour. They work better and longer in the fields than men. The Hutukazi are able to carry on their heads burdens twice as heavy as those which men can carry. It is generally known that there are more old men than old women and that women age more quickly than men. The Rundi refuse categorically the hypothesis that those who work harder die younger. Men and women both insist that women are made for work and that they die younger because of the hardships of child-bearing. It is nonetheless believed that the male role is more important than that of the female in procreation. Woman, says the proverb, is only the passive earth; it is the man who provides the seed.

Stronger than men, women are thought to be less agile. Conse-

Women of Burundi: A Study of Social Values

quently, in domestic battles, the husband can vanquish the wife. He must, nevertheless, be on his guard if she becomes very angry. For, even though men (as superiors) are able to control their anger, women (as inferiors) are likely to lose their heads. She can take a knife and kill her husband, says the Hutu; she will poison her husband, says the Tutsi. Furthermore, women are regarded as less courageous than men in the presence of enemies; they are more easily discouraged when there is misfortune; they cry more easily; and they do not conceal their emotions. No attention whatever is paid to any evidence which might contradict the stereotype.

A man who is jealous of his wife's lovers is considered an imbecile. Particularly among the rich, a wife can show her fidelity to her husband's interests by going to bed with his superiors, if by this means she can calm the superior or obtain valuable information from him. Out of delicacy, the husband visits his neighbours when his superior comes to call. On the other hand, most family troubles are explained by the presumably unlimited capacity of women for jealousy. At marriage, a Rundikazi is supposed to be a virgin. Once she is married, it is said, she has great and constant need for sexual satisfaction. A man is privileged, if not obliged, to sleep with all his wives, the wives of his brothers and of his parallel cousins, his female cross-cousins, the wives of his male cross-cousins, the sisters and female cross- and parallel-cousins of his wife, and various other ladies. The kinship system is obviously a highly classificatory one. Nevertheless, men must discharge their sexual obligations in secret. If a husband finds his wife in bed with another man, he is morally obligated to beat his wife and to quarrel a little with the man. Far more serious, if a woman sees her husband entering the house of his sister-in-law, there will be no more peace for him at home. A woman, it was explained, is jealous of those with whom her husband sleeps, because the others will perhaps get presents out of him that she wants for herself, or perhaps one of the other women will speak against her to persuade her husband to divorce her. If there appear to be contradictions here, it is probably due to the lack of a truly Rundi perspective.

It is not for nothing, say the Rundi, that the wives of a polygamist are called *abakeba*, rivals.[11] Each woman watches every other wife—the presents she has received from her husband, the size of the property she has been given to cultivate and as an inheritance for her sons, the cows given for her household, the number of children she has, the number of nights the husband spends with her. To calumniate one's *abakeba*, to poison them, to quarrel with them, to give the husband *inzaratsi*—the potion that diverts his love to the one that administers it to him—or to look for magic that will make the husband impotent when he is with other women, every sort of vengeance is normal among the wives of a polygamist. A Tutsi polygamist would not dare to settle his wives on one property. He places them on plots as distant from each other as possible. The Hutu polygamist congratulates himself that he can put all his wives together in one house. He is not rich, hence there are no motives for hatred under his roof. In this the Rundi were not unanimous: The Hutu insist that their wives obey them without backtalk but that Tutsi wives dominate their husbands. Against this idea, the Tutsi protested perhaps too much, while the idea evoked a Mona Lisa smile from the Tutsikazi. The enquirer was unable to seek verification in the houses themselves. There was talk about Tutsi domestic tyrants and a few of them were known, but the bulk of the evidence favours the Hutu point of view.

The contrasts between men and women parallel the Tutsi-Hutu case. Women are stronger than men, but clumsy and less agile; they are less stable and are less able to hide and control their emotions; they are much given to jealousy and competition in seeking the favour of the superior; they work for their husbands; they ask gifts of them. Although women as women are without doubt inferiors, their inferiority by no means excludes the possibility that character and behaviour will be reversed when they are in the roles of superiors.

Distinctions between the sexes begin at birth and increase with maturity. A little boy wears no clothing. His sister, from the first day of her life, wears the *ubudede*, a string of beads worn around her hips, which later in her life will be added to, especially through gifts from her husband. Except for the beads, however, there is very little attention paid to sex differences in infancy. Excepting among the wealthy, introduction to economic and social responsibilities occurs very early. Children, like any inferiors, must work and must obey the instructions and commands of their superiors. Boys are in the charge of their fathers and girls of their mothers. Apprenticeship begins earlier for girls than for boys. When she is three years old, a little girl, Tutsi or Hutu, is already old enough to accompany her mother to the fields and follow her about the house. At six, she knows how to sweep the yard, do a little work with the hoe, and carry on her head a sizeable basket of beans or a large gourd of water. At the same age, her brother, particularly among the herders, begins at last his apprenticeship with his father. Among the Hutu, boys are sometimes instructed by their mother or grand-

Women of Burundi: A Study of Social Values

mother how to farm and to carry burdens on their heads. At 12, boys and girls should be able to work well and independently. If not, they are beaten or deprived of their dinner to encourage them to learn. There is, nevertheless, time to play with other children, the boys with other boys, the girls with other girls.

Moral taboos have no significance before adolescence. Children may eat anything at all, without penalty. A young girl may milk a cow: she is not yet a woman, say the Rundi, she is still like her brother. Brothers and sisters sleep together in the same bed and are covered by the same mat. If sometimes there are sexual experiments, these are not called incest. They are only children, they are not responsible, they cannot sin. At puberty, a young girl is removed from the common bedroom of the children. Boys seem to mature much later than girls. Moreover, the question of the dowry enters to delay their marriage. It is said that girls want to be married very early. By the time they have reached puberty, they have already begun to play with other young girls, each helping the other to develop the private parts to a maximum size in anticipation of the pleasures of the marriage bed. A mother warns her daughter that she must absolutely remain a virgin until her marriage, or, at least, that she does not dare to become pregnant if she has not yet been asked for and paid for. In the past, an unmarried mother-to-be would have been killed and her father's property confiscated. Today, there are illegitimate children, and nobody knows quite what to do with them. (One way in which a disgruntled wife can revenge herself upon her husband is by allowing a grown daughter to become pregnant before she is paid for.) At all events, it is up to the mother of a nubile daughter to watch her carefully.

Very strong taboos forbid all contact between a father and his daughter after she has been weaned, except for mutual greetings and for several minor services which a daughter performs for her father.[12] It is customary for girls to wear only a skirt while working, and in the past, a young girl might wear nothing at all or only a leopard skin around her hips. A father must avert his eyes if a daughter is working with her bosom exposed. If a father wishes some information about his daughter, or if he wishes to say something to her, he must ask his wife to speak to their daughter. If a young girl is to be punished, it is the mother who will beat her, never the father. The same taboos apply to the father's brothers. All are called *data*, father. Fathers never enter the house in which a married daughter lives with her husband. The explanation offered for these strong taboos to separate father from mature

195

daughter is the necessity to prevent incest. The taboo is strong enough to serve as the basis of the oath in court. A man "swears on his daughter", by saying, "If a lie, may I do that act with my daughter, the one named such-and-such".

Despite the physical and social distance between father and daughter, they are jointly interested in the earliest possible marriage for her. She is impatient for the pleasures and privileges of the married woman. He is looking forward to the dowry, which he keeps entirely for himself. It is possible that a mother will do her best to put off the marriage. She does not stand to profit from it at all. On the contrary, the departure of her daughter diminishes the available labour supply for work in the home and in the fields. Young people brought up in the homes of the great must wait a long time before their master or mistress will allow them to leave to be married. The *inchoreke*, young women of good family who are the personal servants of princes and princesses, are often 25 years old before they are married. The *abakamyi*, young men of good family who milk for the great families, are sometimes 35 or 40 at marriage. Among the commoners, the children of the wealthy are able to marry early, the girls at 15 or 16 and the boys at 18. Poor people envy them and have to wait five to ten years longer before they can be married.

A girl's father waits for a visit from a man who is looking for a wife for his son. Sometimes, a boy may ask his father to dower a young girl to whom he has taken a fancy. However, it is the two fathers who decide everything. Neither the girl nor the boy need be formally advised of their father's decisions. Nevertheless, a father will probably tell his son and a mother will tell her daughter. If not, a girl among the Tutsi of western Burundi will guess that she is engaged from the arrival of the prescribed number of pots of beer from the family asking for her and from the gifts of beer and food sent by relatives for the celebration. She will guess the approach of the wedding day most easily from the construction of the *indaro*, a temporary dwelling, in her father's yard, where she will live with her husband for the first year of the marriage. (On the wedding day, the girl's father must absent himself from his house.) If the new husband and wife are satisfied with each other and if they have a child, they will leave to take up permanent residence on the property the young husband has received from his father.

The Tutsi in the east of Burundi and the Hutu marry at the home of the groom's father. It is then the young man who deduces from the activities in the household that he will soon be married. The intended bride should properly be told who her intended bridegroom is so that she can obey the rule forbidding her to look at or speak to the man she is to marry. There are nonetheless young people, orphans or children whose parents are inconsiderate, who do not know until the wedding day that arrangements have been made to marry them. If this happens to a young girl, it is said, she becomes very frightened by the sudden necessity to go perhaps very far away to live with a strange family and with a man whom she has probably never seen. Although the young girl receives new clothes from the family of her bridegroom, although she goes to her new home accompanied by a representative of her family and by her friends and cousins (neither her mother nor her father may attend the wedding at the groom's home), the happy dreams of marriage change into nightmares. The bride is hardly reassured by a wedding ceremony that is a symbolic kidnapping. The hostility between the two patrilineages is supposed to be play-acting, but under the influence of beer, it often becomes genuine quarrelling. Weddings are almost invariably marked by arguments and mutual criticisms which are sometimes very bitter. In truth, hatred for a husband may still burn in the memory of an elderly lady as she speaks of her wedding of 50 years ago, if she had not been told in advance and if her husband on their wedding night behaved like a wild young man and took her by force and against her will. If the groom and parents-in-law are kind, they will be able to calm the fears of a bride. For the four days of the honeymoon, they are indulgent towards her. The husband and his brothers give her little gifts to persuade her to eat, they bribe her so that she will talk to them, and the mother-in-law sends beer and food. In this way, she can become accustomed to her new home.

A father who is wise and kind chooses a good husband for his daughter. He will point out that a bad marriage is not worth the trouble. If soon after the marriage his daughter returns home with a legitimate reason for having left her husband, the father will have to return the dowry and wait for someone else to come and ask for his daughter. It sometimes happens that a father is more interested in the dowry than in the happiness of his daughter. He will then accept the first offer made him, even if it comes from a man he knows is bad, or, scandal of scandals, from an old man. (The latter connotes incest, involving as it does a male of an older generation than the female.) Or, if the father is dead, a girl may be given by her paternal uncle to anyone who comes along. Men of this kind do not allow the women to come back home again when they are dissatisfied with their husbands. An orphan or the daughter of a bad father will have the good luck to please her husband and to have a good life with him only if she is liked by *Imana*.

The dowry represents wealth for the father. The average Tutsi expects to receive a cow for his daughter, an average Hutu eight hoes. However, today the Hutu often and the Tutsi sometimes pay the dowry in cash. For the husband, the dowry purchases the children produced by the woman during the term of their marriage. For the young woman, the dowry is a measure of her social value. She has discussed with other girls how much a man will have to give for her. Young Tutsikazi flatter each other by saying that they are certainly worth four cows—the dowry of a Tutsikazi of a very good patrilineage. A Hutukazi may boast of the 2,500 Congo francs (50 dollars) that were given for her, for everyone knows that 1,500 Congo francs (30 dollars) is the average for a Hutukazi. Or, a poor woman who is slightly mad is overcome by shame, for everyone knows that her father has given her in marriage without demanding a dowry. The more one has given for a young woman, the higher her social status. The wife of a wealthy man will have more clothes and less work, more respect and less hardship, than the wife of a poor man.

Although a young woman looks forward to marriage to rise above her painfully low status as a female child, she knows very well that what lies before her is a lifetime of work and that she will for a long time be under the authority of others. She is in effect sent from her father's household, where she works for her mother, to her husband's household, where she works for her husband and her mother-in-law. Regarding the sentiments of the husband towards his wife, or of men in general towards women, it is enough to mention that in the rich oral literature of Burundi, there is not one poem or song of love. At best, among the *amazina*—praise-poems, most of which praise the king or a generous patron or the man himself as a warrior—there are several which praise a good wife. She is praised for her cleverness, for her indefatigable efforts on behalf of her husband, for the cleanness of the butter she churns, and she may be given the compliment of comparison with a cow. In all truth, a man may sometimes have a great love, or be infatuated with his wife or his mistress. He does not talk about it very much; he would certainly not talk about it with strangers. At all events, love is not relevant to married life except in the general form it takes as the basis of the exchange of gifts and services between superiors and inferiors.

Every married woman of every class and caste works for her husband. Often a bride goes to live in the same household with her

Women of Burundi: A Study of Social Values

mother-in-law or with a sister-in-law, though sometimes she may be alone on a part of her husband's property at some distance from his father's household. The social division of labour assigns to women nearly total responsibility for anything that is related to food, small children and the house. Men are rarely at home. Among the herders, the men are out in the pastures with the cattle. During the dry season, they may have to go for pasture a long way from home and build temporary dwellings for the season. A Hutu farmer works in the fields of his master, and these may be very far from the plot of land granted him for himself and his family.[13] The wives of a polygamist are each in turn necessarily alone. Moreover, men often have to go on trips for their superiors or to look after their own interests. Sometimes a trip lasts only two or three days, sometimes the man is absent from home for several months or for an entire year. We see here the continuing influence of an earlier day of a military, feudal society. Before 1920, every Tutsi was obliged to put in military service at the court of his prince. His wife sent him food, and he visited her at home from time to time, but he had to spend many months in service. Hutu sometimes went to war, but most of them stayed on the property of their feudal masters to work. Even today, young Rundi, both Hutu and Tutsi, leave home to earn money for the dowry and then very soon after marriage leave again to make money for other purposes. They work for their Rundi superiors, or in Uganda, or Tanganyika, or the European cities of Burundi. As administrators, as porters, as cowherds, they travel a great deal. The women are responsible for the household during the frequent and often prolonged absences of the men.

In all other things the inferior of her husband, a Rundikazi is absolute proprietor of the food supply. The land she farms is her husband's. The husband gives her orders to work and decides what will be grown, and the husband inspects the granaries and the pots of butter. However, it is strictly forbidden for men to take so much as a handful of beans, raw or cooked, or a bit of butter without the wife's permission. If one asks what would happen to a man who might steal food from his wife, it is said: that doesn't happen, nobody would drink with that sort of fellow. This rule is taken very seriously. If a man wants food for himself for any reason, he must grow it himself. He may not touch any of the food raised by his wife. It is said that the woman has raised the food even when the farmhands and the serfs of the husband have done the actual work. What is meant is that the household food supply is always under the control of the wife.

199

Hutukazi have as their first duty cultivating the husband's fields. During the two or three weeks before the rainy season, a woman leaves the house each day a little after sunrise, pregnant or a baby on her back and another child trailing behind her, hoe in hand. She must prepare the soil and sow the seed. Once or twice during the rainy season, she must weed the peas, beans and millet. At harvest time, she is again very busy for two or three weeks.[14] She must harvest the crops and must carry it from the fields to her yard in bundles of from 30 to 50 kilograms on her head; there she must dry and clean what she has harvested. Finally, she stores the food in large storage baskets and brews the sorghum beer. Between the planting season and the harvest, there is leisure for visits to her mother or sister, to take it easy at home, to gossip with a neighbour, and to weave baskets.

Daily, a woman must prepare meals, watch and instruct her children, and pick up around the house and yard. In the morning, the pot of beans or peas for the evening meal must be set on the three-stone hearth to cook. In mid-morning, work is stopped for breakfast, the cold leftovers from the previous evening's dinner. If there is no child old enough to send, a woman must herself return at intervals to the house from the fields or from the house of her neighbour to add firewood to the fire. Each day she must draw water from the spring and carry it back in her 20-litre pot on her head to the house, and she must cut firewood and carry it back to the house on her head. Every few days she must sweep the yard and the packed-dirt floors of the house and change the straw on the beds, especially if her husband will be staying with her that night. It is also necessary every week to grind the sorghum, cassava, or maize into flour for *umudsima*, a polenta eaten with each meal. Ordinarily, a woman does the work only for her own house. However, a mother-in-law has the right to assign tasks—other than cooking—to her daughters-in-law. There is especially great need for help when there are visitors. It is necessary to prepare beer and food, and if they stay the night, a bed must be made ready.

When the husband is home, he will probably help his wife to clear a new plot of ground or to sow or harvest, according to the season. If he does not like to do woman's work, he stays at home while his wife goes to the fields or he visits a neighbour who has beer. If the husband is at home, he will probably be the one to chase away the animals who try to get into the yard at night or who are foraging for food in the fields. If he is not home, the wife has to look after these matters. If at night, a hyena, having scented the goat or the sheep in the yard, tries to enter, the woman will pick up a piece of firewood and chase the hyena. However, if she hears thieves or a lion or antelope or wild pigs in the fields, she gives the cry of alarm so that the neighbours will come to help her. One need not think that the Rundi consider a woman courageous who is at home alone night after night with several babies and who chases away wild animals and thieves.[15]

In a Tutsi household, all of the tasks of the Hutu household must be done and in addition those which result from the fact that the houses and the yard are used as corral and barns. If a Tutsikazi is lucky, her husband is wealthy enough to provide her with Hutu to do the farming and with one or more Hutu or Tutsi girls to help her in the house and yard. If this is the case, the Tutsikazi's job is to command and supervise others. However, even a Tutsukazi of a very good patrilineage will very likely have to work at least a little in the fields and do some cooking and other household chores. Whether it is the wife, a daughter, or a servant girl, somebody has to clean the yard after the cows have been taken to pasture. The cow dung has to be collected and taken to the fields where it is needed as fertilizer. Fresh earth has to be spread over the puddles and mud that the cows have left, and it is necessary to look in on the calves that are kept in the various houses of the dwelling unit. If a calf or a child or a Hutu is sick, the mistress of the house must prepare the medicine. The wife of a herder has as her first obligation the proper care of the milk which her husband or the boy who milks the cow gives into her care in the morning and the evening. She lets it accumulate so that she can churn every few days. Then, she must clean the butter and put aside some to be used for cooking, some to be mixed with red ochre to be used as a cosmetic, some to annoint the mats of the bed when her husband is at home. If the family is not rich enough to pay a herd boy and if the sons are still young, the Tutsi husband and wife take turns watching over the cows at night. At dawn, both may sleep: thieves will not come once it is daylight.

The richer one is, the more serfs and servants there are to do the work in the house and the fields and to attend to the cattle. Among the very wealthy, the wife is primarily the administrator of her husband's property. She supervises the workers, she gives them orders, she punishes those who misbehave and those who are lazy, and she receives visitors, who are frequently men of high position. The proper education of a Tutsikazi of good family is the responsibility either of her mother or of the princess in whose household she is brought up. There is hope that a daughter will be married by a wealthy man, that she will be literally a *mwamikazi* who will never have to do menial tasks. Young girls are taught, so that they will be refined, to command and to correct inferiors gently but firmly; to weave pretty baskets; to rub red and yellow ochre on the wooden milk pots which are lined up on a long shelf to display the herder's wealth; to offer beer and food to visitors and to sing and dance, breasts bared, to entertain them. Later, a young woman must learn to cover her face with her scarf, to so arrange her numerous diaphanous white and yellow robes that her entire body is covered, and to engage visitors in conversation while shielded from view by a screen. She must learn how to listen and to understand. If a young girl has noticed that her mother is a good conversationalist, she takes into account the fact that her mother is discreet, intelligent and older than she.

The more closely a woman approximates to the feminine ideal for her caste, the greater her hope for the rewards due to a married woman. A good wife should receive from her husband a quantity of clothes and jewels proportionate to his wealth, permission to go out and to visit where she wishes, permission to drink her husband's beer and to take snuff. In addition she will be praised wherever her husband travels. If the husband has cows, he will give her several so that she and the children will have milk, and he may give her one or more as gifts. If he likes her very much, he will plan in advance the means by which she can remain on his property if he predeceases her. To be a good wife means first of all to execute wifely tasks efficiently. Then, towards her husband and parents-in-law, a good wife is always obedient and respectful, at least while there are outsiders present. Intelligence is a highly desirable characteristic and is indeed indispensable in anyone who will be the wife of a prince. A capable woman will be consulted by her husband, especially if he knows that she is cleverer than he. Among the Hutu, the husband asks advice of an intelligent wife before he goes to ask a cow of a Tutsi, before choosing a wife for their son, before he does anything. Among the Tutsi, a husband who takes pride in his wife's intelligence will consult her before he chooses a serf, goes to his superior to ask for another cow. He does nothing without her advice and boasts about her intelligence and loyalty to his friends. Among the princes, family and economic affairs are hardly distinguishable from affairs of state. Thus, intelligent women come to have a voice in matters of the first importance.

A good hostess who provides food and drink for her husband's visitors need never fear his anger. Just as women speak a great deal of the importance of receiving clothing from their husbands, so men speak a great deal of the importance of a warm welcome for

Women of Burundi: A Study of Social Values

their friends, especially if they are away from home. A wife who always gives abundant beer and food to her husband's friends is, by so doing, showing respect for her husband.

Beauty does not count very heavily, but a man is not displeased if people notice that his wife is attractive and well-fleshed, has a long and narrow nose, a light skin, and is somewhat like a cow. If a woman is fortunate, she will have a child every two years, and the children will not die. One of the most fortunate women of whom the Rundi spoke—a Tutsikazi *imfura*, needless to say—gave birth to a child virtually every 11 months. The husband of a wife who produces many children is a real man, and people always speak highly of the fathers of many children.

A husband supervises his wife, as every superior supervises his inferiors, and he must punish her if she does not do as she ought. Hence, a Tutsi will not hesitate to go to see whether all the clothes he has given his wife are in the baskets that serve as wardrobes for women. He also goes to see if everything is clean. If he is not satisfied, he will warn his wife that she must change her ways. Sometimes she makes excuses. Perhaps she has not worked well because she has been ill, or because she had to do a great deal of work for her mother-in-law, because several of the workers have run off to Uganda, because her husband ordered more work than she had strength to do. A considerate husband will check up on his wife's explanations. If he is satisfied that they are correct, he will do his best to see that she has help, even if he has to help her himself. A man of bad character, however, does not accept any excuses. He will beat his wife, he will insult her, and she can expect to be sent back home, unless she becomes angry and goes back without waiting to be sent.

The Rundi speak a great deal about "good character" and "bad character". Character, for them, explains most of human behaviour. Obviously, the ideal marriage unites a woman of good character with a man of good character. However, there are a great many people of bad character, probably most people. This explains, they say, the numerous quarrels and divorces. People know what they ought to do, but they don't do it. In all truth, a young woman lives like a nomad. She goes from her father's home to the home of her first husband, then after quarrels or divorce back again to her father, then to a second husband, then back to her father, until at last she finds a husband who pleases her and who at the same time is pleased with her. Divorce is forbidden those who are Catholics. Nevertheless, for them as for the other Rundi, married life is no more peaceful than any other interpersonal relationship among the

Ethel M. Albert

Rundi. Peace is always desirable but rarely achieved. The frequent absence of the husband does not seem to diminish the tensions and problems of domestic life. There is a host of reasons to quarrel, to fight, to separate for several days or forever.

A man will be angry with his wife if she has drunk up all his beer, if she has not prepared dinner for him, if she has left the house without his permission, if she has invited company without permission, if she has not done the work he has told her to do, if he comes back home to find her in bed with another man. One quarrel need not destroy a marriage. However, a man is considered perfectly within his rights to send away a woman who is consistently disobedient and lazy, who insults her husband and parents-in-law, who does not offer food and drink to her husband's visitors while he is away from home. A woman suspected of witchcraft will be packed off at the first possible moment. A sterile woman will be retained only in the exceptional case: a man gives the bride-price to have children. Among the Tutsi, a woman who takes the milk to drink for herself instead of churning it into butter for her husband will be humiliated and sent away. Her father-in-law will invite her father to drink beer. Then, he asks the offending woman "to show the butter to the bull", who has been led into the yard for this little "ceremony". She has no butter to show. Her father, furious and humiliated, will take her back home and will punish her. Finally, a talkative woman who discusses her husband's business with strangers will certainly be sent back home. Towards a woman who speaks against her husband, who is engaged in intrigue against him, a husband will have no pity. She will be beaten within an inch of her life and sent back to her father— unless she has been clever enough to succeed in a plot that ruins her husband utterly, while she has arranged to be married afterward by his richer and more powerful enemy.

On her side, a woman does not have to put up with a husband who eats so much of what she has cooked that nothing is left for her, nor with a husband who does not eat what she cooks. Does he think, she wants to know, that she is going to poison him, or is it that he prefers the cooking of his mother or sister-in-law? A man who praises other women need not imagine that his wife will stay with him for long, particularly if she is a Tutsikazi. If he has money and does not give his wife clothes, she will surely become angry. If all her children die, the woman will fear her mother-in-law's sorcery and will leave. If the husband consistently overworks her, if he beats her too much and without legitimate reason, she will go back home. Sometimes the marriage does not last the four days of

Women of Burundi: A Study of Social Values

the honeymoon. The morning after the wedding, it can happen that the young bride will go out into the yard and announce in a loud, clear voice: "I did not come here to go to bed with another girl". She goes home. The boy's father knows that his son is impotent. It is the mother's fault. She must have allowed the dried umbilical cord to fall on the male organ of her newborn son. The cure also is up to her. The parents give their son a great deal of beer so that he will become drunk. The father then leaves the house, and the mother then has intercourse with the son in order to remove the impotence which her neglect caused. If the cure has not failed—and there is great confidence in the probable success of this remedy—the young couple will be reunited and remain together to face the other risks of married life.

When spouses fight, the neighbour-women give advice to the wife and the men to the husband. Both are encouraged to reform. If the wife has become seriously angry, she will leave and stay at her father's for a while. She tells her mother her reasons for having left. If she is wrong, if she has deserved the beating, or if she has refused to do work which a woman is obliged to do, her mother must correct her. Sometimes after two or three days, she returns voluntarily to her husband. However, she much prefers to wait for her husband to come after her and to have to explain his behaviour to her father. If it is the husband who is in the wrong, his mistake will probably cost him a handsome new length of cloth, some money, or some jewellery before his wife will consent to go back to him.

Sometimes the advice of the neighbours and the parents lead at last to marital adjustment. If not, there is a divorce. However, the Rundi say that divorce is no longer reasonable after a man and woman have had two or three children together. Their blood has been mixed. Furthermore, they have had time enough to get to know each other's defects. In addition, to divorce the mother of several children is expensive. The husband takes back the bride-price, but he must pay to have his children. A Tutsi has to give a heifer for each daughter and a bull-calf for each son. The Hutu do not always buy back their children, or else they must wait a long time before they have sufficient hoes or money to redeem them. Occasionally, a man prefers simply to abandon a woman. She and her children remain on the property that the husband has given her, and she must send her sons to stay with their father as soon as they are old enough to work for him. Because he does not take back the brideprice, she cannot remarry. A father may not accept more than one dowry for each daughter. If she wants to remarry, she must get her father or another relative to intervene for her with her husband. If she cannot do anything, she remains married but abandoned. Or, it may happen that an unfortunate Hutukazi without relatives can no longer endure a bad husband or is sent away by her husband or left a widow without property. Women of this kind become vagabonds who wander about the countryside, often with children, and who often enter voluntary slavery for the sake of food and a roof over their heads.

In the household, the mother-in-law is the superior of her daughters-in-law. According to the ideal, she is like their true mother. According to the proverb: the daughter-in-law waits for her mother-in-law's death so that she can at last be the mistress in her own house. A woman has good reason to fear her mother-in-law. She may persuade her son to send his wife away. She can poison a daughter-in-law she does not like, or she can overwhelm her with work. Among sisters-in-law, there is little friendship. The first one to be married into the household has in principle priority over the other sisters-in-law. If the husband of the first-ranking sister-in-law has just made four mortars for grinding grain, his wife will demand all of them for herself. Each of his brother's wives, no doubt, will also demand all four for themselves. The first one will probably have all of them, and the hatred of her sisters-in-law will surely result. Or, a Hutukazi may receive cloth and bracelets from her husband newly returned from Uganda. She loses no time in showing them to her sisters-in-law. The latter promptly ask their husbands for cloth and bracelets. If a woman has many children, her sisters-in-law not so many, or if one of them is preferred by the mother-in-law, the one thus favoured by fortune will be the object of the hatred of the others. This goes on, the men complain, this just goes on and on. Each woman nags her husband. The same story and even worse is told of the wives of a polygamist. One of the wives of a Tutsi or Hutu will normally be kept as the permanent wife, with the privileges of seniority. The second and third wives are often no more than servants, farm labour and child-producing machines. They do not usually last very long. The bride-price is taken back to replace those who die without having produced children and those who run away. The *umutoni*, the favourite wife, is probably not the very first woman that the polygamist married. Although she may at a given moment be the favourite wife, she must exert herself to prevent another from taking her favoured place, as she probably took it away from someone else. A second or third wife who is stronger, more fertile, or cleverer may upset the order of precedence.

Women of Burundi: A Study of Social Values

Many children represent happiness for both men and women in Burundi. Women adore babies, and a pregnant Rundikazi is a happy woman. Only very rarely do women go into the bush to look for the medicines that cause miscarriage. (For unwed mothers, the motivation is obviously different). It is not possible to find a Rundikazi, even a great-grandmother, who will admit that she is *umukechuru*, a woman beyond the age of child-bearing. A woman who is sterile, or who has had only one child and never again conceived believes that she has been cursed by her paternal aunt or is the victim of witchcraft. Some women produce Gargantuas, children they have carried for 11 months, or 15 months or even two years. The Rundi are by no means ignorant of the biological cause and signs of pregnancy.[16] They simply refuse to acknowledge any other alternative conditions than pregnancy or nursing mother. It is also not for a lack of knowledge of the biological facts that men have no interest in the biological paternity of their children. If a brother or cousin is the biological father, this is no more than is to be expected. If it is a stranger who has got his wife with child, he has made the husband a free gift. The father does not reproach his wife if she has conceived during one of his long absences from home, nor is he at all prejudiced against those of his children who have been fathered by other men, when the time comes to choose his heritor.[17]

Among the princes and the Tutsi of the very good patrilineages, the mother does not take care of the children except to nurse them. A governess, a woman from a family only slightly lower in the social scale than that of the child, looks after it. At present, the wealthy send their school-age children to European schools far from home. In the past, young adolescents were sent to be brought up by princes and princesses. Among the commoners, an infant is with its mother day and night. He is carried nude on her naked back and nursed at the first whimper. The mother plays with her baby, especially with her son, tickles it everywhere, and talks baby talk to it. She adores her baby, but the moment she finds herself pregnant again, she immediately weans her child. The child, who is probably between 18 and 24 months old, is abruptly separated from his mother. He is handed over to a brother, a sister, a grandmother, to anyone who will have him. Sometimes, the grandmother or a grown-up sister will permit a newly-weaned child to suck at the dry breast, but soon the child is put on the ground to crawl about, to play, and to learn that life is hard. It is not surprising that the mortality rate of newly-weaned children is very high.

If there has been a divorce, the departing wife takes with her

207

the child she is still nursing but leaves the older children with their father. Once weaned, the child is sent to live with its father. The paternal grandmother or one of the father's wives will bring it up. If the divorced woman remarries and is again pregnant, she sends the weaned infant to his father with no visible regrets. If she is not pregnant, or if she has occasion to speak of her children by her divorced husband, she will express misgivings, for children are rarely kindly treated by a stepmother. She is also unhappy because she no longer has her daughters to help with the work. Moreover, it is nice to have children in the house so that one will not be lonesome. It happens very often that a woman who has many children will send a two or three-year-old to stay with its grandmother or an aunt who is sterile. Little children are really very much liked.

An *umuzungu*, an outsider, may be somewhat confused by the typical Rundi combination of pragmatic considerations with very tender sentiments. It seems a little paradoxical that Rundikazi love the infants they are nursing but pay no attention to children who have been weaned, except to wait for the day when they are old enough to work. In effect, weaning ends the only period of privilege and pleasure before full maturity. The life of young people is a long night of servitude under the exacting supervision of father and mother. In daily life, children have no importance as persons. The inferiors of their parents, they are treated as inferiors. Excepting in very wealthy families, they do not have enough clothing or blankets against the chill of their mountainous country. Children may go to bed without dinner, if the father and mother have eaten all the food or have simply forgotten about them in the midst of a quarrel or a party. Clever young people, nevertheless, learn how to profit from the conflict of jurisdiction between the father and the mother. Both have the right to order the children to work. If a son disobeys his father, he will be punished by a beating or by being deprived of his dinner. An indulgent mother may very well give food secretly to her unfortunate child. If a boy disobeys his mother but he has worked well for his father—for example, he has taken good care of the cows, but he has refused to go for firewood for his mother— the father will not allow the mother to harm the boy. She will have to wait for revenge on the boy until her husband is away from home. The son, if he is intelligent, will find a way to make her forget her anger. Or, he may take refuge with his paternal aunt or grandparents, who are obliged to offer him asylum against her anger. A young girl cannot go for protection to her father, and she can avoid her mother's punishments only by putting herself under the

Women of Burundi: A Study of Social Values

protection of her grandparents. It is best if she is obedient and thus avoid blows and dinnerless nights.

Friendship between a woman and her daughter must wait until the latter is herself a mother. If a married daughter is kind, she will ask her husband for permission to go to help her mother during the busy season. From her married son, a woman expects presents. If he is too poor to give gifts, she will mock and shame him. If he arrives at her home empty-handed, if he comes back from a job in Uganda or the city without something for her, she will be enraged. It means her son does not like her, for he has not given her a present. However, an intelligent woman very early chooses one of her sons as her favourite—usually a different one from the father's favourite. She struggles on his behalf against the other children of her husband, above all against his half-brothers, the sons of his father's other wives. She protects his heritage, she does not remarry even if left a widow very early, she prevents the brothers of her deceased husband from taking possession of her husband's cows or from chasing her and the children off of her husband's property. A widow, particularly among the Tutsi, prefers to remain on the property given her by her husband without remarrying. She is thus finally independent of a husband's authority. To live where her favourite son lives assures her happiness. A good son, it is said, puts the happiness of his mother before that of his wife.

A full analysis of Rundi "Momism" is not possible here. It seems to depend in part on the biological and symbolic importance of food, which the mother gives or refuses at will; in part on the maternal sorcery of sacrificing her own interests for the sake of her sons; in part on the psychological power of which a mother assures herself during her son's infancy by making him very happy when she praises him and causing him great unhappiness and shame when she ridicules him. Children are, in any event, obliged to respect and love their parents, that is to say, to work for them and to obey them.

When a woman is at last a mother-in-law and grandmother, she has reached the high point of her life as a woman. A mother-in-law and her son-in-law, no matter what their caste, address each other as *umufasoni*, noble. Their relationship is one of highly formal respect, politeness of the highest degree, no jokes and no quarrels. A mother-in-law is the uncontested superior of her daughters-in-law. She orders them to work, she must be given respect, she chooses one of them as her favourite—the one who works the most for her, who is most obedient and docile. Towards her grand-

Ethel M. Albert

children, a grandmother may at last dare to indulge openly in revealing her sentiments, without, however, neglecting practical considerations. Grandparents joke with their grandchildren, spoil them, protect them against their parents' anger, and, if they are not believing Christians, they expect their grandchildren will in due course perform the ceremonies in honour of the *imizimu*, the spirits of dead grandparents.

* * *

The most direct route to happiness is conformity to the norms and rules of society. Most Rundi have some roles in which they are superior and others in which they are inferior and the accompanying obligations and compensations. A good wife of a generous and reasonable husband, a good mother of numerous and good children, a good mother-in-law of obedient and industrious daughters-in-law and of respectful sons-in-law, will be a happy woman. Unfortunately, it is necessary to take into account the ever-present and infamous "bad characters", the numberless misfortunes sent by *Imana* when he is in a bad humour, the truth that *Imana*—or, if one prefers, Nature, biology, or genetics—does not always pay attention to social norms. Thus, it can happen that a man is not qualified for the role of patriarch, that he suffers all his life the oppression of a nagging shrew. It can happen that a woman is born too weak for manual labour. If she does not find a kind husband who will carry the burden of the work of the household or a rich one who can provide her with workers, she will die very miserable and very young. It can also happen that a woman is more intelligent and more enterprising than her father, her husband, or her son. A woman of this kind is ordinarily encouraged to make use of her gifts—intelligence must not be wasted—but sometimes an energetic woman is tied to a husband who is cruel and stupid and can do nothing with her good-for-nothing sons. In the social life of Burundi, the motto is, everyone for himself. Each must do what he can with whatever *Imana* has given him.

There are many Rundikazi who are unfortunate and wretched—orphans, the daughters of avaricious and cruel fathers, the wives of bad husbands, childless widows, the poor and the sick—in brief, those who do not have the favour of *Imana*. Let us pass in sad silence from their pathetic lot to the more fortunate women, those who have succeeded, despite the inevitable woes of life, in obtaining at least some measure of happiness, and to the true favourites of *Imana*, the well-born women who are at maturity true matriarchs. The absolute quantity of power and wealth depends upon birth. A

Women of Burundi: A Study of Social Values

mwamikazi and a wealthy Tutsikazi are matriarchs on a much grander scale than is possible for any Hutukazi. Nevertheless, the character model and the methods for success as a matriarch are quite the same. Furthermore, although the methods employed by women are not in every detail like those of men, there is only one character model for the matriarch and the patriarch, that of the superior. By the same token, there is only one character model for those in the roles of inferiors. The latter are always alert to opportunities for asking some good thing of a superior. If one road is closed, it is necessary to find another. If a husband is not generous, a woman will ask one of her brothers for gifts, or she will wait until her sons are grown. When fortunate people have received gifts, they obviously have something to give, and they thus may expect petitioners to come to them for gifts. Yet again, if a man is muddled by drink, his wife or his vassal or someone who wants his favour will make a request of a gift in the presence of others; a promise given, drunk or sober, before witnesses must be respected at the risk of losing one's fair name. The rules of society provide only for a minimum of happiness. One must rely upon intelligence to point the way to supplementary means and to profit from every favourable circumstance.

Like any normal citizen of Burundi, a Rundikazi desires as much power and authority as possible, which is to say, numerous inferiors, including children, workers, feudal followers; wealth, which is to say, for women who can inherit nothing, many gifts from men and from wealthier women; respect and love, which amounts to having many inferiors; elegance, which is again to say many gifts, but also education in the home of a princess; many children, which depends on the will of *Imana;* protection against one's enemies, that is, against one's rivals and one's mother-in-law; and the good luck to retain what has been received from *Imana* and from human beings, which again depends on *Imana* and also on one's own intelligence, courage and strength of character. There is decidedly no psychological conflict in women of strong character, nor is there any conflict between feminine ambitions and social norms. Everything is taken care of by the functional norms of the society.

A woman starts very young to calculate what she needs in order to be happy. From her father she expects little more than that he will find her a husband who is wealthy and reasonable, or better yet, tractable; that he will allow her to return home if she is not satisfied with a husband and will find her a better one; that he will from time to time give her gifts. If a father has a tendency to turn

211

a deaf ear to his daughter's wishes in the matter of changing a husband, she will perhaps make the necessary arrangements on her own initiative with the husband she prefers, and the father will have no choice but to accept the new arrangements. From her husband, a woman expects to receive gifts in proportion to his wealth—clothing, copper bracelets, beads, cows, money. She also wishes workmen and servants, so that she will not have to perform the menial tasks of inferiors; so that she will have a great many inferiors to supervise; so that she will enjoy sufficient energy and leisure for the planning and plotting necessary to increase her wealth and her influence in family affairs, economic matters and politics. As her husband's business partner, an intelligent woman will be consulted at every turn or she may not even wait for her husband to ask her advice. She decides what must be done, and her decisions must be respected. A wife who is well-established will almost certainly be the preferred intermediary of those who seek the favour of her husband. As an intermediary, she receives gifts, particularly pots of beer, to persuade her to intervene with the superior. An intelligent woman who finds herself with more beer than she needs will send a servant to sell it and keep the money for herself. For women in the lower castes, there are various optional roles through which they can earn money. They may sell the excess baskets they weave; they may be midwives; they may be *bapfumu*, physician-pharmacists who sell medicines and amulets; they may be governesses or ladies-in-waiting for good families. A husband takes great pride in a wife who becomes wealthy. Her wealth advertises her cleverness and is at all events obtained at no cost to him. Some women, it is said, are so intelligent that a prince will make them *abashingantahe*, judges and councillors. Women who have this honoured position receive cows, clothing, jewellery and serfs. On occasion, a woman of this kind may be wealthier than her husband, but he has every reason to be pleased to have such a wife. A wealthy woman will keep some of her cows for herself for milk and butter. Others she will give to those who come and ask of her, and these will become her feudal followers who will work for her, respect her, and go about in quest of information for her.

The frequent absences of the husband are opportunities for a woman to show herself capable of managing the property. Work is for inferiors and is not a source of honour. It nevertheless establishes the realistic dependence of the superior upon his inferior, and it forms the solid basis, sometimes explicitly recognized, of the relationship between superior and inferior. A good manager is indispensable to a wealthy man, for he has many feudal vassals, serfs, cows and lands. A woman of a powerful and wealthy patrilineage can be of great assistance to her husband in the matter of forming useful political alliances. The wife will probably have considerable influence with her brothers and perhaps also with her father.

The higher the social status of a woman, the higher will be the social status of her husband, and hence the higher the status of the visitors she entertains. In her role as hostess, a clever woman can profit very materially from the visits of her husband's friends and superiors. If she knows she pleases them, she will do them the honour of asking them for cows and other gifts. If her favourite son is ready to take his place in the world, she will look around among the visitors for a likely prospect of whom her son can ask a cow, if it is a family where the traditional values still prevail, or of whom he can ask for a job, if the son has been trained in European schools. In addition, the fair name of a man among his friends depends in no small measure upon the magnificence of the hospitality provided in his home by his wife and upon the gossip that circulates between the visitors and the wife. If a woman is satisfied with her husband, she will see to it that visitors have a good impression of the man. She will find ways to get information to gauge the friendliness of the visitors towards her husband. She will recognize his enemies and know how to defeat them. If she hears from the visitors that there are rumours to the effect that her husband is no longer loyal to his superior, that he does not take care of the cows which his superior has given him, that he will soon be removed from his position and his wealth taken away from him, she will probably seek means to save him, since his downfall will also be hers. However, if the husband is not clever, if he has not been generous, and if the wife sees a way to move to a more favourable position in another marriage, she will risk adding her calumny to the rest. It does not happen often, but when a woman has succeeded in ruining her husband, men talk about it for a long, long time. A mature woman prefers to stay with her husband and then, as a widow, with her favourite son. Among the men with whom she is in contact—her father, her brothers, her husband, her brothers-in-law, her cousins, her sons, and her visitors—an intelligent woman will certainly find a few who are generous and obliging and through whom she can obtain the wealth and power that she desires.

In all this, it is not to be forgotten that a woman is the inferior of her husband and of his distinguished visitors. To get what is wanted, an inferior must know how to please superiors, unfailingly displaying in public the respect and obedience due them. An intelligent woman makes herself liked or feared, according to the character of the men with whom she is dealing. Occasionally, it is said of a Rundi that "his house is burning", that is to say, despite the show of respect, his wife rules the roost. He is afraid of her, she nags him, she criticizes him, she wants to decide everything, and one fine day she will put poison in his beer, or she will calumniate him. However, a woman need not dominate her husband in so heavy-handed a fashion to earn her laurels as matriarch. She has her own inferiors to dominate, and there are other ways to become the *umutoni* of her husband and the other men. Apart from her ability as the mistress of her house and her generosity as a hostess, apart from all her obligations, a woman as an inferior is likely to understand very well the uses of flattery and subservience. She knows how to be an informant, to calumniate her superior's enemies as well as her own hated rivals, to show herself always loyal and devoted, to make the welfare of her superior her primary concern. She also knows how to satisfy sexual desires, the need for alcohol, and other demands of the body and the spirit. Superiors, apart from their economic dependence upon their inferiors, seem to seek them also for the satisfaction of what appear to be exceedingly urgent needs for love, respect, and loyalty and for entertainment that will take their minds off their troubles. It is to have these needs satisfied that they make presents, that they give what is asked of them. An intelligent woman busies herself with satisfying the desires of her superiors and thereby making herself indispensable to their happiness. Neither the Sophists, nor Machiavelli, nor the courtiers of Louis XIV have anything to teach the Rundi. An intelligent Rundikazi, like any intelligent social inferior, knows that to obtain happiness it is necessary only to say yes—to play along with the internal weaknesses and needs by which the superior is enslaved.

NOTES

[1]*Linguistic note:* Bantu prefixes have been dropped from words that refer to the inhabitants of Burundi. They are referred to as "Rundi" and by their caste-names, Tutsi, Hutu and Twa. Other words of the language retain their Bantu form, e.g., *mwami*, king; *mwamikazi*, queen-mother or princess, *bamikazi* in the plural; *muganwa*, prince, *baganwa* in the plural. The suffix, *-kazi*, designates the feminine. For "Rundi woman," "Tutsi woman," "Hutu woman," or "Twa woman," the Rundi forms will be used, i.e., "Rundikazi," "Tutsikazi," "Hutukazi," and "Twakazi."

Women of Burundi: A Study of Social Values

[2]For the most part, what is here said of Burundi was true also of the people of the neighbouring kingdom of Ruanda. Significant differences will be footnoted. For the hierarchical principle in Ruanda, see: J. J. Maquet, *Le Système des Relations sociales dans le Ruanda ancien*, Annales du Musée Royal du Congo Belge, Tervuren (Belgique), Sciences de l'Homme, Ethnologie, vol. I, 1954.

[3]Burundi is changing its laws. Thus, women and other social inferiors increasingly enjoy legal privileges and rights.

[4]In Ruanda, the queen-mother shared the royal power with her son, the *mwami*. This was not the case in Burundi.

[5]Very little will be said about religion in Burundi. The cult of Kiranga, the ancestor cult, and every other aspect of traditional religion and belief have been legally suppressed. About one-third of the population have been converted to Christianity. Religion, traditional and contemporary, is always important in the life of a society, but it may be concluded from the behaviour, the interests and the values of the Rundi that their society is secular rather than sacred.

[6]The word "caste" is not entirely satisfactory for describing the social distinctions of Burundi. However, there does not seem to be any better translation for the term, *aboko*, which connotes racial differences and to which are attached taboos and marriage regulations which separate rather rigidly these divisions of Rundi society.

[7]Although the terms "Hamitic" and "Bantu" are, properly speaking, linguistic terms, they will be used here, for lack of anything better, in their common acceptation as referring to social-cultural groups.

[8]In Ruanda, the Twa are more respected than the Hutu. Moreover, caste distinctions in Ruanda are social rather than racial. *Cf.* J. J. Maquet, *op. cit.*

[9]When the *mwami* of Ruanda gave a Tutsi wife to a man of an inferior caste, he raised the man to the higher caste.

[10]*Cf.* Jean Hiernaux, *Analyse de la Variation des Caractères physiques humains en une Région de l'Afrique centrale: Ruanda-Urundi et Kivu*. Annales du Musée Royal du Congo Belge, Tervuren (Belgique), Sciences de l'Homme, Anthropologie, vol. 3, 1956.

[11]Since 1952, polygamy is no longer permitted. Nevertheless, there are still a good many plural marriages. In the past, a prince might easily have had 20 wives. The average Rundi, however, would not have been wealthy enough to pay for more than two or three.

[12]These taboos are not known in Ruanda.

[13]The Hutu husband is obliged to build and to make repairs on the house, to take care of the banana grove that encircles the homestead, and to brew banana beer.

[14]In the past, there was only one harvest each year. There are now two, but the second one is relatively light.

[15]Almost nothing is known about the Twa, except that the men go to the marshes for the clay needed by the women to make pots and then sell them. The work in the fields is done by the women, but it appears that the men are often home and help.

[16]It has been suggested that anæmia explains the physiological condition interpreted by the Rundi as a prolonged pregnancy.

[17]Blinded by the ideas of my own culture about men's interest in their children's paternity, I wasted a great deal of time in the field seeking confirmation from Hutu and Tutsi, the Europeanized and the traditional. I was finally convinced of the lack of interest in biological paternity. This is, in any case, in keeping with the rather liberal rules pertaining to sexual relations in the kinship system.

WOMEN OF DAKAR
AND THE SURROUNDING
URBAN AREA

Solange Faladé

A REPERUSAL OF THE ACCOUNTS written by dealers living in Senegal towards the end of the last century[1] raises the question as to whether there is any point in describing once again the life of Wolof and Lebu women in the Dakar urban area, since so little seems to have changed since then. To be sure, the landscape has been greatly altered, and it is no longer an adventure for a European to go unaccompanied from Dakar to Wakam. This does not, however, alter the fact that, in spite of the technological improvements that have been introduced, the living conditions of women have remained almost untouched by them, even in the town. It is true that it is now possible to take a fast train or a taxi to get from one place to another. It is no longer necessary to go to the well to draw water, since there are taps at all the street corners; but the amount of time wasted in awaiting one's turn to fill up one's bowl is still considerable. In short, in all its essentials, the life of a woman today does not appear to be very different from what her mother's or her grandmother's must have been.

My reason for deciding nevertheless to describe the life of Dakar women as it is lived in the middle of the twentieth century is, that it seemed to me important to emphasize this lack of change, which some people—arriving, to my mind, at a too hasty conclusion—have considered to be a state of stagnation. African women, they say, are allergic to progress. I shall not go into the question here as to how much real effort has been made to change their living conditions. But on the hypothesis that such an effort has been made, or might have been made, would these women have accepted a radical change in their lives? In a word, would they not have had

217

a feeling of doubt, however vague, as to whether the change wrought in their lives were really a progressive one, really a step forward?

Since February 1955 I have had repeated interviews of many different kinds with 145 women living in the centre of Dakar or its immediate neighbourhood, as well as in Wakam, N'Gor and Camberen. These women belong to what one may describe as the Senegalese middle class, and represent the large majority of women in the Dakar urban area.

Their husbands are either petty officials or artisans (orderlies, masons, carpenters, plumbers, for the Department of Public Works), or fishermen, merchants, tailors and jewellers. Some of them follow two occupations: they have a trade in the town, and in the winter season return to the land. Their incomes do not seem to be very high. Their wives were usually unable to give me any clear idea as to the exact amounts, as they did not know what their husbands earned. This is not particularly surprising—could every Frenchwoman of the corresponding social class tell exactly how much her husband earned? Finally, to specify further the context of the women interviewed, I might mention that they live in the Medina, the African quarter of Dakar, and usually occupy one room there, varying in size. At N'Gor and Camberen they live in dwellings more or less of the classic type of African hut; in Dakar the dwellings are constructed of wood, very seldom in "hard", to use the term often employed by Africans.

Not all the women are of Wolof origin, but all call themselves Wolof even when they are of Lebu descent (that is to say, Tukulor or Serer). Women of this kind living in Dakar will say: "I have been here for quite a long time now", or "I was born here and even although my parents do not come from here, I live the same way as the other Dakar women do", "I have got into the way of living as the Wolof do, I have become a Wolof". This is something that should be emphasized, because it appears to be a conscious decision on their part: they choose to live like the Wolof.

* * *

I have adopted a very simple method of presentation, by merely following the natural sequence of the interviews. The first contacts were usually made about matters concerning a newly born infant, so I shall begin by talking about birth and about more general topics connected with birth.

How is the arrival of a baby daughter received in a Wolof family? What are the reactions of the parents? As a general rule, they are pleased to have another child. Both Wolof and Lebu are glad when their numbers are increased by the arrival of a new being, whether boy or girl. The father is usually better pleased if the baby is a boy, but a girl is by no means unwelcome, especially if he already has a son.

The mother is always particularly happy to have a daughter. The little girl (unless she is given to some other member of the family) will live with her mother until she gets married, whereas a boy will not be with her for so long. The little girl will be breast-fed for 24 months (six months longer than a boy), which establishes an even closer link between mother and child.

The child, after copying mother in the games she plays, as does every little girl the whole world over, will then gradually learn from her everything that a woman in her social surroundings requires to know. She is very proud if she is allowed to go, when still quite tiny, to buy a sou's worth of salt or a few matches for her mother, and when she is a little older she is usually very willing to give up the game she is playing, leave the other children, and look after the fire and stir the pot while keeping a watch on it. Soon she will be helping her mother to prepare the meals, sweep the house, and do the washing, ironing and mending; and when she reaches the stage of going with her mother to the market, she will learn from her how to make purchases. She will also learn how to look after her brothers and sisters. In this way the childhood, and then the adolescence, of a girl will be spent, divided between play and completing her apprenticeship in the tasks which will be hers when she becomes a woman. During this period, she will have been to the Koranic school; but for girls, attendance is less strict and lasts for a shorter time. As for the French school, only an infinitesimal number of women have attended it, sometimes for three or four years, seldom longer. But none of them uses French as her main language, the reason for which is not hard to seek.

The little girl grows up and the parents begin to have marriage plans for her. It must at once be remarked that neither among Wolof nor among Lebu women is there anything approaching any form of initiation ceremony. There is nothing in the nature of the retreat in the sacred grove such as is found among certain tribal groups in Casamance;[2] and certainly nothing equivalent to the circumcision ceremony among boys, even so far back as the memories of a few of the older women I have questioned go. As for the tattooing of lips and gums (a custom that is fast disappearing), it is questionable whether this should be regarded as a survival

219

of initiation ceremonies, or simply as a form of ornamentation.

Furthermore, it does not appear that this young girl will have received, either from her mother or from some other female relative, what is nowadays so glibly called "sex education". Apart from what she has been able to gather here and there, from an older sister or from an older girl friend, she comes to marriage quite ignorant of such things. Usually, before her marriage she has undergone the physiological change that occurs with the beginning of menstruation, and this has been marked by the ceremonial bath required by custom. But although it is almost always the case that young girls are not considered ready for marriage before they have reached puberty, I must mention that it does sometimes happen that a marriage is consummated before the periods have started. I have myself come across a case of this kind. But for the most part it is thought that a young girl should get married around the age of 16, 17 or 18.

The choice of the marriage partner, whether for a young girl or for a young man who is to be married for the first time, is an affair arranged by the parents.[3] This custom has usually been indignantly denounced, as though such a practice were entirely unknown in Europe, in spite of the fact that it seems to have been more or less the rule there until quite recent times. But let us return to Senegal. There, it is indeed the parents who choose the marriage partner. I do not think it is necessary to regard this as nothing but a heartless trick, or something done for egoistic reasons, on the part of the parents. It is not a question merely of a union between two individuals, but of a union between two families. And the parents have the idea that they know better than the young girl what is likely to make the marriage null or inharmonious. And while it is easy, in theory, to know about the prohibitions of consanguinity (although many of the explanations proffered by the women I have interviewed suggest that practice confounds theory), it may, in practice, be difficult to know who all the so-called sisters and brothers "of the milk" are. Now, the fact of having married a brother "of the milk" is a reason for the annullment of the marriage. The first point (degree of relationship) need not detain us; this is a question of the application of Muslim law. The second point concerns a question of custom, as practised by the Wolof: brothers and sisters "of the milk" include all those who have sucked, even if once only, at the same breast; which means that it is rather difficult to know who they all are.

The parents are also anxious to achieve, as I have said, a harmonious relationship for their daughter, and they think that they

Women of Dakar and Surrounding Urban Area

know, better than anyone else, the character of the girl, and so will be able to choose the most suitable husband for her.

Another important point arises from the fact that all those who regard themselves as "free men" will prefer not to marry into what are regarded as "castes"—that is to say, those who belong to the organizations of jewellers, smiths, cobblers or *griots* (a kind of sorcerer). This social structure deserves more detailed study, which is however, beyond the scope of this essay.[4] In the samples at my disposal there is no case of a free man or woman being married to a woman or man of the caste variety.

Let us return to the future marriage partner. It rarely occurs that her future husband is completely unknown to a young girl before she marries him (four cases only). But it is difficult to draw any conclusions from such a small sample. Perhaps I was lucky in the cases that happened to come my way, and I ought to admit honestly that the marriages in which the couple did not know each other beforehand were not always those in which husband and wife got on least well with each other, in spite of the great anxiety of the women concerned when the decision about their marriage was announced to them. I am talking of marriages which had lasted from ten to 15 years, and, where the situation I have described above was present, it would seem that the bond which held the two partners together sprang from a feeling of gratitude on the part of the girl towards the man who had made a woman of her.

What most often actually happened was, that parents allowed several young men to court their daughter. One of these young men might say to his father that he liked this particular young girl and would like to marry her. The father, after making enquiries from older people and from the persons customarily concerned with these matters, would put out a feeler through a go-between (a friend, a cousin, or the descendant of a family slave) as to whether the young girl and her mother viewed the prospect favourably. I should like to emphasize here what an important say the mother has in the choice of a husband, since this is usually underrated. If the parents of the girl favour the marriage, the kola nuts sent as a formal present to the father are distributed to the people they know. The young man may come to plead his cause. Sometimes it may happen that several young men are after the same girl; in this case, as soon as one of them has been accepted, the others are told about it so that they may retire from the fray. During the engagement, the young man is allowed to pay regular visits to his fiancée, and on every visit he will give a number of presents (kola nuts and other eatables) to his future family-in-law. But as soon as the girl has

Solange Faladé

received from the man chosen for her the special present known as *waronga*, the marriage must take place within the next eight days. I shall not attempt to discuss here the significance of the marriage payment, and shall do no more than note that it was as heavy a burden for the young man of 30 years ago as it is for the young man of today, if the accounts of the mother of one of my informants are to be believed. When the marriage ceremony takes place, the young man must pay a sum of 25 francs, in addition to the marriage payment. The payment of these 25 francs more or less binds the young man, and if they are not paid, the marriage cannot take place. Another essential stage is the consummation of the marriage, although this does not necessarily take place on the same day. But failure to consummate the marriage is a recognized cause of annulment. This is equivalent to saying that impotence on the part of the husband is one of the causes of making a marriage null. This causes a good deal of anxiety among mothers on account of their boys, and it often happens that they will want to see that their little boys are capable of having an erection. If a marriage has to be annulled on account of the impotence of the husband, the girl does not have to return the presents that have been given.

Once the marriage ceremony has taken place, what does the young wife do? Very often, she remains for some time with her parents, perhaps even for several years. The only exception to this is provided by the market-gardeners of Camberen, among whom a young man never marries unless he can provide a roof for his wife.

A man who marries must be in a position to provide for his wife and for his future children, and a woman must be able to look after her husband's house. It is the rhythm of household tasks that will fill her life from then on.

In the first place, the preparation of meals. It is true that women in the Dakar urban area do not have to spend a lot of time, as women in the country do, on the hard tasks of searching for firewood and carrying it home; but the cooking utensils they have at their disposal remain extremely primitive. The food is cooked on a stove, usually of the Madagascan variety, which burns charcoal. The midday meal—rice with fish, or sometimes with meat—takes less time to prepare than the evening one. For all that, there are still endless daily tasks to be performed, and the morning soon goes. After morning prayer at five o'clock, a woman may find time to lie down again and rest. After dressing quickly, breakfast is taken, consisting of coffee or *quinquiliba*, bread, and the remains of last night's supper. Then the children have to be looked after. The

222

breakfast dishes are washed, and the room, which is usually well kept, is cleaned out. Then water has to be fetched, which generally means two or three trips; you set off with the bowl carried on your head to take your place in the queue which is waiting beside the tap, and you have to return several times, each time having to wait your turn. Back home, the wife now dresses herself properly and gets ready to go to the market to buy fish or meat and the condiments required for cooking. Every day, the head of the family hands over to his wife, for her daily purchases, the money known as "spending money"—about 200 francs, which enables a housewife to feed from six to eight people. But the grocery items—rice, oil, and sometimes millet—which constitute the biggest outlay, have been arranged at the beginning of the month by the head of the family. When the meal has been eaten and the dishes washed, the wife can very seldom allow herself much time for resting, for she will have washing and ironing to do. The washing cannot be done any old day, Wednesdays and Fridays being days when it is better not to do it. The taboo concerning Wednesday is very important, for this is the day when husband and wife should abstain from sexual intercourse: a child conceived then might, if it was a boy, be unable to achieve an erection; and if it was a girl, she might have some anatomical defect which would lead to doubts as to her virginity. This taboo concerning Wednesdays is found outside the town as well; for instance, in the areas where rice is cultivated, women do not work in the rice-fields on that day.

The day wears on, and the women must begin to think of preparing the evening meal, which always entails a great deal of work, for millet has to be ground for making the couscous which will be the main dish. The meal is eaten about eight o'clock, after prayer; so often a start has to be made about three or four o'clock.

After the evening meal comes an interval of leisure which can be spent chatting with the other women in the household. The men always stay together.

Once married, the young wife hopes to begin having a child as soon as possible, and every month expects her periods to stop. Her mother is the only person she will tell the news to, and she will say nothing to her husband, who will have to make his own observations about any change that has taken place in his wife. Usually a family pretends not to notice a pregnancy. No direct mention will be made of it. Perhaps this habit of passing it over in silence, which is a very widespread one, is responsible for the Western idea that in some societies women are ignorant of the mechanism of conception. I can only state emphatically that a Wolof woman, like all women the world over, knows quite well what it means to be pregnant. If she keeps silent about it for as long as possible, this is because no direct allusion should be made to her condition, because it might bring her bad luck.

It would be impossible to overestimate the importance of pregnancy to a Wolof woman. Motherhood is one of the things most ardently desired, and childlessness can be a cause for the annulment of a marriage. To be a mother not only ensures the stability of her marriage, but also confers respect upon her as a woman.

However happy the future mother may feel about her condition, she does nothing, throughout her pregnancy, to prepare for the arrival of the child. Nothing is done until the child is actually there, alive and kicking. To see to anything, whatever it might be, beforehand, would somehow be equivalent to expressing a wish that it should not be born.

When the confinement is over, the mother and child are washed according to a certain fixed ritual, and then the mother lays the newly born infant on the bed beside her. Mother and child will spend a week living side by side on the bed, without seeing the light of day, and will have the necessary care taken of them. In particular, the child will be given massage all over its body, a process which, for a girl, does not last longer than a month.

On the eighth day the child will be baptised. Apparently the paternal aunt plays quite an important role in choosing the name of the child. That is the day when the mother can once again cross the threshold of her house and go out-of-doors. Mother and child continue to live together, but before the mother can carry the child on her back, a special ceremony must be performed. Since this name-giving ceremony, carried out according to Muslim law, has been described by other authors, I shall do no more than mention it.

As can be seen from the description I have given of a day in the life of a young wife, there is not much time left between doing the household chores and preparing the meals, which means that the birth of children at fairly short intervals adds considerably to the burden of work of a young mother who is the only wife, *awa*, with no one to help her.

It seldom happens that this woman remains for long the only wife. As soon as the husband can do so, he takes a second wife, then a third, and, very occasionally, a fourth (only one husband in the 120 families of my sample has four wives). If the various wives live together, as is fairly often the case, each of them will take her turn of being, as it is said, "on duty". A rota will be established, whereby each of the women, even if they are not all co-wives, will for several days be exclusively occupied with the housework and more especially, with the cooking. During this time, the others will be occupied with their own affairs: petty trading in pancakes or shelled peanuts, sold at the market or on the doorstep (the profits derived from this trade being their own); or else they will be busy at home sewing or embroidering; or will pay visits to relations. It is with the wife who is "on duty" that the husband will share his bed.

The other co-wives will be busy with their own affairs. The money they earn enables them, of course, to buy cloth or jewellery; but often they spend it on improving the menu when it comes to their turn to prepare the meals. This can be a cause of petty rivalry between co-wives.

It is very difficult, after such a brief enquiry, to say anything about polygyny, especially as regards what the wives themselves think about it. One thing certain is, that it does constitute a problem for them. In some cases, the kind of person the co-wife is likely to be is quite as important a factor as what sort of person the husband is. It must be remembered that the two women, if they share the same dwelling, will spend more time together than either of them will spend with the husband they have in common. If there must be a co-wife, it is generally thought to be preferable that there should be one as soon as possible, for then the two co-wives will be of approximately the same age, and the children of both can look upon them as two "mothers"; whereas if the husband waits too long to take a second wife, she will be of an age nearer to that of her husband's children than to that of their mother. This is the kind of situation that leads to many of the quarrels that take place.

When is a man likely to take another wife? As soon as he feels that he is well enough off to be able to overcome the problems of housing and cost of living, and maintain a second family. First of all, he must have paid off the marriage payment demanded by the parents of the first wife. Then the husband must warn his wife of his intention. If he omits to do this, she has grounds for divorce (which was the case with one of my informants). If the co-wives do not live under the same roof, the husband stays with one for three or four days, and then moves to the other one.

Has any serious attempt ever been made to try and measure the psychological implications of polygyny, apart from the material problems that arise? Women have been asked to express their point of view, but the questionnaire method does not allow for any possibility of arriving at the deeper level of women's views on a practice to which they have always been accustomed and which is an institution that has been presented to them, ever since they were of an age to understand such things, as the normal and desirable form of marriage. Nor should we forget that for the husband polygyny always has a factor of prestige, which in turn reflects back on the wives.

Besides, it is so certain that monogamy has nothing but advantages, however preferable it may be in general and from an absolute point of view? Judgments given in its favour are always made by partisans convinced in advance of its superiority; the least one can say is that they lack objectivity.

The interviews showed that, as far as the women whose daily life I have just described are concerned, polygyny poses two problems.

First of all, the good, or the bad, relations between wives are less a matter of the feelings they have towards the husband than of the sympathy or antipathy which they feel for each other. It is the degree of confidence or mistrust which they have in each other that enables them either to accept sharing, or refuse to share, what is dearest to them—the man who occupies the centre of their lives. Of course the problems of life cannot be translated into such simple terms as these, and unless the observer is aware of the ambivalence underlying such feelings of love and hate, the situation observed or reported may well appear to contradict what I have just suggested. A fact which seems to me to be of fairly common occurrence in Western society may serve to support my thesis, and that is, that it is by no means rare to find that women who seem to feel a great attraction for each other are often rivals for the affection of the same man, if they do not already share it. The decisive role which, in some African societies at least, the chief wife plays in the choice of another legitimate wife is full of significance.

The second big problem arises when the husband, when he is getting on in years, marries a new wife who is much younger than he is. I have noticed that in some cases the young wife in question was obviously of the same age as one of the man's daughters, often as that of his favourite daughter. It is not uncommon that the young wife is even a friend of this daughter. It is then scarcely surprising if this man's new marriage is not always readily accepted either by his wife or by his daughter.

As we have seen, a man's successive marriages are not always without conflicts, and sometimes a divorce takes place. When there has been a divorce, or the annulment of a marriage, the man can remarry immediately, whereas the woman must wait for three months before doing so. If a wife loses her husband, she must wear mourning for four months and ten days.[5] Throughout this period she must stay at home, out of sight of everyone. Her relations will come to help her. If she is pregnant when she loses her husband, the mourning period must last until the birth of the child. Once the mourning is over, she can consider re-marrying if she wants to. Widows and women who have been divorced usually return to their families, and, if they are still young, plans may be made for re-marrying them; if they no longer have a father, it will be a brother who makes the arrangements.

Everything that has been said applies equally to women in Dakar, N'Gor, Camberen and Wakam.

Many of these housewives follow a trade as well or carry on petty commercial transactions. The women of N'Gor, for instance, are fishermen's wives, and have the task of selling the fish their husbands catch. This is a heavy responsibility, and not all of them are able to undertake it, for it is something that requires experience from a very early age. The husbands give their wives a certain percentage on the sales, which belongs to them to do as they please with. During the winter season, the N'Gor woman help with the farming. The peanut crop is their property, and it is often the products of their own labours that they sell on their doorsteps or along the beach.

The women of Camberen are wives of market-gardeners and help their husbands in their work in the gardens and with gathering the crops. It is their job to sell at the market the garden produce (vegetables and flowers), as well as the rabbits reared in the village. They do not receive a percentage on the sales, but their husbands let them have a few vegetables (small cabbages, for instance, or small tomatoes . . .) which they are free to dispose of. The money they make from this belongs to them.

The women of Dakar and the surrounding area have formed mutual aid associations which are usually called "tontines". More precisely, these tontines have been described as a form of "savings bank" without interest. Women living in the same house, if there are enough of them, or in the same district, decide to club together, and everyone contributes a certain sum each week or each month. Sometimes women belonging to such a group live in various parts of the town at quite a distance from each other.

The women choose a responsible person—"the mother"—to collect the contributions and decide, according to a rota, upon the

Solange Faladé

beneficiary who will receive the total sum of the contributions of the week or of the month, a total from which the sum paid to the *griot*, if a dance has been on the programme of the "tontine", is deducted. Everywhere associations of this kind tend to proliferate more and more. Their purpose is primarily a practical one: to oblige women to save money and enable them to dispose, each in her turn, of a sufficiently large sum as to allow purchasing something of value. The associations also have a social purpose: to provide an opportunity for making contacts for women living in a large town (and it should not be forgotten that many families come from inland to settle in Dakar, sometimes without knowing anyone there); and also, in some cases, to provide some recreation for them by holding dances or communal singing.

I have said very little about the religious life of these women. They are all Muslims. None of them has made the pilgrimage to Mecca. In spite of Islam, it can be stated that it is the women who preserve both the spirit and the ritual of the earlier African religion; I need only mention certain dances of possession, or the rites performed at the time of the harvest of the new millet.[6]

Such is the life of the women of Dakar and the surrounding area as I saw it through the interviews I have had since 1955 with several of them.

BIBLIOGRAPHY

BALANDIER, G. and MERCIER, P., *Les Pêcheurs lebou du Sénégal*, I.F.A.N., Études Sénégalaises No. 3, Saint-Louis, Senegal, 1952, 213 pp. ill. maps.
A monograph on village communities in the surroundings of Dakar.

FALADE, S., *Contribution à une étude sur le développement de l'enfant d'Afrique*, Paris, Foulon, 1955.
The psycho-motor development of the African child in Senegal during the first year of its life.

GAMBLE, DAVID P., *The Wolof of Senegambia*, Int. Af. Inst., 1957, 110 pp. ill. maps.
A useful summary of ethnographic information concerning the Wolof and the Serer; the latter are probably an older stratum of the population, but the degree of assimilation is such that it would be difficult to single out traits as being specifically Wolof or Serer. Good bibliography.

MERCIER, P., *L'agglomération dakaroise: quelques aspects sociologiques et démographiques*, I.F.A.N., Études Sénégalaise No. 5, Saint-Louis, Senegal, 1954, 83 pp.

MERSADIER, Y., *Budgets familiaux africains: Étude chez 136 familles de salariés dans trois centres urbains du Sénégal*, I.F.A.N., Etudes Sénégalaises No. 7, Dakar, 1957, 102 pp. ill.

Women of Dakar and Surrounding Urban Area
NOTES

[1] Du Sorbiers de la Tourasse, *Au pays des Ouoloffs* (Mame, Tours, 1897, 8vo). Memories of a Senegal dealer. Other and better-known works could be cited.

[2] An initiation ceremony for girls has been reported as a traditional custom among the Mandinka and Jola, but none among the Wolof. *See* D. P. Gamble, *The Wolof of Senegambia* (International African Institute, 1957), p. 64.

[3] "The first marriage of a young man is generally arranged by his parents and he has little to say in the matter . . ." D. P. Gamble, *op. cit.* p. 65.

[4] In traditional Wolof society members of the royal lineages, nobles and peasants were grouped together in an upper class of free men. Artisans formed castes: smiths and goldsmiths; cobblers, *griots* and musicians. Finally, first-generation slaves, captured or bought, were distinguished from their descendants born in the household, who were called "hut captives".

[5] Traditional customs stipulated a period of mourning for a husband lasting for four months and ten days in the case of a free woman; for two months and five days in the case of a wife of slave origin.

[6] On this point, see in particular the chapter "Vie religieuse traditionelle" in G. Balandier and P. Mercier, *Les Pêcheurs lebou* (I.F.A.N., Senegal, 1952), pp. 111-119.

I. A Coniagui woman. Little girls begin looking after the babies at a very early age.

II. A Bassari woman carrying her youngest child.

III. Coniagui girls wear jewellery from the age of six or seven.

IV. An old woman pouring out the sacrificial beer.

V. A WoDaaBe Bororo woman (Cameroon).

VI. A group of young WoDaaBe girls ready to take part in a dance.

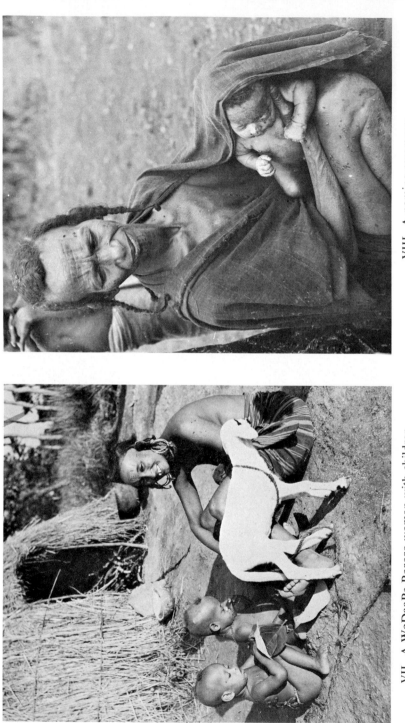

VIII. A naming ceremony.

VII. A WoDaaBe Bororo woman with children.

IX. Natélégé Kitté, woman chief.

X. Nakpangi and Sango.

XI. Songombi, the waif princess.

XII. Nabate, the wife of the ancestors.

XIII. A Tutsikazi.

XIV. A Hutu "matriarch".

XV and XVI. Burundi landscapes.

ANALYTICAL BIBLIOGRAPHY

M. Perlman and M. P. Moal

THE FOLLOWING BIBLIOGRAPHY is an analytical one, since it is our belief that a compilation of this kind is of little use unless it gives some information, however brief, about the content of the works listed. Consequently, it is selective rather than exhaustive, and we have purposely excluded very short articles and those without any scholarly interest. We have also, to our regret, had to omit most of the monographs in which chapters occur dealing with women under one aspect or another (education, work, special rites, beliefs concerning their magic powers, or the female deities in African pantheons) where these are not the exclusive, and indeed where they are not the main, topics of the publications in question. It would have been impossible for us to go through the entire Africanist literature.

The choice of headings may cause some surprise. For one thing, the absence of one on Marriage or on Bridewealth is sure to be remarked upon, since such matters clearly concern women. But they concern the men of a society just as much. And how could we have included works dealing with marriage—with permitted marriage partners, preferential marriages, rules concerning exogamy, rules concerning residence of the married couple—and excluded those discussing kinship structure, embracing topics such as the role of the maternal kin or relations between affines, which come within our field of study? A line had to be drawn somewhere, and this could only be done arbitrarily. Selection was an arduous task. We would not care to claim that we had carried it out entirely successfully.

An asterisk indicates works which could not be consulted, being absent from the shelves of Paris libraries. The date limit for publications was fixed at 1st January, 1960.

D.P.

M. Perlman and M. P. Moal

JOURNALS, CONGRESSES, CONFERENCES

A journal to consult: *African Women*. Published by the Department of Education in Tropical Areas, University of London, Institute of Education.

This journal contains articles principally concerned with the education and training of women and girls, with their new activities, and with social work, mainly in British African territories. The articles are followed by book reviews and by notes and a Personal Column, giving statistics and detailed information about teachers and appointments of women to official posts.

Conférence Inter-Africaine du Travail, 5e Réunion, Lusaka, 1957, *Rapports de la Conférence tenue par la Commission de Coopération Technique en Afrique au Sud du Sahara* (C.C.T.A.).

Appendix III, pp. 131-55, "Emploi des femmes" [Employment of women]: This report summarizes briefly the replies of the governments taking part in the Conference to a series of questions on this topic. Introduction: the sociological, economic and educational factors determining the position of African women wage-earners. Three accounts follow concerning the number and type of occupations in which women are employed, the questions of legal protection and of maternity welfare, and future prospects of employment and training, in British, French, Portuguese and Belgian territories of Africa. Conclusion: except in South Africa, there has been very little advance in the employment of women. [*See also* Inter-African Labour Conference].

Congrès Colonial National, 12e Session, Brussels, 1956, *La promotion de la femme au Congo et au Ruanda-Urundi*. Rapports et Comptes rendus des Assemblées Générales des 23 et 24 novembre 1956, 528 pp. map, bibl.

Reports and communications following upon an enquiry conducted by questionnaire in the Congo, bearing upon four points: Legal and customary status of women; social work as a means of education; education in schools; the training and role of European women.

Congrès constitutif de l'Union des Femmes de l'Ouest Africain (U.F.O.A.), Bamako, July 20-23, 1959.

The aim of this Congress was "to form groups and to unite the women of Africa in the fight for freedom" in order to carry out the following programme: Defence of the rights of women; child welfare; cultural and social activities; the fight for peace and for the independence and unity of Negro Africa. (*La Vie Africaine*, IV (Paris, 1959), 7).

*General Missionary Conference of South Africa, 7th, Lovedale, 1928, *The Realignment of native life on a Christian basis*, Lovedale Institution Press, 1928, 166 pp.

Contains two articles on women: "The reintegration of the social life of native women and girls", by Mrs. Hofmeyr; "Social and medical work for native women and girls in urban areas", by Mrs. Bridgman.

Inter-African Labour Conference, 5th meeting, Lusaka, 1957, *Reports of the Conference held by the Commission for Technical Co-operation in Africa South of the Saraha* (C.C.T.A.), pp. 28-32. [*See also* Conférence Inter-Africaine . . .]

International Institute of Differing Civilizations (INCIDI), 31st meeting, Brussels, 1958, *Women's rôle in the development of tropical and subtropical countries*. Report of the 31st meeting held in Brussels 17-19 September 1958, Brussels, 1959, 543 pp.

Analytical Bibliography

This compilation contains contributions dealing with the following themes as they concern localities: the legal, the social and cultural, the political, and the economic aspects of the role of women; by: Sister Marie-André du Sacré-Cœur (French West Africa [A.O.F.]); F. J. Amon d'Aby (Ivory Coast); E. Mills Scarborough (Liberia); T. Baker (Nigeria); G. A. Costanzo (Italian Somaliland); M. J. Salema (Portuguese African provinces); D. Soyer-Poskin (Belgian Congo); S. Naigisiki (Ruanda); R. Apthorpe (Rhodesia and Nyasaland); E. S. Nyendwoha (Uganda); M. Horrell (Union of South Africa); and Saad Ed Din Fawzi (Sudan).

Louvain, Semaine de Missiologie de Louvain, 20ᵉ Session, 1950, *Le rôle de la femme dans les missions*, Rapports et Comptes rendus, Brussels, Éd. Universelle, 1951, 274 pp.

Four reports concerning African women, by: Dom Gillès de Pélichy, Mother Suzanne Van Roye, the Rev. Father Cornet, Sister Françoise-Marie.

United Nations Organization, Commission on the Status of Women, 6th meeting 1952, *Renseignements sur la condition de la femme dans les territoires sous tutelle*, roneo, 69 pp. (E/CN6/182).

The general condition of women, their legal and political status, opportunities for education and employment . . . in the Cameroons, Somaliland, Ruanda-Urundi, Tanganyika, Togo.

United Nations Organization, Commission on the Status of Women, 11th meeting, 1957, *Le statut de la femme en droit privé*.
Report in *African Women*, II, 4 (1958), 81-2.

SOCIAL AND LEGAL STATUS

General

ATANGANA, N., "La Femme africaine dans la société", *Présence Africaine*, n.s. XIII (Paris, 1957), 133-42.

The African woman and the literature produced by the Colonial Powers (criticism of the writings of Sister Marie-André du Sacré-Cœur). The African woman in traditional society: marriage, bride-wealth, polygyny; these concepts are given their true value in terms of their social context. The African woman and colonization: the disparity between the education of boys and of girls does great harm.

*Aus dem Leben schwarzer Frauen [On the lives of negro women], Bethel, Verlagshandlung der Anstalt Bethel, 1939, 15 pp.

BAEGE, B., *Die Frau im Leben der Naturvölker*, Jena, Thüringer Verlagsanstalt und Druckerei G.m.b.H., 1931, 78 pp. ill.

The life, position and activities of women . . . among certain [primitive] peoples. Refers to South Africa, Transvaal, West Africa.

BRIFFAULT, R., *The Mothers. A Study of the origins of sentiments and institutions*, Allen & Unwin, 1927, 3 vols. bibl.

Various references to African women.

"La Femme dans l'Union Française", *Tropiques*, No. 379 (Paris, 1955), 2-91, ill.

A series of notes and articles on African women, their occupations, rites, dances, etc. Numerous illustrations.

M. Perlman and M. P. Moal

La Femme noire dans la société africaine. Lectures given at the *Institut Catholique de Paris*, 1938-39, by Sister Marie-André du Sacré-Cœur, J. Wilbois, M. R. Randau, the Rev. Father Mazé, M. Danel. Paris, Union Missionare du Clergé, 1940, 172 pp.

The lectures dealt with: family life of African women; economic and social life of African women; African women and native custom; reforms to be introduced, customary and legal reforms.

Femmes Africaines, [No place of publication], [1959], 190 pp. ill.

Testimony of women of the Cameroons . . . etc., met together at Lomé under the auspices of the *Union mondiale des organisations fémines catholiques.* Contributions by Sister Marie-André du Sacré-Cœur, several African priests, African women . . .

"Fostermothers in Africa (*Lactatio serotina*)", *Africa*, XI, 1 (1938), 108-9.

Notes on the fostermothers in Africa who take the place of mothers who have died.

GARNIER, C., "Africaines 1955", *Tropiques*, 53rd year, No. 379 (Paris, 1955), 9-19, ill.

A popularizing article describing negro women of French Africa, their flirtatiousness, their character, the conditions of their married life, their occupations throughout their entire life-cycle. The account is illustrated by examples supplied by direct observation. (*Bibliographie Ethnographique du Congo Belge*, 1955).

[GOLLOCK, G. A., *Sons of Africa*, Student Christian Movement, 1928, 247 pp.
— , *Daughters of Africa*, Longmans, Green & Co., 1932, 175 pp.]

GOURDAULT, J., *La Femme dans tous les pays*, Paris, Lib. Furne, Jouvet et Cie, 1882, 340 pp. ill.

Chapter IX, "A travers le continent mystérieux", deals with various African peoples: Hottentots, Kaffirs, the warrior women of Dahomey, the negroes of Senegambia, the Fulani, the Kanuri.

LANDES, R., "Negro slavery and female status", *African Affairs*, LII, No. 206 (1953), 54-7.

The writer finds a continuity between the status and social position of women in Africa and of negro slaves in both North and South America.

LEMAIRE, C., *Africaines. Contribution à l'histoire de la femme en Afrique*, Brussels, C. Bulens, 1897, 256 pp. ill.

Description of African women and their way of life, first in French West Africa and then in the Congo. Hair styles, ornaments.

LETOURNEAU, C., *La Condition de la femme*, Paris, V. Giard et E. Brière, 1903, 508 pp.

Chapters II and III deal with negro women: their position in the family; their legal status in society, and their work. Chapter IV deals with negro women from a more general point of view.

MERCIER, P., "La femme et les sociétés africaines", *Tropiques*, 53rd year, No. 379 (Paris, 1955), 21-8, ill.

The economic functions and the status of African women vary according to the society in which they live, but their importance and potential activities have already been manifested in several areas.

POIVRE, PASTOR, *Fils et filles d'Afrique*, Paris, Missions Évangéliques, 1946, 208 pp. ill. map.

Analytical Bibliography

Stories adapted from *Sons of Africa* and *Daughters of Africa* by G. A. Gollock [*q.v.*].

REITZENSTEIN, F. F. VON, *Das Weib bei den Naturvölkern. Eine Kulturgeschichte der primitiven Frau*, new revised and enlarged ed., Berlin, Verlag Neufeld und Henius (no date), 386 pp. 219 photo, fig.
Anthropology, sociology, domestic and cultural life of woman among primitive peoples.

REYNOLDS, R., "Women in Africa: notes on religious and social trends", *Antioch Review*, XIV (Yellow Springs, Ohio, 1954), 312-22.
The writer compares the position of women and the changes brought about by religious (Islam, Christianity), and social (division of labour) trends in present and former British territories in East and South Africa.

SCHMIDT, W., "The position of women with regard to property in primitive society", *American Anthropologist*, XXXVII, 2 (Washington, New York, 1935), 244-56.
A communication made to the first Congress of Anthropological and Ethnological Sciences, held in London, 1934. The property of women in primitive societies of hunters, pastoralists and food-gatherers; the African examples are mostly taken from South Africa (Pygmies) and East Africa (Nilotics and Nilo-Hamitics).

VIALLE, J., "Femmes africaines", *Civilisations*, I, 4 (Brussels, 1951), 55-8.
The African woman is first and foremost a mother and a worker. Some examples.

*"Wir verehren die Muttergottes durch unsern Einsatz, für die Gleichstellung der Frau in Afrika", *Christi-Reich*, V (1957), 66-9.
Comments on the attitude of missionaries towards the position of women in native society: woman the basis of the "Sippe", bride-wealth, the role of missions and of the State. (*Bibliographie Ethnographique du Congo Belge*, 1957).

West Africa

AMON D'ABY, F.J., *see* International Institute of Differing Civilizations.

*ARRIENS, C., "Die soziale Stellung der Frau in West Afrika", *Der Erdball*, III, 10 (Berlin, 1929), 36-61, 4 ill.

BAKER, T., *see* International Institute of Differing Civilizations.

BEIER, H.U., "The position of Yoruba women", *Présence Africaine*, n.s. I-II (Paris, 1955), 39-46.
The life of Yoruba women in the town of Ede, where most of them follow the pattern of the traditional way of life; their political, religious, economic position; western influence.

BURNESS, H., "The position of women in Gwandu and Yauri", *Oversea Education*, XXVI, 4 (1955), 143-52.
The position of girls among the Hausa and Fulani and the attitude towards their education.

—, "Women in Katsina province, Northern Nigeria", *Oversea Education*, XXIX, 3 (1957), 116-22, ill.
Notes on the position of girls and married women in a highly Islamized society (tendency towards the seclusion of wives whenever economically possible); general attitude of mistrust towards the education of women and girls.

235

M. Perlman and M. P. Moal

*Comhaire-Sylvain, S., "The status of women in Lagos", *Pi Lamba Theta Journal* (Seattle, Wash., March 1949), 158-63.

DELAFOSSE, M., "Coutumes observées par les femmes en temps de guerre chez les *Agni* de la Côte d'Ivoire", *Revue d'Ethnologie et de Sociologie*, IV (Paris, 1913), 266-8.

The dances of Baule women and their licentious songs insulting the leader of the enemy and singing the praises of the village head and his warriors. Victory goes to the side on which the women have done the most singing and dancing.

DONNER, E., "Das Leben der Frau in den Urwaldgebieten von Liberia", *Mitteilungen der anthropologischen Gesellschaft in Wien*, LXVI (Vienna, 1936), pp. [6]-[7].

Once she is married, a woman goes to live in her husband's village, but is regarded as a stranger there. She can, however, belong to women's associations and play her part in this polygynous society. The writer describes her daily life and her work.

DUGAST, I., "Autobiographie d'une femme banen", *Bull. de la Société d'Études Camerounaises*, VI (Douala, 1944), 83-96.

The writer, during four consecutive evenings, took down the life-history of a Banen woman, called Kubong, of the Ndogbiakat tribe.

FORTES, M., *The dynamics of clanship among the Tallensi*, O.U.P., 1945, 270 pp. map.

Chapter IX (pp. 147-53) deals with the role of women in clan organization and with the concept of a "clanswoman".

HARRIS, J. S., "The position of women in a Nigerian society", *Transactions of the New York Academy of Sciences*, II, 5 (New York, 1940), 141-8.

Ibo women have a definite influence on society, acquired through their role in everyday life and also because of the courts of law which they hold among themselves.

HAUFERLIN, C., "La vie d'une femme dans un village de Dahomey", *Le Courier de l'UNESCO* (Paris, March, 1957), 4-10, ill.; (May), 14-15 and 32-3.

The writer describes the traditional daily life of women at Mitro, a small village in Dahomey.

HERSKOVITS, M. J., "A note on 'woman marriage' in Dahomey", *Africa*, X (1937), 335-41.

These marriages between women, which also exist in Nigeria (Ibo), in the Sudan (Dinka, Nuer) and in the Transvaal (Bavenda), take a number of forms in Dahomey which may be divided into two categories, the characteristics of which are described by the writer.

*HIMMELHEBER, U., *Schwarze Schwester*, Bremen, Schünemann, 1956.

The life-cycle of the Dan women of Liberia.

HINTZE, V., "Mutterrechtliche Züge in der Sozialordnung der Akan", *Deutsche Akademie der Wissenschaften*, V (Berlin, Institut für deutsche Volkskunde, 1952), 61-9.

Life is regulated by a material principle *abusua* and a spiritual principle *ntoro*. *Abusua* can only be transmitted by women or by succession. The *ohemaa* or queen-mother is the female chief of the country.

JOSEPH, G., "Condition de la femme en Côte d'Ivoire", *Bulletins et Mémoires de la Société d'Anthropologie de Paris*, XIV, 5 (Paris, 1913), 585-9.

Customs regulating marriage, bridewealth, polygyny, the home life of a mar-

Analytical Bibliography

ried woman [Ivory Coast]; because of her work and the indispensable services she renders, she has great influence. The chief wife has a privileged position.

LABOURET, H., "Situation matérielle, morale, et coutumière de la femme dans l'Ouest Africain", *Africa*, XIII (1940), 97-124.

Women's work, woman's position in the household; her legal status in customary marriage; female solidarity; the effects of education.

*LÉGER, J., "La femme en pays dogon", *Vivante Afrique*, CXCV, 22 (Namur, 1958), 10-12.

Privileged position of Dogon women, their occupations, rights and privileges. (*African Abstracts*, X, 2 (1959), 62).

LEITH-ROSS, S., *African women, a study of the Ibo of Nigeria*, Faber, 1939, 367 pp. ill. maps.

Daily life of Ibo women in four villages, their occupations, rights, views . . . Remarks concerning those who, in the main centres, are in close contact with Government, with commercial activities and with European missionary activities.

LESTRANGE, M. DE, "La journée de Madame Nemmé, femme coniagui de la Guinée française", *Geographia*, I (Paris, 1951), 43-7, ill.

Daily life and work of a Coniagui woman.

LITTLE, K. L., "The changing position of women in the Sierra Leone Protectorate", *Africa*, XVIII, 1 (1948), 1-17.

The life of a young Mende girl from her birth until her marriage and widowhood. European influence is giving birth to a new type of society.

——, The position of women, in *The Mende of Sierra Leone*, (Routledge and Kegan Paul, 1951), pp. 163-74.

Tension between the sexes; the difficulties encountered by educated women; the position of unmarried women, without family attachments, in the towns.

MARCHAL, R. P., *La condition de la femme indigène. Étude sur le problème de l'évolution des coutumes familiales dans quelques tribus de l'A.O.F. Observations sur le même sujet relatives à l'Algérie*, Lyon, Chronique sociale de France, 1930, 24 pp.

Consists of two parts: the position of girls and women among certain tribes of French Sudan and of the Upper Volta, as laid down by custom; the civilizing role of the Government, which is, to give women a sense of their own importance and of their responsibilities by means of administrative measures.

MARIE-ANDRÉ DU SACRÉ-CŒUR, Sister, "La femme mossi, sa situation juridique", *L'Ethnographie*, n.s. XXXIII-XXXIV (Paris, 1937), 15-33, ill. map.

Mossi women have no legal rights in so far as the free disposal of their own persons is concerned. In marriage, they are goods which are given, taken, inherited. Respect for native custom has prevented reforms of any kind. The writer is of the opinion that the time has come to assist progressive changes in custom by means of reforms with legal backing.

——, "La condition de la femme au Mossi", *Grands Lacs*, 54th year (Namur, 1937-38), 177-81.

Some notes on the position of women in Mossi society, before and after marriage.(*Bibliographie Ethnographique du Congo Belge*, 1938).

——, *La situation juridique de la femme indigène dans la boucle du Niger*, Rapports et Comptes rendus du Congrès internationale de l'évolution culturelle des peuples coloniaux (Paris, 1938), pp. 96-102.

237

M. Perlman and M. P. Moal

A summary of her lecture: the legal position of women (particularly among the Mossi) in marriage and at the death of their husband.

—, "La condition de la femme indigène en A.O.F.", *Afrique Française*, Renseignements Coloniaux, 49th year (Paris, 1939), 121-6.

In French Sudan and the Ivory Coast women are not free, in particular, not free to choose a husband. This is something several administrative decrees are attempting to change.

—, *La Femme noire en Afrique Occidentale*, Paris, Payot, 1939, 278 pp. 2 maps, ill. bibl.

Woman in the family: ideas on marriage, prestige of motherhood. Woman in society: legal status and economic life of women. Aesthetic appreciation. Women and the native religion. Women and foreign influences: Islam, Christianity, the European administration.

—, *see* International Institute of Differing Civilizations, 1958.

MERCIER, P., "Le consentement au mariage et son évolution chez les Betammadibe", *Africa*, XX, 3 (1950), 219-27.

Before marriage, Somba women can lead a life of sexual freedom. They have the right to choose their husband and their consent is required.

MILLS SCARBOROUGH, E., *see* International Institute of Differing Civilizations, 1958.

NICOD, A., *La femme au Cameroun*, Paris, Société des Missions Évangéliques, 1927, 82 pp.

Notes on the life of women in South-West Cameroon (Banem, Duala, Bakaka). They are slaves to custom, and for the clan are merely something of economic value, although quite a high one. There follows the description of various measures taken since 1917.

PAILLOUX, R., "La place de la femme chez les Babemba", *Grands Lacs*, X (Namur, 1953), 9-16 and 37-40.

The first part deals with the important place of women in Babemba society; the writer refutes the idea that the woman is her husband's slave and that native marriage is a form of purchase. The second part deals with the relations between husband and wife, and mother and children, and with the Church's contribution towards education.

PAULME, D., Women in society, in *Organisation sociale des Dogon* (Paris, Ed. Domat-Montchrétien, 1940), pp. 259-70.

Dogon women enjoy great material and economic independence, but are excluded from political and ritual affairs. Role of the maternal kin in the social strucure.

—, "The social condition of women in two West African societies", *Man* XLVIII (1948), 44.

Review of a lecture given at the Royal Anthropological Institute on the position of women among the Dogon and Kissi.

—, "Un mouvement féminin en pays kissi", *Notes Africaines*, XLVI (IFAN, Dakar, 1950), 43-4.

Account of an incident [among the Kissi] which demonstrates that the women have their own activities from which men are entirely excluded.

PRÉVAUDEAU, M. M., Individual life, in *Abomey la mystique* (Paris, Éd. Albert, 1936), pp. 87-98.

Analytical Bibliography

This chapter is mainly concerned with the life of a Dahomey woman (confinement, marriage, work laid down by custom) and with the origin of the Amazons.

PROST, R. P., Marriage and the condition of women, in "Notes sur les Songhay", *Bull. de l'IFAN* (Dakar, 1954), 193-213.

Privileged position of Songhay women. Notes on customs observed during confinements, taboos imposed on married women, status of widows.

"Quelques coutumes particulières du mariage au Cameroun", *Togo-Cameroun* (Paris, 1929), pp. 58-64, ill.

A series of short articles, on, among others: Woman in the light of Bulu custom (economic value of women); life of native women among the Yaunde (status, from the point of view of work, of the chief wife, *Ekomba*, of the favourite wife, *Mgbock*, and of the other wives of a chief) widows in Duala custom.

RATTRAY, R. S., The family: the wife, in *Ashanti law and constitution* (Oxford, Clarendon Press, 1929), pp. 22-32.

Women are of great importance in this matrilineal society. They retain membership of their clan and the clan name and transmit them to their children. If they reside with their husband, they remain independent and retain ownership of their belongings.

*REIN-WUHRMANN, A., *Lydia: ein Frauenleben aus dem Grasland von Kamerun*, Basel, Baseler Missionsbuchhandlung, n.d., 31 pp. [Tr. by M. Bryan, *Two women of the Cameroons: Lydia and Margaret*, (abridged) Sheldon Press, 1931, 32 pp.]

ROMERO MOLINER, R., "Notas sobre la situación social de la mujer indigena en Fernando Póo", *Cuadernos de Estudios Africanos*, XVIII (Madrid, 1952), 21-38.

The legal status of the African woman: it is that of an object, not of a subject, under the law. Women are sold, loaned or inherited. Colonial influence is changing the biological structure of society.

*SCHMIDT, A., "Aus dem Leben der Eingeborenen im Grasland von Kamerun", *Die Frau und die Kolonien*, VII, (1941), 49-51.

— , *Uber die Wesensart der Frau in Nsei, Bezirk Bamenda, Kamerun*, Vienna, Institut für Völkerkunde der Universität, 1947, 158 pp. (Doctoral dissertation).

— , "Feld-Forschungen über das Leben der Frau im Grasland von Kamerun, 1938-1939", *Archiv für Völkerkunde*, IV (Vienna, 1949), 165-85.

The writer describes the daily life of women in Nsei, a village in the Bagenda district (Cameroon). They live within the narrow framework of family life and work all day in the fields. From the age of ten, girls are under the strict control of their parents, who prepare them for marriage. Women belonging to the same family live in close contact with each other.

— , *Die rote Lendenschnur. Als Frau im Grasland Kameruns*, Berlin, D. Reimer, 1955, 197 pp. ill.

The writer gives a day-to-day account, with ethnological, sociological, economic and religious information, of Nsei and its people, the men, the women, the king. A particular feature is that men and women agree that women are of greater value as workers in the fields than as mothers. The grandmother looks after the children while the mother works in the fields. (*Afrika und Ubersee*, XL (1956), 134).

SMITH, M. F., *Baba of Karo: a woman of the Muslim Hausa*, Faber, 1954, 299 pp., map.

239

Autobiography of a Hausa woman recounting her childhood and various marriages. It is of general interest. Describes the customs concerning women of her time.

SMITH, M. G., "The Hausa system of social status", *Africa*, XXIX, 3 (1959), 239-52.

Pp. 244-46: status of women. Marriage more important than descent. It frequently occurs that a woman contracts three or four marriages. Views regarding the *karuwai* (prostitutes).

"Status of women in West Africa", *African Women*, I, 3 (1955), 63-6.

Their social position is high owing to their economic activities. The article deals mainly with the Ibo of Nigeria.

TALBOT, A. P., *Woman's mysteries of a primitive people. The Ibibios of Southern Nigeria*, Cassel, 1915, viii + 252 pp. ill.

The life of women from birth to death; prenatal and natal customs; role during war; magic and religion.

— , Woman, marriage, etc. in *Life in Southern Nigeria*, (Macmillan, 1923), pp. 203-14.

Legal status of married women.

TARAORE, D., "Yaro Ha ou mariages entre femmes chez les Bobo Niéniégue", *Journal de la Société des Africanistes*, XI (Paris, 1941), 197-200.

Marriage between women practised by the Bobo Nieniege (Ivory Coast): to avoid an unhappy old age, Nieniege women who have passed child-bearing age without having had any children attempt to assure themselves by indirect means of the services of a fictitious progeny to be attained by Yaro hâ or marriage between women.

TARAORE, M., "Prêt des femmes en pays soussou (Guinée)", *Notes Africaines*, XXIX (IFAN, Dakar, 1946), 12-13.

Notes on the [Susu] marriage custom known as *gine yefu*, literally "woman loaned". (*Bibliographie Ethnographique du Congo Belge*, 1946).

TEMPLE, O., "Women in Northern Nigeria", *Blackwood Magazine*, CXVII (Edinburgh, 1914), 257-67.

Daily life of women, in particular Nupe women, their occupations, the customs with which they must comply in marriage, marriage offers, mourning, etc.; their high degree of freedom.

VIARD, R., Position of Gere women, in *Les Guérés, peuple de la forêt*, (Paris, Éd. Géographiques, Maritimes et Coloniales, 1934), pp. 128-39.

Status according to customary law of girls, married women, mothers, widows; attitude of the administration towards custom.

WESTERMANN, D., *Autobiographies d'Africains*, Paris, Payot, 1943.

Pp. 236-45: life of Mme Marthe Afemele Kwami, of Togo, the daughter and the wife of teachers.

WILBOIS, J., *L'action sociale en pays de missions*, Paris, Payot, 1939, 150 pp.

The greatest need is for legislation that will change the position of women in French Africa.

Central Africa

CATTEEU, O. P., "La femme congolaise", *Grands Lacs*, 63rd year, No. 2 (Namur, 1947), 5-14.

The life of Mamvu women: birth, family life, widowhood; the feminine soul.

Analytical Bibliography

COLLARD, J., "La fem ae dans la sensibilité bantoue", *Synthèses*, 11th year. No, 121 (Brussels, 1956), 288-91.

Some notes, in a discussion of a film on Bantu art, on relations between men and women: as a wife, the woman is entirely dependent on the man; as a mother, she is transformed.

*CONSTANCE-MARIE, Sister, "Het jonge meisje in Kongo" [The young girl in the Congo], *Nieuw Afrika*, 69th year (Antwerp, 1953), 163-9.

Position of girls in native society, marriage, the role of the clan on this occasion among the Bira of Ituri.

CORNET, R. P., *La femme en régime matriarcal*, Rapports et Comptes rendus de la XXᵉ Semaine de Missiologie de Louvain, 1950, Brussels, Éd. Universelle, 1951, pp. 192-209.

Among the Bashila, the clan is of prime importance and women are regarded by the clan merely as an economic asset. Their dignity as individuals is not respected.

CYFER-DIDERICH, G., *Le statut juridique de la femme indigène au Congo Belge*, Brussels, Conseil National des Femmes belges, 1950, 32 pp.

Position of native women from the point of view of custom: marriage, separation, rights and duties of wives, system of ownership, the widow, polygyny and its effects; the writer also discusses native women who have been educated, emancipated, and culturally assimilated.

— , "La condition juridique de la femme au Congo Belge", *Civilisations*, 1, 4 (Brussels, 1951), 59-67.

In the Belgian Congo the position of women is still conditioned by the old rules of customary law which underlie the legal system. Restrictions have been introduced by a series of decrees and legal enactments, particularly as regards bridewealth, polygyny and education.

*DARTEVELLE, A., "La femme: étude de sa condition et de sa situation sociale chez les Ba-Vili (Congo français)", *Bull. de la Société Royale Belge d'Anthropologie et de Préhistoire*, LIV (Brussels, 1939), 99-100.

A summary of the writer's communication concerning native women among the Ba-Vili of the French Lower Congo. Various aspects of their position in society and in the family are examined. (*Bibliographie Ethnographique du Congo Belge*, 1941).

*DE BOECK, J., "Enige nota's over het inlandsch huwelijk bij de Ekonda (Leopoldmeer)", *Congo*, I, 4 (Brussels, 1933), 547-54.

Marriage and the position of women in the traditional setting of Konda society.

DECAPMAKER, "Sanctions coutumières contre l'adultère chez les Bakongo de la région de Kasi", *Congo* (Brussels, 1939), 134-48.

After recalling the customs regulating marriage, the author discusses the sanctions applied to women in cases of adultery both before the arrival of the Whites (death, enslavement, or payment in kind), and after.

DE MAN, M., "Het social statuut van de vrouw in Belgisch-Kongo", *Zaïre*, IV, 8 (Brussels, 1950), 851-69.

The writer discusses first the position of women of other races, and then of native women, in the Belgian Congo. (*Bibliographie Ethnographique du Congo Belge*, 1950).

*DOUCY, A., "Réflexions sur le rôle de la femme indigène au Congo Belge", *Bull.*

M. Perlman and M. P. Moal

de l'Union des Femmes Coloniales, 26th year, No. 4-5 (Brussels, 1955), 4-5, ill.
Problem of the education of native women: they remain under the pressure of the influence of the clan even when transplanted to non-traditional surroundings. (*Bibliographie Ethnographique du Congo Belge*, 1955).

FRANÇOISE-MARIE, Sister, *La femme indigène dans la législation coutumière au Nepoko*, Rapports et Comptes rendus de la XXe Semaine de Missiologie de Louvain, 1950, Brussels, Éd. Universelle, 1951, pp. 210-23.
Legal situation of unmarried and of married women, problem of bride-wealth.

*GERDA, Sister, "La femme ruandaise hier et aujourd'hui", *Trait d'union*, 7th year, XLIV (Antwerp, 1957), 11-14, ill.
Former condition of women among the Tutsi: daily routine; motherhood. Women today: contribution of Christianity, future outlook. (*Bibliographie Ethnographique du Congo Belge*, 1957).

GILLES DE PELICHY, DOM, *Condition de la femme d'apres le droit coutumier de l'Ouest Africain*, Rapports et Comptes rendus de la XXe Semaine de Missiologie de Louvain, 1950, Brussels, Éd. Universelle, 1951, pp. 155-77.
Colonialist literature makes out women to be miserable creatures. A study of traditional institutions (the writer has made a study of the Sudanese tribes of the Gulf of Guinea) shows that African customary law pays great respect to the dignity of women, especially of the mother.

JAULIN, R., Questions concerning women, in "Eléments et aspects divers de l'organisation civile et pénale des groupes du Moyen-Chari: groupe sara madjingaye et groupe mbaye", *Bull. de l'IFAN*, XX, B, 1-2 (Dakar, 1958), 170-84.
Legal and actual position of Sara women following upon their desire for emancipation; bridewealth, sanctions, women's work.

KAGAME, A., "Les organisations socio-familiales de l'ancien Ruanda", *Mémoires de l'Académie Royale des Sciences Coloniales*, Classe des sciences morales et politiques, XXXVIII, 3, Brussels, 1954, 8vo, 355 pp.
Chapter II (pp. 71-94) is on the family and kinship. Women do not belong permanently to their natal families; they share completely in the life of the man they marry.

*KELLERSBERGER, J. S., *Congo crosses. A study of Congo womanhood*, Boston, Central Committee of United Studies and Foreign Missions, 1936, 222 pp. map, fig. ill.
The writer, a Protestant missionary in the Belgian Congo, discusses in an interesting manner the life of Congolese natives, particularly the life of women, their role in society, their occupations, marriage, children's education, and the influence of missionary work on the native mind. Good illustrations. (*Bibliographie Ethnographique du Congo Belge*, 1936).

MACLATCHY, A., Condition of women, in "L'organisation sociale de la région de Mimongo (Gabon)", *Bull. de l'Institut d'Études Centrafricaines*, I, 1 (Brazzaville, 1945), 68-9.
Before marriage, women enjoy complete sexual freedom. As married women, they have great influence, as was shown by a strike of protest organized by all the wives.

MAKONGA, B., "La position sociale de la mère", *Problèmes Sociaux Congolais*, *Bull. du CEPSI*, XVII (Elisabethville, 1951), 243-59.
Among the Luba-Katanga, woman, especially in her role as mother, is the basic element in society, and has ownership of personal property.

Analytical Bibliography

*MARIA HELENA, Sister, "De vrouw in Congo bij de Ngbandi" [Woman among the Ngbandi of the Congo], *Xaveriana*, XLVIII, (1927), 32 pp.

Women's role in the principal events of native life among the Ngbandi.

MULENZI, J., "La femme dans la société ruandaise", *Échanges*, XXVI (Paris, 1956), 30-4.

Ruanda women always play an important role. Their free consent is required for marriage, they become the guardian of their children on becoming a widow and inherit their husband's property. The education of their children is entirely in their hands up until the children are ten years old.

NAIGISIKI, S., *see* International Institute of Differing Civilizations, 1958.

PAILLOUX, R., "La place de la femme chez les Babemba", *Pères Blancs*, XCVIII (Paris, 1952), 10-15; XCIX, 9-14, ill.

African women have never been the slaves they have been made out to be, any more than bridewealth was a form of sale, but rather a sign of respect towards women and a protection for the wife's position. Relations between husbands and wives and parents and children, although they may follow a different pattern from ours, are based on love and affection.

PEERAER, S., "Toespraken tot jonggehuwden bij de Baluba (Katanga)", *Kongo-Overzee*, V, 5 (Antwerp, 1939), 241-76.

Advice to young married couples, especially to the young wife, the future mother, the young housekeeper. These counsels are still handed down today.

PLESSERS, R. P., "Les *Bakaji ba mpinga* (femmes de remplacement) chez les Baluba du Lubilash", *Bull. des Juridictions indigènes et du Droit coutumier Congolais*, 13th year, No. 5 (Elisabethville, 1945), 130-2.

Bride-price being high, the Baluba of Lubilash claim another woman to replace a wife that has died. A cause of conflict. How to remedy this. (*Bibliographie Ethnographique du Congo Belge*, 1945).

*RIEHL, A., "A familia indigena no Congo", *Portugal em Africa*, III, 14 (Lisbon, 1946), 88-98.

Notes on the indigenous family among the Mayombe: betrothal, marriage, divorce, rights of women, prostitution.

SIQUET, M., Legal and customary status of women, in *La Promotion de la femme au Congo et en Ruanda-Urundi*, Congrès National Colonial, 12th session, Brussels, 1956, pp. 197-251.

Report on four topics: Condition of women under Congolese customary law before coming under European influence; condition of women under present-day customary law; legal impediments to the advance of Congolese women and proposals for removing them; status of Congolese women under statutory law and proposals for possible modifications.

SOHIER, A., *Évolution de la condition juridique de la femme indigène au Congo Belge*, Contribution to the 24th session of l'Institut Colonial International, Rome, 1939, Brussels, 1939, pp. 149-217.

Study of the legal status of native women, both as girls and as married women, in customary law, and then in the legal system of the independent Congo State.

*— , "L'évolution de la condition juridique de la femme indigène aux colonies" *Bull. de l'Union des Femmes Coloniales* (Brussels, 1939), No. 105, pp. 156-8; No. 106, pp. 178-80; No. 107, pp. 203-4; No. 108, pp. 230-31; No. 109, pp. 255-6; No. 110, pp. 282-3.

M. Perlman and M. P. Moal

Notes on the general situation of native women before the European occupation. (*Bibliographie Ethnographique du Congo Belge*, 1939).

SOYER-POSKIN, D., *see* International Institute of Differing Civilizations, 1958.

STAPPERS, L., "Bandala-Mumba, vrouwen van gazagsdragers bij de Baamilembwe", *Kongo-Overzee*, 16th year, V (Antwerp, 1950), 249-52.

Among the Bamilembwe the wives of certain officials can obtain a title which distinguishes them from other women, a title much sought after and which is only granted on payment of a large sum. (*Bibliographie du Congo Belge*, 1950).

VAN CAENEGHEM, R., "Étude sur les dispositions pénales coutumières contre l'adultère chez les Baluba et les Bena Lulua du Kasai", *Bull. du CEPSI*, VIII (Elisabethville, 1949), 5-46.

Legal dispositions against adulterous women; conception of the word *disandi* (adultery).

South Africa

AKELEY, M. L. J., "The Swazi queen at home; intimate observations on love, life and death in South Africa's timeless Swaziland", *Natural History* (New York, June 1938), 21-32.

Notes accompanied by numerous illustrations concerning village life. The education of girls among the Swazi of South Africa.

APTHORPE, R., *see* International Institute of Differing Civilizations, 1958.

*BRADLEY, K., "My cow, my wife and my old clay pipe", *African Observer*, VII, 3 (1937), 33-7.

Summary of the ways and customs of the Ba-Ila of Northern Rhodesia, particularly the relations between men and women before marriage; brief comments on marriage and adultery. (*Bibliographie Ethnographique du Congo Belge*, 1937).

*CASQUEIRO, M. VON BOSSE, "A mulher indigena", *Boletim da sociedade de estudos coloniais de Moçambique*, XXI (Lourenço-Marques, 1951), 5-25.

CHILD, H. F., "Family and tribal structure: status of women", *Nada*, XXXV (Salisbury, 1958), 65-70.

Concerning the status of Matabele women. Formerly every woman, of whatever tribe and whoever she might be, remained a minor all her life.

EARTHY, E., *Valenge women. The social and economic life of the Valenge women of Portuguese East Africa*, O.U.P. for Int. Af. Inst., 1933, 251 pp. maps.

The author writes of the social and economic life of Valenge women, among whom she lived as missionary for 30 years.

*ENNIS, E. L., "Women's names among the Ovimbundu of Angola", *African Studies*, IV, 1 (Johannesburg, 1945), 1-8.

Women's names among the Ovimbundu reveal the customs, beliefs and psychology of this people. (*Bibliographie Ethnographique du Congo Belge*, 1945).

*FRAZAO, F. S., "A mulher na familia gentilica", *Mensario administrativo*, No. 55-56 (Luanda, 1952), 9-22.

*GUTMAN, B., "Die Frau unter den Bantunegern", *Evangelische Missionsmagazin*, LXVIII (Basel, 1924), 331-5.

244

Analytical Bibliography

HORREL, M., see International Institute of Differing Civilizations, 1958.

JUNOD, H., Life-cycle of a woman, from birth to death, in *Mœurs et coutumes des Bantous*, (Paris, Payot, 1936), Vol. I, pp. 162-205.
The writer studies the condition and activities of women before marriage (games, initiation), and after (conditions of married life, taboos, confinement, widowhood . . .).

KUNENE, D. P., "Notes on *hlonepha* among the southern Sotho", *African Studies*, XVII, 3 (Johannesburg, 1958), 159-82.
Hlonepha = to respect. Out of respect, a married woman must observe a certain number of taboos, in particular, she must avoid saying certain words and names in the presence of certain male relatives of her husband (her father-in-law, her husband himself, etc.). Distribution of this custom, reasons for it.

*MAXEKE, C. M., "Social conditions among Bantu women and girls", *Christian studies and Modern South Africa* (Fort Hare, 1930), 111-17.

*MEDGER, R., "Die Stellung der Frau bei den Dschagga nach den Stammeslehren", *Afrika Rundschau*, VIII (Berlin [?], 1942), 98-105.

*POSSELT, F., "The story of the Princess Mepo", *Nada*, VII (1929), 115-17.

SALEMA, M. J., see International Institute of Differing Civilizations, 1958.

*SHROPSHIRE, D. W. T., *The Bantu woman under the Natal code of native law*, Lovedale, Lovedale Press, 1941, 47 pp.
The results of an enquiry conducted by the author on the question of customs regulating the position of Bantu women in Natal (family, widowhood, emancipation, bridewealth, care of children).

SIMONS, H. J., "African women and the law in South Africa", *The Listener*, LV, No. 1416 (1956), 626-7 and 644.
In South Africa, the native woman lives under three legal systems (customary law, native law, European law) without any of them according her a position equal to that which she in fact holds, in virtue of her influence, her economic independence, and her social and political dynamism.

*SLOAN, A., "The black woman", *Nada*, I (Salisbury, 1923), 60-9.
Life and occupations of Shona women.

WEITZECKER, G., "La donna fra i Basuto", *Archivio per la antropologia e la etnologia*, XXXI (Florence, 1901), 459-78.
Brief account of position and activities of women . . . in the family, in society, and in relation to religion; refers to birth, namegiving, puberty and initiation, clothing and ornament, marriage. (*Bantu Studies* (1934), 325, I. Schapera).

*WILLOUGHBY, W. C., *Race problems in the New Africa*, Oxford, Clarendon Press, 1923, Part II, pp. 46-138.
Contains notes on the position of women among the Tswana (Bechuana), education and initiation.

*WILSON, B. M., "The position of women in South Africa", *The East and the West*, XIV (1916), 61-8.

East Africa

BROWN, E. F., "Hehe grandmothers", *Journ. of the Roy. Anthr. Inst.*, LXV (1935), 83-96.

M. Perlman and M. P. Moal

Importance of the grandmother in the social and family life of the Bantu of Tanganyika: she looks after the education of her grandchildren and presides at the excision ceremonies for girls. She knows a great deal about medicine.

*CHRAPKOWSKI, M. ,"Ostafrikanische Frauen", *Der Erdball*, IV (Berlin, 1930), 341-4.

COSTANZO, G. A., *see* International Institute of Differing Civilizations, 1958.

CULWICK, A. T. and G. M., "Fostermothers in Ulanga", *Tanganyika Notes and Records*, I (Dar-es-Salam, March 1936) 19–24.

Notes on fostermothers among the Wabena of Ulanga, and on the system under which they operate. (*Bibliographie Ethnographique du Congo Belge*, 1936).

DRIBERG, J. H., "The status of women among the Nilotics and Nilo-Hamitics", *Africa*, V (1932), 404-21.

Division of labour between the sexes according to their physical capabilities; the position of women is not an inferior one.

FAWZI, SAAD ED DIN, *see* International Institute of Differing Civilizations, 1958.

*INTMANN, B., "Die Wertschätzung der Frau unter den Ostafrikanern", *Der Erdball*, VIII (Berlin, Aug. 1931), 312-20.

MACVICAR, T., "The position of women among the Wanguru", *Primitive Man*, VII, 2 (Washington, 1934), 17-22.

Domestic, economic, social, political and religious life of Wanguru women (Tanganyika). Theoretically they are inferior to the men, but they often have a great deal of influence which enables them to participate in the public life of the tribe.

NYENDWOHA, E. S., *see* International Institute of Differing Civilizations.

FAMILY LIFE

Girls

BÉART, C., "Intimité: les lettres de la fiancée", *Présence Africaine*, VIII-IX (Paris 1950), 271-88.

An attempt to analyse the private thoughts of educated girls in Dahomey from study of the letters written by one to her fiancé. (*Bibliographie Ethnographique du Congo Belge*, 1950).

BRAUSCH, G. E. J. B., "Les associations prénuptiales dans la Haute Lukenyi", *Bull. des Juridictions Indigènes et du Droit coutumier congolais*, 15th year, IV (Elisabethville, 1947), 109-29, map.

These [prenuptial] associations, which have their socially sanctioned rites and ceremonies, demonstrate the complete sexual freedom of girls among the Ohindu and, to a lesser extent, among the Nkutshu. The writer studies the sexual, social and economic functions of these associations as well as their legal status.

CULWICK, A. M., "New ways for old in the treatment of adolescent African girls", *Africa*, XII, 4 (1939), 425-32.

Changes brought about by the Berlin mission (at Maneromanga, Tanganyika) in the practice of seclusion of girls (from the onset of menstruation until marriage).

Analytical Bibliography

DOOLEY, C. T., "Child-training among the Wanguru", *Primitive Man*, VIII, 1 (Washington, 1934), 27-30.
Makes a special study of girls' games.

*EDME, P., "Kunda Kalumbi, fille d'Afrique", *Jeune Afrique*, 7th year, XIX (1953), 41-6; XX (1953), 32-5.
The life of African girls. An example of colonialist literature.

"L'Enfant dans la famille gabonaise", *Bull. de la Société de Recherches Congolaises*, 2nd year (Brazzaville, 1923), 15-22.
The life of children among the Mpongwe, Benga, Sekiani, Kele and Pahouin. Rights and obligations of the mother, of the children. Girls before marriage have almost complete sexual freedom; on marrying, they pass from being under their father's authority to that of their husband.

HAUSER, J., "Notes sur quelques attitudes de la collégienne dakaroise", *Bull. de l'IFAN*, XVIIB, 1-2 (Dakar, 1955), 203-9.
The compositions written by pupils of the Delafosse School at Dakar during several months of attendance there supply the writer with useful information as to the attitudes of schoolgirls towards our civilization. Systematic analysis of these compositions. (*Bibliographic Ethnographique du Congo Belge*, 1955).

HULSTAERT, G., "La coutume nkundo (mongo) et le décret sur la fille indigène non pubère", *Congo* (Brussels, Oct. 1937), 269-76.
A study of the custom of marriage of girls before puberty as practised by the Nkundo of Equatorial Africa; the manner in which it is carried out, its legal and moral aspect as seen by the natives.

*MAKANYA, V. S., "The problem of the Zulu girl", *Native Teachers' Journal*, X (Pietermaritsburg, Natal, 1931), 116-20.

MOHR, R., "Ricerche sull'etica sessuale di alcune popolazioni dell' Africa centrale e orientale", *Archivio per l'Antropologia e la Etnologia*, LXIX, 3-4 (Florence, 1939), 157-315.
A systematic account of the documentation concerning premarital and marital sexual ethics among the peoples of the Upper Nile and in the region of Lake Victoria. Three points are discussed: prohibition of sexual relations before marriage; sexual freedom before marriage; premarital pregnancy in relation to the type of culture and of social organization.

OMINDE, S. H., *The Luo girl from infancy to marriage*, Macmillan, 1952, 69 pp. ill.
Divides the physical and mental development of Luo girls (East Africa) into five stages: infancy (until two years of age); childhood from two to six years of age, after which the separation of the sexes occurs; school age, from six to 11; adolescence; marriage and the life of a married woman.

PAUWELS, H., "Fiancée et jeune mariée au Ruanda", *Zaïre*, V, 2 (Brussels, 1951), 115-35.
The rites which Ruanda girls must undergo before betrothal and up until marriage.

RATTRAY, R. S., The education of girls, incision, etc., in *The tribes of the Ashanti hinterland* (Oxford, Clarendon Press, 1932), Vol. I, pp. 163-70.
According to a Nankane informant, in his tribe (and in most of the tribes in the northern areas of the Gold Coast), girls are brought up by their mothers, who gradually train them for their future life as a wife. At puberty, they have to undergo excision [clitoridectomy], an operation which gives them the dignity of womanhood and exhibits their moral worth if it has been found that their virginity is intact, virginity being an essential social value.

247

M. Perlman and M. P. Moal

TWALA, R. B., "*Umhlanga* (reed) ceremony of the Swazi maidens", *African Studies*, XI, 3 (Johannesburg, 1952), 93-103.

An organization among Swazi women for cutting the *umhlanga* (reeds) for use in chiefs' dwellings. This task is entirely undertaken by girls (*see* Initiation)

*VAN CAENEGHEM, R., "Hoe een negermoeder haar dochter opvoedt bot het hywelijk", *Band*, 3rd year, X (Leopoldstad, 1944) 390-5.

How a Luba mother prepares her daughter for marriage.

Fertility

BERESFORD STOOKE, G., "Ceremonies designed to influence the fertility of women", *Man*, XXVIII (1928), 177.

Various fertility ceremonies carried out by the Akamba (Kenya). They are only held for menstruating women. The treatment is said to be infallible.

BRASSEUR, M., "La protection de la mère et de l'enfant dans la formation médicale de Kitangue", *Aide médicale aux Missions*, 26th year, IV (1954), 140-7.

Deals with the Pende and Chokwe tribes of Chikaga territory. The *Kampugu* are the women who come to consult the doctor about childlessness; the writer investigates the causes for this, and makes proposals for remedying it (gynaecological, prenatal consultations); the infant clinics show encouraging results. (*Bibliographie Ethnographique du Congo Belge*, 1954).

EKALLE, S., "Croyances et pratiques obstétricales des Duala", *Bull. de la Société d'Études Camerounaises*, XIX-XX (Duala, 1947), 61-92.

Magical protection, fertility rites and taboos.

JEFFREYS, M. D. W., "A contraceptive girdle from Calabar Province, Nigeria", *Man*, XLIV (1944), 70.

Description of a contraceptive girdle worn by an Ibibio girl.

MASSÉ, L., "Contribution à l'étude de la nuptialité et de la fertilité dans l'agglomération de Kanise", *Études Sénégalaises*, V (Saint-Louis, Senegal, IFAN, 1954), 41-67.

A study of the correlation between celibacy, monogamy and polygyny, and social and professional categories. The marriage rate is variable. Polygyny appears to dimish the fertility of women. Numerous tables.

ROMERO MOLINER, R., "Notas sobre la situación social de la mujer indigena en Fernando Póo", *Cuadernos de Estudios africanos*, XVIII (Madrid, 1952), 21-39.

The fertility of Bubi women: their precocious sexual life brings about barrenness caused by frequent gynaecological infections. Fertility is much reduced after the age of 30.

SCHMIDT, A., "The water of life (female fertility rite at Bamessing village, Bamenda division, British Cameroons)", *African Studies*, XIV, 1 (Johannesburg, 1955) 23-8.

Describes a female fertility rite among the Bamenda of the Cameroons. Its aim is to wash away the sin which has made the woman barren in the waters of the river which flows from the fertility altar *Funbeko*. (*Bibliographie Ethnographique du Congo Belge*, 1955).

*Shaw, M., "Fertility dolls in Southern Africa", *Nada*, XXV (Salisbury, 1948), 63-8, ill.

These are dolls which women and girls carry on their backs so that they

Analytical Bibliography

shall not be barren. The dolls described here come from the Zulu, Swazi, Matabele, Basoto, Bechuana, Balenge and Ovambo. (*Bibliographie Ethnographique du Congo Belge*, 1955).

TALBOT, P. A., *Some Nigerian fertility cults*, O.U.P., 1927, xxii + 140 pp.

The writer deals with two tribes, the Ibo and the Ijo, and describes certain sexual taboos which on some occasions may, or even must, be violated (a kind of catharsis).

*TANNER, R. E. S., "Sukuma fertility: an analysis of 148 marriages in Mwanza district, Tanganyika", *East African Medical Journal*, XXXIII, 3 (Nairobi, 1956), 94-9.

The fertility of a Sukuma wife varies between polygynous and monogamous unions and with the length of marriage. (*African Abstracts*, 1957).

VERBEEK, A., "Anticonceptionele middelen (Nkundo)", *Aequatoria*, XIV, 1 (Coquilhatville, 1951), 26-8.

Deals with the Injolo, a group of the Nkundo. The contraceptive methods of these people consists of douching in which preparations of herbs with abortive properties are used.

WHITE, C. M. N., "Conservatism and modern adaptation in Luvale female puberty ritual", *Africa*, XXIII, 1 (1953), 15-24.

Formerly a woman's most important attributes were fertility and the ability to be a good housewife. The older generation still insists on the importance of fertility magic, but to the young girls fertility is no longer either admirable or desirable.

ZAAL, C., "Bij de Nzakara, *Bendo*, een fetisj voor de vrouwen" [*Bendo* a female fetish], *Kongo-Overzee*, XXIV, 1-2 (Antwerp, 1958), 80-9.

A fertility fetish, the *bendo* is a shrub planted with its roots in the air behind the hut. It becomes the object of a cult if a birth in fact takes place.

Birth: Mother and child

ABBATUCCI, S., "La maternité en Afrique noire", *Outre-mer*, IV (Paris, 1931), 420-35.

Very interesting documentation concerning the peoples of former French African colonies, in particular the Bambara and Sara of French East Africa [A.E.F.]. (*Bibliographie Ethnographique du Congo Belge*, 1931).

ACQUAYE ELMINA, J. R., "Fanti native customs about conception and birth", *Anthropos*, XXIII (Posieux (Freiburg), 1928), 1051-3.

Fanti customs about conception and birth (Gold Coast). Confinement, death in childbirth of the woman.

ALBERT, A., "Coutumes des Bandjouns à la naissance, au mariage et à la mort" *Missions Catholiques*, (Lyon, 1937), 117-21 and 138-43.

Various Banjun (Cameroon) customs concerning birth, particularly the birth of twins.

BA, A. H., "Le couteau de la maternité", *Notes Africaines*, XVII (Dakar, 1943), 3-4.

A legend explaining why Fulani women and women of other Sudenese tribes never leave a baby alone without placing a knife by its head as protection against the spells of the anti-maternity demon.

BARNES, H. F., "The birth of a Ngoni child", *Man*, XLIX (1949), 87-9.

The birth of a Ngoni child and the customs concerned. Description of the birth.

249

M. Perlman and M. P. Moal

BLANLUET, J., "Enquête sur l'enfant noir en A.O.F.: l'Enfant Gourounsi", *Bull. de l'Enseignement de l'A.O.F.*, XXI, 78 (Dakar, 1932), 8-19.
Notes on birth and relations between parents and children.

BOKETSHU, B., "La grossesse et l'enfantement chez les Nkundo", *La Voix du Congolais*, VI, 46 (Kalina, 1950), 26-8.
If a Nkundo woman wants to have a child she invokes the spirit *elima* and eats a tree-frog; conception, some medicines for pregnant women.

BOLYA, P., "Étude ethnographique des Mongo", *Voix du Congolais* (Kalina, 1957), CXXXVIII, 696-9; CXXXIX, 776-8; CXL, 862-5.
Brief general notes on various [Mongo] customs, particularly about birth; the mother must spend a period in seclusion (*jule*). Customs concerning birth in urban centres.

CARDINALL, A. W., Birth and marriage customs, in *The Natives of the Northern territories of the Gold Coast* (Routledge, n.d. [1920]), pp. 66-81, ill.
Customs for the birth of the first child, taboos during pregnancy; the mother readmitted to society three days after the birth if it is a boy, four if it is a girl.

CYRILLE, G., "Enquête sur l'enfant noir en A.O.F.: le petit Dahoméen", *Bull. de l'Enseignement de l'A.O.F.*, XXI, 79 (Dakar, 1932), 79-90.
Birth [in Dahomey]; the mother's influence on the child's upbringing during infancy.

EKALLE, S., "Croyances et pratiques obstétricales des Duala", *Bull. de la Société d'Études Camerounaises*, XIX-XX (Dula, 1947), 61-92.
Detailed notes on: magical protection, fertility rites, taboos, the methods of the midwives in certain cases.

ELLISON, R. E., "Marriage and child-birth among the Kanuri", *Africa*, IX, 4 (1936), 524-35.
Notes on marriage and birth among the Kanuri of Northern Nigeria. The writer shows how traditional Islamic practices (the Kanuri have been Mohammedans for several centuries) are modified and complemented by local custom and by superstition. (*Bibliographie Ethnographique du Congo Belge*, 1936).

EVEN, A., "La grossesse, la naissance et la prime enfance chez les Bakota du Haut-Ogooué et du nord de Mossendjo (Moyen Congo)," *Bull. de la Société de Recherches Congolaises*, XXVI (Brazzaville, 1938), 5-21.
Taboos about pregnant women [among the Bakota]. Simulated confinement of the husband. Earliest stages of the baby's upbringing.

GROSPERRIN, H., "Quelques coutumes ewé en matière d'accouchement", *Annales de médecine et de pharmacie coloniales*, III (Paris, 1935), 822.
Notes on the persistence of native customs [concerning confinements among the Ewe] in spite of the increase in European maternity hospitals and clinics.

HILLS-YOUNG, E., "Charms and customs associated with child-birth", *Sudan Notes and Records*, XXIII, 2 (Khartoum, 1940), 331-5.
Customs and charms concerning birth and fertility.

HUBER, H., "Schwangerschaft, Geburt und frühe Kindheit im Brauchtum der Bat-Ewe (Ghana)", *Annali Lateransi*, XXI (Vatican, 1957), 230-44.
Ewe rites of magic protection, special rites for the birth of twins. The woman is confined at her mother's.

KAMMER, M., "The customs observed as regards miscarriage among the Barotse", *East African Medical Journal*, XVIII, 2 (Nairobi, 1941), 56-9.
A period of mourning follows a miscarriage.

Analytical Bibliography

KOHLER, M., *Marriage customs in Southern Natal*, Pretoria, Department of Native Affairs (*Ethnological Publications* IV), 1933, 103 pp. ill.
Contains some notes on the birth of the first child.

—, "Menstruation, Schwangerschaft und Geburt in Afrika", *Wissenschaftliche Zeitschrift*, Friedrich-Schiller Universität, III, 1 (1953-54), 129-42.
Customs associated with the onset of menstruation among African women, coitus, pregnancy, birth, the umbilical cord, the placenta, the couvade. Brief survey of the relevant bibliography. (*Bibliographie Ethnographique du Congo Belge*, 1954).

Labracque, E., "Accidents de la naissance chez les Babemba", *Anthropos*, XXV (Posieux (Freiburg), 1930), 730-1.
Customs concerning still-born and premature babies, and the death of women in child-birth.

*LAIDLER, P. W., "Native (Bantu) beliefs concerning pregnancy and child-birth, their effects on public health administration, and the effects of detribalisation or urbanisation upon these ancient customs and upon infantile mortality rates", *South African Journal of Science*, XXVIII (Johannesburg, 1931), 418-22.
Notes on sexual practices and on birth among the natives of East London.

LAIGRET, J., "De quelques coutumes indigènes concernant les accouchements", *Bull. de la Société de Recherches Congolaises*, VI (Brazzaville, 1925), 11-14.
In the Congo basin delivery sometimes takes place "through the rear passage", when there has been a large tear in the tissue connecting the vagina and the rectum. The child is delivered with the help of experienced midwives.

LEBEUF, J. P., "Sur la naissance en général et sur celle des jumeaux en particulier chez les Kotoko", *Bull. du Musée d'Ethnographie du Trocadéro*, XI, 6 (Paris, 1939), 545-53.
Ethnographic information concerning birth rituals among the Kotoko (Chad).

LESTRANGE, M. DE, "Mères et enfants en Afrique noire", *Le Concours Médical* (Paris, 1954), 4367-70.
The article is about the Coniagui and Bassari of French Guinea: desire for children: sexual freedom of girls; abortion; pregnancy; confinement. Infancy, feeding and upbringing, the love of mothers for their sons.

LEYDER, J., "La naissance chez les Bwaka (Ubangui)", *Bull. de la Société Royale de Géographie*, LVII (Brussels, 1933), 109-27.
The writer examines the customs and practices associated with fertility, their origins and social significance; the state of the pregnant woman, geophagy, confinement and subsequent rites among the Bwaka of Ubangi.

MALCOLM, W. G. B., "Notes on birth, marriage and death ceremonies of the Eyap tribe, central Cameroon", *Journal of the Roy. Anthr. Inst.*, LIII (1923), 388-401.
The first part of this article is on natal and prenatal customs: the mother is given infusions to drink at certain specified times during pregnancy.

MARIE-ANDRÉ DU SACRÉ-CŒUR, Sister, "La mère et l'enfant en A.O.F.", *L'Ethnographie*, n.s. XXXVII (Paris, 1939), 71-82.
Customs concerning birth, name-giving, and children's upbringing. Influence of Christianity and decrease in mortality. (*Bibliographie Ethnographique du Congo Belge*, 1939).

251

M. Perlman and M. P. Moal

MAURICE, P. M., "La naissance au pays des Bapimbwe", *Bibliotheca Africana*, IV, 1 (Innsbruck, 1930-31), 79-86.

Before giving birth, a pregnant woman is surrounded with magic protections. The midwives, who belong to a corporation called *malombwe*, deliver the child and preside at all the ceremonies; there are special ceremonies for the death of a pregnant woman, for the birth of the first child, differing according to its sex, for the birth of twins, regarded as maleficent deities (to be exorcised by adoration and insult). The care of the child until the age of two.

— , "La naissance chez les Bapimbwe", *La Géographie*, LXIV (Paris, 1935), 309-16.

Notes on the bringing up of children and on birth among the Bapimbwe of Northern Rhodesia.

MOLLER, M. S. G., "Bahaya customs and beliefs in connection with pregnancy and child-birth", *Tanganyika Notes and Records*, L (Dar-es-Salam, June 1958), 112-17.

Taboos during pregnancy; after birth, the solemn burial of the placenta, often regarded as the dead brother of the newborn child. The custom of *bisisi*, the status of mother and newborn child.

NDONGO MBA, M. A., "Costumbres y creencias pamues sobre el nacimiento", *Africa*, XIV, 192 (Madrid, 1957), 14-15.

The birth of a boy is celebrated by a great feast. Customs at the birth of twins. Children belong to the man who has paid bridewealth. The mother must paint herself red with camwood powder.

*NGOI, P., "La grossesse et l'enfantement chez les Nkundo", *Aequatoria*, VII, 1-2 (Coquilhatville, 1944), 14-24 and 63-70.

NIAKATE B., "Naissance et baptême chez les Saracolés de Bakhounou (cercle de Néma, Soudan)", *Notes Africaines*, XXIV (Dakar, Oct. 1944), 22.

Some customs at the birth of a Sarakole child, compared with those among the Bambara.

OLIVIER, G. and AUJOULAT, L., "L'obstétrique en pays yaoundé", *Bull. de la Société d'Études Camerounaises*, XII (Duala, 1945), 7-71.

Notes on marriage, initiation of girls, pregnancy, taboos, confinement, delivery, the newborn child. Notes on the fertility of women, obstetrical physiology and pathology in maternity cases. (*Bibliographie Ethnographique du Congo Belge*, 1945).

ORTOLI, H., "Les rites de la maternité chez les Dogon de Bandiagara", *Bull. de l'IFAN*, III, 1-2 (Dakar, 1941), 53-63.

Notes on conception, pregnancy, abortion among the Dogon.

PAGES, A., "Rwanda belge. Cérémonies qui entourent la naissance d'un enfant et la réclusion de la mère", *Congo*, II, 2 (Brussels, 1934), 205-26.

An important contribution to the study of the rites and ceremonies that precede, accompany, and follow birth among the Banyaruanda. Seclusion of the new mother, churching rites, name-giving ceremony, the situation of the mother of a large family, associated religious beliefs. (*Bibliographic Ethnographique du Congo Belge*, 1934).

PAULME, D., Birth, in *Organisation sociale des Dogon* (Paris, Domat-Montchrétien, 1940), pp. 421-57.

Notes on the beliefs, customs, rites, from conception until the giving of its name to the newborn child. The birth of twins.

Analytical Bibliography

RUAM, O. F., *Chaga childhood. A description of indigenous education in an East African tribe*, O.U.P., 1940, 422 pp.

Chapter II (pp. 67-102) deals in detail with prenatal preparations: education of the parents; birth; moral test of the father and mother.

RWITZA, K. J., "Natal customs in Bukoba", *Tanganyika Notes and Records*, L (Dar-es-Salam, June 1958), 104-5.

Some taboos and rules to be observed before and after birth. Name-giving ceremonies, when the child cuts its first tooth.

SIEBER, D. and J., "Das Leben des Kindes im Nsungli-Stamm", *Africa*, XI, 2 (1938), 208-20.

Rites at birth and at weaning (about the age of two). The mother brings up the children, until the age of six in the case of boys.

STAPPERS, L., "Het Intreden van het kind bij de Baamilembwe" [Entry of the child among the Bamilembwe], *Kongo-Overzee*, XVIII, 1 (Antwerp, 1952), 1-5.

Description of various customs observed during pregnancy, confinement customs, ceremonies following birth, for name-giving, the first time the child leaves the house . . . followed by a prayer (pp. 6-7) said by the mother at the time of birth.

*TEICHLER, "Wie die Hayafrauen Geburtschilfe treiben", *Das Hochland*, VII (Oldeani, 1937), 177-82.

THOMAS, N. W., Birth, twins and circumcision, in *Anthropological report on Sierra Leone*, Part I (Harrison, 1916), pp. 108-18, ill.

Birth customs are fairly simple, the most striking feature being the departure of the woman from her husband's house one month before the birth takes place, to have her confinement at her father's house.

— , "Birth customs of the Edo speaking peoples", *Journ. of the Roy. Anthr. Inst.*, LII (1922), 250-8.

TRAVELE, M., "Usages relatifs aux naissances survenues hors du village en pays bambara", *Revue d'Ethnographie et des Traditions populaires*, V (Paris, 1924), 373-4.

Wherever a birth may have taken place, no care may be taken [of mother and child] until they have returned to the village.

WAGNER, G., Birth, in *The Bantu of North Kavirondo* (O.U.P. for Int. Af. Inst., 1949), Vol. I, pp. 295-332.

Pregnancy, birth, name-giving ceremony.

WALK, L., "Die ersten Lebensjahre des Kindes in Südafrika", *Anthropos*, XXIII (Posieux (Freiburg), 1928), 38-109.

Pregnancy, confinement, birth of the first child, care [of mother and child], ceremonies . . .

WILSON, M., The ritual of birth and abnormal birth, in *Rituals of kinship among the Nyakyusa* (O.U.P. for Int. Af. Inst., 1957), pp. 130-71.

"The procreation of children is an ultimate value of Nyakusa society . . . but . . . under certain conditions it is hedged about with taboos."Among births regarded as abnormal, that of twins takes first place.

Married women

ALBERTO, M. S., "Problemas do 'Bem Estar Rural' moçambicano. A mulher indigena moçambicana perante a estructura familiar da tribo", *Boletim da*

253

M. Perlman and M. P. Moal

Sociedad de Estudos Moçambique, XXIV, 83 (Lourenço-Marques, 1954), 93-104.
  A lecture given by the writer on the position and social conditions of native women within the tribal structure of the indigenous family of Mozambique. Their position, in both patriarchai and matriarchal societies, is a subordinate one. In polygynous households the chief wife has some privileges.

BIRAHIM, B., "Les Bobos, la famille, les coutumes", *Éducation africaine*, n.s. XXIII (Dakar, 1954), 61-75.
  The author gives reasons why Bobo women enjoy a strong position.

*CURRYER, W. H. S., "Mothercraft in Southern Nigeria", *United Empire*, XVIII, n.s. 2 (Feb. 1927), 78-81.

*FRAZAO, F. S., "A mulher e o casamento", *Mensario Administrativo*, LI-LII (Luanda, 1951), 47-58, ill.

HAUMANT, J. C., The condition of women, in *Les Lobi et leur coutume* (Paris, P.U.F., 1929), pp. 104-15.
  Adolescent girls are free to refuse the husband chosen for them by the family and to choose one for themselves.

KAGAME, A., Woman in the home, in "Les organisations socio-familiales de l'ancien Ruanda", *Mémoires de l'Académie Royale des Sciences Coloniales*, XXXVIII, 3 (Brussels, 1954, 8vo), 233-49.
  The wife looks after the domestic economy. She is also her husband's counsellor. She carries out the less arduous tasks. When she is pregnant, the husband is attentive.

KANE, E., "La disposition des cases des femmes dans le carré du mari commun (Sénégal)," *Notes Africaines*, XXVI (Dakar, IFAN, 1945), 11-12.
  The various arrangements [of wives' huts within the courtyard of their common husband] always give pre-eminence to the chief wife, or the one who is in charge.

*KOEUME, E., *The African housewife and her home*, Nairobi, Eagle Press, 1952, 186 pp.

KUPER, H., "The marriage of a Swazi princess", *Africa*, XV, 3 (1945), 145-56.
  Description of the wedding ceremonies at the marriage of Princess Bahashule to a chief with the name of Nkonjane. Her position after marriage.

*Macpherson, K., *Mothercraft in the tropics*, Cassel, 1947, 205 pp.

*MAREE, M. C., *The Nyasa woman at home and in Southern Rhodesia*, Proceedings of the South Rhodesia Missionary Conference, Salisbury, 1928, pp. 46-7.

MARIE-ANDRÉ DU SACRE-CŒUR, Sister, "La condition de la femme indigène dans la boucle du Niger", *Revue d'Histoire des Missions*, 14th year (Paris, 1937), 471-7.
  The writer discusses the condition of Mossi, Gurunsi, Dagari and Bobo women; their place in the family, how they get married. (*Bibliographie Ethnographique du Congo Belge*, 1937).

*NTHALA, S. Y., *Nchowa [a novel about an African woman]*, Longmans, 1949, 117 pp.

PAUWELS, H., "Fiancée et jeune mariée au Ruanda", *Zaïre*, V, 2 (Brussels, 1951), 115-35.
  A newly married woman does not begin to work until 15 days after she is married; her social life, after a period of seclusion lasting two months.

Analytical Bibliography

*REYHER, R. H., *Zulu woman*, O.U.P., 1948, 282 pp.

Without being an enthnographic study, this book has a certain documentary interest, since it gives the impressions of a woman, Christina Sibiya, the wife of Solomon king of the Zulus, about her home surroundings and her position as co-wife. (*Man*. LXII, 1948).

——, *The Fon and his hundred wives*, New York, Doubleday & Co., 1952, 318 pp. 40 ill. map; Gollancz, 1953, 302 pp.

The writer attempts to describe the thoughts and feelings of the wives of a polygynous husband.

SHAPERA, I., *Married life in an African tribe*, London, Faber; New York, Sheridan House, 1940, 364 pp. ill. map.

Married life, relations between husband and wife, and parents and children; legal status of married, divorced and widowed women.

*SOHIER, A., "Le rôle de la femme dans la famille congolaise", *Etapes*, 5th year, XXI (Brussels, 1947), 93-7.

The family is not the same thing among black people as among white. With the latter, it is a household, with the former, a part of kinship. The conception of the role of the woman in the household explains many customs, especially marriage customs. (*Bibliographie Ethnographique du Congo Belge*, 1947).

VAN CAENEGHEM, R., "La femme du Lupangu", *Zaïre* (Brussels, 1952), V, 464-86; VI, 569-95.

Mukawo is the special relation which exists between the co-wives of one husband. The wives exercise continuous pressure and control over their husband.

*WARD, E. H., *The Yoruba husband-wife code*, Washington, Catholic Univ. of America, 1937 (Anthropological Series, No. 4).

*WERNER, A. and HICHENS, W., *The advice of Mwana Kupoua upon the wifely duty*, Medstead, The Azanian Press, 1934, 95 pp. ill.

A poem composed by a woman in the nineteenth century, translated from the Swahili. Advice to her daughter. (*Africa*, VIII, 236-7).

Widows—Mourning

*CHAPMAN, J., "La femme pendant les funérailles", *Ébur*, I (Abidan, 1954) 8-18.

CHARDEY, F., "Deuil et veuvage au Togo Sud", *Anthropos*, XLVI, 3-4 (Posieux (Freiburg), 1951), 622.

Mourning is rigorously observed by both men and women and lasts from eight to 16 days. Taboos concerning the widow: among the Fanti she is bound hand and foot, beaten. The ceremonies terminate with visits of thanks to the relatives.

EISELEN, W., "Die posisie van die weduwee bij die heidense en bij die kristelike Batau", *Bantu Studies*, IX (Johannesburg, 1935), 281-5.

Shows changes in the life of widows since the introduction of Christianity.

HOLAS, B., "Le Kouna (un cas de prophylaxie magique contre des décès consécutifs de femmes enceintes dans le pays guerzé)", *Notes Africaines*, LII (Dakar, 1953), 16-18, ill.

Description of a magic ceremony among the Gerzé, carried out following upon the successive deaths of several pregnant women.

——, "Décès d'une femme guerzé (cercle de Nzérékoré, Guinée française)", *Africa*, XXIII, 2 (1953), 145-55.

M. Perlman and M. P. Moal

Detailed description of funeral rites among the Gerzé on the occasion of the death of a woman.

*JUNOD, H. A., "The fate of widows among the Ba-Ronga", *Report of the South African Association for the Advancement of Science*, Cape Town, Johannesburg, 1909.

Detailed description of special rites of purification and of mourning; the husband's kin inherit the widow. (I. Schapera).

LESTRANGE, M. de, "L'enterrement de Tyira, femme bassari", *Marco Polo*, XVIII (Paris, 1956), 20-7, ill.

Funeral rites: burial, sacrifice to the soul of the deceased.

MAURICE, P. M., "La maladie et la mort chez les Bapimbwe", *Bibliotheca Africana*, IV, 2 (Innsbruck, 1930-31), 22-32.

The duties of the surviving spouse; the widow forms part of the inheritance, the man to inherit her being chosen by family council.

ORTOLI, H., "Le décès d'une femme enceinte chez les Dogon de Bandiagara", *Bull. de l'IFAN*, III, B, 1-4 (Dakar, 1941), 64-73.

The death of a pregnant woman is exorcised by a series of rites in which religion, magic and medicine are closely intertwined. (*Bibliographie Ethnographique du Congo Belge*, 1941).

RATTRAY, R. S., Widows and "in-laws" at funerals, in *Religion and art in Ashanti* (Oxford, Clarendon Press, 1927), pp. 171-4, ill.

Widows (*kunafo*) have to observe certain rites, mainly of protection, for a year after the death of their husband. The levirate is practised.

— , Funeral customs: the funeral of an old woman, in *The tribes of the Ashanti hinterland* (Oxford, Clarendon Press, 1932), Vol. I, pp. 186-9.

A narrator of the Nankane tribe describes the funeral rites of his tribe, a special feature being that a married woman has two funerals: one in her husband's village, the other in her father's.

*SENDANYOYE, G., "De la situation des veuves et de leur déplacement en dehors de la résidence maritale", *Bull. de Jurisprudence de Ruanda-Urundi*, X (1952), 515-17.

The status of a widow varies according to whether she has any children or not. (*Bibliographie Ethnographique du Congo Belge*, 1952).

*— , "Jugement annoté: veuvage. Droits de la veuve sur les biens de son mari. Droit du tuteur sur les orphelins", *Bull. de Jurisprudence du Ruanda-Urundi*, I (1926), 36-7.

A court decision at Nyanza (Ruanda): if it is the case that a stepmother does not have the orphaned children of her deceased husband under her care, she has no right to farm all the lands or to make use of all the property of the deceased. (*Bibliographie Ethnographique du Congo Belge*, 1946).

INITIATION

*BAL, A., "La claustration des jeunes filles chez les Ngbandi et les Ngombe de Lisala", *Trait d'Union*, III, 4 (Antwerp, 1934), 3.

A contribution to the study of marriage customs of the Gombe and the Ngandi in the Congo-Mongala-Ubangi region.

BALANDIER, G., "Danses de sortie d'excision à Boffa, Guinée française", *Notes Africaines*, XXXVIII (Dakar, 1948), 11-12.

Analytical Bibliography

Description of a Susu initiation ceremony: the placing of the people taking part and of the orchestra; *tyamba* or the bird-mask the central personage in the dance. (*Bibliographie Ethnographique du Congo Belge*, 1948).

BETTELHEIM, B., Girls' rites, in *Symbolic wounds. Puberty rites and the envious male* (Glencoe (Ill.), The Free Press, 1954), pp. 239-60.
Several examples taken from the Luvale, Cewa and Chaga to illustrate general points.

BLOHM, W., "Die christliche Familien-Gemeinschaft in Xosa Volkstum. Beobachtungen in Ost-Südafrika", *Africa*, VI (1933), 431-55.
Traditions have survived, in particular the *intonjane*, "consecration" of girls. After a 14 days period of seclusion, the girl is purified and returns to her parents.

BOYLE, C. V., "The marking of girls at Ga-Anda", *Journ. of the South African Soc.*, XV (1916), 361-6, 4 pl.
These tattooings which cover almost the entire body have an important social significance: they mark the stages of the social life of a girl from the time when her marriage is arranged by her parents (often when she is only a few days old) until the day when her marriage takes place.

*BRIOD, R., "Rites d'initiation. La jeune fille zambézienne et sa préparation à sa vie de femme", *Nouvelles de Zambèze* (1931), 1-18.

BROWNLEE, F., "The In-Tonjane ceremony", *Bantu Studies*, III, 4 (Johannesburg, 1929), 401-3.
Puberty rites for girls in Fingoland (Union of South Africa): the period of seclusion, very strict, lasts for from three to four months, and is obligatory before marriage.

BRYK, F., *Die Beschneidung bei Mann und Weib. Ihre Geschichte, Psychologie und Ethnologie*, Neubrandenburg, G. Feller, 1931, 319 pp. 7 pl. 55 ill.
Circumcision and excision rites and ceremonies among various peoples; information about Equatorial Africa and also, mainly, about East Africa.

BURTON, W. F. P., "The secret societies of Lubaland (Congo Belge)", *Bantu Studies*, IV, 4 (1930), 217-50.
The first part deals, not with secret societies, but with initiation societies. Girls are initiated in two stages: *kwikana* and *butanda*, the first being a preparation for the second, which is the real initiation from which the girl emerges purified and a woman.

CESTON, J. M., "Le gree-gree bush (initiation de la jeunesse) chez les Nègres Golah, Liberia", *Anthropos*, VI (Posieux (Freiburg), 1911), 729-54.
Among the Gola there are two gree-gree: that of the women is called *sande*. It is an initiation into the life of the tribe, and an education. At the head of the gree-gree is the "devil", then her Assistants, the Assistants' Assistants, and the Girls, that is to say, the new initiates, whose age varies; they are usually not married, although there is no strict rule. The duration of the ceremony varies. There are coming-out ceremonies.

CHÉRON, G., "La circoncision et l'excision chez les Malinké", *Journal de la Société des Africanistes*, III (Paris, 1933), 297-303.
Girls undergo clitoridectomy between the ages of 13 and 15. They are then known as *solimamusso*. The aim of the operation is to give a woman beauty. The oldest of the girls taking part is called *Kuntigi* (head).

CLAYES, P. F., "Gaza", *Congo*, II (Brussels, 1934), No. 2, pp. 223-41; No. 3, pp. 381-96; No. 4, pp. 506-33.

257

M. Perlman and M. P. Moal

Male and female (pp. 506-33) circumcision among the Bwaka of Ubangi. The ceremonies for each sex are held separately. Descriptions of the preparations, the operations, the taboos to be observed.

COSTERMANS, B., "Sipema: Puberteits-ceremonie bij de Logo-Avokaya", *Zaïre*, IV, 2 (Brussels, 1950), 167-79.

Among the peoples of the north-east of the Belgian Congo, boys and girls have operations performed on their teeth. Among some tribes, these operations are supposed to ensure a woman's fertility. These customs are disappearing rapidly.

DETHIER, F. M., "De quelques effets juridiques de la 'gaza ya se' ou excision", *Bull. des Juridictions Indigènes*, XV, 1 (Elisabethville, 1947), 6-8.

During the period of initiation, a certain number of taboos have to be observed: sexual, concerning the family of the initiate and the guests at the ceremony; alimentary, which concern the initiate only and last until the birth of her first child. As well, legal ties link the *buganza* (the initiate's sponsor) with the parents by means of a system of mutual guarantees. Any infraction brings judicial sanctions and court cases.

*DOSSOU-YOYO, M. M., "Circoncision et excision chez les Bariba", *Notes Africaines*, XIX (Dakar, 1943), 10-11.

DROUREGA, M., "Initiation of a girl in the Acenga tribe, Katondwe Mission, Luengwa District, Northern Rhodesia", *Anthropos*, XXII (Posieux (Freiburg 1927), 620-1, 1 pl.

Interesting documentation on the initiation rites of a young girl among the Acenga. (*Bibliographie Ethnographique du Congo Belge*, 1925-30).

*EARTHY, E. D., "Initiation of girls in the Masi Yeni district", *Annals of the Transvaal Museum*, XI (Pretoria, 1925), 103-17.

Detailed description of girls' puberty rites among the Lenge and Chopi.

— , "Notes on some agricultural rites practised by the Valenge and Vachopi (Portuguese East Africa)", *Bantu Studies*, II (Johannesburg, 1925), 193-7.

The cycle of initiation rites for girls follows the cycle of the agricultural year, the important ceremonies coinciding with growth of the crops and the agricultural rites.

*EMA, A. J. U., "Fattening girls in Oron, Calabar Province", *Nigeria*, XXI (Lagos, 1940), 386-9.

ESTERMANN, C., "La fête de puberté dans quelques tribus de l'Angola méridional", *Bull. de la Société Neuchâteloise de Géographie*, XLVIII (Neuchâtel, 1941-42), 128-41.

Description of the rites marking the nubility of girls among the Ambo, Herero, Nyaneka . . . These rites, which are still almost the same today, show variations between one tribe and another, but all have the character of a rite of passage with a period of seclusion and changes in hair style and dress. They last for a varying amount of time, and marriage does not always follow immediately.

*FRANZ, H. M., "Mädchenbeschneidung in Nord-West Transvaal", *Die Brücke*, *Wissenschaftliche Beilage*, II (1929), 1-5.

Interesting notes on the schools of initiation for girls. (I. Schapera).

FROELICH, J. P., "Les sociétés d'initiation chez les Moba et les Fourma du Nord-Togo", *Journal de la Société des Africanistes*, XIX, 2 (Paris, 1949), 99-141, ill. map.

Analytical Bibliography

Two kinds of initiation for girls: the first, *kpankpankwondi* (pp. 115-18) occurs in cases where the girl refuses to marry the husband chosen for her; this is an individual initiation with a four months' period of seclusion. The second, *markwondi*, includes excision and a period of seclusion lasting 45 days. This is a group initiation, for girls of varying ages.

GANAY, S. de, "Symbolisme de quelques scarifications au Soudan français avec l'excision", *Comptes rendus des Scéances de l'Institut français d'Anthropologie* (Paris, 1947-49), 7-8.

Marka women receive scarifications at the times of the main events in their life: initiation (excision), marriage, confinement. They are tests of endurance and of adult womanhood.

GEIGY, R. and HÖLTKER, G., "Mädchen-initiationen im Ulanga-Distrikt von Tanganyika", *Acta Tropica*, VIII (Basel, 1951), 289-344, ill.

This initiation, which does not include any operation, begins at the onset of menstruation; it continues during a period of isolation which sometimes lasts as long as three years, during which the girl learns from some of the old women everything concerning married life in the form of maxims, songs, ritual manipulations, etc. Certain fertility rites play an important role. The last chapter gives some information about pregnancy and the first confinement.

GROSS, B. A., "Pour la suppression d'une coutume barbare: l'excision", *Notes Africaines*, XLV (Dakar, Jan. 1950), 6-8.

Various examples taken from Africa (the Banda of Ubangi).

GUTMANN, B., "Druchstücke aus den Kerbstocklehren für Mädchen nach dem Mreho lo Ljango", *Zeitschrift für Eingeborenen Sprachen*, XV (Berlin, 1925), 1-19.

Fragments of songs collected during the period of seclusion which forms part of initiation, being followed by ceremonies in which the whole village takes part.

HARLEY, G. W., "Notes on the Poro in Liberia", *Papers of the Peabody Museum of American Archaeology and Ethnology*, XIX, 2, Cambridge (Mass.), Harvard University, 1941, 40 pp. ill.

Corresponding to the *Poro*, the initiation society for boys among the Geh and the Gio, is the *Sande*, the initiation society for girls, a special study of which is found on pp. 27 ff.

HARRIES, L., "The initiation rites of the Makonde tribe", *Communications from the Rhodes-Livingstone Institute*, No. 3, 41 pp. polyc.

The initiation of girls or *Ciputu* (pp. 24-41) is obligatory before puberty; it is carried out in several stages and is accompanied by songs which the author has notated.

*HILLS, Y. E., "Female circumcision in the Sudan", *Anti-Slavery Reporter*, V, 1 (1949), 13-15.

An operation performed upon little girls of four to ten years old, among the peoples of north and central Sudan; the author describes a barbarous scene at Omdurman. (*Bibliographie Ethnographique du Congo Belge*, 1949).

HOERNLE, A. W., "Certain rites of transition and the conception of *!nau* among the Hottentots", *Harvard African Studies* II (Cambridge (Mass.), 1918), 65-82.

Puberty rites for women (pp. 70-82): at the onset of menstruation, girls must spend a period of seclusion (in practice softened and abridged) as well as performing rites of passage which liberate them from their state of *!nau* and give them a status in a new social group.

259

M. Perlman and M. P. Moal

HOERNLE, A. W., "An outline of the native conception of education in Africa", *Africa*, IV (1931), 145-63.

The education of young girls is under strict social control and is carried out within the framework of the age-classes. Initiation at puberty takes various forms, but always includes detailed instruction about adult life, particularly sexual instruction, which takes place during a period of seclusion of varying length. The writer describes two initiation ceremonies for girls, among the Zulu and the Hottentots.

HOLAS, B., "L'évolution du schéma initiatique chez les femmes oubi (région de Tai, Côte d'Ivoire)", *Africa*, XXVII (1957), 241-50.

With the introduction of modern ways of life, customs lose their rigidity. Thus the date fixed for initiation ceremonies [among the Ubi] is made to fit in with the official calendar of events and with the requirements of the coffee plantations. The length of time spent in continuous seclusion is reduced.

HUBER, H., "Cérémonie pour les filles pubères d'origine adangme à Anécho (Togo)", *Bull. de l'IFAN*, XX, B (Dakar, 1958), 417-31, 5 phot.

A rare Adangme custom still practised at Anecho.

——, "Initiation to womanhood among the Sε (Ghana)", *The Nigerian Field*, XXIII, 3 (1958), 99-119, ill.

Initiation ceremonies, although they have been reduced to a period of seven weeks, and the age of initiates has been raised, still occupy an important place,

JEFFREYS, M. D. W., "The Nyama society of the Ibibio women", *African Studies*, XV, 1 (Johannesburg, 1956), 15-29.

The Nyama is an Ibibio women's society; it has the duty of performing clitoridectomy on girls, having some connection with fertility; the operation is performed shortly before marriage.

JONES, N., "Initiation rites among the Matabele", *Man*, XXI (1921), 147-50.

Rites that are on the way to becoming extinct or modified. As far as girls are concerned, the ceremony is individual and lasts for four days.

KIRK-GREENE, A. H. M., "A Lala initiation ceremony", *Man*, LVII (1957), 5-11.

Ceremonies for girls who have reached puberty. They receive certain scarifications, three in number. These puberty rites, which do not include excision, are obligatory before marriage.

*KOHLER, M., *Marriage customs in Southern Natal*, Pretoria, Dept. of Native Affairs (Ethnological publications, IV), 1933, 103 pp. ill.

These notes concern the Ama-Khuze and the Ama-Baca among the Kaffirs and Zulus of Natal. The first part deals with puberty rites for boys and for girls and with relations between the sexes before marriage.

KRÜGER, F., "Tlôkwa traditions", *Bantu Studies*, XI (Johannesburg, 1937), 85-115.

The *Byali* (pp. 102-2), when girls assemble for initiation, lasts several months. The girls live together in seclusion. There is no operation, but scarifications on the thighs.

LAMBIN, R., "Notes sur les cérémonies et les épreuves d'émancipation et d'initiation chez les Kissiens", *Bull. de l'IFAN*, VIII, 1-4 (Dakar, 1946), 64-70.

Excision takes place at an age which varies as between north and south. The *toma boudod* "consecrates" the girl. It is also his initiation.

LEAKEY, L. S. B., "The Kikuyu problem of the initiation of girls", *Journ. of the Roy. Anthr. Inst.*, LXI (1931), 277-85.

Analytical Bibliography

Great changes have taken place in the attitude towards the initiation of girls, due to the influence of European moral ideas. To suppress it altogether would be an error, as was proved by the hostile demonstrations of 1930. The writer suggests preserving the educational side of initiation while suppressing the undesirable elements (clitoridectomy, sexual practices).

LESTRANGE, M. DE, "Sociétés secrétes, circoncision et excision en Afrique Noire", *Le Concours Médical* (Paris, Nov. 1953), 3815-18.

These sexual mutilations are rites which give access to adult society. Coniagui girls undergo clitoridectomy about the age of 17 during the course of an important ceremony. Only then may they have children, and later get married.

MAHLOBO, G. W. K. and KRIGE, E. J., "Transition from childhood to adulthood among the Zulus", *Bantu Studies*, VIII (Johannesburg, 1934), 157-91.

The first part (pp. 157-66) describes the ear-piercing ceremony (*Qumbhuza*) in which boys and girls of the same *intanga* (age-class) take part.

MAIR, L., "A Yao girl's initiation", *Man*, LI (1951), 60-3.

Description of a ceremony at which the writer was present, at the initiation of girls among the Yao of Tanganyika Territory. (*Bibliographie Ethnographique du Congo Belge*, 1951).

MALCOLM, L. W. G., "Note on the seclusion of girls among the Efik of old Calabar", *Man*, XXV (1925), 113-14, phot.

Before marriage, every girl must spend some time in the "fattening hut", the length of time varying according to the social position of the parents.

MAYER, P., "Gusii initiation ceremonies. Initiation of girls", *Journ. of the Roy. Anthr. Inst.*, LXXXIII (1953), 26-36.

Description of the initiation of Gusii girls (Kenya), including clitoridectomy and a period of seclusion in the mother's hut, during which they learn songs and are initiated into the mysteries. Apparently these rites survive for the girls more than for the boys.

— , "*Ekeigoroigoro*: a Gusii rite of passage", *Man*, LIII (1953), 3-6, ill.

This "revelation of images" is independent of the initiation ceremonies, which it precedes; in principle it should precede marriage for both boys and girls. The images are made by a group of five girls (the leader's function being hereditary) who are initiated but unmarried, and who perform the revelation to the novices.

MENGRELIS, T., "Fête de la sortie de l'excision au pays mano, Guinée française", *Notes Africaines*, XLIX (Dakar, 1951), 11-13.

Description of the initiation of girls among the Mano of French Guinea. The rites and ceremonies which accompany the return to the village of the girls who have undergone the ceremony.

— , "La sortie des jeunes filles excisées en pays mano(n)", *Études Guinéenes*, VIII (Conakry, 1952), 55-8.

The coming-out rites take place after the swearing-in feast according to a fixed order of ceremonies, the first of the initiates heading the procession. But it is not until the following day that the initiates return to society.

— , "La sortie des initiés en pays guerzé", *Notes Africaines*, L (Dakar, 1951), 44-6, ill.

The dances at the coming-out of the initiates [among the Gerzé].

*NDAU, "The Mula custom", *Nada*, IV (Salisbury, 1926), 69.

Notes on initiation rites for girls in Northern Rhodesia.

M. Perlman and M. P. Moal

NZEKWU, O., "Iria Ceremony", *Nigeria*, LXIII (Lagos, 1959), 341-52, ill.

The only traditional ceremony still in existence among the Okrika, it has probably survived owing to its social function (it marks the entry of girls into womanhood) and its moral function (to protect the virginity of girls). Description of the ceremony. Numerous photographs show the costumes worn by the young initiates when they emerge from their seclusion.

PAULME, D., "L'initiation des jeunes filles en pays kissi (Haute-Guinée)", *Conferencia Internacional das Africanistas* (Lisbon, 1947), V, Part II (Lisbon, 1952), 303-31.

Initiation of girls at Nongoa in 1946. The *bundo* ritual. Description of all the stages of initiation and of the rites among the Kissi. (*Bibliographie Ethnographique du Congo Belge*, 1952).

PEPERTY, R., "La circoncision et l'excision chez les Tankambas de la subdivision de Tanguieta (Dahomey)", *Conférence des Africanistes de l'Ouest*, 1945 (Paris, 1951), fasc. 2, pp. 274-80.

The circumstances in which the ceremony takes place, the age of the patients, their costume, those who perform the operation, chronology of the ceremony. (*Bibliographie Ethnographique du Congo Belge*, 1951).

PIRES, A. E., "*Ofundula*. Festa cuanhama da puberdade feminina", *Mensario Administrativo*, XX-XXI (Luanda, 1949), 45-52, ill.

Description of the rites and ceremonies in which Kwnayama women of Angola take part at puberty (*Bibliographie Ethnographique du Congo Belge*, 1949).

RAMSEYER, P., "La circoncision chez les Bassouto", *Revue d'Ethnographie et des Traditions Populaires*, IX (Paris, 1928), 40-70.

The female circumcision ceremony *lebollo;* origin of the term, rites and ceremonies.

RAUM, O. F., "Female initiation among the Chaga", *American Anthropologist*, n.s. XLI (New York, 1939), 554-65.

Notes on the initiation of girls before marriage, among the Chaga in the region of Kilimanjaro. (*Bibliographie Ethnographique du Congo Belge*, 1939).

RICHARDS, A. I., *Chisungu: a girl's initiation ceremony among the Bemba of Northern Rhodesia*, Faber, 1956, 224 pp. ill. map, bibl.

The writer describes in detail the *chisungu*, the girls' initiation ceremony among the Bemba, at which she was present in 1931. Interpretation of the symbols used in the rites, and of the various stages of the *chisungu*.

SCHNELL, R., "La fête rituelle des jeunes excisées en pays baga (Basse-Guinée)", *Notes Africaines*, XLIII (Dakar, 1949), 84-6.

Description of the ceremonies which celebrate the recovery of the girls who have been excised among the Baga of French Guinea.

SCHULIEN, P. M., "Die Initiationszeremonien der Mädchen bei den Atxuabo von Portugiesisch-Ostafrika", *Anthropos*, XVIII-XIX (Posieux (Freiburg), 1923-24), 69-102.

After the ritual dances performed by former initiates, the future initiates are secluded in an initiation hut, where they undergo clitoridectomy, which is regarded as a test and not as an end in itself. After a night spent in drinking the *nipipa* (a drink made from rice, honey and water), they return to their own huts.

SEGY, L., "Initiation ceremony and African sculpture", *The American Imago*, X, 1 (New York, 1953), 57-82.

Initiation signifies entry into society. It is often confused with entry into

Analytical Bibliography

a secret society, fulfils an educative role (concerning the history and institutions of the tribe), and provides for women a training in adjustment to men.

SICARD, H. VON, "Die Initiation im Monomutapa-Reich", *Ethnos* I-II (Stockholm, 1941), 42-7.

According to the information provided by the literature on the subject, initiation, from the 15th until the 17th c., existed for girls as much as for boys, which does not seem to be the case any longer in the areas concerned, particularly since the introduction of Christianity. (*Bibliographie Ethnographique du Congo Belge*, 1941).

SOURIN, R. P., "L'initiation des jeunes filles chez les Kabrés (Nord Togo)", *Notes Africaines*, XXXVI (Dakar, 1947), 18-21.

Account of the initiation rites for Kabre girls; they represent the transition from childhood to adulthood.

SPAGNOLO, L. M., "Some notes on the initiation of young men and girls in the Bari tribe", *Africa*, V (1932), 393-403.

The *Bero na kö'disi*, a rite of passage for girls, consists of several stages: at 15, 17, 18, 19, 20 years of age. *Karin ti ber na kö'disi*, the names of the age-classes in several Bari tribes.

THILENIUS, G., "Die Mädchenbeschneidung der Basotho", *Archiv für Anthropologie*, XIII (Braunschweig, 1915), 72-5, ill.

The initiation takes place between May and September as soon as there are thought to be enough girls of between ten and 15. It includes all sorts of very painful physical tests of endurance, of which clitoridectomy is one. During the operation the girl must not show that she is suffering, under penalty of punishments which may even go so far as being put to death.

TWALA, R. G., "Umhlanga (reed) ceremony of the Swazi maiden", *African Studies*, XI, 3 (Johannesburg, 1952), 93-104.

The task of gathering reeds for the royal and chiefly dwellings is kept for girls, and it is accompanied by carefully organized ceremonies of a religious nature which form an initiation, particularly a sexual initiation.

VAN BUGGENHOUT, H., "Coutumes d'initiation", *Bull. des Juridictions indigènes et du Droit coutumier congolais*, I, 1 (Elisabethville, 1933), 8.

Notes on girl's initiation rites and ceremonies held within the family framework, such as are found among the Balunda, Chokwe, Dembo, Aluenan ad Kawonde of the High Kasai, in the Belgian Congo and in Angola.

VASSAL, J., "Une mutilation des organes génitaux des femmes noires banda: le ganza", *La Presse médicale*, LXXVI (Paris, 23 Sept. 1925), 1275-8.

Description of a [Banda] ceremony during which the women undergo the *ganza* (=excision), followed by dances. This operation is performed on a fixed date, but the age of the patients varies between 15 and 25. The men are present at the ceremony.

VILLENEUVE, A., DE, "Étude sur une coutume somalie: les femmes cousues", *Journal de la Société des Africanistes*, VII (Paris, 1937), 15-32.

Excision and infibulation are practised [in Somaliland] on girls before puberty by their mother or by the *gedda* (grandmother). The husband makes an opening at the time of marriage, and a second is necessitated at confinement, after which the torn tissues heal again immediately.

WALK, L., "Initiationszeremonien und Pubertätsriten der südafrikanischen Stämme", *Anthropos*, XXIII (Posieux (Freiburg), 1928), 861-966, bibl.

M. Perlman and M. P. Moal

Description of initiation rites in various South African tribes: they include a period of seclusion (except among the Matabele) which—among the Bechuana for example—may last as long as three months. Entry into adult life is marked by mutilations, tattooings, excision, a change in clothing and ornaments.

WENS, A. F., "Coutumes d'initiation", *Bull. des Juridictions indigènes et du Droit coutumier congolais*, I, 1 (Elisabethville, 1933), 9.

Among the Balumba, only the girls go through the ceremony of *kisungu*.

WHITE, C. M. N., "Conservatism and modern adaption in Luvale female puberty ritual", *Africa*, XXIII, 1 (1953), 15-24.

Changes are at present taking place in puberty rites. Their importance lies in their being one of the integrative factors in social life. They include sexual instruction and instruction in the use of contraceptives.

WHITE, C. M. N., CHINJAVATA, J. and MUKWATO, L., "Comparative aspects of Luvale puberty ritual", *African Studies*, XVII, 4 (Johannesburg, 1958), 204-20, bibl.

Luvale and Bemba puberty rites are compared, and then the parallel female and male Luvale rites in their order: entry, seclusion, coming-out rites.

WILLOUGHBY, W. C., "Notes on the initiation ceremonies of the Bechwana", *Journ. of the Roy. Anthr. Inst.*, XXXIX (1909), 228-45.

Mostly on ceremonies for boys but with reference to parallel ceremonies for girls.

WILSON, M., The ritual of puberty and marriage, in *Rituals of kinship among the Nyakusa* (O.U.P. for Int. Af. Inst., 1957), pp. 86-129.

"The puberty ritual for girls . . . is fused with the marriage ritual." They undergo a period of seclusion, and at the onset of menstruation are given a treatment to fortify them, instruction in the duties of a wife, and an examination for virginity. Feasts are held in a girl's own and in her husband's family to celebrate her maturity and virginity.

ZABOROWSKI, M., "De la circoncision des garçons et de l'excision des filles comme pratiques d'initiation", *Bull. de la Société d'Anthropologie de Paris*, V, 4th series (Paris, 1894), 81-104.

On the aims and functions of circumcision and excision. Many examples from Africa.

WOMEN'S ASSOCIATIONS—AGE GRADES

BALDE, S., "Les associations d'âge chez les Foulbé du Fouta-Djallon", *Bull. de l'IFAN*, I, 1 (Dakar, 1939), 89-109.

Deals with the associations formed by Fulbe [Fulani] children from the age of four, girls as well as boys. Later these associations become the *gire* (*yirde* for girls) which have their own organization and strict discipline. Membership ceases about the age of 30 or 40.

BLACKING, J., "Fictitious kinship among girls of the Venda of the Northern Transvaal", *Man*, LIX (1959), 155-7.

This is a traditional institution which operates during initiation and which now extends to primary and secondary schools: every girl is initiated in three stages (the author gives details) by her "mother", a former initiate, whose

264

Analytical Bibliography

"daughter" she becomes. In the schools, there is the same relationship, but here the mother is a "play mother". This relationship seems to continue at least until marriage. In the course of this article the author also mentions: the social stratification (nobles/commoners) which is emphasized at initiation by having separate schools whenever possible; the position of women among the patrilinear Venda—they appear to be servile but in fact have considerable personal influence; moreover it would appear that the more women are able to preserve their traditional institutions and club together, the better they will be able to retain their influence.

BURTON, W. F. P., "The secret societies of Lubaland (Congo Belge)", *Bantu Studies*, IV, 4 (Johannesburg, 1930), 217-50.

The secret society *Bunbudye* has both men and women as members; the latter can be at the head of communities. Organization, activities, initiation of new members, hierarchy. Women play a less important part in the two other societies studied, the *Bakasanji* and the *Tupoyo*.

COMHAIRE, J., "La vie religieuse à Lagos", *Zaïre*, III, 5 (Brussels, 1949), 549-56.

Yoruba market-women form an important class at the head of which is the *Iyalode* (Mistress of the markets). This class calls itself the Women's Party and the Muslim influence is considerable. For women Islam means progress.

DONNER, E., "Togba, a women's society in Liberia", *Africa*, XI (1938), 109-11.

Notes on a women's society to protect the village against leopards and "human leopards", which exist among the Dan and the Mano of Liberia. (*Bibliographie Ethnographique du Congo Belge*, 1938).

EVEN, A., "Les confréries secrètes chez les Babamba et les Mindassa d'Okondja", *Bull. de la Société de Recherches congolaises*, XXIII-XXIV (Brazzaville, 1937), 31-112.

(See following reference).

—, "Les propriétés maléfiques et bénéfiques du sexe de la femme selon les croyances des Babamba et des Mindassa (Moyen Congo, A.E.F.)", *Bull. et Mém. de la Société d'Anthropologie de Paris*, X, 8th series, 1-3 (Paris, 1939), 51-72.

The Babamba and Mindassa of Ogoue believe that woman's sexual nature contains beneficent and maleficent powers which a woman may unleash either consciously (the evil spell of *okaghi*) or unconsciously (during menstruation and confinement). From this arises a woman's way of behaving due to her strong feeling of sexual shame and also to her desire to neutralize these powers, and the *Lissimbu* or *Yandza* is a women's association formed in order to mobilize the protective aspect of these powers by means of ceremonies which are in the nature of a cult of deceased initiates, a form of totemism, and the worship of the protective powers. The main feature of the cult consists of ceremonies of initiation to the society, during which the initiates learn about the taboos they must observe in order to control the powers within them. Numerous mimed dances are performed in the course of these ceremonies.

FORDE, D., "Ward organization among the Yakö", *Africa*, XX (1950), 267-89.

The *Ekuruso* is an association for women of matrilineal descent, with ward organization. It includes a man who is known as "the companion of the women". Another association, the *Oyonko*, is a kind of dance club. The women's associations maintain a system of social control independent of that of the men.

GREEN, M., *Ibo village affairs*. Sidgwick & Jackson, 1948, 362 pp. map.

265

M. Perlman and M. P. Moal

The result of fieldwork in the villages in the bush. The writer wanted to find out if there were any women's secret societies. She came to a negative conclusion.

HARLEY, G. W., "Notes on the Poro in Liberia", *Papers of the Peabody Museum of American Archaeology and Ethnology*, Harvard University, Cambridge (Mass.), XIX, 2 (1941), 40 pp. ill. map.

Corresponding to the *Poro*, the boy's initiation society among the Mano, the Geh and the Gio of Liberia, is the *Sande* society for girls.

HOLDING, E. M., "Some preliminary notes on Meru age-grades", *Man*, XLII (1942), 58-65.

Men's and women's age-grades in all the Meru clans. Their importance.

—, "Women's institutions and the African church", *International Review of Missions*, XXXI, 123 (Edinburgh, 1942), 290-300.

Concerning the Meru of Kenya: importance of their women's institutions, need to know about them and study them so as to make them useful allies in solving certain social problems. The writer makes a special study of girls' initiation and of the Council of women. (*Bibliographie Ethnographique du Congo Belge*, 1943).

JEFFREYS, M. D. W., "The Nyama society of Ibibio women", *African Studies*, XV, 1 (Johannesburg, 1956), 15-28, ill.

Nyama is the name of a women's society in Nigeria which has the duty of looking after the initiation of girls before marriage. Women of all ages can be members. This custom is tending to disappear under the influence of Christianity.

"Lagos women's play", *Nigeria*, LVIII (Lagos, 1958), 225-37, ill.

The Lagos Child Welfare Mother's Union makes use of the theatre as a means of propaganda against the lax morals of town life. The plays, written by women for women, take up popular themes all to the glory of feminine qualities.

LAMBERT, H. E., *Kikuyu social and political institutions*, O.U.P. for Int. Af. Inst., 1956, 149 pp.

Chapters IV, VI, VII and IX are about age-classes, their ritual, organization, social and political functions.

LITTLE, K. L., "The changing position of women in the Sierra Leone Protectorate", *Africa*, XVIII (1948), 1-17.

Notes on the functions of women in secret societies such as the *Sande* and the *Poro*. They hold hereditary offices and positions of leadership. In some cases, women are appointed as paramount chiefs.

—, "The Poro society as an arbiter of culture (Sierra Leone)", *African Studies*, VII, 1 (Johannesburg, 1948), 1-15.

Women may become members of the society under certain conditions. There is only one woman member in each society.

MACLATCHY, A., The women's society, in "L'organisation sociale de la région de Mimongo (Gabon)", *Bull. de l'Institut d'Études Centrafricaines*, I, 1 (Brazzaville, 1945), 81-2.

The women's society is called *Niembe* in distinction to the men's society *Mwiri*. It is a kind of defensive syndicate against the male element. Initiation is preceded by a severe novitiate.

MAHLOBO, G. W. K. and KRIGE, E. J., "Transition from childhood to adulthood among the Zulus", *Bantu Studies*, VIII (Johannesburg, 1934), 157-91.

Analytical Bibliography

Age associations (pp. 158-9) exist for both boys and girls. The members of an association or *intanga* call each other *ntanga*, "my equal".

MAUNY, R., "Masques mende de la société bundu (Sierra Leone)", *Notes Africaines*, LXXXI (Dakar, 1959), 8-13, ill.
The *bundu* society is a women's society, parallel to the *Poro* for the men. By means of this society, women exert considerable political influence.

O'KELLY, E., "Corn mill societies in Southern Cameroons", *African Women*, I, 1 (1955), 33-5.
Women's societies originally formed to play the role of co-operatives and to buy machines. Extension of their activities.

PEDRALS, D. P. de, "Une curieuse fondation, le Yéhoué", *Encyclopédie mensuelle d'outre-mer*, 5th year, IV, 43 (Paris, 1954), 107-8, ill.
The *Yehue* is a kind of secret sect, an association of a magical-cum-social nature, composed of women, and with its own rites. Its unavowed aim seems to be to offer concerted resistance to an oppressive patriarchate. (*Bibliographie Ethnographique du Congo Belge*, 1954).

ROUCH, J. and BERNUS, E., "Notes sur les prostituées *toutou* de Treichville et d'Adjamé", *Études Éburnéennes*, VI (IFAN, 1957), 231-42, tables.
The *tutus* or "English prostitutes" come exclusively from British territories (Nigeria, Ghana) and belong to three ethnic groups: Fanti, Krobo, Ibo. They are strictly organized into chiefdoms, and have a president at their head. The article studies the history of their installation, their social organization, the economic aspect, their relations with the autochthonous peoples and the ties they maintain with their native countries.

TASTEVIN, C., *Société secrète féminine chez les Bakoko du Cameroun*, XVIᵉ Congrès international d'anthropologie et d'archéologie préhistorique, VIᵉ assemblée générale de l'Institut international d'anthropologie, Brussels, 1936, pp. 901-6.
The fetish of the secret society *ko*, if it is to be efficacious. must have along with it some pieces of human remains taken from corpses. A woman must be a responsible person if she is to become a *koko*. (*Bibliographie Ethnographique du Congo Belge*, 1936).

TURNBULL, C. M., "Initiation among the BaMbuti Pygmies of the Central Ituri", *Journ. of the Roy. Anthr. Inst.*, LXXXVII, 2 (1957), 191-216.
The women's society *Alima* is essentially religious; at puberty girls enter it after an initiation period of one month.

ZUGNONI, J., "*Yilede*, a secret society among the Gbaya (Kreish), Aja, Banda tribes of the Western district of Equatoria", *Sudan Notes and Records*, XXVI, 1 (Khartoum, 1945), 105-11.
A secret society of Banda origin, the members of which are mainly women. Its aims are independence in relation to one's husband and with regard to motherhood, mutual aid, satisfaction of personal revenge. It has initiation rites for both men and women. Its effects on the birth-rate. (*Bibliographie Ethnographique du Congo Belge*, 1945).

WORK

AMES, D., "The economic base of Wolof polygyny", *South Western Journal of Anthropology*, XI, 4 (Albuquerque, 1955), 391-403.

M. Perlman and M. P. Moal

Polygyny remains resistant to outside influence, husbands and wives both finding it advantageous. A study of the daily tasks of a woman and of the activities of co-wives over a period of ten days.

APPIA-DABIT, B., "Quelques artisans noirs", *Bull. de l'IFAN*, III, 3-4 (Dakar, 1941), 1-44, ill.

Magic prayers, techniques employed by women dyers in French Guinea, women potters of French Guinea and Senegal.

BALANDIER, G., "Note sur l'exploitation du sel par les vieilles femmes du Bargny", *Notes Africaines*, XXXII (Dakar, 1946), 22.

How old Senegalese women extract salt by evaporation, along the sea-shore, lagoons connected by marshes. (*Bibliographie Ethnographique du Congo Belge*, 1950).

BAUMANN, H., "The division of work according to sex in African hoe culture", *Africa*, I, 2 (1928), 289-319, 2 maps, bibl.

This article deals with the role of women in the development of hoe culture.

BELCHER, A., "The future of pottery for African women", *African Women*, II, 2 (1957), 28-9.

In 1955 women-potters at Karura and Kangemi formed co-operatives and gave instruction in making kilns. Local production may increase owing to the facility of procuring raw materials.

BEURNIER, R., "Artisans et artisanes do Saint-Louis-de-Sénégal", *Outre-mer* (Algiers, Dec. 1937), 279-300.

Dyeing in particular is a trade carried on solely by women.

BINET, J., "Condition des femmes dans la région cacaoyère du Cameroun", *Cahiers Internationaux de Sociologie*, XX (Paris, 1956), 109-23.

New activities open to women: trade, crafts, plantation work . . .

*CAPELLE, G., "Emploi du personnel féminin dans les entreprises du Congo Belge", *Bull. de l'Institut interafricain du travail*, (Brazzaville, March 1959).

COMHAIRE-SYLVAIN, S., "Le travail des femmes à Lagos", *Zaïre*, V (Brussels, 1951), No. 2, pp. 169-87; No. 5, pp. 475-502.

Enquiry into girls' schools in Lagos (Yoruba). Women who do not work are rare and come mostly from monogamous families not of Yoruba origin. In trade, the commonest occupations are shopkeepers, export merchants, brokers, pawnbrokers, market saleswomen and shop assistants. Women are also found in industry, teaching, and in the professions.

DUVIEUSART, E., Congolese women in trade, in "Note sur le commerce indigène dans les grands centres extra-coutumiers du Congo Belge", *Problèmes Sociaux Congolais*, XLV (Elisabethville, 1959), 80-1.

About 50 per cent of traders are women. Some of them are hawkers, but most of them trade in the markets. Their trading is not organized, except for the Lokele women of Stanleyville, whose monopoly and influence are associated with superstitions.

ELKAN, W., "The employment of women in Uganda", *Bull. de l'Institut Interafricain du travail*, IV, 4 (Brazzaville, 1957), 8-23.

"In Uganda and East Africa generally, women form an insignificant proportion of the total labour force and are virtually excluded from manufacturing industry." Outside agriculture, women are employed as teachers, nurses and prostitutes. The employment of a larger number of women would be a means of diminishing the instability of the labour force, but the prospects

Analytical Bibliography

of doing so are hedged in by severe limitations both in demand and supply. Employment of women, see Inter-African Labour Conference.

*Fosbrooke, J., "Masai women and their work", *Crown Colonist*, XIV (1944), 313-14.

Guelfi, L., "La femme noire et les formes modernes du travail", *Conseil National des Femmes françaises*, (Paris, Oct. 1957), 7-14.

Having noted the importance and the economic freedom of women in traditional societies (referring chiefly to the Dogon and the Malinke), the writer studies the new forms of economic activitity which African women are embarking upon, with varying degrees of preparation, in: European and African plantations of an industrial kind, hospital work, research, office work, trade, dressmaking, domestic work, industry. The writer also studies legal protection of working women.

Harris, J. S., "Papers on the economic aspect of life among the Ozuiten Ibo", *Africa*, XIV, 1 (1943), 12-23.

Economic activities of boys and girls of various age-classes. Division of labour between the sexes.

Hauferlin, C., "La femme africaine: une méconnue", *Marco Polo*, XXVIII (Paris, 1957), 59-68, ill.

Daily life of a Dahomeyan "business woman" at Miro, a village in South Dahomey.

Hellmann, E., Rooiyard, Economic life: Revenue contributed by women, in "Rooiyard: a sociological survey of an African slum yard", *The Rhodes-Livingstone Papers*, Rhodes Livingstone Institute, No. 3 (1948), 37-53.

"Under tribal conditions the Bantu woman was an economic asset; on her work in the fields the family was dependent for its subsistence. In an urban area . . . [as here, in Johannesburg] she is of no less economic importance but the nature of her work has changed." Most women earn a living by brewing and selling beer illicitly, although some are employed by Europeans. Owing to this economic activity, they have become independent and influential members of the family. This fieldwork was done in 1933-34, but the findings are still valid for many districts of Johannesburg and other urban centres.

Kaberry, P. M., *Women of the Grassfields. A study of the economic position of women in Bamenda, British Cameroon*, H.M.S.O., 1952, xxi + 220 pp., 21 pl. maps (Colonial Research Publications No. 14).

Land tenure, agriculture, division of labour, standards of living.

Kouaovi, B. M., "Les Tagalakoy ou porteuses d'eau du Niger", *Encyclopédie mensuelle d'outre-mer*, V, 53 (Paris, 1955), 46-7, ill.

The *tagalakoy* are the women who sell water at Niamey, and who not only are "characters" but have artistic leanings as well. (*Bibliographie Ethnographique du Congo Belge*, 1955).

Lebeuf, J. P., "Foyers kotoko", *Journal de la Société des Africanistes* (Paris 1942), pp. 260-3.

These fixed fireplaces are modelled by women.

"Législation sur le travail des femmes en Afrique au sud du Sahara", *Bull. de l'Institut interafricaine du travail*, II, 2 (Brazzaville, 1955), 29-50.

A study of legislation concerning the employment of women, based on the archives of the [Inter-African Labour] Institute up to 30 September 1954.

*Longmore, L., "Infant mortality in the urban Africa. The African attitude

269

towards it in the Witwatersrand", *South African Medical Journal*, XXVIII, 14 (Cape Town, 1954), 295-8.
Contains references to the employment of women.

*MAQUET, E. and WILDE, R. DE, "Les tâches quotidiennes de la paysanne rouandaise", *La Femme et le Congo*, 27th year, No. 158 (Brussels, 1957), 6-9, ill.
Illustrations showing the daily occupation of Ruanda women with comments by E. Maquet. (*Bibliographie Ethnographiques du Congo Belge*, 1957).

*MUKELEBWE EBWE, "Aujourd'hui ou demain, la femme congolaise au travail", *La Voix du Congolais*, 9th year, No. 88 (Kalina, 1953), 474-6.
The writer puts forward several arguments in favour of the moral education of native women. (*Bibliographie Ethnographique du Congo Belge*, 1953).

MURRAY, K. C., "Women's weaving among the Yoruba at Omu-aran in Ilorin Province", *The Nigerian Field*, V, 4 (1936), 182-91, ill.
They do not weave as a regular activity, but only as the need arises. Description of the work and of the techniques employed.

NEMO, J., The economic role of women, in *Contributions à l'étude démographique et sociologique d'une ville du Togo: Palimé* (Paris, Ministère de la France d'Outre-Mer, 1958), pp. 67-74 (*Documents et statistiques*, No. 22).
The writer discusses the social significance of the economic activities of women. Three traditional occupations are still found: agriculture, dressmaking, petty trade; the last is the most important of these occupations and forms a new economic sector occupied entirely by women, that of the middleman. This accentuates the economic independence of women. Recently an upper social stratum has come into being, recruited from the Westernized well-to-do, and forming a new bourgeoisie.

NSIMBI, M. B., "Village life and customs in Buganda", *Uganda Journal*, XX, 1 (Kampala, 1956), 27-36.
Division of labour between the sexes.

OTTENBERG, P. V., The changing economic position of women among the Afikpo Ibo, in Bascom, W. and Herskovits, M.J., *Continuity and change in African cultures* (University of Chicago Press, 1959), pp. 205-23.
Pottery, trade, agriculture, are the traditional economic activities of women at Afikpo, a rural community in Nigeria. The introduction of cassava, a crop cultivated solely by women, has enabled them to become economically independent and to extend their activities.

PAULME, D., "La femme africaine au travail", *Présence Africaine*, XIII (Paris, 1952), 116-23.
Sexual division of labour; economic independence of women owing to aptitude for trade which enables them to accumulate possessions quite separate from those of their husband.

— , "Peintures murales et pierres kissi", *Marco Polo*, XX (Paris, 1956), 43-54, ill.
Decoration, done by women, of replastered hut-walls, mostly representing scenes of agricultural or domestic work.

PAUWELS, M., "Les couleurs et les dessins du Ruanda", *Anthropos*, XLVII, 3-4 (Posieux (Freiburg), 1952), 474-82, ill.
It is only Tutsi women who use the colour red. It is also the women who maintain the traditional knowledge of the meaning of the designs they use in basketwork.

Analytical Bibliography

"Pottery in Ghana", *African Women*, II, 4 (1958), 84-5.
Pottery is women's work.

STRANGWAY, A. K., "The advance of African women in Angola", *African Women*, I, 4 (1956), 79-84.
A new division of labour between the sexes and new responsibilities for women among the Ovimbundu.

"Travail coutumier et la situation sociale en Afrique noire française", *Bull. de l'Institut interafricain du travail* (Brazzaville, Dec. 1953), 528-43.
Repercussions of the new economic and social structure on the African family and on women's work.

"Women of Ghana make successful traders", *Ghana to-day*, III, No. 19 (1959).
A very brief article showing the aptitude of women for trade. They are beginning to organize themselves.

ORNAMENTS

ALEXANDER, D., "Notes on ornaments of the Wondeo pagans who are a section of the Marghi pagans (females only)", *Man*, XI (1911), 1, 4 photos.
Some notes on feminine ornaments from childhood to marriage.

APPIA-DABIT, B., "Notes sur quelques bijoux sénégalais", *Bull. de l'IFAN*, Series B, V, 1-2 (Dakar, 1943 [1948]), 27-33.
Tukulor and Wolof jewellery in filagree gold, alloyed with copper.

ARNOT, A. S., "Reproductions of five Aro Ibo designs used by women for skin decorations", *Nigeria*, XIV (Lagos, 1938), 113.
Five reproductions without text.

"Bijoux en paille et poupées de cire sonrai à Tombouctou", *Notes Africaines*, LI (Dakar, 1951), 84-8, ill.
Jewellery in plaited and coloured straw worn and made by women.

BLANCHARD-ZABOROWSKA, R. and JOYEUX, C., "Sur quelques coiffures indigènes en Afrique Occidentale Française", *Revue anthropologique*, LVI (Paris, 1920), 124-8, ill.
Hair styles for children, young women, and the mother of a circumcised boy, in the Upper Volta.

BOHANNAN, P., "Beauty and scarification among the Tiv", *Man*, LVI (1956), 117-21, ill.
Women have scarifications on the face and on the body, usually the back and the legs.

BOYLE, V. C., "The marking of girls at Ga-Anda", *Journal of the African Society*, XV (1915-16), 361-6, 4 pl.
The first tattooings at five years old, then at seven and at nine. Then a woman's whole body is tattooed all over. The Twa markings are slightly different.

CRASTE, L., "Variations sur la coiffure féminine en A.O.F.", *Monde Colonial Illustré*, 26th year, No. 225 (Paris, 1948), 99-101.
A series of sketches of [French] West African women, showing the great variety of hair styles.

DECORSE, J., "Le tatouage, les mutilations ethniques et la parure chez les populations du Soudan", *L'Anthropologie*, XVI (Paris, 1905), 129-47.
Mutilations of women's ears, nose and lips for aesthetic purposes.

271

M. Perlman and M. P. Moal

DELONCLE, P., *La parure féminine aux colonies*, Paris, Agence des Colonies, 1945, 32 pp. ill.

All varieties of femine ornament: hair styles, jewellery, clothing. Africa is particularly noted for hair styles.

DUPUIS-YAKOUBA, A., Jewellery, hair styles, in "Notes sur Tombouctou", *Revue d'Ethnographie et de Sociologie*, V (Paris, 1914), 254-9, ill.

Account, with drawings, of the various types of jewellery in use at Timbuktu; hair styles according to age, class (free women, slaves).

GEO FOURRIER, G., The "Femmes à plateaux" [Disc-women], *La Nature*, No. 2928 (Paris, 1934), 400-3.

The writer rejects the theory that Sara women wear discs as a protection against being carried off in raids, or that the wearing of discs is out of respect for the totem of the tribe. He thinks it is to be explained by the exaggerated liking for adornment found in African women.

*GOEMAERE, G., "Le pagne", *Jeune Afrique*, 7th year, No. 21 (1954), 28-30.

On the multi-coloured cotton gowns worn by Congolese women today, and on the charm of this "national costume". (*Bibl. Ethn. du Con. Bel.* 1954).

HERZOG, R., "Der *rahat*, eine fast verschwundene Mädchentracht im Ostsudan", *Baessler-Archiv*, n.f. IV, 1 (Basel, 1956), 1-12, ill, bibl.

Introduced from Arabia, the *rahat* was worn by girls, and destroyed by the husband on the day of their marriage. It was a fringed leather sash decorated with glass beads, cowries, etc. according to the region. It has practically disappeared.

HOLAS, B., "Notes sur le vêtement et la parure baoulé", *Bull. de l'IFAN*, Series B, XI, 3-4 (Dakar, 1949), 438-57.

Historical development of Baule costume; clothing, ornaments, hair styles, amulets, facial scarifications.

HUNTINGFORD, G. W. B., "Notes on the charms worn by Nandi women", *Man*, XXVII (1927), 209-10.

Nandi women wear charms round their neck designed to protect them against various misfortunes.

LAFON, S., "La parure chez les femmes peul du Bas-Sénégal", *Notes Africaines*, XLVI (Dakar, 1950), 37-41.

Description of hair styles, jewellery, ornaments and bracelets of Fulani women. It is the hair style that distinguishes Wolof Fulani women; their hair is less fuzzy, longer, and is braided and coiled. (*Bibliographie Ethnographique du Congo Belge*, 1950).

LEBEUF, J. P., "Les bijoux parlants des femmes kanouri", *La Terre et La Vie*, IX, 4 (Paris, 1939), 124-5.

Description and meaning of the little cylinders of brightly painted millet stalks worn by Kanuri women (North Cameroon) in their ears.

—, *Vêtements et parures du Cameroun français*, Paris, Arc-en-Ciel, 1946, 47 pp. 50 pl. in colour.

Album of coloured illustrations.

LE GAL, J. R., "La parure de la femme en Afrique Équatoriale", *Sciences et Voyages*, XXIX (Paris, Sept. 1947), 283-4, ill.

Metal necklaces and bracelets are favoured, as well as mutilations and scarifications (lips, ears). But it is above all the hair style to which women give most attention.

Analytical Bibliography

LEMBEZAT, B., *Éve noire*, Neuchâtel, Paris, Éd. Ides et Calendes, 1952, 64 pp.
Album of photographs of African women, mostly from the Middle Congo and French Cameroon, commented by B. Lembezat.

LEQUES, R., "La mode actuelle chez les Dakaroises (étude de psychologie sociale)", *Bull. de l'IFAN*, Series B, XIX, 3-4 (Dakar, 1957), 431-45, ill.
Results of an enquiry in which 4,000 women were questioned, mainly about colours.

LEVARE, A., "En Guinée pittoresque: coiffure et toilette féminine chez les Foulbés", *Bull. de la Société de Géographie*, CIII (Algiers, 1925), 329.
Costume of a Fulani woman: it consists of two gowns, one worn on top of the other, and a *bubu* or *tigare* in muslin covering the whole body. The hair style is very complicated.

LHOTE, H., "Bijous en paille de Tombouctou", *Notes Africaines*, XXXII (Dakar, 1946), 4-8, ill.
Description of the straw jewellery (chains, rings, earrings) worn by women of modest means in Timbuktu.

MARIE-ANDRÉ DU SACRE-CŒUR, Sister, "Propos sur le vêtement en Afrique" *Rhythmes du Monde*, IV (Lyon, 1946). 61-70, ill.
Account of traditional clothing in Africa: notes concerning the wearing of ritual clothing and colours.

MURAZ, G., "Les cache-sexe du centre africain", *Journal de la Société des Africanistes*, II, 1 (Paris, 1932), 103-11, 32 photo.
Among the Sara of Chad.

MURAZ, G. and GETZOWA, S., "Les lèvres des femmes "Djingés" dites femmes à plateaux", *L'Anthropologie*, XXXIII (Paris, 1923), 103-25.
The discs which Sara-Jinge women wear in their lips are a part of betrothal rites and a sign of coquetry rather than a form of passive defence against slavery.

PATENOSTRE, DR, "La coiffure chez les Peuls du Fouta-Djallon", *Outre-Mer*, III, 4 (Algiers, 1931), 406-19, ill.
Description of hair styles ancient and modern of the Fulani women of Fouta Djallon and of some hair ornaments.

PAULME, D. and BROSSE, J., *Parures africaines*, Paris, Hachette, 1956, 94 pp. phot. map.
The origin, meaning, social role and rules concerning ornaments, tattooing and masks in Africa.

PAUWELS, M., "La mode au Ruanda", *Kongo-Overzee*, XIX, 2-3 (Antwerp, 1953), 234-58, ill.
Ornaments and clothing of girls and women. Hair styles.

"Penteados e adornos femininos das indigenas de Angola", *Boletim General das Colonias*, XXVI, No. 310 (Lisbon), 137-41, 3 phot.
Concerning an exhibition of jewellery and feminine onaments of Angola held in Lisbon; imaginative ingenuity displayed by the women, particularly with regard to hair styles.

PROST, A., "Les ornaments de nez en Afrique", *Notes Africaines*, LXXII (Dakar, 1956), 110-12.
The wearing by women of a metal ring in the right nostril, recorded from Timbuktu to Abéché, is also found among the Zande.

SCHULIEN, M. P., "Kleidung und Schmuck bei den Atchwabo in Portugiesisch Ostafrika", *Anthropos*, XXI (Posieux (Freiburg), 1926), 870-920, ill, bibl.

M. Perlman and M. P. Moal

The writer deals with the importance of clothing among the Atchwabo, the rites and customs in which it plays an important role, jewellery regarded as ornament or as charms, tattooing of children decided upon by the mother.

THIAM, B., "La coiffure 'gossi' et les bijoux qui lui sont assortis", *Notes Africaines*, XLV (Dakar, 1950), 9-11, ill.

Description of hairdressing done with sisal, worn by Wolof, Diula, Tukulor, Serere and Bambara women, and the jewellery worn with it.

*VAN DEN BROUCKE, A., "Haartooi bij de Basuto vrouwen", *Dietschland Zuid-Afrika*, 1st year, 2 (Steenbrugge (Transvaal), 1937), 38-40.

Some notes, with drawings, on how Basuto women arrange their hair. (*Bibliographie Ethnographique du Congo Belge*, 1937).

VASSAL, G., "Parmi les femmes kouyou sur le Congo", *Monde Colonial Illustré*, VIII (Paris, 1924), 186, ill.

Some notes on tattooings and hair styles along the Kuyu near Mossaka.

"Le Vêtement dans l'Union française", *Tropiques*, No. 357 (Paris, 1953), special number.

Articles by Messrs. Labouret, Lhote (on the Saharan frescoes), Muraz (Sara, Bassari), Le Rumeur (Sahara), Lem (African drapery), Aerts (concerning African "haute couture"), accompanied by numerous photographs.

POLITICAL ACTIVITIES

ALPORT, C. J. M., "Kenya's answer to the Mau-Mau challenge", *African Affairs*, LIII (1954), 241-7.

This is followed by a note (p. 247) on the role of women in the Mau-Mau movement: they were food-carriers for the troops and played an important role because of their desire to acquire more land.

*BAZELEY, W. S., "Manyika headwomen", *Nada*, XVII (Salisbury, 1940), 3-5.

On the Manyika institution of headwomen: their influence is great, and probably goes back to matriarchal times. A list of the most important head-women with a biographical sketch of each one. (*Bibliographie Ethnographique du Congo Belge*, 1950).

BIEBUYCK, D., "De mumbo-instelling bij de Banyanga" [The Banyanga institution of the *mumbo*], *Kongo-Overzee*, XXI, 5 (Antwerp, 1955), 441-8; summary in *African Abstracts*, VII (1956), 120-1.

The *mumbo*, principal wife of the political chief, becomes the real or the fictitious mother of the heir to the chiefdom.

"The Chieftainship in Basutoland", *African Studies*, IV, 4 (Johannesburg, 1945), 157-79.

Judgment of a case in favour of the wife of a chief who had assumed the regency, which was a recognition of the *de facto* individual and political rights of women according to customary Law among the Sotho.

DE HEUSCH, L., *Essai sur le symbolisme de l'inceste royal en Afrique*, Brussels Institut de Sociologie Solvey, 1958, 274 pp.

See in particular Chapter III, on "the royal triad": the king's mother and sister share his throne.

DESCAMPE, E., "Note sur les Bayanzi", *Congo*, I, 5 (Brussels, 1935), 685-8.

Documentation on the woman known as *mfumu nkento*, or wife of the chief's clan, her social position.

Analytical Bibliography

HINTZE, V., "Mutterrechtliche Züge in der Sozialordnung der Akan", *Deutsche Akademie der Wissenschaften*, V (Berlin, Veröffentlichung Institut für deutsche Volkskunde, 1952), 61-9.

The *ohemaa* or queen-mother is a woman-chief among the Akan-speaking peoples (Ghana).

JOSEPH, H., "Women and passes", *Africa South*, II, 2 (Cape Town, 1958), 26-31.

The fact that women in the Union of South Africa are obliged to carry identity papers has aroused in them a resistance which is sometimes passive and sometimes active and expressed in public demonstrations.

KRIGE, E. J. and J. D., *The realm of a rain-queen*, O.U.P., 1943, 336 pp. 4 maps, ill.

In particular, Chapter X ("Cogs in the political machinery"), which discusses the political system, with its institutions centred on the queen; and Chapter XI ("The genius of juridical adjustments") which studies the juridical system.

"Lady Paramount Chief: Mme Ella Koblo Gulama, from the Mende of Sierra Leone", *West Africa*, No. 2141 (1958), 391.

Mme Gulama, a district head, is also the first woman deputy. A biographical notice of her.

MACKLIN, R. W., "Queens and kings of Niumi", *Man*, XXXV (1935), 67-8.

Originally, Niumi was reigned over by queens. Then the men revolted. List of the queens of Niumi.

MARIE-ANDRÉ DU SACRÉ-CŒUR, Sister, "L'activité politique de la femme en Afrique Noire", *Revue juridique et politique de l'Union Française*, 8th year (Paris, Oct.-Dec. 1954), 476-97.

Importance of the women's political movement.

MUNONGO, A., "Mort de la mugoli (reine) Mahanga, ancienne femme du Mwami Msiri et mère du chef Mafinge Mulongo", *Bull. du CEPSI*, XVII (Elisabethville, 1951), 260-3.

Biographical sketch of the widow of Msiri, who died 25 Feb. 1951, her character, her social role and her influence.

PEDRALS, D. P. de, "Une curieuse fondation, le Yéhoué", *Encyclopédie mensuelle d'outre-mer*, 5th year, IV, 43 (Paris, 1954), 107-8, ill.

A secret society of a magical-cum-social nature, exclusively composed of women, the Yehue exerts considerable influence. The writer regards it as a movement of concerted resistance against an oppressive patriarchate.

*SAAKSE, J., "The visit to Mujaji, the rain-queen", *Nada*, XXIX (Salisbury, 1952), 83-6.

The rain-queen of the Lovedu must make way for her successor by committing suicide; the present queen has put an end to this custom. This article is an account of the new practice. (*Bibliographie Ethnographique du Congo Belge*, 1951).

*SEABURY, R. I., *Daughter of Africa*, Boston, Pilgrim Press, 1945, 144 pp.

Biography of Mina Soga, an African woman who is a Christian leader.

STORME, M., "Ngankabe, la prétendue reine des Baboma", *Mémoires de l'Académie Royale des Sciences Coloniales*, classe des Sciences morales et politique, Histoire, n.s. VII, 2 (Brussels, 1956, 8vo), 79 pp. maps.

Biography of Ngankabe: she was not, strictly speaking, queen, but her energy enabled her to exploit fully the powers which she derived from her social rank of *nkum'okare*, princess.

M. Perlman and M. P. Moal

TEW, D., "A form of polyandry among the Lele of the Kasai", *Africa*, XXI, 1 (1951), 1-12.

Description of the institution known as *hohombe* (wife of the village) among the Lele of the Kasai; her connection with the political organization of the village. (*Bibliographie Ethnographique du Congo Belge*, 1951).

VANSINA, J., "Lààm, gezongen kwaadsprekerij bij de Bushong", *Aequatoria*, XXVIII, 4 (Coquilhatville, 1955), 125-30.

Taunts made by women in public which have moral and social repercussions and act as a form of sanction.

YOULOU-KOUYA, H., "Une adoratrice du *Nkouémbali*", *Liaison* (Brazzaville, 1957): No. 57, pp. 27-8; No. 58, pp. 54-6, ill.

A few words concerning the circumstances attending the death of Queen Ngalifourou (20 April 1956). Her political influence and religious role.

RITUAL FUNCTIONS

BALANDIER, G., "Femmes 'possédées' et leurs chants", *Présence Africaine*, V (Paris, 1948), 749-55.

About the Lebu of Senegal. The crisis of possession regarded as highly important: consecration of the possessed person (*lefohan*). It is followed by dances and the sacrifice of an animal which is eaten.

COMHAIRE, J., "La vie religieuse à Lagos", *Zaïre*, III, 5 (Brussels, 1949), 549-56.

An increasing number of women [in Lagos] are becoming Mohammedans. Islam represents progress to them, and they have so much influence that it is possible that, owing to them, Mohammedanism will spread to the detriment of the Christian religions.

EARTHY, E. D., "The customs of Gazaland women in relation to the African church", *International Review of Missions*, XV (Edinburgh, 1926), 662-74.

Description of ritual practices associated with the life of women: discusses how they might be adapted to Christian principles.

EVEN, A., "Les propriétés maléfiques et bénéfiques du sexe de la femme selon les croyances des Babamba et Mindassa (Moyen Congo, A.E.F.)", *Bull. et Mém. de la Société d'Anthropologie de Paris*, X, 8th series, 1-3 (Paris, 1939), 51-72.

The beneficent and protective powers attributed by the Babamba and Mindassa to a woman's sex are called into operation by the women's association known as *Lissinbu* or *Yandza*, by means of ceremonies of a ritual nature, including dances and songs with exorcising powers. The writer concludes that for these tribes, men and women, in a mystic far more than in a physical sense, are two kinds of being very different from each other.

FALKNER, D., "Witch or what?" *Nigeria*, XXIII (Lagos, 1946), 105-11.

History of a young girl from the surroundings of Lagos, regarded by her family as a witch. How she became one and how she was cured.

GLUCKMAN, M., "Zulu women in hoe cultural ritual", *Bantu Studies*, IX (Johannesburg, 1935), 255-71.

Sexual division of labour; the hoe culture is done by women. But women play a very small part in the ritual ceremonies associated with it, except in the rites addressed to *Nomkubulwana*, a sky goddess and the only goddess among

276

Analytical Bibliography

the Bantu of the South-East. The men are strictly excluded from these rites.

HUNTINGFORD, G. W. B., "Notes on the charms worn by Nandi women", *Man*, XXVII (1927), 209-10, ill.

Charms made of vegetable matter against illness and the evil eye.

KABORE, D. Y., "Les mangeuses d'âmes chez les Mossi", *Notes Africaines*, XXIV (Dakar, 1944), 17-18.

The Mossi believe that there are women who "eat" the souls of new-born children and of adults. How they are discovered and combated.

KOUROUMA, K., "Sur une formule de purification des femmes en pays somba", *Notes Africaines*, LXIII (Dakar, 1954), 82-3.

A purification formula [Somba] pronounced by future brides after the *Diokointidi* ceremony, the aim of which is to initiate women into adult life and give recognition to their social status.

KRIGE, E. J. and J. D., *The realm of a rain-queen*, O.U.P., 1943, 336 pp. 4 maps, ill.

See Chapters I, VIII, XIII and XV, on the cults of the drum and of the rain, ancestral cults, and fertility rites.

MANDRIN, J., "Les sorciéres mangeuses d'âmes", *Grands Lacs*, 54th year, No. 4-5-6 (Namur, 1937-38), 189-90.

Notes on some Mossi beliefs and superstitions [concerning the "eaters of souls"].

MOORF, G., "The Ila Oeo festival at Ozuakoli", *Nigeria*, LII (Lagos, 1956], 61-9, 12 phot.

An Ibo ceremony which takes place twice annually: it marks the end of the agricultural cycle and is placed under the female sign.

REHSE, H., "Die Priestersprache und die Frauensprache der Basinza", *Zeitschrift für Kolonialsprachen*, VI (Berlin, 1915-16), 244-50.

[Article on the language spoken by priests and the language spoken by women among the Basinza.] A rather simple form of esoteric language which women use among themselves. A glossary accompanies the article.

RUFFIN-PIERRE, M. P., "Femmes 'zebola' ou femmes hantées par un esprit", *Voix du Congolais*, XIV (Kalina, 1947), 613-14.

Operations carried out by means of sorcery which have to be undergone by Mongo women who are supposed to be haunted by a spirit.

ZENKOVSKY, S., "Zar and tambura as practised by the women of Ondurman", *Sudan Notes and Records*, XXXI,1 (Khartoum, 1950), 65-81.

Zar and *tambura* are the names of ceremonies held in order to calm the spirits. The dance of possession is performed by women. The ceremony lasts for one or for two days. On the second day an animal is sacrificed.

EDUCATION—EMANCIPATION

African Women, a review published by the Department of Education in Tropical Areas of the University of London. It is particularly concerned with education and with the teaching of African girls and women. It contains information about the new professions open to women and nominations of native women to official posts.

M. Perlman and M. P. Moal

BALDE, S., "L'éducation de la fille dans l'ancienne famille foulah", *Outre-Mer*, 9th year, IV (Algiers, 1937), 322-30.

Some notes on the education of girls, the position of married women, and the effects of colonization on Fulani women.

—, "La femme foulah et l'évolution", *L'Éducation africaine*, XCVIII (Gorée, 1937), 214-19.

The first part deals with the traditional education of [Fulani] girls. The second, with the effects of colonialization on the way of life of Fulani women: a women's emancipation movement indicates the women's desire to liberate themselves from the masculine yoke.

BERGERET, Y., "A training centre for home and family life", *Interna tional Review of Missions*, XLI, 164 (Edinburgh, 1952), 496-502.

Some notes on the life of Bangante (Bamileke) women. Need for the education of girls. Programmes and methods of the Centre for Evangelical Missions of the Cameroons.

BINET, J., "Condition des femmes dans la région cacaoyère du Cameroun", *Cahiers Internationaux de Sociologie*, XVI (Paris, 1956), 109-223.

Women of today [in the cocoa-growing areas of French Cameroon] are becoming emancipated, particularly from the point of view of the work they do; there are among them a large number of retailers of foodstuffs which they buy in the rural districts. This branching-out in their activities is being done in close association with their husbands and their husbands' families.

BOLAMBA, A. R., *Les problèmes de l'évolution de la femme noire*, Élisabethville, L'Essor du Congo, 1949, 167 pp.

Contains statements of sound principles, with a high aim, put into everyday language, and accompanied by practical examples taken from everyday life. Why African women must be educated and given a new moral outlook. The role of women in the home, the family, the education of children. (*Bibliographie Ethnographique du Congo Belge*, 1949).

BRANDEL, M., "The African career woman in South Africa", *African Women*, II, 2 (1957), 36-8.

New, westernized way of life of professional women. The principal professions open are: nurse, teacher and social worker.

—, "Urban Lobolo attitudes: a preliminary report", *African Studies*, XVII, 1 (Johannesburg, 1958), 34-50.

The institution of the *lobolo* or matrimonial compensation is being adapted to modern conditions. The writer analyses the attitudes of a group of African professional women. Her conclusion is that the change in the status of women is the main factor in the changes in *lobolo* in the towns. It still corresponds to the price of a child, and remains a means for uniting two families. (A review of this article by Professor Vilakazi and Mrs. Brandel's reply can be found in *African Studies*, XVIII, 2 (1959), 80-4).

BURNESS, H. N., "The position of women in Gwandu and Yauri", *Oversea Education*, XXVI, 4 (1955), 143-52.

These are two districts of Northern Nigeria inhabited mainly by Hausa and Fulani: position of girls before marriage, the importance of marriage, general attitude towards education of women. (*Bibliographie Ethnographique du Congo Belge*, 1955).

BURNET, A. M., "Women at Makerere", *African Women*, II, 4 (1958), 78-81.

Analytical Bibliography

The main careers open to women are still those of nurse and teacher, but new possibilities are opening up.

'Calabar", *Nigeria*, LII (Lagos, 1956), 70-88, ill.
Pp. 83-8, the liberation of Efik women from customs.

*"Career women of West Africa", *West African Review*, XXVI, No. 331, (Liverpool, 1955), 290-6.

"The Chieftainship in Basutoland", *African Studies*, IV, 4 (Johannesburg, 1945), 157-9.
Judgment in a case brought against the chief wife of a deceased chief, upon her having assumed the regency; the fact that the judgment was in favour of the woman is proof of the changes taking place among the Sotho in their ideas about the rights of women.

CHILD, H. F., "Family and tribal structure: status of women", *Nada*, XXXV (Salisbury, 1958), 65-70.
The status of Matabele women. "The emancipation of African women is an evolutionary process which law cannot control and today growing numbers are found at work away from their homes."

CLAY, G., "The demonstrations in South Africa. What makes the women march?", *New York Herald Tribune*, New York, 10 Sept. 1959.
A report of the demonstrations of September 1959 in South Africa, led by women. An account of their living conditions.

COULIBALY, O., "Sur l'éducation des femmes indigénes", *L'Éducation Africaine*, No. 99-100 (Gorée, 1938), 33-6.
The African attitude towards the disequilibrium and the faults arising from the present education of girls.

*DARDENNE, E., The role of women in African social and economic development, in *New Education Fellowship*, *6th World Conference, Nice*, London, 1932.

DARLOW, M., "The African townswoman in Northern Rhodesia", *African Women*, I, 3 (1955), 57-9.
Women form a third of the urban population; their ages vary from 20 to 40 years. Mention of the educational social centres open to women, particularly the experiment at Fort Jameson.

*DAVIES, H. O., "Emancipation of women in West Africa", *West African Review* (Liverpool, Feb. 1938), 13-15.

DAVIS, J. M., Importance of women's education (Bantu), in *Modern Industry and the African* (1933), pp. 326-9.
The first part deals with the traditional education of children, upon which women, as guardians of tradition, have great influence. The second part deals with the influence of Christianity. The education of boys and girls should be more even, so as to avoid the present lack of balance.

DEBRA, A., "La femme noire dans les centres extra-coutumières et les camps de travailleurs congolais", *Bull. du CEPSI*, IX (Elisabethville, 1949), 131-41.
Lack of morals of African women, once they are outside the framework of ancestral customs. (*Bibliographie Ethnographique du Congo Belge*, 1949).

DE CARVALHO, A., "Instrução e educação da mulher africana", *Portugal em Africa*, XIII, 74 (Lisbon, 1956), 65-75, table.
The progress of education and the teaching of women in the diocese of Lourenço Marques. A table gives statistics from 1885 to 1954.

DENOEL, L., A summary of the replies obtained in answer to a questionnaire sent

M. Perlman and M. P. Moal

out in the Belgian Congo, in *La Promotion de la femme au Congo et au Ruanda-Urundi*, Congrès National Colonial, 12th session, 1956, pp. 325-42.

Position of women and girls in traditional and non-traditional surroundings. Their attitudes, desire for emancipation. Obstacles to emancipation, means for promoting it.

DEVAUX, V., "La femme congolaise et la civilisation européenne", *Grands Lacs*, 65th year, VII (Namur, 1949-50), 5, ill.

Women in the Congo have been later in coming into contact with European civilization than the men, fewer of them have done so, and under less favourable conditions. How to deal with the question of their education. (*Bibliographie Ethnographique du Congo Belge*, 1950).

*DOBSON, B., "Woman's place in East Africa", *Corona*, VI, 12 (1954), 454-7.

Notes on the position of native women in East Africa, traditional forms of education; how best to promote their emancipation, especially by means of schools. (*Bibliographie Ethnographique du Congo Belge*, 1954).

DOUGLAS, R. L., "Education for African girls", *West African Review*, XXVI, No. 335 (Liverpool, 1955), 743-8, ill.

The problem of women's education in Africa; how it presents itself in the various British African territories. (*Bibliographie Ethnographique du Congo Belge*, 1955).

DRICOT, F., "Jeunesse féminine dans un camp de travailleurs au Katanga", *Cahiers des Auxiliaires laïques des Missions*, 10th year, 3 (Brussels, 1951), 25-35.

Problems posed by the persistence of customary ideas in bringing up girls (initiation, the prohibition against girls who have reached puberty living with their parents) in non-traditional surroundings [a workers' camp].

DURTAL, J., "Ou en est la femme noire?", *Hommes et Mondes*, XXVIII, 111 (Paris, 1955), 366-76.

Position and outlook of the emancipated young [African] woman; obstacles to women's emancipation (mainly bridewealth and customary marriage).

DUTILLEUX, G., "La femme détribalisée du centre extra-coutumier", *Bull. du CEPSI*, VI, 14 (Élisabethville, 1950), 100-14.

The writer studies the problems posed [by detribalized women in non-traditional surroundings] and how they appear to women interviewed in Elisabethville; in particular, prostitution arising from the shortage of women; the instability of marriage, and conflicting ideas of men and women on marriage; women seek for some kind of security by joining women's associations.

— , "L'opinion des femmes du centre extra-coutumier d'Élisabethville sur le mariage, la famille, l'éducation des enfants", *Bull. du CEPSI*, XVII (Elisabethville, 1951), 219-23.

Takes up problems raised in the foregoing article.

"L'Éducation de la population africaine féminine dans un milieu industriel du Haut-Katanga", *Problèmes Sociaux Congolais, Bull. du CEPSI*, XLIV, Elisabethville, 1959.

This booklet contains a series of articles concerned with problems of the education of women (schools, adult education) and of children in industrial surroundings; social work and medicine in the Belgian Congo.

*EVANS, J. D., "Education of the Sudanese girl", *Oversea Education*, II (1930), 25-32.

280

Analytical Bibliography

"L'Évolution de la femme africaine", *L'Afrique en marche*, XII-XIII (Paris, 1958), 38-40, ill. table.

Historical outline of votes for women, their political role, percentage of women's votes.

L'Évolution de la femme et de la famille en Afrique [changes in the position of women and in the family in Africa], in *Problèmes sociaux africains*, Comptes rendus des entretiens internationaux sur l'Afrique, CHEAM, Paris, 23-28 Oct. 1950, pp. 22-30.

Contributions by Miss Gwilliam, S. A. Ogilvie and Sister Marie-André du Sacré-Cœur on the position and role of women in the new African society, the position of women wage-earners or wives of wage-earners; importance of the education of women for the development of family life.

FORTES, M., *Social and psychological aspects of education in Taleland*, O.U.P., 1938, 64 pp. pl. (Memorandum 17, Supplement to *Africa*, XI, 4).

This study contains a survey of the social environment of the children, attitude of parents and children; games; a synoptic chart of the education of children of both sexes aged from three to 15 years.

GILLARD, M. L., "La condition de la femme noire", *Centre d'Études et de documentation sociales de la province de Liège*, VIII, 10 (Liège, 1954), 549-59.

General comments on what Belgium has done for the Congo, especially for Congolese women.

*GWILLIAM, F. H. and READ, M., *Report on the education of women and girls in Northern Rhodesia*, 1947, Lusaka, Government Printer, 1948, 8 pp.

Need for varied careers for Africans; increased roll at secondary schools. (D. Forde, ed., *Annoted Bibliography of Tropical Africa*, New York, The Twentieth Century Fund, 1956).

— , *Report on the education of women and girls in Nyasaland*, Aug.-Sept. 1947, Zomba, Government Printer, 1948, 8 pp.

Education in hands of missions; demand for government action; women should be trained in home economics, literacy and as matrons. (D. Forde, ed., *Annotated Bibliography of Tropical Africa*).

HELLMAN, E., "Rooiyard: a sociological survey of an African slum yard", *The Rhodes-Livingstone Papers*, No. 3, 1948, 125 pp.

In particular the chapter: "Economic life: revenue contributed by women" (pp. 37-53); the revenue is to a large extent acquired by the brewing and (illicit) sale of beer. This trade is changing the status of women, for they are acquiring independence and control of their own lives (widows and women who have been abandoned prefer to make their own living by this trade rather than return to their own families). The trade has given rise to an association of the nature of a mutual aid society or a savings bank. These data collected in Johannesburg in 1933-34 are still valid, and for other urban centres as well.

HOLAS, B., "L'évolution du schéma initiatique chez les femmes oubi", *Africa*, XXVII, 3 (1957), 241-50.

Initiation customs among Ubi women (Ivory Coast) are in the process of changing owing to new social conditions.

HOLLEMAN, J. F., "The African woman in town and tribe", *The Listener*, No. 1,436 (4 Oct. 1956), 496-7 and 509.

In a rural environment a woman is dependent on her family. In an urban environment kinship relations weaken and new relations of equality arise between husband and wife.

M. Perlman and M. P. Moal

HULSTAERT, G., "L'instruction des filles", *Aequatoria*, 14th year, IV (Coquilhat-ville, 1951), 128-9.

The real causes of backwardness of African women of the Congo.

HUNTER, M., "The effects of contact with Europeans on Pondo women", *Africa*, VI (1933), 259-76.

Revolutionary changes in economic life and the breakdown of the former system of social organization (*ukulobola*) have created a new conception of the social position of women. Women are becoming emancipated from every point of view.

IYEKI, J. F., "Un pas de plus vers la promotion de la femme noire", *Voix du Congolais*, 12th year, No. 129 (Kalina, 1956), 859-63.

["One step further in the advance of women"]. The writer had had a conversation with Mme Nkumu, the first Congolese woman to have a seat on the City Council of Leopoldville. (*Bibliographie Ethnographique du Congo Belge*, 1956).

JAHODA, G., "Boys' images of marriage partners and girls' self-images in Ghana", *Sociologus*, n.s. VIII, 2 (Berlin, 1958), 155-69, table.

As a form of test, the writer showed pictures of girls in African dress and girls in European dress to 60 Accra schoolboys and 60 schoolgirls aged from six to 18 years, and asked for their opinions. He thus showed the attitude of educated boys towards marriage and the girls' views on their future.

KAGAME, A., Girls' education, in "Les organisations socio-familiales dans l'ancien Ruanda", *Mémoires de l'Académie royale des Sciences coloniales*, Classe des Sciences morales et politiques, XXXVIII, 3 (Brussels, 1954, 8vo), 250-5.

The traditional education of Ruanda girls, given by their mothers, is a whole-time preparation for married life.

LEAKEY, L. S. B., "The Kikuyu problem of the initiation of girls", *Journ. of the Roy. Anthr. Inst.* XLI (1931), 277-85.

The writer discusses the reasons for Kikuyu opposition to changes in their custom of girls' initiation and makes his own suggestions about the matter. (*See* Initiation).

LE BER. A., DEMBA E. and KI, J., "Éducation de la femme", *Servir Outre-mer*, IX (Paris, Secrétariat social d'Outre-mer, 1952), 27-54.

Three essays on the education of African women: what has been done, what still requires to be done.

LEBLANC, M., "Problèmes de l'éducation de la femme africaine", *La Revue Nouvelle*, 13th year, XXV, 3 (Brussels, 1957), 257-75.

"The mother . . . is the repository of the traditional values of Bantu cosmology . . . If we knew more about the cosmology by which their behaviour is inspired, we might find the real motivations of the Bantu soul which could become the driving-force for new forms of education." The problem in fact is that of "changing the attitudes of both men and women in the Congo". [Trans. of excerpts from original text].

*LE GOFF, G., "L'enseignement des filles en A.O.F.", *L'Éducation Africaine*, 26th year, XCVII (Dakar, 1937), 189-99.

Girls are educated by their mothers; it is a practical education, carried out by performing the daily tasks. Three stages for girls' education, programmes.

*— , "L'éducation des filles en A.O.F.: l'éducation d'une fillette indigène par sa famille", *Oversea Education*, XVIII, 4 (1947), 547-63, ill.

282

Analytical Bibliography

Description of the education of a girl in French West Africa: village life described, and how the mother educates her child. The difficulties met with when children are sent to school. (*Bibliographie Ethnographique du Congo Belge*, 1947-48).

LEITH-ROSS, S., "The rise of a new elite among the women of Nigeria", *International Social Science Bulletin*, VIII, 3 (Paris, UNESCO, 1956), 481-8.

Extension of education, consequences. The position of a feminine elite seems more secure since the women have not moved so far away from the masses.

Liaison, Brazzaville, 1957: No. 57, pp. 5-7; No. 58, pp. 30-4.

Two articles: the first by an African woman ("Homme africain, qu'as-tu dans la tête?" [African man, what is in your mind?]), accusing men of negligence and laziness; the second by an African man ("La corruption des mœurs des femmes dites évoluées" [The corruption of morals of women who are supposed to be emancipated]) who replies that the flightiness of African women is undeniable and often comes from their parents.

LITTLE, K. L., "The changing position of women in the Sierra Leone Protectorate", *Africa*, XVIII, 1 (1948), 1-17.

After describing the life of a Mende woman from birth on in the old society, the writer then discusses the position of women in the new society in formation, where money and economic activity are the criteria of social status. The status of women is not very high, as their economic activities are on quite a small scale.

— , "Two West African elites", *International Social Science Bulletin*, VIII, 3 (Paris, UNESCO, 1956), 495-8.

At Keta, Nigeria, associations have been formed, some of which are exclusively for women, such as the Keta Women's Institute, which serves both to channel women's opinions and as a pressure group.

LOMBARD, J., "Cotonou, ville africaine. Tendances évolutives et réaction des coutumes traditionelles", *Bull. de l'IFAN*, XVI, 3-4 (Dakar, 1954), 341-77.

Chapters V and VI deal with changes in the family [in the town of Cotonou] and more particularly in the behaviour of women, who, because of being away from the family head and from the village, feel freer to act as they choose. They often refuse to countenance polygyny and the men are thus led to contract unions with unattached women. The break with the family environment gives rise to an increase in prostitution. A reaction is forming to this development, one feature of which is that girls are being sent back to the village, from the age of ten until marriage, in order to be given the traditional upbringing.

*LONGMORE, L., *The dispossessed: a study of sex-life of Bantu women in urban areas in and around Johannesburg*, Cape, 1959, 334 pp.

*MACMATH, A. M., "Developments in female education in Sierra Leone", *Oversea Education* (Oct. 1939), 30-4; (Apr. 1943), 108-12.

MACNAMARA, C. T., "Women are going to school in Africa", *World Mission*, X, 1 (New York, 1959), 18-28.

With the disappearance of former laws many of the obstacles to women's education have gone. Mostly about Kenya.

MAGDALEN, SISTER, "Education of girls in Southern Nigeria", *International Review of Missions*, XVII, 67 (Edinburgh, 1928), 505-14.

Some principles to follow in order to give girls a sound Christian education without making too abrupt a break with native customs.

M. Perlman and M. P. Moal

MARIE-ANDRÉ DU SACRÉ-CŒUR, SISTER, "Vers l'évolution de la femme indigène en A.O.F.", *Le Monde Colonial Illustré*, 16th year, No. 178 (Paris, 1938), 68-9.

The second part of this article [on the advance of native women in French West Africa] studies the changes in customs that have actually taken place, which must be followed by legal reforms that will give women their liberty.

— , Education and the African woman, in *Rapports et Comptes rendus de la* 24e *Semaine de Missiologie de Louvain*, 1954, (Brussels, Desclée de Brouwer), pp. 44-62.

The situation as regards the education of girls and women in French Africa, the Belgian Congo and Ruanda-Urundi, and Uganda.

— , *Civilisations en marche*, Paris, Grasset, 1956, 252 pp. ill. maps.

The writer raises the problems of family life in Uganda, in the Belgian Congo and Ruanda Urundi, and shows how important it is for the social and cultural development of Africa as to whether women are to form a feminine élite or simply be housewives. The importance of the work of the Christian missions is underlined, and also the obstacles still in the way of women's emancipation.

— , "Évolution de la femme africaine", *Grands Lacs*, No. 188 (Namur, 1956-57), 16.

In workers' camps, Congolese women have a lot of time on their hands which they should be taught to employ usefully. As well as being educated to become wives and mothers in monogamous families, they should be given some preparation for playing their part in public affairs.

MARTHEY, J., "L'œuvre missionaire pour la population féminine au Congo", *Revue de l'Histoire des Colonies*, XLIV, 154 (Paris, 1957), 79-101.

The author studies the educational, family-welfare and social work of the Missions among the Bateke.

MAUNIER, R., "La femme noire en Afrique française", *Le Monde Colonial Illustré* (Paris, 1939), pp. 143-4.

In particular, the position of women [in French Africa] and the changes brought about by legislation.

*MAXEKE, C. M., The progress of native womanhood in South Africa, in J. D. Taylor (ed.), *Christianity and the natives of South Africa, a yearbook of South Africa Missions*, Lovedale, Institution Press, 1928, 503 pp.

MIKOLASEK, M., "Some attempts at feminine education in the Cameroons", *International Review of Missions*, XLI (Edinburgh, 1952), 493-5.

Attempts to educate Bamileke women and girls by combining Western and native principles.

*MISSIA, "L'éducation de la femme en pays kivu", *Afrique Ardente*, 19th year, LXXXII (Brussels, 1954), 14-18.

Some notes on social relations in the region of Kivu: kinship rights, inheritance. (*Bibliographie Ethnographique du Congo Belge*, 1954).

MOBE, A. M., "Encore un mot au sujet de la prostitution", *Voix du Congolais*, 10th year, XCV (Kalina), 82-7.

Some aspects of prostitution in the Belgian Congo: its principal causes (extremely high bride price, polygyny, exodus of young men to the industrial centres . . .), ways of combating it.

*NEATBY, H., "The contribution of educated African women to the Uganda of today", *East and West Review*, XX, 3 (1954), 67-72.

About half the African women who have received a good education are

Analytical Bibliography

capable of taking their place in society as equals with men and are capable of leading a feminine movement.

*NGONYAMA, S., "The education of the African girl", *Nada*, XXXI (Salisbury, 1954), 57-8.

Family resistances which still have to be overcome by every girl who wants to go to school in Southern Rhodesia. (*Bibliographie Ethnographique du Congo Belge*, 1954).

*NICOLLET, A., "La femme, la famille et les changements économiques en Afrique Noire", *Cahiers de Sociologie économique*, I (Le Havre, June 1959).

OTTENBERG, P. V., The changing economic position of women among the Afikpo Ibo, in W. Bascom, and M. J. Herskovits, *Continuity and change in African cultures* (University of Chicago Press, 1959), pp. 205-23.

In a rural environment such as Afikpo, the introduction of cassava has led to an increase in women's personal resources. They no longer depend on their husbands for subsistence and make a larger contribution to the family budget. They assume more authority, and the most interesting thing is, how they spend their increased income: instead of buying traditional titles to prestige as the men continue to do, they prefer to spend it on material improvements and on sending their children to school. Some notes comparing the activities of women in semi-urban with those in urban surroundings.

PETIT, M., "Les filles noires devant l'école familiale", *La Nouvelle revue pédagogique*, XII, 1 (Tournai, 1957), 35-8.

Education must be organized in a way that takes account of the fact that African girls pass from childhood to adult life without any transition period; hence it is necessary to create a "timespace", that is to say a period of adolescence during which girls can be given an education both mental and practical.

PETRE. M. M., "Promotion féminine dans un centre extra-coutumier d'Afrique centrale", *Perspectives de catholicité*, 16th year, IV (Brussels, 1957), 43-52.

Aspects of the advance of women due to Christian missions and their work, at Kindu, Belgian Congo.

POWDERMAKER, H., "Social change through imagery and values of teen-age Africans in Northern Rhodesia", *American Anthropologist*, LVIII (Washington, New York, 1956), 783-813.

The attitudes of Bemba adolescents towards traditional or European ways of life differ as between girls and boys. Generally speaking, the girls are more sensitive to manifestations of racial prejudice and more hostile to the Whites than the boys; the latter, because of their closer contact with Europeans, have become more open to influence. The position of women in traditional society provides a natural explanation for the girls' attitude. Both girls and boys want to be educated and want to live in the towns and escape from the toils of heavy labour.

READ, M., *Migrant labour in Africa and its effects on tribal life*, Montreal, International Labour Office, 1943, 27 pp.

The writer studies the migration of men in Nyasaland and southwards, and raises the problem this involves of the position of women left alone in the villages, upon whom necessity imposes an ever increasing economic independence.

RÉTIF, A., "Vers la libération de la femme camerounaise", *Études*, 88th year, CCLXXXIV, 1 (Paris, 1955), 80-8.

In traditional society, a woman is dependent on her family, then on her

M. Perlman and M. P. Moal

husband, this dependence being aggravated by the degradation of the payment of bridewealth. Education ought to be at once practical and moral, designed to teach women their proper value.

*REYHER, R. H., *Zulu woman*, O.U.P., 1948, 282 pp.

Without being an ethnographic study, this book has a certain documentary interest, since it gives the impressions of a woman, Christina Sibiya, the wife of Solomon king of the Zulus, about her home surroundings and her position as co-wife, and shows how this woman, who was an educated Christian, adapted to a traditional environment. (*Man* (1948), No. 162).

SCHAPERA, I., "Premarital pregnancy and native opinion. A note on social change", *Africa*, VI (1933), 59-89.

Changes in traditional attitudes towards premarital sexual relations and pregnancy under European, and particularly Christian, influence. Customary sanctions have almost disappeared, and religious sanctions only touch a very small proportion of the population. A certain amount of licence ensues. Detailed study of these changes among the Kxatla.

SENGHOR, L. S., "L'évolution de la situation de la femme en A.O.F." *Marchés Coloniaux*, 6th year, CCXXVI (Paris, 1950), 541-2.

In the old form of society, a woman was not regarded as "inferior": she was a person, in the same way as a man was. Nowadays, all the girls on leaving school (to become teachers, midwives, nurses, stenographers, and soon lecturers, doctors, lawyers) earn their own living and are less and less willing to accept inequality.

SHANNON, M. I., "Women's place in Kikuyu society. Impact of modern ideas on tribal life. A long-term plan for female education", *African World*, (Sept. 1954), 7-10.

There have not yet been many changes in the position of Kikuyu women. The chief reforms needed concern bridewealth, and education, which at present does not last long enough and offers too narrow a choice of careers.

SIMONS, H. J., "African women and the law in South Africa", *The Listener*, LV, 1416 (1956), 626-7 and 644.

Native women in South Africa are in the process of disengaging themselves from the tutelage imposed on them by the three legal systems in force. They are becoming increasingly important as a social factor, particularly, they constitute a dynamic force in the face of masculine conservatism.

*SIRET, M., "La situation des femmes abandonnées et des femmes seules dans les centres extra-coutumiers d'Usumbura", *Bull. du CEPSI*, XXXII (Elisabethville, 1956), 250-68.

In an introductory note the demographic situation in Usumbura is discussed, the reasons why women are abandoned by their husbands, their position, the position of widows, possible solutions. (*Bibliographie Ethnographique du Congo Belge*, 1956).

SOHIER, A., "Évolution de la condition juridique de la femme indigène au Congo Belge", *Comptes rendus de la 24e session de l'Institut Colonial International*, Rome, 1939, (Brussels, 1939), pp. 149-217.

A study of the legal status of unmarried and married native women, first in customary law, and then in the legal system of the Independent Congo State.

— , "La réforme de la dot et la liberté de la femme indigène", *Bull. des Juridictions indigènes et du Droit coutumier congolais*, 18th year (Elisabethville, 1950): No. 7, pp. 217-21; No. 9, p. 286.

Analytical Bibliography

Concerning legislative measures limiting the amounts paid in bridewealth and declaring null any marriage concluded without the consent of the woman.

SOHIER-BRUNARD, Mme., The lack of preparation of the native women of the Congo for the tasks imposed on them by contact with our way of life, in "L'Enseignement à dispenser aux indigènes dans les territoires non autonomes", *Cahiers de l'Institut Solvay*, I (Brussels, Lib. Encyclopédique, 1951), 74-87.

Boarding schools and mixed schools are needed and women must gain economic independence; the article also studies the work done by the Social Centre and the consequences of the suppression of polygyny brought into force in 1950.

*"South African Institute of Race Relations. The employment of native girls trained in domestic service at native training institutions", *South African Outlook*, LXII (1932), 6-9.

"Status of women in Togoland and the Cameroons", *African Women*, I, 4 (1956), 95-8.

New activities, political and, especially, professional, for women. Girls' education, obstacles encountered.

STRANGWAY, A. K., "The advance of African women in Angola", *African Women*, I, 4 (1956) 79-84.

New division of labour between the sexes among the Ovimbundu. New responsibilities assumed by women.

TARDITS, C., Woman against the lineage, in *Porto-Novo. Les nouvelles générations entre leurs traditions et l'occident* (Paris, The Hague, Mouton, 1958), pp. 59-76. (École Pratique des Hautes-Études, Le Monde passé et présent, 1re sér., Études, No. 7).

The writer describes the results of an enquiry into the attitude of educated women on various problems: bridewealth, marriage, the question of who children should belong to, inheritance of property. With regard to the last three points, women are ready to welcome innovations, but they want to preserve the system of bridewealth. There is "an aspiration among women to see changes in the role of the patrilineage as a regulating factor . . ., an endeavour . . . towards easing and consolidating conjugal relations by weakening the ties binding a man to his kin". [Trans. of excerpt from text].

THURNWALD, H., *Die schwarze Frau im Gestaltwandel Africas. Eine sociologische Studie unter ostafrikanischen Stämmen*, Stuttgart, Kolhammer, 1935, 167 pp. eight ill.

[The negro woman in changing Africa; a sociological study among East African tribes]. Two approaches: the life of women in a changing world, biological factors, social and family status; analysis of the changes, economic, religious and cultural influences.

— , "Zur Frage der Erziehung ostafrikanischer Frauen und Mädchen", *Koloniale Rundschau*, 33rd year, 3-4 (Berlin, 1942), 130-58.

Contribution [on the question of the education of East African women and girls] to the general problem of African education. Chiefly concerned with the former German East Africa. (*Bibliographie Ethnographique du Congo Belge*, 1942).

THURNWALD R., *Black and White in East Africa. The fabric of a new civilization, a study in social contact and adaptation of life in East Africa* (With a chapter on women by H. Thurnwald), Routledge, 1935, 419 pp.

Changes in family life and in the status of women.

TULLAR, L. E. and AKINSEMOYIN, K., "Woman's Part in the new West Africa", *West African Review*, XXI, 269 (Liverpool, 1950), 136-8.

Views of an American missionary and an African student on the part to be played by women in the new West Africa.

*WATERS, M. M., "The need to-day of native women and girls", *South African Outlook*, LIX (1929), 97-9, 113-15.

*WELSH, J., "The goal of women's education in Africa", *Oversea Education*, IX, 2 (1940), 65-72.

Women qualified for scientific careers.

*"What is being done in the East African territories: opportunities of advancement for African women", *East Africa and Rhodesia*, XXVII, n.s. No. 1384 (1951), 893-906.

*WRONG, M., Education of African women in a changing world, in *Yearbook of Education*, (Evans, 1940), pp. 497-520.

YACINE, D., "A travers la famille en Guinée française", *L'Éducation Africaine*, CII-CIII (Gorée, 1939), 42-52.

Mention of intellectual education for Muslim and Christian girls, and moral education given by their mothers.

SCHOOLS

Journal to consult: *Oversea Education. A Journal of Educational Experiment and Research in Tropical and Sub-Tropical Areas.* Quarterly, published by the Colonial Office.

"African schoolgirls in Tanganyika", *African Women*, II, 2 (1957), 31-4.

Discusses general matters: their place of origin, standard of living, mental capacities.

"Aperçu sur l'éducation en Afrique tropicale britannique", *Notes et Études documentaires*, No. 2124, Paris, Présidence du Conseil, 10 Jan. 1956, 15 pp.

A general review of education in West and East Africa, Zanzibar, and British Somaliland. There is a general lack of advance in the education of girls, which presents problems of organization, of material, of personnel, as well as social problems. The solutions adopted for the education both of girls and of adults vary from one area to another.

*"The Arab girls' school of Zanzibar", *Oversea Education*, I, 4 (1930), 125-30.

*BELL, J., "Early days of girls' education in Somaliland", *Oversea Education*, V, 3 (1953), 110-17.

BERGERET, Y., *Banganté (un internat de jeunes filles au Cameroun)*, Paris, Soc. des Missions Évangéliques, [1954?], 40 pp. ill. maps.

Description of the life of native girls at the boarding school at Bangante, Cameroon. Training in domestic science, education; difficulties encountered.

BONGONGO, L., "De l'éducation de nos filles", *La Voix du Congolais*, 5th year, XLV (Kalina, 1949). 465-71.

The new conditions of family life demand that girls' education should no longer be limited to primary education in the vernacular.

*BROOMFIELD, G. W., "Education of African women and girls in Tanganyika", *Bull. of Educational Matters*, III, 2 (1929), 2-8.

Analytical Bibliography

COMHAIRE, J., "Enseignement féminin et mariage à Lagos, Nigeria", *Zaïre*, IX, 3 (Brussels, 1955), 261-77.
List of educational facilities for girls in Lagos. Educational standards. Preparing girls for a future as wife and mother is clearly insufficient.

CONGLETON, F. I., "Some problems of girls' education in Northern Nigeria", *Oversea Education*, XXX, 2 (1958), 73-9.
The writer replies to questions concerning changing attitudes towards women's education, women's educational needs, the organization of education in Northern Nigeria (primary and secondary), and suggests a method of teaching by educative games.

*COOPE, K. B., "The training of women teachers", *Oversea Education*, IX (1938), 21-2.

*CURRYER, W. H. S., "Mothercraft in Southern Nigeria", *United Empire*, XVIII, 2 (1927), 78-81.
Description of the Mary Slessor Institute for girls at Aro Chuku; its influence on the Aro.

DARKE, M. E., "The education of girls and women in British Somaliland", *Oversea Education*, XXX, 4 (Jan. 1959), 160-3.
Progress in female education is extremely slow owing to the opposition of the people (Islamized). The success of the government school opened in 1953 at Burao opens up new possibilities for the education of girls as well as of women.

Development of African teacher training, secondary schools and the education of girls, Entebbe (Uganda) Government Printer, 1954, 50 pp.

"L'École d'apprentissage pédagogique en milieu rural", *Revue pédagogique congolaise*, III (Elisabethville, March. 1956), pp. IX-XVI.
Need to create monitors, especially for the first class.

"L'Enseignement féminin du second degré et les professions féminines en A.O.F.", *L'Éducation Africaine*, XXIII (Gorée, 1954), 5-11.
List of technical and professional openings for girls in secondary schools.

"Girls' education in Nyasaland", *African Women*, I, 3 (1955), 61-3.
Although always lower than that of the boys, the number of girls attending school has greatly increased. Some statistics on school attendance.

"Growing up in Nigeria", *African Women*, II, 4 (1958), 73-8.
A Nigerian woman teacher recounts her memories of her education according to traditional methods, then at primary and secondary schools. She discusses her criticisms and the obstacles standing in the way of girls' education.

GUEYE, F. P., "L'enseignement des filles au Sénégal et dans la circonscription de Dakar", *L'Éducation Africaine* (Gorée, 1934), 191-3.
Article on general matters in which the author discusses the obstacles in the way of girls' education and the new direction it should take.

JANISCH, M., "Reinforcements for African girls' education in Kenya", *Oversea Education*, XXVI, 4 (1955), 152-5, ill.
Progress made by missions and government in education; scholastic education; measures taken for raising the standards of this at the capital.

JEANNE DE LA CROIX, Sister, "L'enseignement menager et familial au Congo", *Rapports et comptes rendus de la 24e Semaine de Missiologie de Louvain, 1954*, (Bruges and Paris, Desclée de Brouwer, 1954), pp. 121-31.
Organization of schools of domestic science, general problems, situation of pupils on leaving school.

289

M. Perlman and M. P. Moal

KING, E. R. G., "On educating African girls in Northern Rhodesia", *The Rhodes-Livingstone Journal, Human Problems in British Central Africa* X (Livingstone, 1950), 65-74.

Education of girls is still behind that of boys. It is mainly held back by public opinion, and by the early age at which girls marry. The lack of women teachers necessitates mixed schools, the disadvantages of which are greater then the advantages. Girls who have been to school are faced with an acute problem presented by the very limited professional openings (teaching and nursing careers) and by the difficulties of their situation, particularly as regards lodgings, as girls working in urban surroundings away from their families.

LADURANTIE, G., "Quelques aspects actuels de l'enseignement des filles au Cameroun", *Encyclopédie mensuelle d'Outre-mer*, XXXIX (Paris, 1953), 310-12.

The results of an enquiry conducted by the *Union féminine civique et sociale* show that education has consequences diametrically opposed to those aimed at. The education of girls should be seen as resting on a moral and practical basis suitable for African life.

LE GOFF, G., "L'Enseignement des filles en A.O.F.", *L'Éducation Africaine* XCVII (Gorée, 1937), 48-58.

Three points: education of the native girl in family life; what French schools have done and must still do; a new three-stage organization of education.

PRIOR, K. H., "Rural training at Asaba", *Nigeria*, XLVII (Lagos, 1955), 184-212, ill.

Education of girls in various domestic tasks.

"Le Problème de l'Enseignement dans le Ruanda-Urundi", CEPSI, *Mémoires*, I, 1958.

Women's education is treated in a special chapter, pp. 87-111.

ROBERTSON, M. K., "A Girls' school in British Somaliland", *Oversea Education*, XXX, 4 (1959), 164-9.

Description and programme of the first government school for girls, opened at Burao in 1953.

*ROSS, McGREGOR, MRS., Some aspects of girls' education in Africa, in *Education in a changing Commonwealth*, New Education Fellowship (ed.), 1931.

Much still valid: co-education; use of local culture. (D. Forde, ed., *Annotated Bibliography of Tropical Africa*).

"La Scolarisation en Afrique Noire", *Tam-Tam*, 4th year, Nos. 6-7-8 (Paris, 1955), 98 pp. maps, tables.

The situation in female education (pp. 26-9) on 1 Jan. 1954. The proportion of girls undergoing secondary education in relation to the total number attending school barely reaches 1 per cent. On the other hand, a large number of those undergoing technical training are girls, which shows that they take a practical view of education.

*SHARIFF, E., "Girls' education in Zanzibar", *Makerere*, I, 3 (1947), 112-16.

Among the various schools in the protectorate of Zanzibar, the Arab school is the one with the greatest number of pupils. (*African Abstracts*, 1952, p. 186).

SHAW, M., *Les enfants du chef; une expérience d'éducation en Rhodésie du Nord*, Paris, Missions évangéliques, 1947, 209 pp.

An account of daily life in a school for girls run by the Protestant mission at Mbereshi (Lake Moero). How the writer, a Protestant missionary, teaches his pupils.

290

Analytical Bibliography

*Soyer,Poskin, D., Means of education: schools, in *La promotion de la femme au Congo et au Ruanda-Urundi*, Congrés Colonial National, Brussels, 12th session, 1956, pp. 360-430.

After discussing the general situation of girls in traditional and non-traditional surroundings and the attitude of "advanced" men towards the emancipation of women, the writer studies the present structure of girls' education, gives some statistics for 1954, and formulates further aims.

"Status of women in West Africa", *African Women*, I, 3 (1955), 63-6.

The social position of women has always been strong owing to their economic position. The present rate of advance is rapid (especially among the Ibo, Nigeria) owing to the opening of a number of schools and colleges and the entry of girl students to the Universities. Some statistics and the choice of careers open.

Van Roye, Rev. Mother, "L'Éducation de la jeune fille évoluée au Congo", *Bull. du CEPSI*, XVI (Elisabethville, 1951), 150-61.

The educational aims of missions as shown by the example of the boarding school at Mbansa Mboma.

ADULT EDUCATION

*Arnot, A. S., McKennel and Barbour, "Literacy among Calabar women", *Books for Africa*, VIII, 4 (1948), 49-52.

Discussion on external education programmes for Ibo and Efik women. The women's views on education and the language problem.

Boye, Dr, "Les essais de protection de l'enfance et de la maternité en A.E.F.", *A.E.F.*, XXXVI (Brazzaville, 1934), 3-8.

A communication made in May 1931 on the efforts made to teach mothers the rudiments of hygiene in the care of their children, in the [maternity and child-welfare] centres at Bambari and Libreville.

Brausch, G.E.J.B., "L'action en Afrique belge de l'Institut de Sociologie Solvay", *Problèmes d'Afrique Centrale*, 12th year, XLI (Brussels, 1958), 160-4.

Current information on the social and educational centres set up in both urban and rural districts.

*Burman, Garber, N., "An experiment in adult education (Solusi Women's School, Zambesi Union Mission, Southern Rhodesia)", *Oversea Education*, XVII, 2 (1946), 257-9.

Colin, P. M., "Trois femmes congolaises", *Voix du Congolais*, 12th year, CXIX (Kalina, 1956), 125-32, ill.

Some examples of the education at present being given to Congolese women. (*Bibliographie Ethnographique du Congo Belge*, 1956).

— , "Quatre heureuses initiatives pour la formation des femmes congolaises", *Voix du Congolais*, CXXXVI (Kalina, 1957) 522-30, ill.

[These four new enterprises in women's education] are: the government school for women's crafts at Leopoldville; evening classes for Congolese women in the non-traditional industrial centre of N'Djili; French course for Congolese mothers; courses in stenography. (*Bibliographie Ethnographique du Congo Belge*, 1957).

Darlow, M., Education of women and children in external classes, in "L'enseigne-

291

ment à dispenser aux indigènes dans les territoires non autonomes", *Cahiers de l'Institut Solvay*, I (Brussels. Lib. Encyclopédique, 1951), 17-23.

A survey of the British experiment mainly in Kenya and Uganda.

*DUPEROUX, A., "Quelques propos sur l'éducation de la femme noire", *Bull. de l'Union des femmes coloniales*, 22nd year, CXXXVI (Brussels, 1951), 6-8, ill.

Efforts made by the Union Minière of Upper Katanga to improve the lot of the wives of the workers and elevate them morally and spiritually.

*"L'Éducation ménagère de la femme camerounaise", *Bull. d'information et de documentation*, CXV (Yaoundé, 15 Oct. 1955), 18-21.

*FRASER, MRS., *Teaching of healthcraft to African women*, Longmans, 1932, 134 pp. ill.

From her own teaching experience, the writer shows how and to what extent results may be expected; they have so far been encouraging if slow. (*Africa*, 1933, p. 349).

*HARRIS, B., "Women's training centre, Kwadaso", *Community Development Bull.*, IV (1953), 35-6.

A Methodist women's training centre [in Ghana] offers courses for illiterate women and courses in domestic science. Women who have attended later become militant Methodists. (*African Abstracts* 1954, p. 69).

*HASTIE, P., "Women's club in Uganda", *Mass Education Bull.*, II, 1 (1950), 26-30.

Principal activities of these clubs: dressmaking, knitting, child welfare, cooking; there is also some general education given by African girls who have had some teacher's training.

*HAY, H., "An African women's institute, Mindolo, Copperbelt", *Oversea Education*, XV, 3 (1944), 104-7.

*HOLDING, M., "Report on adult literacy among Meru women", *Books for Africa*, V, 2 (1945), 17-22.

*JELLICOE, M. R., "Women's groups in Sierra Leone", *African Women*, I, 2 (1955), 35-43.

Influence of the Social Welfare Department of Mende women's groups on the social life of women in Sierra Leone.

JONES, N., "Training native women in community service in Southern Rhodesia", *International Review of Missions*, XXI (Edinburgh, 1932), 566-74.

The first Jeanes School for women only, the school at Hope Fountain, opened in 1928, accepts girls who have left school and married women with their children, in order to teach them hygiene and domestic science.

KABERRY, P., "Raising the status of women", *Times Survey of the British Colonies* (Dec. 1950), 11-12, ill.

Development of educational centres for women (child welfare, agricultural mechanics . . .).

MANN, M., "Women's homecraft classes in Northern Rhodesia", *Oversea Education*, XXX, 1 (Apr. 1959), 12-16.

The system used here is modelled on the "badges" of the Guides. Centres (of which there are at present 61) have been opened in the towns and villages and give women a practical training in domestic science (attended by 2,000 women). A test has to be passed at each stage.

RHODIUS, G., Social work as a means of educating native women in Belgian African territories, in *La promotion de la femme au Congo et en Ruanda-Urundi*

Analytical Bibliography

Congrès National Colonial, Brussels, 12th session, 1956, pp. 252-9, map.
Account of social work done for Congolese women in the industrial centres and in the villages, and of youth work.

RICHARDS, G. E., "Adult education amongst country women: an experiment at Umm Ger", *Sudan Notes and Records*, XXIX, 2 (Khartoum, 1948), 225-7.
The writer surveys the method employed, the subjects taught (mainly domestic science and hygiene) and the results achieved over a period of 18 months.

*RIVERS-SMITH, S., "Education of the African women", *Bull. of Educational Matters*, II, 3 (1928), 13-23.

*SMITH, M. M., "An embryo Women's rural institute, Nyasaland experiment", *Oversea Education*, XIV, 2 (1943), 67-71.

SPELMAN, N. G., "Women's work in the Gezira, Sudan", *Oversea Education*, XXVI, 2 (1954), 66-9, ill.
Teaching women child-welfare. Development of a sense of individualism and responsibility by means of discussion groups. These experiments have been carried out in the Sudan since 1949; 600 to 700 women annually take the courses.

*WAINWRIGHT, R. E., "Women's clubs in the central Nyanza district of Kenya", *Community Development Bull.*, IV, 4 (1953), 77-80, ill.
Training in domestic science for women in these clubs pays special attention to dressmaking.

INDEX OF AUTHORS
CITED IN THE
ANALYTICAL
BIBLIOGRAPHY

Index of Authors

Index of Authors

297

Index of Authors

Index of Authors

GENERAL INDEX

Aba riots, 113-14
Abayejidu, 96
abduction, marriage by, 68-9
abortion, 36, 177
adolescence, 24-30
adoption, 70, 72, 88, 178
adultery, 9, 13, 100, 133-4, 139, 153-4, 165
African women, see women
age, see seniority
age-classes (age-grades), 12, 25, 52, 112
agriculturalists, 2, 97; attitude of towards nomads, 47-8; see also farmers
Amina, Queen, 95
ancestor cult, 125, 166-7, 170, 175, 176, 178, 215
ancestors:
  bridewealth paid to, 126, 163, 177
  placation of, 127, 151-2, 172
  presentation of wives and of children to the, 11, 127, 128, 141, 161, 163
  the wrath of the, responsible for lack or loss of children, 151, 153, 165
  see also wives of the ancestors
anọnk (Coniagui exogamous matrilineal group), 17ff.
Angwu Tsi (Jukun joint ruler), 100
Ankole, 103
annulment of marriage, see marriage, dissolution of
ants, 146, 176
aristocracy, 125, 126-7, 180, 183
army, service in the French, 20-1, 27, 33, 43
Ashanti, 96, 101
associations, women's, 23, 112-14, 227-8
autobiographies, Coniagui, 18-20, 26-8, 32-4, 35-6, 38-9, 43-4

Baba of Karo, 2, 48
babies, 37, 53-4; death of, 145, 150, 168-9; stillborn, 141-2, 168, 169; see also mother and child
Bachama, 110
Bagirmi, 105, 107, 108
Bakongo, 96
Bamileke, 14, 100, 107
Banda, 124
Bandia, 123, 124, 125, 126-7, 128, 146, 151, 152, 153, 154, 174
Bangassou, Sultan, 122, 128, 130ff, 138, 140, 141, 148, 176
Bantu, 183
bark-cloth, 174
Bassari, 17, 18, 20-2, 24, 30-1, 32, 35, 45
Bateke, 103-5, 118
Bazao-Turunku, 95
bazingers, 134, 145, 167, 169
beads, 29, 139, 194
beating, 23, 39, 40, 41, 42, 43, 138, 171, 190, 204
beer, 41, 196, 197, 200, 202, 203, 204, 205, 212
Behanzin, 96
Bemba, 101, 107
benge (Nzakara chiefs), 123, 124, 125, 128, 158
betrothal, 52, 60, 163, 196, 221-2; child-, 4, 9, 23-4, 31, 56
bilharziosis, 175
Bini, 112
biographies, Nzakara, 121-73
birth, 62-3, 172, 218, 224; see also abortion, babies, child, childlessness, miscarriages
birth rate, declining, 130, 176, 178
"blood", importance to the Nzakara of the factor of, 124, 126
Bolewa, 105
bolo, see commoners
Bororo, 47; see also camp
Bororo women, independence of, 48, 69; reputation of, 47-8; social roles of, 53

301

General Index

breast-feeding, 37, 54, 63, 219; *see also* weaning
bridewealth (bride price), 47, 48, 91, 125, 127, 128, 129-30, 132, 165, 166, 167, 169, 171, 172, 173, 205, 206; *see also* dowry, marriage payments
brothers, full, 79
brothers and sisters, relations between, 56-7
brothers-in-law, 71
budgets, family, 80, 223
Bunda, 111
Bushongo, 101
butter, 75, 76, 80, 198, 201, 204
"butter money", 80
Butwa (a Lunda association), 112

calabashes, 50, 51, 55, 63, 69, 76, 80, 84
calves, tethering of, 51, 64, 76, 79
Camberen, 218, 222, 227
camp, the Bororo 50-2, 57, 63, 64, 65, 71, 72, 76
Candamukulu (Bemba joint ruler), 101
Casamance, 219
castes, 179, 180, 181, 183, 185, 186, 187, 192, 202, 215, 221, 229
Catholicism, 27, 203
cattle, 17, 18, 60, 64, 65, 67, 73, 75, 76, 80, 82, 180, 201; ownership of, 78-9, 82, 83, 84; sale of, 78, 80; *see also* calves, cows, heifers
"cattle complex", 183
Chamba of Donga, 100-1
"character" as explanation of human behaviour, 203
chiefs, role played by women in accession of, 85-6, 111; women, 109-10, 126, 127, 131
child, birth of the first, 12, 62-3, 72
child-betrothal, *see* betrothal
childlessness, 36-7, 62, 72, 121, 127, 132, 151-2, 153, 155, 164, 204, 207, 224; injections for curing, 164, 169, 170, 172
children, desire for and love of, 36, 61, 203, 207, 208, 219, 224 (*see also* mother and child); governesses for, 207; illegitimate, 185, 195; queens and princesses prohibited from bearing, 102, 104, 105, 107;

rights over, 38, 66, 72, 110, 150, 171, 176, 207-8; treated as inferiors, 208; upbringing of, 22-4, 37-9, 54-6, 194-5, 219
Christianity, 32, 185, 215; *see also* Catholicism
circumcision, 38, 219
class distinctions, levelling of, 122, 129
classes, social, 93, 123, 125-9, 180, 218
classes in the Fulani language, 49-50
clinics, 164, 170, 172, 177
clitoridectomy, 10, 24; *see also* excision
clothing, clothes, 5, 22, 70, 80, 83, 87, 129, 135, 146, 147, 158, 162, 186, 194, 195, 197, 202; *see also* gowns, sandals
co-wives, 66-7, 144, 193, 206, 224-5, 226
colonization, effects of, 1, 8, 27, 32-3, 94, 107, 110-11, 121, 122, 123, 129-30; *see also* Whites
commoners, Nzakara, 125, 126, 127-8
concubines, 165; male, 126, 178
consanguinity, prohibitions of, 220
cooking, 76-7; *see also* meals
cotton cultivation, 154, 164, 169
court, the Nzakara Sultan's, 133ff, 138-9, 140, 148
courtyard, the chief's, 137-8, 140, 141, 142, 157, 165, 174; the women's, 131, 146, 147
cousins, 53, 57
cows: given as dowry, 184, 185 (*see also sadaaki*); women compared with, 187, 198, 203
cross-cousin marriage, 185
currency: used for bridewealth, 125; women as a form of, 128, 156

Dahomey, 96
dancers, 132, 184
dancing, 48, 54, 57-8, 62, 140, 147, 157
daughter, *see* father and—, mother and—
daughters-in-law, *see* family, husband's
Daura, Queen of, 96
Delacour, A., 17, 25, 31
descent:
matrilineal, 5, 17, 96; combined with patrilocal residence, 6, 17-18
patrilineal, 179; restrictions on marriage rights imposed by, 107, 109-10

General Index

Dinga, 111
diviners, 127, 132, 135, 136, 142, 148, 151, 159, 165
division of labour, 4, 64, 75-7, 114, 199
divorce, 35, 59, 68, 110, 203, 205, 207-8, 225, 226-7
dolls, 23, 54
dowry, 63; (in sense of marriage payment) 184, 185, 195, 196, 197, 198, 199, 205
Driberg, J. H., 84

education, 201-2; *see also* children, upbringing of, *and* schools
Ekoi, 112
exchange of women, 125, 126, 128-9, 131, 139, 140, 148, 156, 159, 174, 178
excision ceremonies, 24, 36; *see also* initiation
exogamy, 128

family:
    extended, Bororo camp consisting of, 50, 57, 71
    husband's, a woman's position in her, 3, 12, 14-15, 61-2, 71-2
    natal, married women's attachment to their, 3, 42, 73-4, 188
farmers, 179, 180, 187, 199
father and daughter, 55-6, 195-6
father-in-law, 71
favourites, 191-2
fertility, 127, 137, 203; of the soil, women's connection with, 77
feudal society, 179, 183, 199
fidelity, conjugal, among the Rundi, 193; *see also* wives
fishermen's wives, 227
Fong (Bamileke king), 100
food, 7, 37-8, 63, 64, 80, 132, 133, 138, 186, 203, 209, 222, 223; dividing out of, 132, 133; *see also* meals
food supply, Rundikazi the proprietor of the, 199
friendship, 23, 191
Fulani (Fulbe), 4, 12, 47-92, 105; language of the, classes in, 49-50
funerals, 131, 136-7, 144, 147-8, 175, 184

Gara (Chamba king), 100

Gargantuas, 207
Gere, 112
Gezo, 96
gift-giving among the Rundi, 189-92, 211
girls, adolescent, 24-30
Glegle, 96
goats, 76, 83
governesses, 207
gowns, 61, 62, 63, 158, 160, 163
granaries, 131-2, 133
grandparents, 56, 71, 210
griots, 221, 228
Guessain, Robert, 17

hair styles, 47, 61, 91
harem, 131
healers, 88
heifers, 56, 58, 61, 70
herd, master of the, 75
herders, *see* pastoralists
herds, *see* cattle
hierarchy, social: of the Nzakara, 125-9; of the Rundi, 182-4
hoe culture, 183
hoes as bride price, 185
hohombe ("wife of the village"), 111
household, setting up of the joint, 11, 12, 29, 31, 63-4
household tasks, 2, 55, 76, 138, 143, 200, 222-3
Humɔi society, 112-13
Hunter, Monica, 2
hunting, 124, 135, 138, 157, 174
husbands, *see* family, marital relations, marriage, marriage partners, polyandry, polygyny, wives
huts, 23, 28, 38, 40, 41, 42, 50, 51, 63, 64, 73, 131, 136, 138, 140, 142, 145, 146, 152, 154, 156, 157, 160, 163, 165, 168, 172, 218
Hutu, 179, 183, 184, 185, 186, 187, 188, 189, 192, 193, 194, 196, 198, 199, 201, 206, 215; Hutukazi, 183, 185, 186, 187, 192, 198, 200, 206, 211

Ibn Batuta, 96
Ibo, 2, 113-14
illegitimate children, *see* children
illness, 144, 150-1, 153, 154, 166, 175
Ilunga Kibinda, 96

General Index

General Index

patrilineages, Rundi, 179, 184; *see also* lineage segment
patrilineal, *see* descent
peasants, 125
Pende, 111
physical types, 53-4, 185-7
plants, gathering of wild, 29, 32; magic and medicinal use of, 129, 132, 136, 137, 161
play, 23, 54, 195; *see also* work
poison, 129, 134, 191, 193, 206; fear of, 38, 144
political systems: African, 93-4; hierarchical, position held by women in, 97-109; based on kinship, authority exercised by women in, 109-12
polyandry, 119
polygyny (polygamy), 4, 8-9, 32-4, 66-9, 193-4, 206, 215, 224-5; psychological implications of, 225-6
Pondo, 2
Poro society, 112
possession, spirit, 156-7, 166-7
potters, 23, 184
pregnancy, 10, 36-7, 62, 140f, 149-50, 160, 167-8, 207, 223
presents: given by betrothed, 23-4, 60, 61; by husband, 62, 63, 65; by girls to sweetheart, 27, 58; given to girls at excision ceremony, 23, 24; to girls by sweetheart, 154, 155, 160, 171, 177; *see also* gift-giving
primogeniture through the mother, right of, 87, 89
princesses, 125, 146ff, 180, 201
puberty, marriage of girls before they have reached, 220
punishments, 134, 136, 139, 142; *see also* beating

queen-mothers, 99, 184, 215
queens, 97-107
quinine, 164

rain-making, 98
Rançon, A., 17, 25, 30-1, 42
rank, distinctions of, 125; *see also* hierarchy, superiors
residence: matrilocal, 6; patrilocal, 5-6, 65; virilocal, 196

revenge, 18-22, 73
ritual, *see* women, ritual functions of
Ruanda, 99, 215
rubber plantations, 152, 154, 178
Rundi, Rundikazi, 179-215

sadaaki, 4-5, 65, 66, 67, 68, 73, 78, 79, 82, 83, 87, 91
sandals, 53, 61, 62
Sande society, 112
schools, European, 207; Koranic, 219
seclusion, periods of, 10, 11, 24, 61
seniority, 56, 57, 189; *see also* age-classes
Serer, 96, 228
serfs, 179, 180, 190, 201
servants, 128, 131, 140, 146, 196, 201
sex : antagonism, 1-2, 13, 28, 32; differentiation, 49-53, 75, 114, 192-5; education, 220
sexual: escapades, 24; freedom, pre-marital, 3, 9-10, 25, 32, 58-9 (*see also* love affairs); intercourse, taboo on, for mothers of babies, 37, 132, 141, 142, 145, 173, 175; obligations, of Rundi, 193
sheep, 76, 83, 90
Shilluk, 107
sisters, *see* brothers and—
sisters-in-law, 66, 71-2, 206
slave trade, 176
slave-wives, 165, 178; *see also* Kafi, biography of
slaves, 125, 126, 127, 128-9, 133, 137, 138, 139, 142-3, 146-7, 149, 152, 156, 165, 174, 175, 178, 206
smallpox, 136
So, 95
society, stratified, 2, 125; *see also* hierarchy
soldiers, 131, 133, 134, 135, 138; *see also* bazingers
Songhai, 95
Songombi (Nzakara princess), 122, 123; biography of, 146-55
sorcery, 88, 142, 175, 204; *see also* witchcraft
sororate, 74, 92
spitting, magic, 88
sterility, *see* childlessness
superiors and inferiors, 180, 188-92, 198, 203, 211, 213-14

General Index